Straight Writ Queer

# Straight Writ Queer

*Non-Normative Expressions of Heterosexuality in Literature*

*Edited by* RICHARD FANTINA

*Foreword by* CALVIN THOMAS

McFarland & Company, Inc., Publishers
*Jefferson, North Carolina, and London*

LIBRARY OF CONGRESS CATALOGUING-IN-PUBLICATION DATA

Straight writ queer : non-normative expressions of heterosexuality in
    literature / edited by Richard Fantina ; foreword by Calvin Thomas.
        p.    cm.
    Includes bibliographical references and index.

    ISBN-13: 978-0-7864-2638-6
    (softcover : 50# alkaline paper) ∞

    1. Sex customs in literature.   2. English literature — History
and criticism.   3. American literature — 20th century — History
and criticism.   4. Sodomy in literature.   5. Heterosexuality in
literature.   6. Homosexuality in literature.   I. Fantina, Richard.
PR149.S5S77   2006
820.9'353 — dc22                                            2006023123

British Library cataloguing data are available

©2006 Richard Fantina. All rights reserved

*No part of this book may be reproduced or transmitted in any form
or by any means, electronic or mechanical, including photocopying
or recording, or by any information storage and retrieval system,
without permission in writing from the publisher.*

Cover photograph © 2006 PhotoAlto

Manufactured in the United States of America

*McFarland & Company, Inc., Publishers
    Box 611, Jefferson, North Carolina 28640
        www.mcfarlandpub.com*

# Table of Contents

*Foreword: Crossing the Streets, Queering the Sheets, or:*
*"Do You Want to Save the Changes to Queer Heterosexuality?"*
    CALVIN THOMAS      1

*Preface*      9

*Introduction*
    RICHARD FANTINA      11

## Part I: Imperfect Sodomy and Queer Chastity

1. Back Door Sex: Renaissance Gynosodomy, Aretino, and the Exotic
    CELIA R. DAILEADER      25

2. Pegging Ernest Hemingway: Masochism, Sodomy, and the Dominant Woman
    RICHARD FANTINA      46

3. Queer Desire and Heterosexual Consummation in the Anchoritic Mystical Tradition
    SUSANNAH MARY CHEWNING      68

4. Deviant Celibacy: Renouncing Dinah's Little Fetish in *Adam Bede*
    KATE FABER OESTREICH      82

## Part II: The Victorians, of Course

5. The Mark of the Brotherhood: Homosexual Panic and the Foreign Other in Wilkie Collins's *The Woman in White*
    RICHARD NEMESVARI      95

6. "A rod of flexible steel in that little hand": Female Dominance and Male Masochism in Mary Elizabeth Braddon's *Aurora Floyd*
   DENISE HUNTER GRAVATT — 109

7. "Was ever hero in this fashion won?" Alternative Sexualities in the Novels of George Meredith
   MELISSA SHIELDS JENKINS — 124

8. *She:* Rider Haggard's Queer Adventures
   SHANNON YOUNG — 134

## Part III: The Incommensurability of Sex/Gender/Desire

9. Strange Anatomy, Strange Sexuality: The Queer Body in Jeffrey Eugenides' *Middlesex*
   ZACHARY SIFUENTES — 145

10. Freudian Foreplay: Lesbian Failure and Freud's Desire in "The Psychogenesis of a Case of Homosexuality in a Woman"
    ASHLEY T. SHELDEN — 158

11. Latent Lesbians and Heterosexual Narrative: Tracing a Queer Poetics in Fay Weldon's Fiction
    LORENA RUSSELL — 170

12. Stepping into the Same River Twice: The Tragic Sexual Mulatto and Subversion of the Inside/Outside Dialectic in the Novels of E. Lynn Harris and Alice Walker
    GRACE SIKORSKI — 183

13. "Beautiful, or thick, or right, or complicated": Queer Heterosexuality in the Young Adult Works of Cynthia Voigt and Francesca Lia Block
    DEBORAH KAPLAN *and* REBECCA RABINOWITZ — 197

## Part IV: Instabilities and Wayward Subversions

14. Nom de Guerre: Homosociality in Timothy Findley's *The Wars*
    SHELTON WALDREP — 209

15. Granville Barker's Effeminate Heterosexuals: The New
    Drama's New Men
    ANNE STILES                                                      219
16. "The most primeval of passions": Incest in the Service
    of Women in Angela Carter's *The Magic Toyshop*
    MADELEINE MONSON-ROSEN                                           232
17. "If thou art God, avenge thyself!" Sade and Swinburne
    as Christian Atheists
    CAROL POSTER                                                     244

*About the Contributors*                                             259
*Index*                                                              263

# Foreword: Crossing the Streets, Queering the Sheets, or: "Do You Want to Save the Changes to Queer Heterosexuality?"

CALVIN THOMAS

> As the point of convergence for a potentially infinite number of non-normative subject positions, queer is markedly unlike those traditional political movements which ground themselves in a fixed and necessarily exclusionist identity. In stretching the boundaries of identity categories, and in seeming to disregard the distinctions between various forms of marginalized sexual identification, queer has provoked exuberance in some quarters, but anxiety and outrage in others.
> Annamarie Jagose, *Queer Theory: An Introduction* [101]

> If it aims effectively to intervene in the reproduction of [social] reality ... then queer theory must always insist on its connection to the vicissitudes of the sign, to the tension between the signifier's collapse into the letter's cadaverous materiality and its participation in a system of reference wherein it generates meaning itself. As a particular story ... of why storytelling fails, one that takes both the value and the burden of that failure upon itself, queer theory ... marks the "other" side of politics.
> Lee Edelman, *No Future: Queer Theory and the Death Drive* [7]

The "spectre of the queer heterosexual" (Schlichtler 547) has haunted queer theory, and annoyed or appalled identity politics, from the very first moments of queer theory's all too maculate conception. If Teresa de Lauretis is generally credited with the first "high-profile" titular use of the term "queer theory" in the feminist journal *differences* in 1991, the oxymoronic phrase "straight queer" was already circulating in an anonymously authored pamphlet in London in the same year.[1] The term, or some variation thereof, or some allowance for the possibility of non-heteronormative heterosexualities, appears or is alluded to in numerous articulations from the antifoundationalist founders of queer theory whose critical work permeated the 1990's: Eve Sedgwick, Alexander Doty, David Halperin, Lauren Berlant, Michael Warner, Leo Bersani, Judith Butler, etc. I have quoted the relevant passages from these and other authorities too often and in too many discursive arenas to trundle them out again here.[2] Rather than defensively re-rehearse these critical legitimations of the question of queer heterosexuality, then, I will turn to one authoritative formulation that interests me for reasons that are sexual and aesthetic but not *prima facie* "political."

Eve Sedgwick's "Queer Performativity: Henry James's *The Art of the Novel*" was the lead essay in the inaugural issue of *GLQ: A Journal of Lesbian and Gay Studies*. In it she observes that "there are some lesbians and gays who could never count as queer, and other people who vibrate to the chord of queer without having much same-sex eroticism, or without routing their same-sex eroticism through the identity labels lesbian or gay" (13). Of course, one can imagine the umbrage taken in response to Sedgwick's claim by "some lesbians and gays" who had long suffered being pejoratively called "queer" but who were now being told that they "could never count as queer" now that "queer" was being resignified as affirmatively "hot"—though here I don't mind re-telling what Andrew Parker calls "a pretty fair joke: 'What's the difference between gay and queer?' 'There are no queer Republicans'" (80).[3]

But there are, it seems, queer heterosexuals, and regarding the question of the way queer theory opens the possibility of thinking about such a torquedly rhetorical figure, the point is that queer theory's great intervention has been to denaturalize and disrupt the common-sense assumption (surely held by "some lesbians and gays" as well as the majority of straights) that one *must* have a coherent sexual identity of some sort, that eroticism of any and all kinds *must* be routed through *some* regulatory political fiction of personhood that can (and must) be affixed with a clearly legible label. Following from Michel Foucault, queer theory problematizes or abrades any smooth conflation of eroticism with identity, of sexuality with the "truth" of one's "personage." As a "project of creative abrasion" (Hall 71), queer theory sexually identifies sexual identification itself as the coreless core of the problem, and the anti-labelous label "queer" thus presents itself not as an alternative identity but as an alternative *to* identity, "less an identity than a *critique* of identity" (Jagose 131), as an "anti-identitarian identity" (Bersani 101), as "an identity without an essence" (Halperin 62), as what "can never define an identity [but] only ever disturb one" (Edelman 17).

A person who is drawn, however tremblingly, to what disturbs identity may ironically be identified or even self-identify as one of what Sedgwick calls those "other people who vibrate to the chord of queer without having much same-sex eroticism." Indeed, such a person may turbulently vibrate to the queer chord without having had *any* recognizably same-sex eroticism at all. Of course, consciously or not, everyone has had *some* same-sex eroticism, if not as a polymorphously perverse infant, then as a (no matter how furtively or infrequently) masturbating adult. We can (and do) forget about our ambisexual infantile pleasures. But masturbation is, after all, an unavoidably thoughtful (i.e., fantasy-dependent) and unavoidably same-sex activity, and I am not alone among queer theorists in associating the turbulence of solitary sex with the disturbances of identity formation. Sedgwick includes "masturbators" in her queer list in *Tendencies* (8); Leo Bersani considers "Who are you when you masturbate?" to be a valuably unanswerable question in *Homos* (103); and, in his book *Queer Theories*, Donald E. Hall writes that "the challenge of queer theorization ... is to return to those 'sites of becoming,' and more importantly *un*becoming, wherein identity is temporarily constructed, solidified, and then threatened or rendered inadequate in its explanatory power," and suggests "one of those hopelessly complicated and therefore highly intriguing sites is the relationship between solitary or masturbatory sexuality and the question of identity" (Hall 109). Hall continues by stressing "the problem of how ideas, images, and fantasies contribute to — perhaps are fundamental to — sexuality" and rephrases Bersani by asking the "identity-complicating" question: "'What do we think when we masturbate?'" (110). Or, to give the question another twist, we might ask "With whom do we think are we having sex when we have sex with and by ourselves?"

In *Of Grammatology*, Jacques Derrida (a "heterosexual" theorist without whom queer theory as we know it would have been unlikely), writes extensively and exorbitantly about what Jean-Jacques Rousseau was thinking not only when he jerked off but when he resorted to the "dangerous supplement" of *writing*. Derrida allows us to see the correspondence between the disturbing, disrupting, or disseminating play of self-presence/self-absence implied by solitary same-sex eroticism and what he elsewhere calls the "non-self-identity" of the sign. In the essay "Ellipsis" in *Writing and Difference*, Derrida writes, "As soon as a sign emerges, it begins by repeating itself. Without this, it would not be a sign, it would not be what it is, that is to say, the non-self-identity which regularly refers to the same. That is to say, to another sign, which will itself be born of having been divided. The grapheme, repeating itself in this fashion, thus has neither natural site nor natural center" (297).

I will not rehearse Derrida's arguments any further. I will only share what I think as I am *signing* off — unnaturally, graphemically, self-repetitively and self-disturbingly — here: to wit, that there is to my way of thinking a "queer" connection between the "identity-complicating" problem of "how ideas, images, and fantasies contribute to — perhaps are fundamental to — sexuality" and the no less turbulent question of how signification, language, ideas, images, and fantasies contribute and are anti-foundationally fundamental not only to *writing* but to the trembling formation of *social reality itself.* In stressing this strange connection, I mean to twist the subtitle of this collection of essays to suggest not simply that there are "Non-normative Expressions of Heterosexuality in Literature" (which the contributors to this volume very productively explore) but that literary expression itself queers heterosexuality, that writing itself, always already beside itself, is what can never define but only disturb identity, and that the "defamiliarization" (Schlovsky 12) or "encounter with strangeness" (Bloom 3) that is the essenceless essence of aesthetic experience is part of what makes a "world that must be made to mean" (Stuart Hall 1050) as queer as it is, and will continue to make this "world queerer than ever" (Warner xxvii). In other words, though the point may be not simply to analyze the world but to change it, things as they are *are* changed on the blue guitar, provided that we who vibrate to the chord of queer know how to listen, provided that we hear "queer" as "a site of permanent becoming: 'utopic in its negativity ... curv[ing] endlessly toward a realization that its realization remains impossible'" (Jagose 131; Edelman, "Queer Theory" 345), and, finally, "provided we recognize ourselves as always already altered by the symbolic — by language. Provided we hear in language ... that basic incompleteness that conditions the indefinite quest of signifying concatenations. That amounts to joying in the truth of self-division" (Kristeva 89).

In juxtaposing, as I just have, an allusion to the words inscribed on Karl Marx's tomb with a line from a poem by Wallace Stevens (in which Stevens plays the "blue guitar" as a metaphor for the poetic imagination), and in capping off with a purely poststructuralist quip from Julia Kristeva, I allude to the tensions among politics, aesthetics, and theory that have always characterized queer critical inquiry.[4] If there has been a hierarchy of urgent concern structuring this *troika*, and there has, then politics has understandably and rightly taken first billing. After all, "queer" got started not in academic hallways but in the activist streets. Thus academic straight intellectuals (like me) who have gotten mixed up with or blundered into queer theory attempt to justify their involvement in terms of potential use-value to transformative queer politics. Consider, for example, the phrasing from Judith Butler's *Bodies That Matter* that first activated my own oxymoronic impulse toward "straight-queer" affiliation: Butler writes of the word "queer" as a "discursive rallying point" for a number of socio-political sexual subjects, including, last and least, "straights for whom the term expresses an affiliation with antihomophobic politics" (230). Without diluting the commitment to antihomophobic politics, and without erasing or easing the tensional differences among different subjects' political, aesthetic, and theoretical experiences (of marginalization and of privilege), can one nonetheless suggest that what the three registers have in common is a desire, "utopic in its negativity," for transformation? Can one not insist that the point about "the world" *is* still to change it, and that things as they are *are* changed on the blue guitar, and that we are all always already altered by language, if not always in the same way, *and* that all of these changes can be intellectually constellated as "notes" comprising the mordant, vibrant chord of queer? Can one not insist, with Lee Edelman, that "[i]f it aims effectively to intervene in the reproduction of such a reality ... then queer theory must always insist on its connection to the vicissitudes of the sign" (*No Future* 7)? Can one, even one such as myself, not insist but suggest, again with Edelman, that if queer theory "marks the 'other' side of politics" (7) then it does so in the same, discursively self-shattering or identity-disturbing way as "I mark(s) the division" (Derrida, *Glas* 165)?[5]

If queer does mark the other side of "the street" (taken as a metonym for the directly political), then that other side (of identity) can be "a site of permanent becoming" to which some heterosexuals desire to cross over. And to the extent that some of them have come across — and I remind the reader that "the word queer itself means *across*" (Sedgwick, *Tendencies* xii) — they have done so not so much "in the sheets" (taken as a metonym for fucking) as "*on* the sheets" (taken as a metonym for writing), though the marks or stains may be of a similar disorder.[6] They have "taken the textual for the political," a confusion that, as I take it, is as new as Derrida's "there is nothing outside of the text" (*Of Grammatology* 158) and as old as the invention of *polis* and papyrus.[7] Queer heterosexuals, like some other queer theorists, have taken "the world" as textually construed and hence susceptible to change. In other words, without the remarkable sheets (i.e., literary expressions of non-normative desire) the streets would not be *crossable*— in the queerest sense of that word.

Hence the first part of the title of this foreword — which I thank Richard Fantina for asking me to write — to the remarkable volume *Straight Writ Queer: Essays on Non-normative Expressions of Heterosexuality in Literature*, which you will thank Richard Fantina for having put together, and the contributors for having written. As for the second part of the title: depending on your word-processing program, you may have already figured it out. The file-name for this writing has been "queer heterosexuality," and each time I exit this file I am asked the same question — "Do you want to save the changes in queer heterosexuality?" — in response to which I of course always click yes (even if I do want to lose myself in language, I am loathe to lose any "changes"). In closing here, I will say that if you want to save the changes in queer heterosexuality, or if you want to make changes of your own, you should read the following very closely.

## Notes

1. See De Lauretis, "Queer Theory: Lesbian and Gay Sexualities," but be aware that De Lauretis dismissed the term "queer theory" three years later as a "vacuous creature of the publishing industry" ("Habit Changes" 297). As for the anonymously authored pamphlet, it was called "Queer Power Now" and it declared, "Queer means to fuck with gender. There are straight queers, bi-queers, tranny queers, lez queers, fag queers, SM queers, fisting queers" (cited in Sullivan 44).

2. See my "Straight with a Twist," "Cultural Droppings," "Is Straight Self-Understanding Possible?" and "Must Desire Be Taken Literally?"

3. The temperature reference alludes to the opening line of Berlant and Warner's "What Does Queer Theory Teach Us About X?": "Queer is hot" (343).

4. Marx's epitaph is of course the eleventh of the "Theses on Feuerbach": "Philosophers have only analyzed the world; the point is to change it." The Stevens line is from "The Man with the Blue Guitar" (*Collected Poems* 165).

5. Derrida's sentence enacts the problem of subjective self-division in language: on the one hand, as I write I make marks, and each mark, as a signifier, implies, whatever else it signifies, its own self-division, its non-self-identity (because the signifier is different from the signified, the word from the thing, etc.). But "I" is also just such a mark, a self-divided or non-self-identical sign, so every time I make a divisive mark, and all marks are divisive, "I" is (not am but is) marked as well. Derrida is alluding

to the grammatical deformation of Artur Rimbaud's "*Je est un autre*" ("I is an other") as well as formulations like this one from Jacques Lacan: "I identify myself in language, but only by losing myself in it like an object" (*Écrits* 84).

6. I am indebted here to Ann Powers for the "streets" and "sheets" analogies. See her "Queer in the Streets, Straight in the Sheets: Notes on Passing."

7. Of all the critical points made against me by Annette Schlichtler in "Queer At Last?: Straight Intellectuals and the Desire for Transgression," the charge that I "take the textual for the political" (552) is both the most naïve and the one I would least want to deny. I respond to Schlichtler at greater length in "On Being Post-Normal: Heterosexuality After Queer Theory," in the forthcoming *Critical Inqueery: A Reader*, edited by Noreen Giffney and Michael O'Rourke.

## *Works Cited*

Berlant, Lauren, and Michael Warner. "What Does Queer Theory Teach Us About X?" *PMLA* 110.3 (1995): 343–49.
Bersani, Leo. *Homos*. Cambridge: Harvard University Press, 1995.
Bloom, Harold. *The Western Canon*. New York: Harcourt Brace, 1994.
Butler, Judith. *Bodies That Matter: On the Discursive Limits of "Sex."* New York: Routledge, 1993.
De Lauretis, Teresa. "Habit Changes." *Differences* 6.2/3 (1994): 296–313.
———. "Queer Theory: Lesbian and Gay Sexualities." *differences* 3.2 (1991): iii–xviii.
Derrida, Jacques. *Glas*. Trans. John P. Leavey and Richard Rand. Lincoln: University of Nebraska Press, 1986.
———. *Of Grammatology*. Corrected Edition. Trans. Gayatri Spivak. Baltimore: Johns Hopkins University Press, 1997.
———. *Writing and Difference*. Trans. Alan Bass. Chicago: University of Chicago Press, 1978.
Edelman, Lee. *No Future: Queer Theory and the Death Drive*. Durham: Duke University Press, 2004.
———. "Queer Theory: Unstating Desire." *GLQ: A Journal of Lesbian and Gay Studies* 2:4 (1995): 343–46.
Hall, Donald E. *Queer Theories*. New York: Palgrave, 2003.
Hall, Stuart. "The Rediscovery of 'Ideology.'" In *Literary Theory: An Anthology*. Ed. Julie Rivkin and Michael Ryan. New York: Blackwell, 1998. 1050–64.
Halperin, David. *Saint Foucault: Towards a Gay Hagiography*. New York and Oxford: Oxford University Press, 1995.
Jagose, Annamarie. *Queer Theory: An Introduction*. New York: New York University Press, 1996.
Kristeva, Julia. *Powers of Horror: An Essay on Abjection*. Trans. Leon S. Roudiez. New York: Columbia University Press, 1982.
Lacan, Jacques. *Écrits: A Selection*. Trans. Bruce Fink. New York: Norton, 2002.
Parker, Andrew. "Foucault's Tongues." *Mediations* 18:2 (Fall 1994).
Powers, Ann. "Queer in the Streets, Straight in the Sheets: Notes on Passing," *Utne Reader* (Nov/Dec. 1993): 74–80.
Schlichtler, Annette. "Queer at Last?: Straight Intellectuals and the Desire for Transgression." *GLQ: A Journal of Lesbian and Gay Studies* 10:4 (2004): 543–564.

Sedgwick, Eve Kofosky. "Queer Performativity: Henry James's *The Art of the Novel.*" *GLQ: Journal of Lesbian and Gay Studies* 1:1 (1993): 1–16.
_____. *Tendencies*. Durham: Duke University Press, 1993.
Shklovsky, Victor. "Art as Technique." *Russian Formalist Criticism: Four Essays*. Trans. Lee T. Lemon and Marion J. Reis. Lincoln: University of Nebraska Press, 1965. 3–24.
Stevens, Wallace. *The Collected Poems*. New York: Vintage, 1982.
Sullivan, Nikki. *A Critical Introduction to Queer Theory*. New York: New York University Press, 2003.
Thomas, Calvin. "Cultural Droppings: Bersani's Beckett." *Twentieth Century Literature* 47:2 (Summer 2001): 169–196.
_____. "Is Straight Self-Understanding Possible?" *Transformations: The Journal of Inclusive Scholarship and Pedagogy* 13:2 (Fall 2002): 17–24.
_____. "Must Desire Be Taken Literally?" *Parallax 25: "Having Sex"* (October-December 2002): 46–56.
_____. "Straight with a Twist: Queer Theory and the Subject of Heterosexuality." In *Genders 26: The Gay 90s: Disciplinary and Interdisciplinary Formations in Queer Studies*. Ed. Thomas Foster, Carol Siegel, and Ellen E. Berry. New York: New York University Press, 1997. 83–115. Reprinted in *Straight with a Twist: Queer Theory and the Subject of Heterosexuality*. Ed. Calvin Thomas, with Joseph O. Aimone and Catherine A.F. MacGillivray. Urbana: University of Illinois Press, 2000. 11–44.
Warner, Michael. "Introduction." *Fear of a Queer Planet: Queer Politics and Social Theory*. Ed. Michael Warner. Minneapolis: University of Minnesota, 1993.

# Preface

*Straight Writ Queer* contributes to the emerging discourse of "Queer Heterosexuality." In the past few decades, there have been numerous queer interrogations of heterosexuality but not many of heterosexualities that are queer. The essays collected here examine queer heterosexual perspectives in literary productions from the medieval era to the present. These papers are informed by an awareness of heterosexuality's cultural hegemony and employ the critical tools to contest it made available by predominantly gay and lesbian scholars. This collection seeks to make queer heterosexuality culturally legible to the majority of undergraduate and graduate students who self-identify as heterosexual and to elaborate on much that gay and lesbian students may already know, if only intuitively. If it succeeds in convincing straight students to understand the cultural construction of many manifestations of their own ideas of sexuality, to identify some of their own heterosexual practices as inherently queer, and to recognize the validity of alternative sexualities, it will have served its purpose. If the collection succeeds in convincing gay and lesbian students of the similarities between themselves and their heterosexual peers, that will be an added bonus.

One of the persistent criticisms of queer theory has been that it appeals only to gay and lesbian students and scholars. This collection seeks to dismiss that critique by demonstrating how queer theoretical tools can be productively employed to investigate what are perceived to be "straight" texts. As this collection demonstrates, canonical works by authors such as George Eliot, George Meredith, Ernest Hemingway and others can be fruitfully interrogated using methods introduced by queer theory. Many of the essays collected here are concise and accessible to students on both the graduate and undergraduate levels as well as to established scholars in the field. The conscious editorial intention is to provide a broad coverage of many periods, authors, and genres.

*Straight Writ Queer* looks at the possibility of "queer straights" and "queer heterosexuality," apparent oxymorons that may seem puzzling concepts at first. Yet if we remember that homosexuality was only defined in the nineteenth century and actually predates the concept of heterosexuality, it becomes obvious that this binary is a rather recent and artificial construction of our "enlightened" age. Many of the sexual practices and gender positions discussed in this collection are poised between the poles of that binary and cannot be classified as either gay or straight, nor as masculine or feminine. This book intends to demystify the concept of queer heterosexuality. While the queer heterosexual may be only now coming out of the closet, these essays demonstrate that s/he has existed for a long time and has a long literary tradition. *Straight Writ Queer* seeks to identify and out the queer heterosexual in both classic and current literature.

This collection grew out of two panels entitled "Literary Representations of Queer Heterosexuality," presented at the 2005 conference of the Northeast Modern Language Association (NEMLA) in Boston. The ten papers presented on those panels engendered a lively debate and led to the conception of the present volume. Additional papers were contributed by scholars already working in this emerging field of study. I would like to thank NEMLA — and especially Michael Schiavi of the GLBT Caucus — for providing us with a forum. Thanks also to all who participated in these panels and other supporters including Sebastian Bach and Giovanna Montenegro. Special thanks go to Denise Gravatt and Zachary Sifuentes who provided important feedback during the editing of this book. And very special thanks to Calvin Thomas for writing the Foreword — RF

# Introduction
RICHARD FANTINA

## *Theoretical Background*

The concept of queer heterosexuality is a relatively new development within queer theory which received its first detailed literary study in Calvin Thomas's edited volume *Straight with a Twist: Queer Theory and the Subject of Heterosexuality* (2000). As Thomas makes clear in his introduction, the intention of that collection was "not to arrogate, confiscate, or seize queer theory's varied concepts and put them to straight use" but to "proliferate its findings and insights" in the exploration of heterosexuality (3). Thomas writes of the sense of validation and "jubilation" he felt upon reading a passage in Judith Butler's *Bodies That Matter* (1993) that suggests that a queer identification is possible, even desirable, for straights (21). As Thomas notes, "straight readers have taken a genuine interest in queer theory and have found much there to be excited about" (1–2). The present volume reflects the excitement of its contributors, and while not all of these scholars are straight intellectuals, the collection owes its inspiration to Thomas's work. To students new to sexuality studies and to queer theory, it may be useful to provide some brief and selective history.

With the rise of feminist and gay activism and the advent of women's studies and gay and lesbian studies as discrete academic disciplines in the 1970s, new opportunities arose to interrogate sexuality in literature. Neglected female authors were rediscovered and the homoeroticism of classical, early modern, and other texts began to be openly celebrated. Feminism and gay and lesbian studies, as Joseph Bristow, Jeffrey Weeks, and others have shown, were identity-based curricula that grew directly out of the cultural upheavals of the 1960s and what Gayatri Spivak calls the "strategic essentialism" (11, 109) that proliferated in their aftermath among such diverse groups as African Americans, Chicanos, Native Americans, women, and gays. Since the late 1980s, with the emergence of queer theory with its decidedly postmodern and "anti-identitarian" focus, broader interpretations of gender in literature began to create a space in which to accommodate a more thorough interrogation of literary sexuality.

Queer theory derives from several critical approaches of which four stand out: Michel Foucault's *The History of Sexuality* (1978), Judith Butler's theory of the "performance of gender," Eve Sedgwick Kosofky's "homosociality," and Adrienne Rich's notion of "compulsory heterosexuality." Foucault's famous assertion that the social construction of the "homosexual" began to emerge only in the nineteenth century has had enormous impact throughout the social sciences and the humanities. Queer theory has generally embraced this concept and, seeking to avoid "anachronistic" labels, often refers to "same-sex" or "homoerotic" desire, rather than to "homosexuality" in literature before the late nineteenth century. The difference in approach between this new model and the earlier gay and lesbian studies' strategic essentialist approach may appear subtle but in fact has significant implications for our understanding of cultural productions from all periods. Butler's *Gender Trouble* (1990) introduced the concept of the "performativity" of gender which opened up new areas of inquiry into biological sex versus gendered behavior. Sedgwick's work, especially *Between Men* (1985) and *Epistemology of the Closet* (1991), and her concept of "homosociality" identifies the contradiction between the demand that males form close bonds and the insistence that homoeroticism has no place within those bonds. Sedgwick suggests that any investigation into cultural phenomena must be flawed if it neglects the importance of the hetero/homo binary. Adrienne Rich developed the important concept of "compulsory heterosexuality" which she refers to as an artificial regime "imposed, managed, organized, propagandized, and maintained by force" and that "the failure to examine heterosexuality as an institution is like failing to admit that the economic system called capitalism or the caste system of racism is maintained by a variety of forces, including both physical violence and false consciousness" (216). Thanks to these critical traditions, heternormativity has been increasingly interrogated in recent years in works such as Jonathan Ned Katz's *The Invention of Heterosexuaity* (1996). Yet even many of the earliest scholars working within gay and lesbian studies, such as Dennis Altman and Lillian Faderman, critiqued the construction of heterosexuality. As early as 1948, Alfred Kinsey in his famous report writes: "Males do not represent two discrete populations, heterosexual and homosexual. The world is not divided into sheep and goats" (qtd. in Archer 123). The Kinsey Report, though an immense bestseller, appeared at a time when heteronormativity was at its height following the validation of traditional notions of masculinity with the Allied victory in World War II. Yet Kinsey's report represents an early crack in the wall.

In her influential introductory text, *Queer Theory* (1996), Annamarie Jagose writes: "Broadly speaking, queer describes those gestures or analytical models which dramatise incoherencies in the allegedly stable relations between chromosomal sex, gender and sexual desire. Resisting that model of stability — which claims heterosexuality as its origin, when it is more properly its effect — queer focuses on mismatches between sex, gender and desire" (3). Many critics now recognize sexual desire as fluid but still subject to the social regime of compulsory heterosexuality that seeks to ensure that an individual's "performance" of sexuality conforms appropriately to his or her gender identity. A wider range of sexual attitudes and practices can now be identified as queer. Queer interrogations of literature seek to find "spaces" where alternative sexualities operate. We have reached the point at which we can now speak of queer heterosexualities.

A conservative criticism of queer theory holds that it represents the concerns of a "special interest" group, that it speaks only to lesbians and to gay men and possibly to some fringe feminists. This criticism persists despite the anti-identitarian stance that has marked queer theory since its inception. Such critiques from traditional quarters could have been anticipated and it is hardly necessary to address them here. But some of the critiques from gay and lesbian scholars deserve attention. The very expansiveness of queer theory has generated criticism from scholars with a progressive social agenda. In her study *Identity Poetics* (2001), Linda Garber points out that queer theory has sometimes appeared to suffer from a "historical amnesia" by neglecting the vital connections to earlier gay and lesbian activism and other identity-based movements. Garber's work is especially important because it focuses upon the contributions to queer theory of lesbians of color such as Audre Lorde and Gloria Anzaldúa. Garber cites the comments of Fadermen who views "with some alarm" queer theory's apparent disregard of the work in identity politics that had defined the gay and lesbian movement since the days of the Stonewall uprising in 1969 which predates the birth of most students. Faderman notes that "[b]ecause we had defined gay and lesbian identity (as fictive and limited as it may have been), and an identity politics that grew out of it, we were able to form our caucuses in professional organizations, agitate to teach gay and lesbian courses, and initiate gay and lesbian scholarship" (qtd. in Garber 188–89). As Valerie Traub notes: "In the college classroom and the public conference panel, no less then on the political stage, the claims of identity are revealed as deeply held investments that demand and deserve attention"(27). The development of gay and lesbian identities was vital to the development of contemporary queer theory and Garber, Faderman, Traub and others are correct to emphasize their importance. David Halperin suggests that one of the reasons for the increasing acceptability of queer theory is because academic departments and institutions have allowed "the 'theory' in queer theory to prevail over the 'queer'" (341) thereby diluting its transgressive potential. The recognition and validation of gay, lesbian, bisexual, transgender, and other alternative sexual identities remains a pressing concern especially in a time of political reaction like the present. Any attempt to fold the issue of sexual identity into the umbrella of "queer" must include a radical critique that, in Michael Warner's words, "rejects a minoritizing logic of simple toleration" (*Fear* xxvi). While some critics within queer theory may be unwilling to support the idea of the present collection which focuses primarily on heterosexuality, this volume nevertheless owes its very existence to those gay and lesbian scholars who have pioneered the field of queer theory and the critique of heternormativity. This collection of essays would have been inconceivable without such groundbreaking work.

In her book published ten years ago, Jagose wrote of the conflict between traditional gay and lesbian studies and queer theory: "If the dialogue between queer and more traditional identity formations is sometimes fraught — which it is — that is not because they have nothing in common. Rather, lesbian and gay faith in the authenticity or even political efficacy of identity categories and the queer suspension of all such classifications energise each other, offering in the 1990s — and who can say beyond?— the ambivalent reassurance of an unimaginable future." The essays in this collection, by identifying inherently queer heterosexual practices and critiquing heteronormativity, suggest possibilities for the "unimaginable future" that Jagose refers to.

In *Straight with a Twist,* Thomas suggests that "what queerly aspiring straights need to interrogate, challenge, and work toward changing is less their own sexual practices than their condition of possibility" (18). But moving beyond Thomas's suggestion, an interrogation of some straight sexual practices demonstrates that many of these can be as subversive to patriarchal values and institutions as same-sex practices. By focusing on some of these transgressive acts and counterhegemonic gender positions, this collection seeks to blur the divide between homo- and heterosexuality, while deconstructing heteronormativity.

In an essay commenting on the work of Thomas, Ann Powers, Clyde Smith, and others, Annette Schlichter writes that "these queer straights' identifications provide a necessary deconstruction of the clear-cut opposition of straight and queer that is still operative in most queer writings" (549). Schlichter notes that "attempts to reconfigure straightness are taking place in various realms of contemporary culture and society" (560) and she points to Madonna, the novels of Kathy Acker, and the popularity of the how-to video *Bend Over Boyfriend* whose target audience is heterosexual couples seeking to reverse traditional sexual positions with the aid of a strap-on dildo. In her weekly *Village Voice* column, "Pucker Up," sexual radical and self-identified lesbian Tristan Taormino gleefully promotes alternative sexualities. In a 2003 article she suggests that "dialogue and diversity within the LGBT community has ushered in a new identity: the Queer Heterosexual," and she adds, "The LGBT movement has had broad, significant effects on sexuality — not just queer sexuality, but the sex lives of everyone" (QH). Taormino's column and her other activities promoting alternative sexualities provide examples of the important work being done on gender and sexuality outside of academic circles. The work of Carol Queen (who co-produced *Bend Over Boyfriend* and co-edited the collection *PoMoSexuals*) provides another example. Other nonacademic works that speak to the aims of this collection are *Transgender Warriors* (1996) by Leslie Feinberg, *My Gender Workbook* (1998) by Kate Bornstein, and *The End of Gay (and the Death of Heterosexuality)* (2002) by Bert Archer, who offers "an obituary, a eulogy, a thanatology, for sexual identity" (24). While Archer's obituary is both utopian and undesirable at this dangerous historical moment, it suggests an outcome that is implicit in many queer theoretical works. Taormino's remark that sexual identities are "simultaneously crucial and insignificant" (SM) may be more to the point, and she advocates a plethora of alternative sexual identities when she writes: "From gay male bears, faeries, drag queens, and twinkies to lesbian butches, femmes, girlfags, and bois-with-an-i-not-with-a-y, we are at the forefront of the gender revolution thanks to our ability to self-identify and to create our own permutations of masculinity, femininity, androgyny, and beyond" (QH). Taunting religious reactionaries, Taormino adds: "So I gladly welcome the queer heterosexuals into the fold. It's the religious right's worst nightmare. We've infiltrated your ranks. Our men have taught your women how to dress better, and our women have sold your women devices to replace your men.... You're having sex like queers and you don't even know it!" (QH). Many heterosexuals have been "having sex like queers," and writing about it, for millennia. The essays collected here point to some of these literary expressions.

This collection seeks to contribute to this discourse on a more purely academic level, perhaps several steps removed from the "street" experiences of writers like Taormino. With few exceptions academia lags years behind the "street" and scholarship has often been slow to react to popular culture. However, there are notable exceptions, especially within queer theory. Alan Sinfield's *Gay and After* and Judith Halberstam's work (with Del LaGrace) on drag kings provide excellent balances of street-level knowledge and scholarship. Jonathan Goldberg's *Reclaiming Sodom* (1994) provides another example. Michael Warner's work for the *Village Voice* and elsewhere also addresses a popular audience. The essay "Queer Nationality" by Lauren Berlant and Elizabeth Freeman in Warner's excellent collection *Fear of a Queer Planet* (1993) also effectively covers popular cultural phenomena and street-level queer activism, although for a scholarly audience. This collection hopes to contribute to the work of closing the gap between the academy and the street and to historicize queer heterosexuality by examining some of these alternative manifestations of desire and performance in cultural productions of many periods. The essays in this collection seek to take up the challenge initiated by feminism and queer theory as the authors explore a variety of works, practices, and positionalities that, while technically heterosexual, contest heteronormativity. Some scholars, such as Jonathan Dollimore in *Sexual Dissidence* (1991)— with its compelling analyses of the work of D.H. Lawrence, Shakespeare's *Othello,* and many other texts—and Christopher Craft in *Another Kind of Love* (1994) with an inspired reading of *Dracula* have touched upon these issues but only peripherally and before a queer heterosexual vocabulary had been elaborated. Thomas's *Straight with a Twist* and Schlichter's essay "Queer at Last" have begun to provide such a vocabulary. We hope that this collection will further advance it.

These essays focus on those "mismatches between sex, gender and desire" that Jagose refers to. The authors here focus on works that register a "disconnect" between the gender of the subject and his or her desire, or the sex of the subject and the "proper" performance of his or her gender. While not all of the authors profiled in these essays represent politically progressive views, all of them, some perhaps unconsciously, depict examples of what we can call, if only anachronistically, a queer heterosexuality. On the question of anachronism and queer theory's general aversion to it, Claude J. Summers, in his introduction to the edited volume

*Homosexuality in Renaissance and Enlightenment England,* provides a useful guideline when he writes that scholars must be "sensitive to the dangers of anachronism" but not "unduly constrained by the tyranny of theory or the anxieties of anachronism" (3). And while several of the contributors to the collection do not engage directly with queer theory and others consciously deploy anachronistic vocabulary, they all owe to queer theory a huge debt for opening up space for such discussions of queer heterosexuality.

## The Essays

This collection begins by grouping thematically two pairs of essays on widely divergent topics — sodomy and chastity. Part II focuses on the Victorians whose legacy made sexual repression a watchword, though since Foucault (and before him Steven Marcus) we know well that a great variety of sexualities were practiced in that era as in all others. Part III focuses on the eternal incommensurability of that triad that Butler has identified as "sex/gender/desire" (GT 6). Part IV explores some particularly wayward interventions and instabilities in literary portrayals of gender and sexuality.

Sodomy has a long and well-researched history. The practice of anal sex was celebrated (under certain circumstances) in classical Greek and Roman culture and since then, most often condemned. Jonathan Goldberg's studies in the recovery of sodomy during the Renaissance in works such as *Sodometries* (1992) and his essays in many collections are indispensable texts on the subject. Students should also consult his historic collection *Queering the Renaissance* (1994). We owe to St. Alphonsus Liguori, an 18th century theologian, the formulation of the distinction between "perfect" and "imperfect" sodomy. Ligouri defined "perfect sodomy" as the "copulation" between two men. This was later extended to include any erotic touching between two persons of the same sex, a very broad definition which led Foucault to call sodomy "that utterly confused category" (HS 101). Because "perfect sodomy," as defined, involves same-sex desires and practices, it falls outside of the focus of this collection. But two of the essays here focus on literary representations of "imperfect sodomy." Foucault describes how a seventeenth century confessional manual portrayed heterosexual sodomy: "[I]f sodomy between a man and a woman is due to a particular taste for the rear parts, then this is imperfect sodomy because the desired part is not natural; the category is still sodomy, but since it is not with the undue sex — since it involves a woman with a man — then the sodomy is not perfect but only imperfect" (*Abnormal* 218). These guidelines, designed to aid priests hearing confessions, give an idea of the kinds of practices that ecclesiastical authorities felt compelled to interrogate, suggesting that such practices were not uncommon.

In her enlightening and highly entertaining essay on Renaissance "gynosodomy," Celia R. Daileader contends that far from being a practice degrading for women, anal sex can endow the female with a great deal of agency. As women often need to direct the movements of the men in this activity, Daileader refers to the "back door's emancipatory potential." Focusing primarily on the work of Thomas Middleton, Daileader writes of the influence on English Renaissance authors of the erotic Italian sonnets of Pietro Aretino, who glorified heterosexual anal intercourse. Quoting from Middleton's *Chaste Maid in Cheapside* (1613), Daileader writes, "'A wise man for love will seek every hole'" (CM, 4.3.11), but she adds that "a wise woman will know where to direct him." Richard Fantina provides another look at heterosexual anal erotics in his essay on the work of Ernest Hemingway. The fiction of this most patriarchal of twentieth-century authors features several instances of male characters being sodomized by their female lovers, most graphically in the posthumous *The Garden of Eden* (1986). This practice, recently dubbed "pegging," has gained considerable popularity in recent years as evidenced by the success of *Bend Over Boyfriend*. Hemingway's masochism and his surprising enthusiasm for passive sodomy when compared to his often aggressively masculine exterior reveals a conflicted career that suggests that he was a victim of a rigidly constructed heterosexuality. His tragedy was that he bought into it so wholeheartedly, despite some of his own deepest impulses and desires, at a cost no one will ever know.

To move from an inherently transgressive practice to a sexual stance more culturally sanctioned, even venerated, two essays in this collection deal with the apparent absence of sexuality through the denials of chastity and celibacy. Susannah Chewning's essay focuses on the anchoritic tradition in Europe of the twelfth and thirteenth centuries. The anchoress was a (typically) young woman who chose to forsake the world and become the bride of Christ. These female urban recluses led sequestered lives in the sacristies of churches in urban areas. They often continued to keep in verbal contact with the outside world as they preached to pilgrims, but they renounced all physical ties. Chewning suggests that these women channeled their heterosexual desires toward the figure of Jesus Christ. Kate Faber Oestreich comments on another religious woman, Dinah Morris in

George Eliot's *Adam Bede* (1859). Oestreich contends that Dinah's initial celibacy in that novel, symbolized by her fetishistic Quaker cap, represents a greater threat to heternormativity than does the sexual transgression of the novel's fallen woman, Hetty Sorel. The essays by both Chewning and Oestreich demonstrate that desires, or even the apparent lack of them, that fall outside of heternormativity are, by their very nature, queer.

Eliot provides just one example of how non-normative sexuality presents itself in the Victorian era, the subject of Part II. The contributors to this collection have found the age of Victoria particularly fertile for explorations of queer heterosexuality. While homosexuality had not yet been pathologized during the mid–Victorian era, an approximation of it had long existed in the Western tradition in the discourses on sodomy. Yet during the reign of Victoria, at least until the trial of Oscar Wilde, allusions to same-sex desire are scarce. Homoeroticism among men was unmentionable, among women unthinkable. When considering whether to criminalize same-sex desire among females, the queen is said to have remarked, "Women do not do such things." Consequently, homoeroticism is often only acknowledged elliptically. In a penetrating study of Wilkie Collins's classic *The Woman in White*, Richard Nemesvari demonstrates how the fear of the homosexual Other, combined with the fear of the foreign Other, informs and complicates the male characters' often queerly distorted relationships with women. Nemesvari addresses the debate on the novel's potential for transgression and decides finally that the author opted for the safety of traditional Victorian values over the subversive sexuality he had temporarily unleashed.

While most Victorian novels enthusiastically endorse patriarchal values, the sensation novels of Mary Elizabeth Braddon often subvert these ideals. In a highly original essay, Denise Hunter Gravatt reads Braddon's *Aurora Floyd* as advocating male masochism *avant la lettre*. Gravatt notes that Braddon's novel predates Sacher-Masoch's *Venus in Furs* (1870) and anticipates many of its themes such as the whip-wielding woman and the submissive man, and moreover that it does so from a female perspective. Because of this, Gravatt's essay suggests that female domination in *Aurora Floyd* represents a more authentic construction than the ritualized fantasies of *Venus in Furs*. Gravatt contends that Braddon's novel queers the institution of matrimony by advocating female domination and male submission as the prescription for heterosexual connubial bliss. Melissa Shields Jenkins turns to the novels of George Meredith to ask the question, "How does one 'learn' heterosexuality?" She argues that in Meredith's first full-length novel, *The Ordeal of Richard Feverel* (1859), his protagonist seeks to "push the boundaries between the writing of sex and the living of it." She goes on to trace the increasingly important role played by feminized men and masculine women in Meredith's later works, as he attempts to forge a place for alternative sexualities in Victorian literature. Shannon Young analyzes the very queer and displaced heterosexuality in Rider Haggard's *She* (1887), which features one of the most dominant phallic women in Victorian literature in the character of Ayesha, while suggesting same-sex desire in the other major characters. Young suggests that Haggard expresses a conflicted, bisexual desire in this novel.

Part III fast-forwards to the twenty-first century, as Zachary Sifuentes explores the hermaproditism in Jeffrey Eugenides's *Middlesex* (2003). Because the protagonist in this offbeat and epic *bildungsroman* is an actual hermaphrodite, or intersexed person, Calliope/Cal experiences heterosexuality queerly whether making love with a man or a woman. Sifuentes argues that the physical body of the intersexual makes claims of stability regarding sexuality both impossible and irrelevant. In some respects, the quintessentially indeterminate character of the hermaphrodite in this Pulitzer Prize–winning novel stands in as a metaphor for the theme of this book.

Psychologists are, perhaps, understandably puzzled by intersexuals. Psychiatry and psychoanalysis also has a long tradition of misunderstanding women. Sigmund Freud — who famously asked, "what do women want?" — felt that perhaps he knew what at least one woman wanted, and found that his own desire corresponded with hers. One of Freud's most controversial analyses of homosexuality appears in his "The Psychogenesis of a Case of Homosexuality in a Woman." Ashley Shelden explores Freud's convoluted negotiations of this woman's desire and finds him hopelessly baffled and far more in need of analysis than she. Freud's unconsciously queer desire both for and of the lesbian girl qualifies him as perhaps the queerest heterosexual presented in this collection. Shelden concludes her essay by repeating Jacques-Alain Miller's rhetorical question asking if the psychoanalyst is a pervert. She answers, in the case of Freud at least, "Certainly. Of course."

Lorena Russell presents another essay dealing with the possibilities of lesbian desire. In her analysis of the controversial works of Fay Weldon, Russell directly addresses the accusations of "homophobia" and "heterosexist" leveled at this author by some critics. Russell contends that Weldon's novels, while often raising lesbian possibilities only to erase or obscure them, are nevertheless both feminist and queer in that they offer such possiblities as viable alternatives in the first place.

Grace Sikorski's essay examines the work of two African American novelists who portray non-normative sexuality. According to Sikorski, E. Lynn Harris's *Invisible Life* is a "passing" novel which in effect justifies the protagonist's felt need to hide his queer impulses while passing as a straight heterosexual man. Harris's hero stands in as both the "tragic mulatto" and "sexual mulatto" because of his bisexual identity. Sikorski contrasts Harris's conflicted vision of sexual plurality with Walker's more life-affirming view in her novel *The Temple of My Familiar,* which offers a positive and spiritual embrace of pluri-sexual identities.

An essay by Deborah Kaplan and Rachel Rabinowitz addresses the fluid gender positions and sexual practices of characters in the young adult fiction of Cynthia Voigt and Francesca Lia Block. The authors suggest that it is idle to pretend that children's books, such as Voigt's *Orfe* (1992) or Block's *Weetzie Bat* (1989), do not contain sexuality; in fact, they often address it more subtly but more honestly than does adult literature. This essay supports the position that the new generation already rejects the primary tenets of heteronormativity, a point echoed in Archer's book referred to above.

Part IV of this collection deals with tenuous or unstable sexual identities and wayward subversions of heterosexual norms. In an essay on Timothy Findley's *The Wars,* Shelton Waldrep suggests that questions about nationalism and sexuality pull at the outer fringes of heterosexuality, threatening to destabilize the concept entirely. Set in World War I, the novel recalls the homoeroticism of poets Rupert Brooke, Wilfred Owen, and Siegfried Sassoon, as the protagonist, Robbie Ross (namesake of one of Oscar Wilde's lovers), connects the novel to the gender battles of the late nineteenth century and the emergence of the fragmented vision of modernism. Waldrep describes how the novel follows this character through a series of violent and ambivalent sexual encounters that problematize the very nature of desire, and finds that in Findley's novel, it eventually becomes clear that the near eroticization of war is also meant to interrogate a model of masculine heroism that frequently appears passive and objectified.

Findley's novel depicts the period that saw the collapse of Victorianism. One of the characteristics of the brief Edwardian period was the prominence of the New Woman. While she was often a figure of ridicule, behind the derision lay an element of envy. The New Woman was coming into her own, as the work of Ibsen, Shaw, Wilde, and others was making abundantly clear. And men were getting increasingly nervous and defensive. Late nineteenth-century novelists such as Olive Scrheiner and Sarah Grand immortalized the New Woman while male authors like George Gissing and Thomas Hardy simultaneously worshipped and reviled her. By the turn of the century and with the advent of the Edwardian era, the New Woman had arrived and nowhere more forcefully than in the theatre. In her essay here, Anne Stiles focuses on one playwright's attempt to confront the New Woman and beat her at her own game. New Woman authors like Schreiner and Grand had advocated a new male sensibility that would give birth to a New Man. In his work, Harley Granville-Barker adapts some of these ideas but while effeminizing and queering his male characters he endows them with some very traditional notions of male supremacy. The result is an odd mix of adulation and resentment that renders Granville-Barker's dramas enduringly enigmatic. Stiles's essay suggests a parallel to late-twentieth century male supporters of feminism who, both envious of and threatened by it, sought to inhabit it for their own purposes.

Madeleine Monson-Rosen examines the work of an underappreciated female author of the late twentieth century. Angela Carter, along with Ursula LeGuin, Monique Wittig, and Octavia Butler, pioneered a feminist science fiction/fantasy genre that continues to the present. In her essay here, Monson-Rosen discusses Carter's novel *The Magic Toyshop* in conjunction with some polemical texts such as *The Sadeian Woman* and reveals how Carter's radical project of demythologization aims at nothing less than the "explosion" of the foundations of patriarchal society. Monson-Rosen describes how Carter queers, burlesques, and valorizes "the most primal of passions," the patriarchal taboo against incest, and turns it into a potentially liberatory outlet. Carter's validation of heterosexual incest represents a radical disavowal of heteronormativity.

In the concluding essay, Carol Poster argues that the irreligiousness of both the Marquis de Sade and Charles Algernon Swinburne belied their faith in the deity. Poster notes that Sade's ideal libertine communities and Swinburne's explicitly iconoclastic poetry represent attempts to defy their Christian heritage. But neither achieved even a modest return for his efforts in the form of official excommunication. Poster, who refers to their work elsewhere as "liturgical pornography," finds that ultimately the fervent blasphemies of "Dolores," in which the Virgin Mary is portrayed as a dominatrix, or the excesses in Sade's *The 120 Days of Sodom*, required an ardent belief even as the authors struggled violently against it.

This collection attempts to offer at least a glimpse at some literary representations of queer heterosexuality. If the essays have a common thread, it lies in a persistent question which, in the words of Debra A. Moddelmog, "asks us to suspect, and finally to critique, those systems of representation that are insufficient and hence disabling to efforts to comprehend the human body and its desires" (99–100). Many more authors and texts could be examined using methods similar to those employed here. We hope that the current collection will help to expand the space devoted to radical subversions of heternormativity by allegedly straight authors and texts in English studies.

## Works Cited

Altman, Dennis, *Homosexual Oppression and Liberation*. New York: Avon, 1971.
Archer, Bert. *The End of Gay (and the Death of Heterosexuality)*, New York: Thunder's Mouth Press, 2002.
Bristow, Joseph. *Activating Theory: Lesbian, Gay, Bisexual Politics*. London: Lawrence and Wishart, 1992.
_____. *Sexuality*. New York: Routledge, 1997.
Butler, Judith. *Bodies That Matter: On the Discursive Limits of Sex*. New York and London: Routledge, 1993.
_____. *Gender Trouble*. New York and London: Routledge, 1990.
Borstein, Kate. *My Gender Workbook*. New York: Routledge, 1998.
Califia. Pat. *Sex Changes*. San Francisco: Cleis Press, 1997, "Introduction" <http://www.sexuality.org/l/transgen/scpc.html> (11 August 2004).
Craft, Christopher. *Another Kind of Love*. Berkeley: University of California Press, 1994.
Dollimore, Jonathan. *Sexual Dissidence: Augustine to Wilde, Freud to Foucault*. London: Clarendon Press, Oxford University Press, 1991.
Feinberg, Leslie. *Transgender Warriors: Making History from Joan of Arc to RuPaul*. Boston: Beacon Press, 1996.
Foucault, Michel. *Abnormal: Lectures at the College de France, 1974–1975*. Translated by Graham Burchell. New York: Picador, 1999.
_____. *The History of Sexuality*. Translated by Robert Hurley. New York: Pantheon, 1978.
Garber, Linda. *Identity Poetics: Race, Class, and the Lesbian Roots of Queer Theory*. New York: Columbia University Press, 2001.
Goldberg, Jonathan, ed. "Introduction" in *Reclaiming Sodom*. London and New York: Routledge, 1994.
_____. *Queering the Renaissance*. Durham: Duke University Press, 1994.
_____. *Sodometries: Renaissance Texts, Modern Sexualities*. Stanford: Stanford University Press, 1992.
Halberstam, Judith, and Del LaGrace. *The Drag King Book*. London: Serpent's Tail, 1998.
Hall, Donald C. *Queer Theories*. New York: Palgrave Macmillan, 2002.
Halperin, David M. "The Normalization of Queer Theory," *Journal of Homosexuality*. Vol. 45, No. 2/3/4. 2003. 339–43.

Jagose, Annamarie. *Queer Theory*. Melbourne: University of Melbourne Press, 1996.
Katz, Jonathan Ned. *The Invention of Heterosexuality*. New York: Plume/Penguin, 1996.
Krafft-Ebing, Richard von. *Psychopathia Sexualis*. New York: G.P. Putnam & Sons, 1965.
Middleton, Thomas. *Chaste Maid in Cheapside*, in *The Collected Works of Thomas Middleton*, ed. Gary Taylor. Oxford: Oxford University Press, forthcoming.
Moddelmog, Debra A. *Reading Desire: In Pursuit of Ernest Hemingway*. Ithaca: Cornell University Press, 1999.
Rich, Adrienne. "Compulsory Heterosexuality and the Lesbian Experience." In *Andrienne Rich's Poetry and Prose: A Norton Critical Edition*, edited by Barbara Charlesworth Gelpi and Albert Gelpi. New York and London: 1993. 203–24.
Schlichter, Annette. "Queer At Last: Straight Intellectuals and the Desire for Transgression." *GLQ*, Vol. 10, No. 4, 2004. 543–564.
Sedgwick-Kosofsky, Eve. *Between Men: British Literature and Male Homosocial Desire*. New York: Columbia University Press, 1985.
_____. *Epistemology of the Closet*. Berkeley: University of California Press, 1990.
Sinfield, Alan. *Gay and After*. London: Serpent's Tail, 1998.
Spivak, Gayatri Chakravorty. *The Postcolonial Critic: Interviews Strategies, Dialogues*. New York and London: Routledge, 1990.
Taormino, Tristan. "Bend Over, Boys!" "Pucker Up" column in *The Village Voice*, March 1–7, 2000 <http://www.villagevoice.com/issues/0009/taormino.php> (12 September 2004).
_____. "The Queer Heterosexual." "Pucker Up" column in *The Village Voice*, April 30, 2003. <http://www.villagevoice.com/issues/0319/taormino.php> (12 September 2004).
_____. "Sex Magic." "Pucker Up" column in *The Village Voice*, October 4, 2004 <http://www.villagevoice.com/people/0440,taormino,57266,24.html> (7 September 2005).
Thomas, Calvin, ed. *Straight with a Twist: Queer Theory and the Subject of Heterosexuality*. Urbana and Chicago: University of Illinois Press, 2000.
Traub, Valerie. *The Renaissance of Lesbianism in Early Modern England*. Cambridge: Cambridge University Press, 2002.
Warner, Michael, ed. *Fear of a Queer Planet: Queer Politics and Social Theory*. Minneapolis and London: University of Minnesota Press, 1993.
_____. "Queer World Making." Interviewed by Annamarie Jagose, *Genders* 31, 2000.
Weeks, Jeffrey. *Sexuality*. London: Routledge, 1986, 2002.

PART I.
IMPERFECT SODOMY AND QUEER CHASTITY

# 1 Back Door Sex
## Renaissance Gynosodomy, Aretino, and the Exotic

CELIA R. DAILEADER

Few current fans of the legendary sixties rock group The Doors are likely to link the song "Back Door Man"—in which Jim Morrison seductively sneers about going in and out of a rear entrance—to an early modern euphemism for anal sex. Yet the modern rock song—its subject illicit, non-monogamous, "straight" sex—occupies a continuum traceable to seventeenth-century England, when shifting ideologies gave rise to a secular and therefore increasingly sexual form of popular entertainment in the commercial theaters.[1] That the back door idiom—though still connotive of transgression—has lost its original anatomical referent should not surprise us, given the rampant homophobia of postwar America and its habit of associating anal eroticism with gay sex. Recent scholarship, however, has questioned the utility of the hetero/homo classification system in comprehending the more fluid erotic economies of early modern English culture, particularly as manifested by the transvestite stage, that matrix of sexual indeterminacy.[2] Moreover, the back door idiom in Renaissance drama does not inevitably invoke male–male sex; very frequently, in fact, it refers to male–female sex. And while Queer theory has shed much light on the various eroticisms of the stage, these gynosodomitical moments remain as yet undertheorized—a footnote in the history of male homoerotic and homosocial relations.[3]

Before we take up these theoretical questions, though, one additional gap must be filled in the above-mentioned historical continuum. Another story lurks behind Jim Morrison's lyrics: in fact, he owed the song to an earlier American musician, the black blues singer Howlin' Wolf. That a white rock star, even one as dark and alternative as Morrison, cannibalized and crafted an eroticized persona from black materials, is no surprise, considering the history of American popular music from Elvis onward. But the "black" substratum of the song's history, along with the early artist's self-caricature as a howling wolf, rings true to the genealogy of the back door as well; this slice of American pop culture curiously replicates the link between bestiality, promiscuity, backwardness, and blackness evident in Renaissance erotic discourses.

In fact, it is arguable that the form of difference English Renaissance culture most frequently associated with back door sex was not gender (women, after all, have anuses too) but ethnicity. This is due to the notoriety of Pietro Aretino's *Sonnetti Lussuriosi* (1525), inspired by and printed with a set of obscene engravings, and flagrantly pro anal sex. Despite suppression by the Pope, "Aretine's pictures"—as they were called—very quickly reached England—either in rumor or in fact—and the name "Aretine" entered the English imagination as a synonym for sexual license of the Italian variety.[4] Thus, to dramatists like Thomas Middleton, whose fascination with "sexual vagaries" stands out even amidst this notoriously bawdy body of plays, sex "after the Italian fashion" was indisputably, anatomically "backward," although references to the practice seldom have much to do with Italy.[5] Interestingly, none of the sixteen sonnets—even the ten which celebrate anal sex—involve homoeroticism. Rather, anal sex is justified for reasons of birth control, pleasure, and fashion, and in only two cases does the female speaker of the pornographic dialogue refuse to engage in the "bestial" act—more frequently, she initiates or encourages it.[6] The Aretinian legacy, needless to say, did little to diminish already flourishing stereotypes of the non–Anglo Other as licentious and sexually depraved, which English authors were quick to anticipate in—if not inevitably to endorse for—their audiences.[7]

An episode from Thomas Heywood's *The Fair Maid of the West, Part 2* demonstrates the xenophobic tendency to lump all less than lily-skinned groups into one seething, hypersexual mass. Here Mullisheg, the Moorish king, emerges after a night in bed with a woman (in fact his own Moorish wife) whom he mistakes for the English heroine:

> Venetian ladies, nor the Persian girls,
> The French, the Spanish, nor the Turkish dames,
> Ethiope, nor Greece, can kiss with half that art
> These English can, nor entertain their friends
> Wi' th' tenth part of that ample willingness
> Within their arms [2.1.13–18].

The irony here is, of course, that Englishwomen are anything but this sluttish — in particular in the arms of a Moor. And the laundry list of darker-complected peoples whose lascivious nature has been outdone by this particularly horny she–Moor presents her as a kind of sexual conglomeration, all wrapped up in one black hide. Also, there is a subtle connection between the darkness that allows for the bedtrick — the logic of which makes this adultery, even though it technically is not — and the racialized language in which it is described. The passage serves as a snapshot of racist, xenophobic paranoia, in which the night teems with animalistic, dark bodies.

I also find this passage interesting because it mentions Venetians and Persians in the same breath. With Venice acting as the geopolitical and mercantile door to the East, the association of Venice — and by extension Italy — with various exoticisms seems natural to Englishmen. Discussing seventeenth- and eighteenth-century fantasies of the Orient, Mladen Dolar considers whether "behind every political concept there is a phantasmatic kernel which effectuates it: it discloses a certain 'economy of enjoyment' that makes it function" (x). Of particular relevance here is the European fascination with the seraglio, representing "the immense sexual lust, the supposed boundless *jouissance* at the core of" Eastern life (xiii). By shifting our vantage-point from all of Europe to the little island of England, however, we may find a corollary to this orientalism in the English fascination with Italian sexual vice. The back door functions in these contexts as an emblem of various cultural fantasies, many of which are not really about sex "after the Italian fashion" or even sex *with* Italians, but about cultural contamination through the adoption of "Italian" sexual mores, particularly by women.[8] From a feminist point of view, therefore, the stakes are very high: erotic agency, variety of pleasure, even reproductive freedom — all may be accessed by or denied women through the back door.[9] The masculinist anxieties which attend to this aperture make for the ambivalence of the examples I will take up: allusions to back door sex range from a sadistic xenophobic misogyny (watch out for those Italians, they'll do you up the ass; if you don't do what I say, I'll do you up the ass) which forecloses the question of female pleasure, to a more playful, carnivalesque treatment which exploits the polymorphous and transgendering erotic potential of the back door, in the process unhinging Anglophile bias to make room for universal lust. All in all, I hope this essay, in exploring Renaissance gynosodomy in all its richness and variety of reference, will redress the critical tendency to speak of sodomy when one means *andro*-sodomy. As we recognized in critiquing the hetero/homo binary, neither body of practices supplies the w/hole story.

First a word or two about the microcosmic referent — the architectural back door. In English drama, the back door is most frequently used as a means of surreptitious exit or entrance, particularly in connection with a sexual tryst. Shylock's daughter elopes, with her father's stolen fortune, out a back door which, according to Frank Whigham, represents the Jew's anality (336–7). The work of Middleton yields a wealth of back door escapades: in *A Trick to Catch the Old One*, and also in *The Witch*, a courtesan flees by this route; in *The Black Book*, a brothel voids its customers out "the back part" (*B*, 44); in *The Changeling*, Beatrice-Joanna is overheard with her lover (*by* two lovers) "in a back part of the house" (*C*, 4.2.91) and is later spied leaving him by "the back door" (*C*, 5.3.11); the heroine of *The Roaring Girl* "[m]ust be let in without knocking" (*R* 7.15–16) through it, so that a "chamber will be made bawdy" (*R*, 7.15.18); *I Honest Whore* refers to "every common hackney that steals out at the back gate of her sweet knight's lodging" (H/W, 2.1.225–27); *Your Five Gallants* features a brothel with "three back doors" (*Y*, 1.1.123), and *Michaelmas Term* describes "a provident back door" as "that thing that's both necessary and pleasant" in a gentleman's lodging (*MT*, 1.1.143–46). Similar back door doings — along with a joke about sex "the Italian way" — take place in Cyril Tourneur's *The Atheist's Tragedy*.[10] And another play of the period, R. A.'s *The Valiant Welshman*, explicitly links back doors and adultery, disdaining a "Bastard, begot at the backe dore of nature" (5.3.42).

By now we are beginning to see the way discussions of the literal back door may open onto larger tropic systems involving abjection at all levels — social, sexual, and racial. Middleton — always quick to turn anatomical humor against men — makes a similar move in *The Nice Valour*; Lapet, whose name is French for "fart," makes his living getting kicked in the butt, with the effect that "His buttocks [are] all black lead, / He's half a negro backward; he was past a Spaniard ... and more Egyptian-like" (*N*, 4.1.217–19). Contextualizing this passage in terms of larger patterns of Anglocentric humor, we can see the way it essentially inscribes an ethnic catalogue on the lower anatomical region. Moreover, Middleton's phrasing "half a negro" — although it seems meant to qualify the degree of blackness — also fleetingly suggests a severing of the torso from the negrified lower body. This creates an image akin to the centaurs described in King Lear's speech which associates the anatomical nether area with darkness: "But to the girdle do the gods inherit; / Beneath is all the fiend's. There's hell, there's darkness / there is the sulphurous pit" (4.5.123–25). In light of this reading, the phrase "negro backwards" begins to look redundant, as backwardness in general or anality in particular seems so readily associated with non–Anglo and particularly non-white peoples (elsewhere in Middleton, the "gypsy" language seems to transpose the words for a woman's "nose" and "ars").[11] Further complicating the ethnic/racial picture is the play's Franco-Italian setting; Middleton, as we shall soon see, very often cites stereotypes arbitrarily, eschewing consistency for comic effect. But there is no mistaking the Aretinian influence of *Nice Valour*'s posterior shenanigans: Lapet not only enjoys getting kicked in the butt; he also has published a book about it, a how-to guide just like "Aretine's Pictures," complete with illustrations.

> LAPET: Nay, but mark the postures.
> The standing of the takers I admire
> More than the givers: they stand scornfully,
> Most contumeliously. I like not them.
> Oh here's one cast into a comely figure.
> CLOWN: My master means him that's cast down headlong.
> LAPET: How sweetly does this fellow take his douse?
> Stoops like a camel, that heroic beast,
> At a great load of nutmegs. And how meekly
> This other fellow here receives his wherret!
> CLOWN: Oh master here's a fellow stands most gallantly,
> Taking his kick in private behind the hangings
> And raising his hips to't [*N*, 4.1.338–50].

Although the passage is clearly homoerotic (as not all sodomy is in Middleton), the author's familiarity with the gynosodomitical source is marked by his use of the word "postures"— here and elsewhere in the text — in reference to Lapet's illustrations; Aretino used the designation "*I positzioni*" when speaking of his pornographic volume, and English authors translated the Italian into "postures," a word which occurs in only one other Middleton play and also in a sexual context. Note also that the requisite bestial comparison involves the exotic camel rather than the domestic ox; the burden of "nutmegs" likewise bears with it the scent of the East.

Some Renaissance authors seem at pains to decide for women whether or not they will find "pleasure backwards." The triply-authored play *The Insatiate Countess*— a gruesome bit of salacious misogynist fantasy, set in Venice, of course — follows its titular nympho-bitch from one sexual conquest to the next, and finally offers the voyeuristic *pièce de résistance* of her on-stage decapitation for her "crimes."[12] But even in this sensationalistic romp, gynosodomy is mentioned only to be dismissed:

THAIS: But you mean they shall come in at the back-doors?
ABIGAIL: Who, our Husbands? nay, and they come not in at the fore-doors, there will be no pleasure in't [2.2.90].

The two women are conspiring to arrange yet another bed trick — with, significantly, the help of "the nigglers our maids" — which will steer their husbands to the wrong beds but the right wives (2.2.59–64).[13] The device operates like the bed trick turned against the Moorish couple in *Fair Maid of the West, Part 2*, in creating the impression of adultery while preserving the technical purity of the conjugal relation: in this respect, the punning rejection of anal sex is consistent with the wives' conservative goals. Oddly, though, the passage, while distinctly antisodomitical, is also distinctly Aretinian: the scene even contains the word *cazzo*, Italian for "cock," a term all over the *Sonnetti* (2.2.90). And the phrasing of "no pleasure in't" may be another clue. One of Aretino's less adventurous heroines complains to her lover, "behind you get all the pleasure / While up front we each get half," and demands that he penetrate her "the proper way or please get out" (*I modi*, 68).

Yet the female speakers of the sonnets do not by any means agree on this practice, a fact which highlights the variety of sexual tastes as well as the delicacy anal sex requires of the penetrator: one woman faults her lover for shifting his weight during anal intercourse and turning the "extreme pleasure" to pain "worse than birth-pangs or shitting." I have mentioned one instance where the female initiates the act; in other cases, the female speaker offers or promises this as a special treat. In further discussion of the anal option, one male recommends it for "the poorly endowed" (not him, he insists), and his partner confirms that women like it both ways; another female says, "it's all the same to me" and describes herself as "aflame" in both orifices.[14]

Of course we cannot assume that the *Sonnetti* bear witness to the desires or experiences of "real" women — particularly considering the drastic shift in tone between this text and his later scurrilous work, *Ragionamento Dialogo*, begun ten years, one war, and one near-fatal stabbing after the scandal caused by his "postures." *Ragionamento* is a lengthy series of dialogues between courtesans and bawds; written in two parts composed two years apart (1534 and 1536), this more acerbic, non-pictorial text begins as a pornographic romp reminiscent of the sonnets but then spirals into the most disturbing depictions of sexuality, stressing disease, poverty, and brutalization as the average courtesan's lot. Within this context, gynosodomy is as potentially degrading as any other sex act, and the older prostitute-speaker bemoans this "modern" fashion (though her colleague defends it as "a dish for gourmets") along with oral sex, both given and received.[15]

But we must resist the temptation to treat either male-authored text as a Kinsey Report of the Renaissance. So rather than launching into a utopian feminist reclamation of these shadowy female personae, I will turn to examine the masculinist anxieties evident in English responses to Aretino. For Jonson's *Volpone* is not the only play in which a depraved Italian sexual appetite is used to scare a woman into chastity. In a passage by Dekker in *I Honest Whore*, the eponymous whore is berated in these terms: "A harlot is like Dunkirk, true to none, / Swallows both English, Spanish, fulsome Dutch, / Back-doored Italian, last of all the French" (H/W, 2.1.353–55).[16] The textual problem of the phrase "Back-doored" also pertains to this discussion; the original quarto text, which read "blackedoor'd," was emended to "Back-door'd," and then re-emended later to "black-beard," on the basis that "the supposition that *back-door'd* can mean *sly* or *devious* ... is rather suspect." Suspect, indeed! Not until 1960 did scholars begin to consider the sodomitical referent. Yet this history of confusions — beginning in the original printed text, with the interpolated "l" — between blackness, backwardness, slyness, and anality, typifies the Italianate exoticism traceable to the impact of Aretino's pornographic text.[17]

The crude and uncomical misogynistic and xenophobic tirade in Dekker's contribution to *I Honest Whore* stands in stark contrast to Middleton's more typically subtle, comic, and even forgiving treatment of "Italian" sexual vice. My personal favorite is a passage in *Michaelmas Term*, when an aspiring courtesan is instructed to "wear your hair still like a mock-face behind; tis such an Italian world, many men know not before from behind" (*MT*, 3.1.18–20). The humor here lies partially in the potential confusion of orifices, but also, subtly, in the more serious anatomical error involved in mistaking heads for tails — an instance of bottoms up burlesque (like the arse/nose reversal mentioned earlier) that Bakhtin would ascribe to the carnivalesque. While Middleton does once again take for granted an association between "backward" sex and Italians, the narrative here undermines the stereotype, as the anatomically benighted men in question are all English. What's Italy got to do with it if the whole world is Italian? As Middleton writes in *The Black Book*: "Knowest thou not that sin may be committed either in French, Dutch, Italian, or Spanish, and all after the English fashion?" (*B*, 22). And that's Lucifer talking: he ought to know.

In any case, one must be careful not to overemphasize the degree to which the back door, in English Renaissance sexual humor, manifests or gives voice to xenophobia as distinct from other cultural anxieties — particularly those which pertain to sex and gender. For this reason, it may be necessary at this point to step back and view this body of rhetoric at its most general, and to look at the way "backwardness" functions as a modifier on the socio-psychological level. The word "backward" is often used as a synonym for ill-behaved or peevish, and when describing women, the modifier is sometimes set in opposition to "forward" in the sense of loose or bold — but I contend that even this latter usage draws its derogatory power (paradoxically) from the association with buttocks and buggery. In my findings, backwardness is quite frequently sexualized. Here are some Middletonian examples:

> The bride cries already and looks t'other way; an you be so backward too, we shall have a fine arseward wedding on't [*F*, 4.1.141–43].
> His goodness has gone backward, and engendered
> With his old sins again [*O*,3.2.77–78].

In the first scene of *The Changeling*, the infatuated hero goes "backward" when he aborts a business trip and begins an ill-fated affair. Similar sexualized uses of the adverb appear in Dekker's *Satiromastix* and *Match Me in London*, and his *Honest Whore, Part 2* equates prostitution itself with a woman's "backward fall" (4.1.390).[18] In two additional Middletonian cases, a woman is labelled "backward" when she resists courtship or marriage — but the context and wording renders the statement highly ironic. Here a courtesan's bawd/mother presents her as a timid, marriageable virgin:

> Always timorsome, always backward!
> ............................................
> She could not endure the sight of a man, forsooth, but run and hole herself presently [*MW,* 4.6.44–50].

As the same play includes a more explicitly anal pun — and does so in reference to the same courtesan (she is conveyed into a secret room, "the key given after the Italian fashion, backward") — it would not be too outrageous to read a sodomitical subtext into the above quote (the ambiguity of "hole" reinforces this reading). Perhaps the implication is that this courtesan — like those who feature in the *Sonnetti* — has been "backward" in bed, and for similar reasons. Here another disguised courtesan is scolded for resisting the advances of a rich old man:

> Come, you widows are ever most backward when you should do yourselves most good; but were it to marry a chin not worth a hair now, then you would be forward enough [*T*,3.1.216–17].

It seems that in all these examples, backwardness does not indicate lack of desire — quite the opposite — but rather the failure of a natural or socially-sanctioned response. I am reminded of a classical reference to a bride so "fearful for her virginity" that she engages in anal sex on her wedding night.[19] A fine way to stick it to the patriarchy! "You want virginity: I'll give you virginity!" The courtesan who "hole[s] herself" in Middleton's *Mad World* has had her virginity sold "fifteen times": anal sex would both duplicate the virginal tightness and preserve the actual hymen, and these customers are just dim enough to fall for it. As the mother/bawd says, the courtesan has "maidenhead enough for old Sir Bounteous still; / He'll be all his lifetime *about it* yet / And as *far* to seek when he has done" (*MW*, 1.2.162–67; my emphases). Perhaps he's impotent; perhaps he's looking in the wrong place — or perhaps a little of both. Can backwardness — and the anal eroticism it often suggests — be read as a badge of female sexual resistance? Given the contraceptive advantage of sodomy, this positive signification is worth considering.

The gendering of backwardness and the back door idiom is a complicated matter, for which we will need to turn to Queer theory. As we have seen in *The Nice Valour*, some of Middleton's buggery jokes transpire between men. Here is another.

> CLOWN: Then in what letter will you have your kicks?
> LAPET: All in Italica, your backward blows
> All in Italica, you hermaphrodite:
> When shall I teach you wit? [*N*, 4.1.242–45].

The conjunction of backwardness and hermaphroditism is no accident; what is unclear, however, is precisely how the gender ambiguity works. Does buggery remind the author of effeminate men (i.e., hermaphrodites) because they are known to practice it, or because the practice itself effeminizes, turning men into hermaphrodites by granting them false vaginas? *Is the anus male or female?* Jonathan Goldberg writes of "the long tradition" by which "masculinity has been attached to the phallus, not the anus, penetrator and penetrated have been hierarchized"— he then goes on to argue against this "easy" supposition, itself a heterosexist construct (*Sodometries,* 121–26). The debate has taken some surprising turns. Jeffrey Masten's essay, "Is the Fundament a Grave?" looks at the two alternative "anal rhetorics" in early modern literature — the first suggested in his title and epitomized by depictions of Edward II's sodomitical execution, the second, its positive inverse, playing on the etymology shared by "fundament" and "foundation," wherein the "fundament is imagined as originary"

(134). This is a brilliant analysis, but there is a serious blind-spot, apparent in this footnote:

> I want to note that my lack of examples of the fundament gendered female may be either the fault of my own research or possibly the property of the discourse: to what extent did medical or religious discourses, for example, conceive of women as having "foundational" body parts? [144 n43].

To the final, rhetorical question, a feminist might offer the bewildered response, "to a very large extent." Apparently, Masten has not noticed the preoccupation in Renaissance medical discourse with the womb — an oversight which becomes even more astonishing considering his reference to the famous title page of Vesalius's *de humanii corporis fabrica*, depicting a female cadaver having its womb dissected.[20] And though I would hate to find myself in a gender tug-of-war with a Queer theorist of Masten's gifts and stature, I cannot help but point out that any figuration of the anus-as-foundational is bound to draw its power from analogy with the womb.[21] Nor does the (male) fundament have a monopoly on grave metaphors — that unfortunate legacy is also due the womb, which even (to my unending feminist chagrin) rhymes with tomb.

At the risk of taking up a chicken and egg dispute, I would like to ask whether anal sex "boys" the girl or "girls" the boy. In Middleton's *More Dissemblers Besides Women,* another of Renaissance drama's ubiquitous cross-dressed female pages becomes the occasion for several "backward" jokes, such as this:

> DONADO: ... You've many daughters so well brought up, they speak French naturally at fifteen, and they are turned to the Spanish and Italian half a year after.
> PAGE: That's like learning the grammar first, and the accidence after, they go backward so.
> DONADO: The fitter for th' Italian: thou'st no wit, boy; Hadst a tutor, he'd have taught thee that [*MD*, 1.4.81–87].

The implication is that the "boy's" tutor would have taught him about Italian *gyno*sodomy by sodomizing *him*. Clearly, arguing whether the passage is either "hetero" or "homo" would be pointless; it is both. The gendered binary flips whenever we change perspective, from the "boy" Donado sees, to the woman beneath his gendered disguise, to the historical boy actor who would have played both — or, don't forget, the gynosodomites in Aretine's pictures who lurk behind these "backward" jokes. A few lines later, this page is praised for "his" voice in terms which continue the gender confusion: "O rich, ravishing, rare, and enticing! Well, go thy ways for as sweet a breasted page as ever lay at his master's feet in a trucklebed" (*MD*, 1.4.100–2). The reference to the sleeping arrangements of boy servants and their masters calls to mind the pederastic potential in the relationship, well documented by scholars such as Alan Bray (68–80). And yet the ambiguously-gendered "breast" keeps us in mind of the female body beneath, and the danger of its unveiling in the pederastic scene. The social practices which permit the sexual use of young boys here place a woman in jeopardy as well; thus, Middleton uses homoerotic innuendo to add to the tension surrounding the "hetero" romantic plot. The confusion — and the dramatic tension it fosters — are brought to a stunningly carnivalesque climax in a later scene. Here the page — whose advanced pregnancy is emphasized by her asides bewailing her aching back — is undergoing a rather painful dance lesson. The instructor complains,

> Open thy knees; wider, wider, wider! Did you ever see a boy dance clenched up? He needs a pick-lock. Out upon thee for an arrant ass, an arrant ass! ... O, I could eat thee up, I could eat thee up, and begin upon thy hinder quarter, thy hinder quarter, I shall never teach this boy without a screw; his knees must be opened with a vice ... [*MD*, 5.1.190–203].

When the page asks for a reprieve from dancing, the instructor makes a further sodomitical threat: "How? such another word, down goes your hose, boy" (*MD*, 5.1.217). Finally, she collapses and goes into labor, crying for a midwife. The dancing-master responds,

> A midwife? by this light, the boy's with child!
> A miracle! some woman is the father.
> The world's turned upside-down: sure if men breed,
> Women must get; one never could do both yet. — [*MD*, 5.1.224–27].

The passage does not directly address the issue of anal sex, but it does offer some insight into how far the dramatist is willing to push the anatomical ambiguity. Middleton seemed to be having fun in the earlier moments of gender confusion, but here the butt (pardon the pun) of the joke is the pederastic tutor, who, faced with the irrefutable proof of pregnancy, persists in boying the girl. This is not to say that the audience couldn't continue to boy (actor) the girl, as "she" is walked offstage to give birth — but to do so is to identify with the object of derision. In sum, the sodomitical thrust of the page sequence is interrupted by sodomitical satire, while the anatomical focus — at the narrative level if not at the level of metatheater — shifts from the anal to the uterine. Admittedly, this is a tenuous resolution, and the text does fleetingly invite us to imagine a boy giving birth — perhaps out his ass. And what would that make of his anus? Something Queerer than I can say.

Other cases are less ambiguous. Dekker, Rowley, and Ford's *The Witch of Edmonton* presents a similar cross-dressing plot, wherein the illegal, second wife of the bigamous hero asks his "boy" servant (in fact, his legitimate, prior wife) to "play the wife" to him, in her stead (*WE*, 3.2.72–78). Clearly, anal sex, to the second wife, would "girl" the boy, working by way of substitution. This interpretation is confirmed a few lines later, when the wife asks the servant to guard her husband, in his travels, against temptation with other women, making all the more apparent the substitutive nature of the aforementioned sex. Sex with the boy is not an issue if the boy is a surrogate wife. That the "boy" is not only a woman, but in fact the hero's only legitimate wife, simply completes the transference.

This is not to say that Middleton offers a definitive solution to the conundrum of the gendered anus; it may well be that the riddle cannot be answered. My intention in pursuing this chicken and egg problem is only to supplement Masten's examples and emphasize those occasions when sodomy is *about women*. Centuries later, Freud would theorize that

> [t]he playing of a sexual part by the mucous membrane of the anus is by no means limited to intercourse between men: preference for it is in no way characteristic of inverted feeling. On the contrary, it seems that *paedicatio* with a male owes its origin to an analogy with a similar act performed with a woman [7:152].

Freud's heterocentrism is not without internal contradictions. Lee Edelman revisits Freud's analysis of the Wolf Man case and unearths the theorist's anxiety that the primal scene — presented in the patient's memory of his parents copulating *a tergo* — made its original impression as male sodomy. Edelman's subtle reading of the psychoanalytic process highlights its retroactive and potentially circular logic, aptly rendered in his coinage of the term "(be)hindsight." As the primal scene, according to Freud, instigates the pre-genital view of intercourse as involving the anus, and because both parents "are believed to possess the phallus" from the child's perspective before "the law of castration," Freud's theory, in Edelman's deconstruction, "presupposes the imaginative priority of a sort of proto-homosexuality," a presupposition which makes for a good deal of waffling and unease on Freud's part (175–76, 180). This is a smart and compelling point, but I would like to pose an alternative critique. If we could return to Freud's source and take the patient's own word for it — that he saw his father engaging in coitus *a tergo* with his mother — why should the scene suggest androsodomy before gynosodomy? It is only if we accept Freud's theory of castration, despite some 70 years of feminist resistance, that we may reconstruct the scene as involving two males (and here I confess a certain vengeful glee in seeing Freud mired in his own phallocentric [il]logic).[22] Indeed, the text is riddled with signs of intellectual strain: Freud writes, "We have been *driven to assume* that ... he understood that women are castrated," and he later admits, in light of the patient's childhood intestinal disorders, "That it should be possible ... for a fear of castration to exist side by side with an identification with women by means of the bowel admittedly involved a contradiction" (17:78–79). Freud's attitude toward the Wolf Man's early "homosexual enthusiasm" is mirrored in his objection to the patient's adult predilection for women with "conspicuous buttocks" and for copulation *a tergo* (the latter is termed "an obsessional neurosis") (17:41). In short, Freud's discomfort with coitus from behind (and seemingly, with women's behinds) is evident. Which came first, the misogynist or the homophobe?

Notwithstanding my alternative reading of the primal scene, Edelman's notion of (be)hindsight may be useful in theorizing all the confusion surrounding anal sex, both in Renaissance drama and in the critical discourse we weave around it.

## *Conclusion*

Obviously, it is a long and winding road which connects the Renaissance back door to the white sixties counterculture version rendered by The Doors. Anality now seems to have little to do with it. It no longer has to. It is my contention that the introduction of birth control to the practices not yet understood as heterosexual allowed for the Queering of vaginal intercourse (evident in Freud's unease with coitus *a tergo*) by rendering it nonreproductive, the site for an "artistic end to a species" such as that which Masten sees in the anus.[23] As one Aretinian hero exclaims, "May my lineage die out with me!" (*I modi*, 74). And this is a male speaking: as Middleton knew, women have had, historically, more to fear from being "poisoned with child" (*G*, 5.2.104), particularly outside of wedlock. "A wise man for love will seek every hole" (*CM*, 4.3.11), but a wise *woman* will know where to direct him. It is here where I see the back door's emancipatory potential.

Modern scholars have been surprisingly timid in approaching gynosodomy in these texts. A case in point is, strangely enough, Lynne Lawner herself, the editor of a modern edition of the Italian erotic volume. Lawner assumes that the real life courtesans on whom the sonnets are based would have found the practice of anal sex repugnant, even abusive, and that they only engaged in it when they "had to." She adds skeptically, "It is possible that many of these women welcomed it, whether because anal sex was a safe contraceptive or because they had ruined themselves in front"—pleasure, it seems, was out of the question. Yet, as we have seen, the *Sonnetti* themselves make the pleasure of both parties a primary concern—what of the courtesan who scolds a male for clumsiness and directs him to assume a more pleasure-giving position? Nor is there any sense that the women engage in certain acts because they "had to"—what of the woman who says, "if you don't like it [vaginal sex], to hell with you" and "get out"? These nuances seem lost on the editor, and in one final effort to come to terms with the sonnets' celebration of gynosodomy, she speculates that

> the interchangeability of the *locus* of pleasure provided a playful way of making a girl into a boy, something many a Renaissance lover enjoyed doing. Courtesans made a special habit of dressing as men.... These disguises aided the women in getting around town somewhat anonymously. At the same time, it allowed women to pander to those men who preferred Adonis to Venus. A special pleasure was elicited from the possession of a woman while imagining she was a boy.

The passage is hard to reconcile with the text it happens to introduce. The word "boy" does not appear in the sixteen sonnets (when Cupid appears once, he is called "bastard"); each poem and image involves a male and a female, and there is no trace of gender-play; no one is mentioned as fond of cross-dressing (every one after all is nude). Nor, for that matter, is any woman described as "ruined in front"—a misogynist (and perhaps classist) phrasing surely, and biologically improbable to boot: the one thing most likely to "ruin" a woman "in front" is not multiple sexual partners but multiple pregnancies (that baby's head is bigger than *any* man's member). Indeed, if anyone in the sonnets is found genitally lacking, it is the male (one man says dolefully, "my small organ makes me despair").[24] Perhaps Lawner's view has been colored by her knowledge of the *Ragionamento*, with its more negative treatment of anal sex: but we are talking about two distinct works, with distinct rhetorical aims, the former to entertain, the latter to disturb. And as for the question of homoerotic desire, there are plenty of Renaissance texts which would support Lawner's speculations about cross-dressing, boying the girl, etc.—but this text is not one of them. The nearly four hundred page *Ragionamento* does include a single reference to men's "use" of the courtesans "as boys" (a phrasing which begs the question of whether boys, when used likewise, are used as women), but again, that is a different book, one remarkable for its variety and abundance of sexual expression. And if there's one thing that unites the two obscene works, it is their emphasis on the fact that "people's habits are more varied than one can imagine"; Lawner's introduction effaces this variety by reducing gynosodomy to one signification.[25] Certainly, the courtesans entertained some men who liked to do it with boys — but I'm not aware that there was any shortage of boys (or men for that matter). And whereas the frisson of a cross-dressed woman might have something to do with male homoeroticism, it seems equally likely to do with the fact that her breeches reveal the shape of her buttocks.

One scholar who has challenged some of our modern critical inhibitions about the body in Renaissance literature and medicine is Gail Kern Paster, whose reading of *Midsummer Night's Dream* unearths the anal subtext involving Bottom and his affair with Titania.[26] Paster notes that Titania's romantic interactions with the (significantly) ass-headed, low-class male include a moment when the queenly figure seems to be administering a purge to her beloved: "Feed him with apricocks and dewberries, / With purple grapes, green figs, and mulberries" (3.1.158–59). Paster boldly writes, "What goes unspoken in these conventional associations of fruit with sexual appetite is ... the erotic promise of the purge, particularly perhaps for Elizabethans accustomed from infancy to this form of bodily culture." Paster goes on to explain that "Bottom's languor" in his later appearance with Titania "may well suggest the post-coital.... But given the pregenital infantilism into which he has lapsed ... the scene is also suggestive of post-purgative release." She concludes that "no interpretive choice needs to be made ... between intercourse and purging. In the psychological formations of Elizabethan culture, they may well have been, or been felt or somehow counted as, the same (132, 141, 142). I would also point out that the eroticized purge — here, curiously, placing the male in the receptive, "feminine" role — would have been equally available to women in the period, a fact which strengthens the case for the historical presence of female anal eroticism.[27] And references to purging do appear in the *Sonnetti* when anal sex is discussed. For instance, one male tells his partner that she will "feel the same benefit from it / That sick men get from enemas."[28] We must remind ourselves that in a world before plumbing and private bathrooms with exhaust fans and deodorizers, anal activity was a less taboo affair.

But little of this has much to do with Italy. And maybe it shouldn't, given the way in which we have seen Italians (and Spaniards, Egyptians,

Ethiopians, and Hebrews) scapegoated for more general masculinist, Anglophile anxieties (sometimes released through humor) about sex. And in fact it turns out that Lawner's squeamishness about anal sex is really about sex in general: however grateful I feel for her edition, which made accessible this centuries old, suppressed material, I was nonetheless puzzled that she does not translate the words *cazzo* (cock), *potta* (pussy), or *cul* (asshole), but leaves them in the Italian and in Italics, and in doing so, she thereby endorses, for the sake of preserving "an 'archaic' flavor" distinct from "pornographic exercises," the notion that *sex is not English* (*I modi*, ix).

Modern Anglophile scholars need to get real about assholes. Despite the fact that we're obsessed with "the body" and love to talk "sex and gender," our scholarship is, well, a bit "anal" when it comes to anal eroticism. Queer theorists are the obvious exception: Jonathan Goldberg even clears a space — for instance, in his discussion of *Romeo and Juliet*'s "open-arse" — for gynosodomy *as* gynosodomy, rather than simply boying the girl.[29] But whereas many non–Queer critics are perfectly happy to endorse Queer theory, there is still the assumption (which, when you think about it, is not a compliment) that the anus is "theirs," not "ours." Implicit in Lawner's condescension toward the Venetian courtesans is a more troubling condescension toward gays. If anal penetration is inherently abusive, how is it *not* abusive in Queer sex? Or are all those happy sodomites out there just confusing the bodily signals of pleasure and pain? And all this prudery about the anus is very odd indeed considering our culture's fascination with the ass. We have the piece of ass, the smart ass, the asshole, the expression, "my ass!" We have the pain in the ass, the dumbass, the jackass, the kick in the ass. Nobody loves a tightass. And in choosing a mate, many want a nice ass. The ass is the butt of invective and the aim (puns intended) of the erotic gaze. It seems the more we abject it the more it haunts us. Like the East, like our origins, it's always back there; it is that bodily thing of darkness that we must, ultimately, acknowledge as our own.

## *Acknowledgment*

Daileader, Celia R. "Back Door Sex: Gynosodomy, Aretino, and the Exotic." *ELH* 69:2 (2002), 303–334. © The Johns Hopkins University Press. Reprinted with permission of The Johns Hopkins University Press.

## Notes

1. On the precise logic of this transition, see Celia R. Daileader, *Eroticism on the Renaissance Stage: Transcendence, Desire, and the Limits of the Visible.*
2. See, for instance, Foucault, 101; Bray, 7–32; Goldberg, 1–26; and Smith, 3–29.
3. A case in point here is an article on female sodomy which appeared just after I had completed this essay; this recent piece, though groundbreaking in its own right, is not about female anal sex specifically but about lesbian eroticism. See Helmut Puff, 41–56.
4. Giulio Romano, Marcantonio Raimondi, Pietro Aretino, and Count Jean-Frederic-Maximilien de Waldeck, *I Modi, The Sixteen Pleasures: An Erotic Album of the Italian Renaissance,* ed. and trans. Lynne Lawner, 3.
5. Kenneth Tynan notes that "where sexual vagaries are concerned there is more authentic reportage in *The Changeling* and *Women Beware Women* than in the whole of the [Shakespeare] First Folio" (*The Observer,* 8 July 1963). Thomas Middleton, *A Mad World, My Masters,* in *The Collected Works of Thomas Middleton,* ed. Gary Taylor, 3.3.64–65. Hereafter all plays by Middleton will be abbreviated from this edition and cited parenthetically by act, scene, and line. Hereafter abbreviations will be as follows: *A Trick to Catch the Old One* will be abbreviated as *T*; *The Witch* as *W*; *The Black Book* as *B*; *The Changeling* as *C*; *The Roaring Girl* as *R*; *1 Honest Whore* as *H/W*; *Your Five Gallants* as *Y*; *Michaelmas Term* as *MT*; *The Nice Valour* as *N*; *A Game at Chess* as *G*; *Women Beware Women* as *WW*; *Mad World* as *MW*; *More Dissemblers Besides Women* as *MD*; *A Chaste Maid in Cheap Side* as *CM*; *A Fair Quarrel* as *F*; and *Old Law* as *O*.
6. *I modi,* 62, 68, 72, 76, and 78. Aretino's later, more complicated, satirical work on the lives of the courtesans, *Ragionamento Dialogo,* paints a darker picture of the practice — and of sex in general — but it is to the pictures that we owe the vast majority of references to Aretino in English drama.
7. Middleton was so fascinated with the *Sonnetti Lussuriosi* that he even named two of his characters after them: the lascivious Lussurioso of *The Phoenix* and a character of the same name and like disposition in *The Revenger's Tragedy.* On the impact of Aretino on Jacobean drama overall, see Lynda E. Boose, 185–200. See also Daileader, "The Uses of Ambivalence: Pornography and Female Heterosexual Identity," 73–88.
8. Demonization of Italians as "sodomites" played a similar role in French nationalist discourse. See Rebecca E. Zorach, 581–609.
9. Guido Ruggiero examines several cases involving "heterosexual anal intercourse" brought before 14th and 15th century Venetian courts; noting the general leniency of the court, the historian comes to the conclusion that in Venice, "heterosexual anal intercourse was more a viable form of birth control for some than an illicit form of sexuality" (121).
10. Cyril Tourneur, *The Atheist's Tragedy.* An amorous male invites a woman to "dance ... after the English manner" rather than "the French or Italian" who dance "preposterously, backward" (2.5.62–65); a back door escape is then necessitated by the arrival of her husband.
11. In *More Dissemblers Besides Women,* an Italian joins a group of gypsies, blackening his face with bacon grease. The following lesson ensues:

DONDOLO: I pray, captain, what's Gypsy for the hind quarter of a woman?
CAPTAIN: *Nosario.*

DONDOLO: *Nosario.* Why, what's gypsy for my nose then?
CAPTAIN: Why, *arsinio.*
DONDOLO: *Arsinio?* Faith, methinks you might have devised a sweeter word for't [*MD*, 4.2.208–15].

12. I owe this notion of the decapitation as a pornographic moment to Leah Guenther's essay "'Take Me Out o the Scaffold': Female Decapitation in Renaissance Drama" (unpublished manuscript).

13. Martin Wiggins glosses "nigglers" thus: "the word may mean 'idlers' or 'lascivious people.' Given the emphasis on darkness in this passage, it is also possible that the printer's copy read 'niggers' (not then an offensive term), indicating that the maids are black; this would suit the Venetian context" (347 n59). Given all the evidence for a racialized back door, I find the latter interpretation most compelling.

14. *I modi*, 90 ("extreme"; "worse"), 64 ("poorly"), 74 ("it's"; "aflame").

15. Aretino, *Dialogues*, 42, 284.

16. All references to Dekker's work are from *The Dramatic Works of Thomas Dekker*, vol. 1. (ed. Fredson Bowers). On Dekker's authorship of this scene, see MacDonald P. Jackson, 79, 102–3. See also David J. Lake, 60–61.

17. See Cyrus Hoy, 2:37–40.

18. In *Satiromastix*, a bridegroom robbed of his nuptials by a lascivious king complains, "All other Bride-grooms long for Night ... / But backward runnes the course of my delight; / The day hath turn'd his back, and it is night," 5.1.310–18. In *Match Me in London*, the heroine feigns madness to escape another lustful Tyrant. She explains, "My wits like Bels / Are backward rung, only to fright the Tyrant / That whilst his wild lust wanders, I may flye / To my sweet husbands armes." The male whom she addresses—a scorned and bitter former suitor—says, "Once hence, you may flye / To the Straights, then crosse over to Barbary: / So th'art a Strumpet" (5.2.26–29, 5.2.40–42).

19. Amy Richlin, 16–17.

20. On the fascination with the womb in early modern anatomy, see Jonathan Sawday, 222.

21. A compatible Queer reading of the anus as male uterus can be found in Elliott Trice's discussion of earlier medical treatises, "Lurking in the Lure: Analyzing the Scene of Fourteenth and Fifteenth Century Medical Perception." It is to Trice that I owe the decision to discard the essay's original coinage of "heterosodomy," opting instead for the more flexible notion of "gynosodomy."

22. For a thorough and compelling debunking of Freud's theory, see Taylor, *Castration: An Abbreviated History of Western Manhood*.

23. Masten (135) borrows the phrase from Guy Hocquenghem, who in *Homosexual Desire* applies it to "the homosexual" (100). I am aware that my notion of the Queer vagina is a utopian vision: child-free "hetero" couples in post-modern western culture are still greatly pressured to reproduce, despite the obvious environmental and personal disadvantages, and surgically sterilized individuals carry a stigma which, though certainly less severe than the stigma attached to homosexuality, is cut of the same ideological fabric. Clearly, heteronormativity hurts not only gays.

24. *I modi*, 44 ("It"), 68 ("if you"), 45 ("the interchangeability"), 86 ("bastard"), 76 ("my").

25. *Ragionamento*, 284, 197.

26. See also Bruce Thomas Boehrer, 123–50.

27. For an intriguing discussion of an alternative "strap-on fantasy," see Goldberg's

introduction to *Reclaiming Sodom*. Goldberg describes an image of male anal penetration by a female, using it "to counter the prevailing tradition that has seen sodomy as a practice that males engage in with each other" (3).

28. *I modi*, 72. Paster's discussion of eroticized purging also invites us to consider the way in which this could function in the period's nearly invisible lesbian culture; women would administer purges not only to boys, but to girls.

29. Goldberg's analysis of the various erotic triangulations of the play foregrounds Mercutio's historically censored statement:

> If love be blind, love cannot hit the mark.
> Now will he sit under a medlar tree
> And wish his mistress were that kind of fruit
> As maids call medlars when they laugh alone.
> O Romeo, that she were, O that she were
> An open-ars and thou a poperin pear! [*Romeo and Juliet*, 2.1.33–38].

The trajectories of transgressive desire evident in this passage and others (for instance, Juliet's "strange love" speech, where she imagines Romeo taking night from behind), point up, in Goldberg's analysis, the play's resistance to an erotics based on "the formations of gender difference as the homo/hetero divide imagines them" (*Queering the Renaissance*, 225). What we might read in the "open-ars" as well as the text's "open Rs"— that is, the chain of alliteration joining Romeo, Rosaline, the name of the rose, and the rosemary strewn on Juliet's corpse — is a space for "anyone — man or woman" to indulge in "(un)productive desires" (232; 218–35). Similarly, Goldberg cautions readers not to assume, in light of the homosocial banter at the end of *Henry V* (the king jokes about catching Katherine "in the latter end" [5.2.332]), "that anal sex marks the difference between hetero- and homosexuality" (156).

## *Works Cited*

Aretino, Pietro. *Dialogues*. Trans. Raymond Rosenthal. New York: Marsilio, 1994.
\_\_\_\_\_. Giulio Romano, Marcantonio Raimondi, and Count Jean-Frederic-Maximilien de Waldeck. *I Modi: The Sixteen Pleasures, an Erotic Album of the Renaissance*. Lynne Lawner, ed. and trans. Evanston: Northwestern University Press, 1988.
\_\_\_\_\_. *Ragionamento-Dialogo*. G. De Sanctis, ed. 3rd edition. Milan: Mursia, 1973.
\_\_\_\_\_. *I ragionamenti*. Rome: Newton Compton, 1972.
Barksted, William, and Lewis Machin (from a draft by John Marston). *The Insatiate Countess*. In *Four Jacobean Sex Tragedies*. Ed. Martin Wiggins. Oxford: Oxford University Press, 1998.
Boehrer, Bruce Thomas. "Bestial Buggery in *A Midsummer Night's Dream*." In *The Production of English Renaissance Culture*. Ed. David Lee Miller, Sharon O'Dair, and Harold Weber. Ithaca: Cornell University Press, 1994. 123–50.
Boose, Lynda E. "The 1599 Bishop's Ban, Elizabethan Pornography, and the Sexualization of the Jacobean Stage." In *Enclosure Acts: Sexuality, Property, and Culture in Early Modern England*. Ed. Richard Burt and John Michael Archer. Ithaca: Cornell University Press, 1994. 185–200.
Bray, Alan. *Homosexuality in Renaissance England*. London: Gay Men's Press, 1982.
Daileader, Celia R. *Eroticism on the Renaissance Stage: Transcendence, Desire, and the Limits of the Visible*. Cambridge: Cambridge University Press, 1998.

———. "The Uses of Ambivalence: Pornography and Female Heterosexual Identity." *Women's Studies* 26 (1997): 73–88.

Dekker, Thomas. *The Dramatic Works of Thomas Dekker*, vol. 1. Ed. Fredson Bowers. Cambridge: Cambridge University Press, 1966.

Dolar, Mladen. Introduction to Alain Grosrichard, *The Sultan's Court: European Fantasies of the East*, trans. Liz Heron. London: Verso, 1998.

Edelman, Lee. *Homographies: Essays in Gay Literary and Cultural Theory*. New York: Routledge, 1994.

Fletcher, John. *The Tamer Tamed*. Ed. Daileader and Taylor. Revels Plays. Manchester: Manchester University Press, forthcoming.

Foucault, Michel. *The History of Sexuality, Volume I: An Introduction*. New York: Random House, 1978.

Ford, John. *The Lover's Melancholy*. Ed. R. F. Hill. Revels Plays. Manchester: Manchester University Press, 1985.

Freud, Sigmund. *The Standard Edition of the Complete Psychological Works of Sigmund Freud* (1901–1905). Ed. and trans. James Strachey, with Anna Freud. 24 vols. London: Hogarth, 1953.

Goldberg, Jonathan, ed. Introduction to *Reclaiming Sodom*, ed. Jonathan Goldberg. New York: Routledge, 1994.

———. "Romeo and Juliet's *Open Rs.*" In *Queering the Renaissance*. Ed. Jonathan Goldberg. Durham, NC: Duke University Press, 1994.

———. *Sodometries: Renaissance Texts, Modern Sexualities*. Stanford: Stanford University Press, 1992.

Heywood, Thomas. *The Fair Maid of the West, Part 2*. Ed. Robert K. Turner, Jr. Regents Drama Series. London: Edward Arnold, 1968.

Hocquenghem, Guy. *Homosexual Desire*. Trans. Daniella Dangoor. Durham, NC: Duke University Press, 1993.

Masten, Jeffrey. "Is the Fundament a Grave?" In *The Body in Parts: Fantasies of Corporeality in Early Modern Europe*. Ed. David Hillman and Carla Mazzio. New York: Routledge, 1997.

Middleton, Thomas. *The Collected Works of Thomas Middleton*, ed. Gary Taylor. Oxford: Oxford University Press, forthcoming.

Paster, Gail Kern. *The Body Embarrassed: Drama and the Disciplines of Shame in Early Modern England*. Ithaca: Cornell University Press, 1993.

Puff, Helmut. "Female Sodomy: The Trial of Katherina Hetzeldorfer (1477)." *Journal of Medieval and Early Modern Studies* 30 (2000): 41–56.

R. A. *The Valiant Welshman* (STC A 3698). I2R, 5.3.42.

Richlin, Amy. *The Garden of Priapus: Sexuality and Aggression in Roman Humor*. Oxford: Oxford University Press, 1983.

Romano, Giulio, Marcantonio Raimondi, Pietro Aretino, and Count Jean-Frederic-Maximilien de Waldeck. *I Modi, The Sixteen Pleasures: An Erotic Album of the Italian Renaissance*. Ed. and trans. Lynne Lawner. Evanston, IL: Northwestern University Press, 1988.

Ruggiero, Guido. *The Boundaries of Eros: Sex Crime and Sexuality in Renaissance Venice*. Oxford: Oxford University Press, 1985.

Jonathan Sawday. *The Body Emblazoned: Dissection and the Human Body in Renaissance Culture*. London: Routledge, 1995.

Shakespeare, William. *The Complete Works of William Shakespeare*. Ed. Stanley Wells and Gary Taylor. Oxford: Oxford University Press, 1986.

Smith, Bruce R. *Homosexual Desire in Shakespeare's England: A Cultural Poetics.* Chicago: University of Chicago Press, 1991. 3–29.
Taylor, Gary. *Castration: An Abbreviated History of Western Manhood.* New York: Routledge, 2000.
Tourneur, Cyril. *The Atheist's Tragedy.* Ed. Brian Morris and Roma Gill. New York: W. W. Norton, 1976.
Whigham, Frank. "Reading Social Conflict in the Alimentary Tract: More on the Body in Renaissance Drama." *ELH* 55 (1988).
Zorach, Rebecca E. "The Matter of Italy: Sodomy and the Scandal of Style in Sixteenth-Century France." *The Journal of Medieval and Early Modern Studies* 28 (1998): 581–609.

# 2 Pegging Ernest Hemingway
## *Masochism, Sodomy, and the Dominant Woman*

### RICHARD FANTINA

Although many critics now readily dismiss the old Hemingway myth of machismo, few seem prepared to acknowledge the masochism that prevails in much of his work. The ideal Hemingway woman, as revealed as early as *The Sun Also Rises* (1926), demonstrates power and a will to dominate. This becomes particularly apparent in the posthumous *The Garden of Eden* (1986), in which Hemingway celebrates a woman who controls the sexual relationship with her husband, and who initiates female-on-male sodomy. Since its publication, the dominance of Catherine Bourne in that novel has led scholars to reappraise the foundations of Hemingway's machismo, which coexists with an alternative, masochistic sexuality.

Hemingway's work does not feature incidents of female domination in the sense of the woman with the whip who so intoxicated Leopold von Sacher-Masoch. But despite the absence of the dominatrix, submissive sexuality reveals itself more subtly and at times more dramatically than in the ritualized fantasies of *Venus in Furs* (1870). Although little attention has been devoted to its appearance in Hemingway's texts, male heterosexual masochism represents to some a legitimate, alternative form of masculine sexuality and has been the focus of study in recent gender theory. This essay seeks to locate Hemingway's work within this discourse. Although psychoanalysis necessarily informs this discussion, the purpose here is not to offer another psychoanalytic interpretation but to discuss Hemingway's work in the tradition of literary masochism and the critical responses to it.

Psychoanalysis has a long history of diagnosing masochism both as feminine and as misdirected homosexuality all the while trying to "cure" it. This attitude has been increasingly challenged in recent years. Carol Siegel writes of the tendency of psychoanalysis toward a "nonsensical conflation of male homosexuality with submissively expressed male heterosexuality and its touting of female masochism as essential femininity" (16). Gilles Deleuze's *Coldness and Cruelty* (1969) places masochism within a tradition of masculinity that had been denied or disparaged by psychoanalysis. Deleuze insists on masochism as an arena in which masculinity can assert itself. The avowal of masochism as a tenable masculine position allows for new interpretations of some classic literature. Elements in much of Hemingway's work indicate a masochistic sensibility coexisting with his cult of traditional masculinity. As an artist, Hemingway expresses an alternative masculinity that on the surface seems diametrically opposed to that which he publicly embraced, but both paradigms of masculinity (and others, including gay models) now have a more recognized validity despite a century-long tyranny imposed by the Victorians. Hemingway's embodiment of diverse models of masculinity may be his greatest legacy.

Traditionally, when critics comment on masochism in Hemingway they generally do so idiomatically, without touching on the sexual implications, by referring to the many physical wounds his characters suffer. Yet the wounded heroes exhibit a non-genital sexuality and occasionally submit to passive sodomy. Their general physical and psychological submission to women who alternately punish, humiliate, and nurture these suffering men, sufficiently demonstrates masochism. Revisionist criticism of Hemingway that questions his status as the ultimate American macho began well before the publication of *The Garden of Eden* (1986) with Aaron Lathan's 1977 essay, "A Farewell to Machismo" and Gerry Brenner's *Concealments in Hemingway's Work* (1983). Mark Spilka's *Hemingway's Quarrel with Androgyny* (1990) portrays its subject as almost a feminist. More recently Carl P. Eby unequivocally identifies *Hemingway's Fetishism* (1998), and in *Reading Desire* (1999), Debra A. Moddelmog finds "transgressive desires" (84) in Hemingway's work. As these and other authors have established, Hemingway need no longer to be interpreted one-dimensionally as the prototypical he-man, but while pointing to Hemingway's "homoerotic wishes" (Brenner 20), "suppressed femininity" (Spilka 204), "transvestic impulses" (Eby 212), and "'queer' desires" (Moddelmog 42), none have acknowledged his masochism.

## Masochism and the Erosion of the Phallus

Some contemporary critics see male masochism as a liberating sexual practice. Kaja Silverman argues at length in favor of masochism's politically subversive potential. She seeks in alternative masculine sexualities "the historical moment at which the equation of the male sexual organ with the phallus could no longer be sustained" (2). She inquires into "the larger political implications of these 'deviant' masculinities, some of which indeed say no to power" (2). Exploring the possibilities of a "model for a radically reconstituted male subjectivity," Silverman seeks modes of countering what she calls the "dominant fiction" of "the unity of the family and the adequacy of the male subject" and believes that "[m]ale masochism represents one way of doing so" (16, 213), largely because its imagining of sexual pleasure is essentially non-genital. Silverman specifically searches for works in which the male sex organ has lost any true correlation to the phallic signifier. According to Silverman, this dislocation can occur at times when "history may manifest itself in so traumatic and unassimiliable a guise that it temporarily dislocates penis from phallus, or renders null and void the other elements of the dominant fiction" (47). Silverman sees this historical trauma in the post World War II era. However, we find similar trauma in the post World War I era. Greg Forter writes of this period and the response of American modernists, including Hemingway, as a "reaction to the loss of masculine authority and potency" before "the onslaught of a destructive and emasculating modernity," a reaction characterized by nostalgia for a "disappearing ideal of male autonomy" (25). Silverman states that the belief system of modern Western Civilization "depends upon the preservation of two interlocking terms: the family and the phallus" (48). Hemingway's work can be seen as subversive to both these ideas. The nuclear family plays virtually no role in Hemingway's fiction and the phallus is notable for its absence.

*The Sun Also Rises* has assumed such canonical status that few now marvel that the main character, Jake Barnes, lacks a full complement of male genitalia. With his wound, Jake represents the embodiment of what Silverman calls "phallic divestiture" (9, 160). That an author so identified with traditional masculinity as Hemingway could render a character like Jake Barnes seems more remarkable today perhaps than when the novel first appeared. The abolition of the phallic signifier in the hero of *The Sun Also Rises* conforms to Silverman's reading of a cultural production that consciously undermines an obsolete equation of the penis and phallic power. This novel's enormous appeal to three generations of readers provides evidence of the resonance that such an emasculated character engenders. That three generations of readers can consider Jake Barnes an anti-hero for their times points to the negation of phallic hegemony on some level. In this sense, the novel does indeed question the concept of traditional masculinity. Hemingway implicitly condemns contemporary Western standards of manhood but while indulging in the depiction of wounded masculinity he projects a self-conscious vision of a restructured male subjectivity. The new construction would elevate the more sensitive qualities of Jake Barnes, and combine them with the solitary, heroic qualities that Hemingway invests in the matador, Pedro Romero.

The dislimbed Jake Barnes in *The Sun Also Rises* is only the most pronounced example of the negation of the phallus. Hemingway's novels and stories contain many treatments of heterosexual love. Hemingway was, after all, heterosexual. While Jake remains the only major Hemingway character actually to lack a complete penis, the other heroes rarely make use of that organ in lovemaking. Hemingway's narrators seldom dwell on genital penetration. There are exceptions but these usually prove the rule. One exception, the early story, "Up in Michigan," specifically presents penetration but remarkably from the point of view of the penetrated woman. In *For Whom the Bell Tolls* (1940) there is little doubt that Robert Jordan penetrates Maria in the famous scene where the "earth move[s]" (175) and again in Chapter 37. Yet some of the most prolonged discussion of penetration takes place in a passage where it never actually occurs. Maria, who has been raped by fascists, regrets that she cannot give herself to Robert because "there is a great soreness and much pain" (368). Maria and Robert discuss, but reject, alternatives to Robert penetrating her. Robert does not insist on having sex with Maria and declines her generous offer when she asks, "Is there not some other thing I can do for thee?" (369). Robert remains content to lie in suspense by Maria's side and to defer sexual gratification.

This element of suspense has been noted by many commentators on masochism. Deleuze writes that "[w]aiting and suspense are essential characteristics of masochism" (70). Gaylyn Studlar writes: "Masochistic pleasure does not reside exclusively in the whip or the kiss but also in the suspenseful anticipation of bringing the fantasy to life" (24). The deferral of male sexual gratification characterizes masochistic literature. Certainly, Jake Barnes suffers from this suspension of sexual satisfaction throughout *The Sun Also Rises*. In *For Whom the Bell Tolls*, after Robert declines Maria's offer of some alternative sexual favor he lapses into "a voluptuousness of surrender into unreality that was like a sexual acceptance of something. ... the delight of acceptance" (370). Robert here, despite his disappointment, demonstrates that, in Studlar's words, "pleasure is taken in desire unfulfilled" (126). Studlar also remarks that, "[s]tillness within movement creates a mystical suspension of time reflecting the ultimate masochistic entrapment of infantile fixation" (129). In *Across the River and into the Trees* (1950), Renata controls Colonel Cantwell's sexual performance, telling him when to move and when to keep still. She directs his movements: "'Please don't move,' the girl said, 'Then move a great amount'" (143). The colonel willingly submits to Renata's commands and her entrapment of him in their encounter in the gondola and as Michael Reynolds notes, "Cantwell brings the young girl to a sexual climax" (216).

In a perceptive reading of *Across the River*, John Paul Russo argues that in this scene, Renata "experience[s] three orgasms to Cantwell's none" (166). Russo, like Brenner (161), identifies the first orgasm at the point in which the narrator remarks that "the great bird had flown out of the closed window" (ARIT 144). After this, while the colonel is eager to gratify Renata again, she tells him: "But it is too soon now. Don't you know how a woman feels?" When *she* is ready, after the colonel pours her a drink, Renata asks/orders him: "Let's do it again, please, now I am in the lee" (145). The colonel and Renata cover themselves for shelter and at the point of her orgasm, "the girl had shifted too, under the blanket, with the wind getting under the edge of the blanket; wildly" (145). Afterwards, exalting in her satisfaction while appropriating the colonel's military identity, Renata triumphantly declares, "I just took the city of Paris" (146). Renata suggests the third orgasm when she asks the colonel: "Do you think we could once more if it would not hurt you?" (147). The colonel places Renata's pleasure before his own and neither insists upon, nor is he offered, any corresponding sexual release as he remains in a suspenseful anticipation which is gratification in itself. Like many women in contemporary erotic masochistic literature, Renata confirms, in Russo's words, her "sexual terror" over the colonel (167). As Russo puts it: "Renata has satisfied her selfish desire: She has experienced three orgasms, avoided sexual penetration, and refused orgasm to her partner" (167). The colonel gratefully submits to this treatment just as in much masochistic fiction the dominant woman declines genital penetration and denies orgasm to the submissive man. In Renata and the colonel, Hemingway created characters who embody several of the qualities of the dominatrix and her slave.

## Hemingway and the Masochistic Aesthetic

Several commentators, such as Deleuze, Studlar, and Leo Bersani have remarked on the aesthetic nature of masochism.[1] A pictorial representation of the beloved constitutes a ubiquitous fetish for the masochist. In the opening chapter of Sacher-Masoch's novel, Severin expresses his devotion to Titian's *Venus with a Mirror*, whom he renames "*Venus in Furs*. You are cold and yet you fire the hearts of men. ... cruel goddess of beauty" (154). Lisa Starks, commenting on the masochistic aesthetic in Shakespeare's *Antony and Cleopatra*, writes of its "emphasis on the frozen scene of artistic contemplation" (60). Starks identifies such a scene in the famous description of Cleopatra on her barge. In a passage in *The Sun Also Rises*, Brett Ashley assumes center stage in a similar *tableau vivant*. During the fiesta in Pamplona before the running of the bulls, Jake as narrator describes how the local Spaniards, joined by tourists, revel in the street: "Some dancers formed a circle around Brett and started to dance.... Brett wanted to dance but they did not want her to. They wanted her as an image to dance around" (155). The crowd transforms Brett into a virtual statue and continues to revel with pagan abandon. This conjures up the image of woman as sacred and immobile, a representation of a goddess with the power to nurture or destroy. Deleuze finds that for the masochist, "women become exciting when they are indistinguishable from cold statues in the moonlight or paintings in darkened rooms" (69). Studlar echoes this point when she writes that, "paintings and statues, like masks and dolls, exemplify the iconic suspension of spatial and temporal laws, the delay of gratification, and masochistic contemplation in the art model" (153).

On a cold morning in Venice in *Across the River*, Colonel Cantwell asks Renata to pose: "Turn your hair sideways on top of this bridge and let it blow obliquely" (187), and as she assumes this position the colonel simply admires her impervious, statue-like beauty (187). Earlier the colonel, like Severin, expresses his admiration for Titian saying, "he painted some wonderful women" (24). Later, Renata presents to the colonel a portrait of herself which recalls Botticelli's *The Birth of Venus*: "I look as though I were rising from the sea without the head wet" (93). The gift overwhelms the colonel and leads him to tell her, "I love you very much. You and you portrayed on canvas" (137). That evening, the colonel props up the portrait in his hotel room and spends much of four chapters (XV–XVIII) in conversation with the pictorial stand-in for his beloved. He addresses the portrait: "I wish your mistress was here and we could have movement" (166). These chapters demonstrate an extreme form of devotion to a female subject and highlight traits already apparent in the earlier portrayals of Jake Barnes, Frederic Henry, and Robert Jordan.

At one point during the colonel's vigil, he imagines that the portrait replies to his remarks in an insulting manner: "You low class soldier" (161). Verbal abuse characterizes another essential component of masochism — the humiliation of the subject. In this regard, several similarities between *Venus in Furs* and *The Sun Also Rises* reveal themselves. Brett's public affair with the young bullfighter receives Jake's humiliating acquiescence. Brett tells the adoring Jake: "I'm mad about the Romero boy. I'm in love with him I think" (182). Similarly, in *Venus in Furs*, when Wanda first lays eyes on the Greek she instructs Severin to "find out immediately about the man we saw.... Oh, what a man!" (247). At Brett's insistence, Jake helps arrange her love affair with Romero. She tells Jake, "Oh, darling, please stay by. Please stay by me and see me through this" (184). While they sit at a table in the café watching the bullfighters and their entourage at another table, Brett gives Jake his orders: "Ask him to come over to have a drink" (184). This reprises the scene in *Venus in Furs* in which Wanda, wishing to arrange a rendezvous with another suitor, orders the adoring Severin to "[t]ake this letter to Prince Corsini" (226). Reflecting on her cruelty, Brett muses, "I've always done just what I wanted," and "I do feel such a bitch" (184). Jake does as he is told and introduces her to Romero and even translates for the bullfighter when his imperfect English fails him. Brett then dismisses Jake and he leaves the café as "[t]he hard-eyed people at the bullfighter table watched me go" (187). Twenty minutes later Jake returns to the scene of his public humiliation and finds Brett and Romero gone.

The rival for the affections of the superior woman represents, according to Deleuze, "the hope of a rebirth of the new man that will result from the masochistic experience" (66). In *Venus in Furs*, this role falls to the Greek, says Deleuze, because "when he is idealized he foreshadows the outcome of masochism and stands in for the new man" (66). In *The Sun Also Rises*, Romero provides this same model. Spilka, in an early essay, rightly sees Romero as one of "the few remaining images of independent manhood" to whom Jake attempts to measure up ("Death of Love" 90). The humiliation of the subject in both *Venus in Furs* and *The Sun Also Rises* serves a higher purpose than degradation for its own sake. In both cases it leads potentially to a renewed masculine awareness. In the fantasy of *Venus in Furs*, Severin's final outrage at being whipped by the Greek with Wanda's encouragement leads him to reject his masochism, although many find a lack of sincerity in Sacher-Masoch's prescribed "cure." Jake Barnes, on the contrary, does not disavow his masochism at the end of *The Sun*

*Also Rises*. Jake rescues Brett and when she remarks on the "damned good time" they could have had, he replies, "Yes ... isn't it pretty to think so?"— implying, perhaps, a willingness to continue with her and endure more suffering if she wills it (247).

Earlier in the novel, when Jake asks Brett to live with him, she replies, "I don't think so. I'd just *tromper* you with everybody. You couldn't stand it" (56). Jake assures her that he could because, "I stand it now" (56). Jake acknowledges his humiliation and accepts it, even invites it, just as Severin does in *Venus in Furs*. Jake as narrator exhibits a superior attitude toward the lovesick Robert Cohn who "follow[s] Brett around like a poor bloody steer" (142). Brett's humiliation of Cohn earns him Jake's contempt because Cohn cannot accept the suffering she metes out to him, unlike the masochistic Jake who embraces it.

In his chapter, "Perversion, Pornography, and Creativity," Eby comments on the role of humiliation in the manuscript of *The Garden of Eden*. Referring to the unconventional hairstyles of Nick Sheldon and David Bourne, which they sometimes feel obliged to hide, Eby writes that "[t]he very fact that the male protagonist needs to be coerced into wearing the fetish implies a reluctance on his part that is inseparable from an element of humiliation," and asks, "how, then, is humiliation related to the preservation of masculinity and how can humiliation excite?" (258). Eby answers his question by citing a case history involving verbal humiliation and cross-dressing, without, however, calling it masochism. Humiliation, as endured by Severin in *Venus in Furs*, is as important to that novel, and to masochism in general, as the physical pain suffered at the hands of the dominant woman.

Pain, of course, represents another essential element in masochism. In addition to Jake Barnes, many other Hemingway characters suffer from a great variety of wounds. Colonel Cantwell in *Across the River* has a crippled hand and welts on his face from battle scars. Harry, in *To Have and Have Not* (1937), gets his arm shot off. An unnamed alcoholic vet in the same novel confesses to the "secret" of how he can take so much punishment from constant beatings. "It don't hurt," he says, "Sometimes it feels good" (203). The colonel echoes this sentiment when Renata visits his hotel room in *Across the River* and "kissed him hard so that he could feel the sweet salt of the blood inside his lips. And I like that too, he thought" (106). Frederic Henry is wounded in *A Farewell to Arms*. Robert Jordan suffers a wound that will lead to his death in *For Whom the Bell Tolls*. The list could go on. But in addition to wounds caused by violence, by the penetration of bullets and shrapnel, Hemingway's male heroes occasionally get penetrated in the bedroom.

## Sodomy, Masochism, and Homophobia

Bersani's work suggests that the position of the passive partner in sodomy is inherently masochistic. Submitting to sodomy can be both painful and humiliating, what Bersani calls "a self-debasement" ("Rectum" 220). Heterosexual sodomy with the man in the passive role is an integral element in much contemporary erotic masochistic literature. In Hemingway's work the male heroes seldom penetrate women but rather are sometimes penetrated themselves. Arguably, the most vivid description of penetration in Hemingway's work occurs when Catherine Bourne sodomizes her husband in *The Garden of Eden*. Catherine returns to the hotel one day and surprises her husband David with her haircut, "cropped as short as a boy's" (14–15). Later, in bed together, David calls her "girl," but Catherine rejects this. "Don't call me girl" she orders him and then asks, "Will you change and be my girl and let me take you?" She continues: "I'm Peter. You're my wonderful Catherine…" (17). Catherine's appropriation of the phallic name Peter gives some indication of what transpires here.

> [David] lay there and felt something and then her hand holding him and *searching lower and he helped with his hands* and then lay back in the dark and did not think at all and only *felt the weight and the strangeness inside* and she said, "Now you can't tell who is who can you?" [emphasis added, 17].

Later, the narrator relates that

> [Catherine] made the dark magic of the change again and he did not say no when she spoke to him and asked him the questions and he felt the change so that *it hurt him all through* and when it was finished after they were both exhausted she was shaking and she whispered to him, "Now we have done it. Now we have really done it" [emphasis added, 20].

This description remains uncharacteristically explicit for Hemingway. A crossed-out phrase in the unpublished manuscript contains more graphic detail describing how David feels "something that yielded and entered" (qtd. in Moddelmog, 69). What "yielded" can only be David's sphincter and what "entered" refers to the device — her finger(s) or some object — that Catherine uses to penetrate him. Yet even the edited language of the posthumously published version leaves only the instrument that Catherine uses to the imagination of the reader.

Although Leslie Fiedler contends that Hemingway "is much addicted to describing the sex act" (316), love scenes in the novels and stories usually receive scant description. Often Hemingway uses a single word, such as "Then" (*SAR* 55) or "Afterwards" (*IITS* 296) to inform the reader that lovemaking has taken place. For example, Brett Ashley and Jake Barnes, despite his debilitating wound, apparently manage to consummate their relationship during "Then" and "Then later" gaps in the seventh chapter of the *The Sun Also Rises*. Critics have speculated on what goes on here. Kenneth Lynn suggests that when Brett sends Count Mippipopolous away from the flat, she and Jake "make love in a fashion often associated with lesbian as well as heterosexual intercourse" (324), implying oral sex. Spilka, satisfied that Jake and Brett merely exchange "fervent kisses," disagrees and asserts that Hemingway would not have been "ready, at this early stage of the sexual revolution, for those oral-genital solutions that recent critics have been willing to impose upon him" (203). While Spilka may be correct that an "oral-genital solution" does not take place here, his remark seems to advance the untenable idea of oral sex as an invention of the late twentieth century. More convincingly, J. F. Buckley holds forth "the possibility of masturbation, oral sex, or other expressions of desire" (79), which could include sodomy. Others suggest that Brett uses her hand to stimulate the remains of Jake's genitals. Yet just before the crucial gap, Jake, as narrator, tells the reader: "I was lying with my face away from her," (56) which affords another possible reading. This position — Jake with his back to Brett — can suggest either the manual manipulation by her hand or Brett's anal penetration of Jake, anticipating the more explicit sodomy in *The Garden of Eden*. Discussing this passage Wolfgang E.H. Rudat makes a case that Jake, despite his wound, retains the ability to engage in "anal homosexual intercourse" (176) and implies that Hemingway created a gay, or at least a gay-friendly, character. But this ignores the possibility of anal heterosexual intercourse with the man in the passive role which the passage suggests. No other man is present as Brett has already sent the count away, so homosexuality is not an immediate issue. As Lynn points out, an "artful vagueness" conceals what actually takes place here (324). Yet clearly, Hemingway does not present Jake as homosexual (or gay-friendly, either) but rather as almost heroically and defiantly heterosexual. If we choose to interpret Brett, a self-described "chap" (22, 32, 57) with her short hair "brushed back like a boy's" (22), as a precursor to Catherine Bourne in *The Garden of Eden*, sodomy becomes a logical explanation.

Hemingway's creation of Jake Barnes represents the conflict between sexual desire and social ideology. Silverman advocates the need to determine the "libidinal politics" of cultural creations that demonstrate alternative masculinities (296). "We need to begin thinking seriously," she writes, "about the political implications of desire and identification" (296).

In the character of Jake, we can perceive how sexual desire is at odds with traditional masculine identification. Ira Elliott, referring to Jake's hostility to the gay men in the third chapter of the *The Sun Also Rises*, writes that "inasmuch as Jake considers himself to be heterosexual, the novel posits the site of sexuality in gendered desire rather than sexual behavior" (86). Jake's self-identification as heterosexual, combined with his crippling wound, limits his choices for sexual fulfillment. Elliot writes that "what distinguishes Jake from the homosexual men is gender performance and erotic object choice" (86). Jake "performs" traditional the masculine gender that includes the choice of women as erotic objects, but his performance of sexuality subverts this paradigm so that the woman must possess the phallus so he can receive it.

Elliott also refers to two incidents where women, Brett and the prostitute Georgette, "press" against Jake's body in nonsexual situations, and surmises that Jake "desires more than he can do; he wants not just 'pressing' but penetration" (90). Elliott suggests that Jake desires to penetrate women. However, Hemingway's creation of this character implies the opposite, that Jake was written without a complete penis precisely so he could *not* penetrate but only be penetrated, and only by women, thereby retaining a heterosexual masculine identification. Forter writes convincingly of "Hemingway's commitment to masculinity as a principle of penetration" but suggests that on another level the novel hints at "the loss of phallic manhood in the name of a recovered capacity for receptivity" (33). Such receptivity can find physical expression in the act of sodomy. This contradiction may help explain the enormous appeal and influence of Hemingway's work. His writings allow the solace of surrender inherent in masochism and passive sexuality while reinscribing traditional canons of masculinity.

Another incident of sodomy in Hemingway's work occurs in Part III, Chapter III of *Islands in the Stream* (1970) in which Thomas Hudson dreams that he is in bed with his ex-wife, unnamed in the published novel but called Jan in the manuscript (Eby 264–268). Hudson asks Jan, "Who's going to make love to who?" She answers him: "Both of us.... Unless you want it differently." Hudson then says, "You make love to me. I'm tired." To which she responds, "You're just lazy. Let me take the pistol off and put it by your leg. The pistol's in the way of everything." The description of the phallic pistol as "in the way" can be interpreted as another example of Hemingway's dismissal of male genital sexuality as an aggressive force. But Hemingway goes further here. Hudson has "moistened" the pistol which Jan apparently is either now holding or positioning by his leg.

Hudson suggests that Jan, "Lay it [the pistol] by the bed. ... And make everything the way it should be." At this point in the dialogue, the narrator reports: "Then it was all the way it should be and she said, 'Should I be you or you be me?'" Hudson gives Jan "first choice" and she says, "I'll be you. To which Hudson responds, "I can't be you but I can try." She tells him, "It's fun. You try it. Don't try to save yourself at all. Try to lose everything and take everything too."

During this dialogue some unspecified activity transpires and since it occurs in a dream an exact interpretation is impossible. But a plausible explanation is that Jan has not laid the pistol "by the bed" but rather that she sodomizes Hudson with it. She asks, "Are you doing it?"

He responds, "Yes. ... it's wonderful." Then she asks him, "Do you know now what we have?" Which can mean — do you know now what we women feel when we are penetrated? Hudson replies, "Yes I know. It's easy to give up."

Finally he asks Jan to "hold me so tight it kills me." He awakens from the dream to feel "the pistol holder between his legs" (333–334). In the light of all this, the possibility that Hudson dreams that his ex-wife sodomizes him with the pistol does not seem outlandish. In reviewing some unpublished sections of the original manuscript, Eby describes how Hudson, "can feel a faintness spread from the base of his spine up through his torso" and "something inside him feels weak and 'destroyed'" (266). Though Eby does not suggest sodomy here, the passage he discusses certainly does.

Other Hemingway protagonists sleep with their pistols. At least three times in *For Whom the Bell Tolls* (76, 279, 389), Robert is awakened and immediately feels "the butt of the pistol that lay alongside of his bare right leg" (389). In *True At First Light* (1998), Papa calls his pistol "my best friend and severest critic" as he feels it "lying comfortably between my legs" (281). Harry Morgan in *To Have and Have Not*, who has lost an arm in a gun battle, also has a gun but he does not sleep with it. Instead, when he makes love with his wife, the stump of his arm stands in for his penis in loveplay (114) — another clear example of Silverman's "phallic divestiture." Despite the literalness with which Hemingway displaces the male phallus, on another level his work does not oppose Silverman's "dominant fiction." Silverman refers to "individual men who embraced lack at the level of their unconscious fantasies and identities" (52) and Hemingway conforms to this view. One can see the wound of Jake Barnes in *The Sun Also Rises* as a rejection of the patriarchal mandate, but through a groveling embrace of his suffering and emotional trauma, he endeavors to emerge as a newly reconstituted man. Anita Phillips writes that "[a] man does remain a man even after erotic humiliation, and men involved in masochism may symbolically endanger their masculinity in order to test and fulfill themselves as men" (30). Despite Jake's lack, he recuperates the function of the phallus. The mutilated hero emerges uncertainly triumphant at the end of the novel, vanquishing his genitally-complete competitors by his ability to successfully negotiate the female Other in the person of Brett Ashley. Of course, this also means that he must submit to her, which he has been doing all through the novel anyway.

Hemingway's characters present obvious conflicts in masculine identity. David Bourne in *The Garden of Eden* allows himself to be sodomized and called "girl" by his wife, while in much of his work Hemingway seems to vent an unbridled homophobia. To examine the apparent paradox of Hemingway's masochism and his homophobia it may be useful to look at Bersani's comments on sodomy and the "self-shattering" of masochism. As Bersani describes it, the passive partner in sodomy necessarily positions himself or herself masochistically. Bersani's primary interest lies in gay male masochism but his argument can apply more broadly. For instance, D.H. Lawrence in *The Rainbow* and *Lady Chatterley's Lover* presents sodomy as appealing so long as it is performed by the man on the woman. In Lawrence's view sodomy on the man would represent a violation of the "phallic consciousness." Hemingway, for all his affirmation of male values and his aversion to homosexuality, does not present anything similar to Lawrence's phallic consciousness and his work instead endorses sodomy on the male if performed by a female. Rather than exalting the male phallus, Hemingway's work consistently seeks to dethrone it. And though he celebrates sodomy on the man, Hemingway remains opposed to homosexuality. Bersani calls homophobia, "the vicious expression of a more or less hidden fantasy of males participating, principally through anal sex, in what is presumed to be the terrifying phenomenon of female sexuality" (*Homos*, 78). Part of Bersani's argument suggests that homophobia stems from homoerotic fantasies repressed because they appear to place the passive partner in a female position. This may approximate Hemingway's route to homophobia. His awareness of sexual "difference" led him to associate it with female sexuality and while part of him embraced it, another part recoiled from it.

While male-on-female and male-on-male sodomy both have long literary traditions, novelists seldom portray female-on-male sodomy in their fiction. Hemingway's overt use of such sodomy as the expression of the physical love between Catherine and David Bourne in *The Garden of*

*Eden* remains remarkable because of this rarity. Even though *Venus in Furs*, the master text of masochism, does not discuss it, sodomy has come to occupy a prominent place in the erotic literature of hetero- as well as homosexual masochism. Lawrence, of course, features male-on-female sodomy in his novels. Jean Genet features male-on-male sodomy throughout his work. James Joyce, much admired by Hemingway, presents a rare instance of female-on-male sodomy in the form of fisting in *Ulysses* (440). Hemingway's depiction of the lovers in *The Garden of Eden*, although the actual mechanics remain unclear, also undeniably includes female-on-male sodomy.

While Bersani may claim a privileged position for sodomy within homosexuality, he does not deny this "self-shattering" to women or to heterosexual men. He writes that: "The investigation of human sexuality leads to a massive detachment of the sexual from both object-specificity and organ-specificity" (*Freudian Body* 39). Bersani asserts that "*masochism serves life*" and that it "developed as an evolutionary necessity" (emphasis in original, 39, 41). "Human sexuality," he continues, "is constituted as a kind of psychic shattering, as a threat to the stability and integrity of self—a threat which perhaps only the masochistic nature of sexual pleasure allows us to survive" (61). This idea comes very close to the French euphemism for sex—*le petite mort*. Masochism, Bersani believes, lies at the very core of all sexuality. Further, he writes: "Sexuality—at least in the mode in which it is constituted—could be thought of as a tautology for masochism" (39). He goes on to say:

> We desire what nearly shatters us, and the shattering experience is, it would seem, *without any specific content*—which may be our only way of saying that the experience [of sex] cannot be said, that it belongs to the nonlinguistic biology of human life [emphasis in original 40].

If, as Bersani contends, both sexual object and organ are nonspecific, the desire to be sodomized can be either heterosexual or homosexual, and any similarly-shaped object can serve as well as an erect penis, depending on the desire of the male or female individual involved. Sodomy remains a polymorphous practice that transcends categories of gender and sexual preference.[2]

Sodomy from both male and female points of view forms the subject of the essays in Jonathan Goldberg's *Reclaiming Sodom* (1994). Although gay and lesbian perspectives predominate, Goldberg introduces the volume with a discussion of an example of female-on-male sodomy from the perspective of the woman who initiates the encounter. Goldberg suggests that "the act of sodomy enables the productive confusions and rigorous questioning of a range of presumptions and conventions governing gender, sexuality and the relations of fantasy and acts" (3). One of these presumptions equates sodomy solely with male homosexuality. Columnist Tristan Taormino writes: "It's a falsehood that *all* gay men have anal sex, and it's equally mythic that gay men have more anal sex than straight people or lesbians" (emphasis in original, Taormino). Regarding a man's desire to be sodomized by a woman and a woman's desire to penetrate a male lover, Goldberg finds that "the possibility of desiring 'the same' has to do with the fact that men and women both have anuses, can locate their desires there (hence, the woman's fantasy about penetrating a man also lights on the anatomical place both genders share as sexual site)" (1). In this sense we can see how men and women can attempt to approximate the common experience of non-genital sexuality that characterizes Hemingway's work, however elliptically. This reflects Moddelmog's comment on *The Sun Also Rises*: "The text asks us to suspect, and finally to critique, those systems of representation that are insufficient and hence disabling to efforts to comprehend the human body and its desires" (99–100). Yet despite the attraction of sodomy Hemingway easily maintains his claim to a manifestly heterosexual masculinity.

A heterosexual man's experience of consensual sodomy ought to be permitted its own heterosexual reactions. David Bourne's reaction to sodomy in *The Garden of Eden* approximates Bersani's "self-shattering" *jouissance*. Bersani's suggestion that for many gay men sodomy "has the terrifying appeal of a loss of the ego, of a self-debasement" ("Rectum" 220), can apply just as easily to heterosexual men or to women. With regard to Hemingway, what remains important in Bersani's analysis is the emphasis on the masculine. Bersani writes that for the homosexual, "[i]t is not a woman's soul in a man's body" that matters but rather "the incorporation of woman's otherness" (*Homos* 60). For Hemingway's male characters, the incorporation of women's otherness into their sexuality does not decrease their masculine identification any more than it does for Bersani's gay man. The heterosexual David Bourne shares the masculine identification that prevails in much of Bersani's view of the gay man. Hemingway, of course, also identifies most emphatically with the masculine, and with phallocentric power arrangements as well. Here we can see how Hemingway's masochism may not be entirely progressive. In this sense, *The Garden of Eden* appears less transgressive than some scholars suggest. Hemingway, after creating Catherine as a representative of a subversive sexuality, intervenes on David's behalf to destroy her. In the manuscript, as Eby (33, 248–49) and Moddelmog (65) point out, Marita takes Catherine's place in gender-crossing. But while Marita assumes the sexual role of "the boy," she does not threaten David by taking on other prerogatives of the phallus in the social realm.

## The Dominant Woman

Hemingway's construction of Catherine in *The Garden of Eden* can be compared to Sacher-Masoch's creation of the dominatrix Wanda in *Venus in Furs*. Having based his novel on his actual experiences, Sacher-Masoch in effect created the women who dominated him throughout his life. The difference between Sacher-Masoch and Hemingway lies in the latter's creation of Catherine as a work of the imagination, with no acknowledged basis in fact. In both cases, according to the formula articulated in *Venus in Furs* and restated by Deleuze, "the masochist manipulates the woman into the ideal state for the performance of the role he has assigned to her" (124). The masochist voluntarily surrenders the function of the phallus to the woman in a self-conscious act of abdication, and as Eby notes, "[w]omen with phallic attributes abound in Hemingway's fiction" (43). In *The Garden of Eden*, David consensually puts himself at the disposal of his audacious wife, never sure where her sexual whims may take them. This sexuality involves the switching of traditional sexual roles and sodomy performed on David by Catherine. David enjoys the adventure for a time, but finally he rebels, not so much at Catherine's domination of the sexual relationship, but against her intrusion into the male domain of art. His desire demands a dominant, phallic woman yet his code of traditional masculinity reins her in if she crosses social boundaries.

The question of the role of the dominant woman in the masochistic scenario has vexed scholars for some time. Siegel and Silverman find progressive and empowering qualities for women within male masochism. And Taormino writes: "As women, since we are already positioned as the receptive, penetrated partner, we need only reorient ourselves to focus on the other orifice" and adds that this gives men the chance to "know what it's like to give it up" (Taormino). Her comment echoes Thomas Hudson's remark in *Islands in the Stream*: "It's easy to give up" (334). Transgendered author and activist, Pat Califia, agreeing with Taormino, writes: "It's wonderful to fuck someone in male persona," but cautions that "it is difficult even for polymorphous perverts to create top/bottom roles that do not share the worst characteristics of polarized, dichotomous genders" (*Sex Changes*). This comment highlights the debate as some scholars question heterosexual male masochism as an alternative to patriarchal dominance.

Sabine Wilke believes that "[t]he functioning of the male masochist's pleasure. ... rests upon the suspension of the woman's desire" (qtd. in Boxer, B11). Suzanne R. Stewart agrees with Deleuze when she asserts that "[t]he masochist remains at all points the stage director of his fantasy" (5), but discounts any subversive potential. This manipulative aspect of masochism can, on one level, fit neatly into an analysis of Hemingway (as well as Sacher-Masoch) for he controlled his texts to accommodate sexually dominant women or women who become sexually dominant at his characters' behest. According to Stewart, "[t]he masochist himself created this Cruel Woman as aesthetic object and in that move attempted to reassert control, both over the means of cultural production and over the woman's body" (13). And while she allows that masochism radically subverts "bourgeois liberalism," Stewart adds that

> [S]uch subversions remained politically ambiguous at best, for they were predicated on silencing women whose position as victims of a sexual hierarchy had been triumphantly usurped by a male claim to the margin that, once so claimed, became the new center [13–14].

Hemingway's "claim to the margin" resonates in his alienated heroes. Though Stewart confines her analysis to *fin-de-siècle* Europe she finds long-lasting effects from what she sees as masochism's role in preserving phallocentric hegemony. If her theory can be updated and can include Hemingway, his masochism emerges as a protected enclave of male domination in the guise of submission, and would not have reached into a larger social sphere and translated into a perception and endorsement of women's equality.

In another critique Nick Mansfield maintains that, "the masochistic subject combines genders without deconstructing the opposition between them" and "wants to own the feminine without ever giving up anything masculine" (46). Mansfield finds a spurious transgression in masochism which masks an abiding sexism. "The gender-crossing of the masochist," he writes, "does not trigger an identical transformation in the woman" (46), but rather, "[t]he woman is derealized by being given a meaning only within the huge and shifting parameters of masculinity" (20). Agreeing with many that the masochist controls the fantasy, Mansfield finds the woman as the real victim. But this view neglects to consider that in masochism, the woman is not sacrificed upon an altar of male aggression.

On the contrary, her central role in the masochistic scenario calls upon her to provide the aggression.

Such critiques, while centering on gender and sexuality, raise masochism above the physical where it must remain grounded. They fail to recognize the importance of masochism's determination not to seek to physically dominate women but rather to submit the male body to the female body and affect an exchange of sexual power. Siegel writes of this empowerment: "[M]asochism can, in essence, transform the male body from an instrument of punishment for women into a medium through which women can generate pleasure for both themselves and their partners" (119). The negative critiques neglect this primary materiality of masochism in an effort to locate it ideologically. Deleuze emphasizes this when he asserts that "[m]asochism in its material aspects is a phenomenon of the senses" (101). Siegel writes that "Deleuze's theory can attract a feminist reader because he envisions the body of the male masochist as the site of *both* the subversion of patriarchal law and its confirmation" (emphasis in original 111). Her argument suggests not that male masochism overthrows patriarchal law but that it deconstructs it. Masochistic artists can subvert certain patriarchal values while upholding others. To see masochism one-dimensionally, solely as a tool of the powerful, seeks to conform it to a narrow political concept, and misses its many nuances. Hemingway's depictions of wounded masculinity and submission to women unquestionably subvert patriarchy but his ideological focus remains within it. This conflict reveals the divide in Hemingway's artistic expression as he goes from radically undermining the phallus to overt support of other trappings of patriarchal power.

The analysis of the cultural texts of masochism for political ramifications employed by Stewart and Mansfield in one direction and Silverman and Siegel in another has limitations in its application to Hemingway because of his enduring complexity. While it cannot be denied that Hemingway held phallocentric social views, a binding relation between these views and his masochism does not convincingly emerge. However, Stewart's analysis of heterosexual male masochism suggests some of the conflicts between Hemingway's desire and his ideology. Part of Stewart's thesis, that male masochism grants woman a pyrrhic victory of the will, conforms to the mode of Hemingway's art. He creates his dominant women to satisfy his sexual desire but leaves most significant social action to his men. However, while Stewart's analysis may apply in some respects to Hemingway as an individual artist, it fails to credit masochism in general for its approach to a significant exchange of sexual power.

## Conclusion

We have seen how Hemingway's work often dethrones the male phallus and how it celebrates sodomy performed on the man by the woman. As Eby points out, Hemingway's dominant woman "assumes her phallic attributes at the expense of her man" (84). Eby's work convincingly demonstrates Hemingway's fetishism in its many forms and as Deleuze asserts, "there can be no masochism without fetishism" (32). If, as psychoanalysis claims, the fetish is the symbolic image or substitute for the female phallus, Hemingway invests his women with phallic agency in the sexual realm. Hemingway endows these women with a variety of fetishes and his male heroes submit to them masochistically.

Brett Ashley, the "chap," represents the first of the overtly phallic women with her short haircut and promiscuous ways. Women with guns appear in the African stories and in *Islands in the Stream*. Much of Hemingway's work, according to Jeffrey Meyers, "emphasizes (as in 'Fathers and Sons') the connection between shooting and sex" (273). In "The Short Happy Life of Francis Macomber," Margot's rifle is a phallic projection of sex and death. When she shoots her husband, Margot perpetrates the ultimate act of penetration of the male body. Helen in "The Snows of Kilimanjaro" and Miss Mary in *True at First Light* are avid shooters, while Debba, in the same novel, appropriates the holster to Papa's pistol which "she truly loved" (281) and is often described as pressing it hard (248) or holding it tight (278). In both *To Have and Have Not* and *Islands in the Stream*, the heroes are mortally wounded by gut shots. Though neither description of the shootings in those novels contain overt sexual allusions, they provide two more examples of the penetrated male body and can be seen as metaphors for sodomy and masochism. Meyers also notes the sexual aspects of Hemingway's portrayal of bullfighting in *The Sun Also Rises* and *Death in the Afternoon*, which Edward Said calls a "studious rendering of the mechanics of ritualized suffering" (233). The killing of bulls and goring of matadors represent more penetration and wounding of male bodies. Moddelmog also notes "images of sexual foreplay and consummation" in the "meeting of bull and bullfighter" (96) and other scholars have recognized the sexual content as well.

Catherine Bourne in *The Garden of Eden* represents an accumulation of other Hemingway compulsions including hair and racial fetishes. Hemingway portrays submission to such women, sometimes specifically through sodomy which literally endows the woman with the phallus, as enormously appealing to his sexual masculinity but dangerous to his social masculinity. But since homosexuality was not an option for Hemingway, he needs the phallic woman to perform the chosen sexual act and to otherwise dominate his male heroes.

Hemingway's work incorporates much of masochism's subversive potential. Yet his simultaneous championship of so much that upholds and even exaggerates traditional masculinity considerably weakens any effort to locate his work as an unambiguous model of transgression. In his written work, Hemingway most often chooses to conceal or obscure desires that do not conform to the prevailing ideal of masculinity. He accepted this ideal for the most part, and when he avows his masochism directly he does so almost defiantly, seeking to incorporate it into his own personal code of manhood. We can be grateful to Hemingway for his radical subversion of some twentieth-century manifestations of patriarchy, but we can hardly pretend that this was his project.

## *Acknowledgments*

This essay was originally published with the title "Hemingway's Masochism, Sodomy, and the Dominant Woman" in *The Hemingway Review*, Vol. 23, No. 1, Fall 2003. © 2003 The Ernest Hemingway Foundation. All Rights Reserved.

Thanks to Bruce Harvey, Mary Free, and Richard Sugg at Florida International University who read and provided helpful comments on an early draft of this essay. Special thanks to Carl P. Eby who has generously encouraged this work for nearly two years. I would also like to express sincere gratitude to the Hemingway Society for their award of a Smith-Reynolds Founders Fellowship and to the Northeast Modern Language Association (NEMLA) for the award of a Summer Research Fellowship.

## *Works Cited*

Bersani, Leo. *The Freudian Body: Psychoanalysis and Art*. New York: Columbia University Press, 1986.
\_\_\_\_\_. *Homos*. Cambridge: Harvard University Press, 1995.
\_\_\_\_\_. "Is the Rectum a Grave?" In *AIDS, Cultural Analysis, Cultural Activism*. Ed. Douglas Crimp. Cambridge: MIT Press, 1988. 197–222.
Boxer, Sarah. "Masochism Finally Gets Even." *New York Times* 27 January 2001: B9–11.
Brenner, Gerry. *Concealments in Hemingway's Works*. Columbus: Ohio State University Press, 1983.
Buckley, J. F. "Echoes of Closeted Desires: The Narrator and Character Voices of Jake Barnes." *The Hemingway Review* 19.2 (Spring 2000): 74–87.
Califia, Pat. Introduction to *Sex Changes* San Francisco: Cleis, 1997. Society for Human Sexuality. 9 July 2003. *http://www.sexuality.org/l/transgen/scpc.html*.

Deleuze, Gilles. *Coldness and Cruelty*. In *Masochism*. Trans. Jean MacNeil. New York: Zone, 1991. 15–142.
Eby, Carl P. *Hemingway's Fetishism: Psychoanalysis and the Mirror of Manhood*. New York: SUNY Press, 1998.
Elliott, Ira. "Performance Art: Jake Barnes and 'Masculine' Signification in *The Sun Also Rises*." *American Literature* 67.1 (March 1995).
Fiedler, Leslie. *Love and Death in the American Novel*. Rev. ed. New York: Stein and Day, 1975.
Forter, Greg. "Melancholy Modernism: Gender and the Politics of Mourning in *The Sun Also Rises*." *The Hemingway Review* 21.1 (Fall 2001): 22–37.
Goldberg, Jonathan, ed. *Reclaiming Sodom*. New York and London: Routledge, 1994.
Hemingway, Ernest. *Across the River and into the Trees*. New York: Scribner's, 1950.
\_\_\_\_\_. *The Complete Short Stories*. New York: Scribner's, 1987.
\_\_\_\_\_. *For Whom the Bell Tolls*. New York: Scribner's, 1940.
\_\_\_\_\_. *The Garden of Eden*. New York: Macmillan, 1986.
\_\_\_\_\_. *Islands in the Stream*. New York: Scribner's, 1970, 1997.
\_\_\_\_\_. *The Sun Also Rises*. New York: Scribner's, 1926.
\_\_\_\_\_. *To Have and Have Not*. New York: Scribner's, 1937.
\_\_\_\_\_. *True at First Light*. New York: Scribner's, 1999.
Joyce, James. *Ulysses*. 1922. New York: Vintage, 1986.
Lathan, Aaron. "A Farewell to Machismo." *New York Times Magazine* 16 October 1977. 52–55, 80–82, 90.
Lynn, Kenneth. *Hemingway*. New York: Fawcett-Columbine, 1987.
Mansfield, Nick. *Masochism, The Art of Power*. Westport, CT: Praeger, 1997.
Meyers, Jeffrey. *Hemingway: A Biography*. New York: Harper and Row, 1983.
Moddelmog, Debra A. *Reading Desire: In Pursuit of Ernest Hemingway*. Ithaca, NY: Cornell University Press, 1999.
Phillips, Anita. *A Defense of Masochism*. New York: St. Martin's, 1998.
Reynolds, Michael. *Hemingway: The Final Years*. New York: W.W. Norton, 1999.
Rudat, Wolfgang, E.H. "Hemingway's Sexual Otherness: What's Really Funny in *The Sun Also Rises*." In *Hemingway Repossessed*. Ed. Kenneth Rosen. Westport, CT: Praeger, 1994.169–179.
Russo, John Paul. "To Die Is Not Enough: Hemingway's Venetian Novel." In *Hemingway in Italy and Other Essays*. Ed. Robert W. Lewis. New York: Praeger, 1990. 133–180.
Sacher-Masoch, Leopold von. *Venus in Furs*. In *Masochism*. Trans. Jean MacNeil. New York: Zone Books, 1991. 143–272.
Said, Edward. *Reflections on Exile and Other Essays*. Cambridge: Harvard University Press, 2000.
Siegel, Carol. *Male Masochism, Modern Revisions of the Story of Love*. Bloomington and Indianapolis: Indiana University Press, 1995.
Silverman, Kaja. *Male Subjectivity at the Margins*. New York and London: Routledge, 1992.
Spilka, Mark. "The Death of Love in *The Sun Also Rises*." In *Hemingway and His Critics*. Ed. Carlos Baker. New York: Hill and Wang, 1961. 80–92.
\_\_\_\_\_. *Hemingway's Quarrel with Androgyny*. Lincoln and London: University of Nebraska Press, 1990.
Starks, Lisa S. "'Like the lover's pinch, which hurts and is desired': The Narrative of

Male Masochism and *Shakespeare's Antony and Cleopatra.*" *Literature and Psychology* 45.4 (1999): 58–73.
Stewart, Suzanne R. *Sublime Surrender: Male Masochism at the Fin-de-Siècle.* Ithaca: Cornell University Press, 1998.
Studlar, Gaylyn. *In the Realm of Pleasure: Von Sternberg, Dietrich, and the Masochistic Aesthetic.* New York: Columbia University Press, 1988.
Taormino, Tristan. "Bend Over, Boys!" *Village Voice* 1–7 March 2000. 9 July 2003 <http://www.villagevoice.com/issues/0009/taormino.php>

# 3 Queer Desire and Heterosexual Consummation in the Anchoritic Mystical Tradition

SUSANNAH MARY CHEWNING

Queer theory and medieval mysticism are both extremely elusive concepts, and both seem, in spite of a growing critical emphasis, to defy formal definition and control. Critics who use queer theory understand it in a variety of ways; in fact, one could argue that it is this multivocity among queer theorists that (although often frustrating to those who seek to understand it) keeps it *queer*; that is, critics' failure to fully know it reinscribes its ultimate unknowability and usefulness as a mode of both intellectual and political inquiry. Medieval mysticism is not any more clearly definable in that, although we who study it think we know what it means (an encounter with the transcendent presence of the Divine), its very nature makes that transcendent moment ineffable, and thus outside of both theological and critical discourse. In spite of the difficulty with *knowing* either fully, it is my intention with this paper to look at the commonalities between queer theory and mysticism, in an effort to illuminate the ambiguities of both.

Alicia Solomon and Paisely Currah define *queer theory* in their introduction to *Queer Ideas* as a "theoretical framework that unsettles binaries, seeks to explode the formation of fixed categories or norms, and works to reexamine the direction of the arrows between cause and effect [that] challenges the way knowledge production is domesticated and made subservient to hegemonic cultural norms" (11). While this definition serves as a solid beginning point for an examination of queer theory, it seems important (in the context of this study) to examine medieval approaches to the subject, as well. Carolyn Dinshaw, in her book *Getting Medieval*, points out similar distinctions and problematizes any examination of sexuality in relation to medieval culture: "the analysis of same-sex sexual relations, even as they cannot be clearly distinguished from opposite-sex sexual relations, implicates such relations in a larger confusion of the natural and the unnatural (that binome that would seem so clear in medieval discourse) and thus suggests that determinate oppositional structures are not going to hold very well in analyzing medieval sexual discourse" (11). Glenn Burger and Steven Kruger, in *Queering the Middle Ages*, also look at both acts and their analysis by arguing that queer theoretical thinking suggests that "effects are often constructed after the fact as essences, origins, and causes— with the human subject itself, for instance, being an effect of a psychic process that is retrospectively misrecognized as the cause of interiority" (12–13). In his recent book, *Queering Medieval Categories*, Tison Pugh approaches a definition of *queer* from the perspective of action and classification when he writes: "sexual acts position one another either inside or outside the realm of the heteronormative, and cultural assumptions about the meanings of various sexual acts thus lead to classifications of the people who engage in such acts" (1). Pugh cites Michel Foucault who defined sexuality according to various binaries, including "licit and illicit, permitted and forbidden" (qtd. 1) with the obvious logical step that that which is queer resides in the categories of illicit and forbidden. Karma Lochrie wisely reminds us that "the distinctions that are made in the Middle Ages never prove so clear-cut as we think they are, nor so intrepid as we sometimes claim them to be in our queer studies" ("Presidential Improprieties" 91). Theodora Jankowski, addressing queer notions of Renaissance virginity writes: "I use the term "queer" not only to define varieties of nonheterosexual activity, but also to define nonproductive heterosexual and nongenital activity" (6). All of these contributions to my understanding of queer theory and its application to medieval studies have assisted me in defining it as I have in what follows, but perhaps it is Ed Cohen, not a medievalist, but one who defined himself (in 1989) as "an openly gay man writing and teaching about the historical articulations of gender, class, age, and nationality" (162), who best expresses my take on the *raison d'être* for queer theory. Cohen sees what he does as a critic and a scholar very simply. He writes: "we fuck with categories" (174–75).

## I.

In her *Getting Medieval*, Dinshaw addresses what she sees as the "unspeakability" of *queer history*.[1] She does not deny that critics are attempting to speak of such history now, but rather argues that, as with most issues of sex and, at least for the medieval audience, unnatural acts (acts "aeynes kynde" as Dinshaw defines them), until the application of postmodern criticism it has been impossible to speak (perhaps due to our own lack of understanding of Otherness) of that which we now seek to understand as *queer*. This unspeakability is a shared quality for that which is *queer* and that which, at least in terms of medieval language and understanding, is transcendent, more specifically, the transcendence of the mystical experience. Elsewhere[2] I have argued that the mystic (whether biologically male or female) is feminized in the experience of transcendence in mysticism. It is my argument that the Otherness of the mystic extends beyond any construction of femininity and can be seen as queer, that is, beyond traditional categories of sexuality and gender; just as Monique Wittig sees the lesbian as "beyond the categories of sex (woman and man)," ("One Is Not Born a Woman" 53). I see the mystic beyond these simple categories, as well. In part this is due to her position as both sexualized and chaste: chaste in her experience and sexualized in her awareness of herself in relation to earthly men and to Christ. Such sexualized chastity is problematic,[3] but not unique in the works of medieval mystics. Both lover and virgin, sexualized and chaste, the mystic is thus part of the heterogenous and indeterminate *queerness* described by Dinshaw (and by other recent queer medieval critics)[4] and, through the language that is most often used in mysticism, equally representative of heterosexual patterns of desire.

Medieval mysticism is simultaneously spoken and unspeakable; deeply felt and inaccessible; transgressive and orthodox; queer and heterosexual. The mystic must recount to her audience an experience that she herself cannot fully understand. Mystics often speak of being silenced in the presence of the divine and yet knowing and being known fully in the encounter. Julian of Norwich, for example, describes what she considers to be "þe onspekabyl passion of Criste," and yet she endeavors, even though it can't really be known, to express this passion in her *Shewings*. She writes

> For just as he was most tender and most pure, so he was most strong and powerful to suffer. And he suffered for the sins of every man who will be saved; and he saw and he sorrowed for every man's sorrow, desolation and

anguish, in his compassion and love. For as much as our Lady sorrowed for his pains, so much did he suffer sorrow for her sorrows. And furthermore, since since his sweet humanity was more honourable by nature [*Showings, Long Text* XX: 739–44].[5]

Julian's description here of the "sweet manhood" of Christ refers to a paradox of desire as it is so often expressed in medieval mysticism: the medieval mystic's expression of erotic desire for Christ may (sometimes) be queer, but most often its nature is expressed using the heterosexual language of marital union (*brautmystik*) and consummation. The Otherness of the mystic makes her queer, but she is left with the phallocentric language of desire, indeed the only language that her culture permits her to use in expressing that desire.[6]

Mysticism is first and most importantly an alternative means of expression. It is the expression of that which, like the semiotic (and the poetic) has been made silent and wordless by the Symbolic Order; the mystic is always one who is different. My reading of mysticism situates the mystic outside of the established order of the Church in much the same way the theories of French feminism situate the poetic writer outside of the Symbolic Order: both the mystic and Hélène Cîxous' writer of *écriture féminine* write from and about that which is immanent, rather than that which is established by the Word of patriarchy. The focus of much of my own research has been the late twelfth and early thirteenth century anchoritic texts associated with *Ancrene Wisse*, texts often examined together in what is called the Wooing Group.[7] Anchoritic writers can be characterized by their sense of isolation from the Christian community—in some ways, a self-imposed exile; their sense of urgency with respect to union with the Divine through worship and contemplation; their isolation from others and their avoidance of human contact in favor of Divine union. While its proponents include Bernard of Clairvaux, whose theology is ruled by the idea of Divine love, the central metaphor for anchoritic spirituality is an abjection of self and of human existence through asceticism of both mind and body.

Anchoritic mysticism is queer in ways that other forms of mystical expression are not, in part because of the extreme isolation of the anchoress (or anchorite in the case of a man) in her anchorhold, an enclosed residence attached to a medieval church which would provide her both sensual and cultural isolation, and because she was viewed in her own time (and clearly in ours) as simultaneously subject and object, One and Other, enclosed and exposed. Dinshaw's definition of the heterogenous nature of queer history provides a means of understanding the anchoress as both within and outside of social and theological control, something not achieved by any other member of medieval religious culture. The anchoress is both one who participates in the patriarchal culture of the Middle Ages and one who resists that culture. She follows a strict rule of behavior prescribed for her by a male mentor; she is chaste; she is expected to spend her time in prayer, in contemplation, and in silent reflection — speaking to no one, touching no one (including herself), and looking upon nothing but the altar and her own sinful soul. At the same time she expresses her desire quite openly, using erotic and often extremely sensual language to describe her love for Christ and her own experience of divine transcendence. In the texts associated with the Wooing Group, Christ takes on both the masculine and the feminine, the abject and the empowered, and through a transference of gender identity, allows the feminine speaker (and reader) to reach beyond her state as culturally defined, oppressed feminine object and attain a sense of transcendent subjectivity.[8]

## II.

In *On Lofsong of Ure Louerde*, the descriptions of Christ fluctuate from line to line with images of his death interspersed with images of his immortal life:

> May the strong streams and the flood that flowed from your wounds to heal humanity clean and wash my sinful soul. Through your five wounds, opened on the cross, driven through and sorrowfully filled up with nails, heal me, sorely wounded with deadly sins through my five senses [Savage and Watson 326].

This passage is a good representation of what occurs for the speaker(s) of the Wooing Group during the mystical experience. They begin as sinful, fallen, penetrated female bodies who are eventually brought to the glory of the resurrection through Christ's fallen and resurrected body and through the intellectual exchange that takes place during the moment of transcendence. Central to their understanding of the potential for their spiritual perfection is the knowledge and understanding of their own physical and earthly abjection. Once they surrender to that notion of their own physical inadequacy and sin, they are enabled to reach beyond the body and participate in the word-less, body-less experience of mysticism.

The question of subjectivity — of the reader and of the speaker of the poem — is important here; how does the subjectivity of the feminine speaker develop — after all, as a woman it is subjectivity that the speaker of the texts is most emphatically denied by her culture. The mystic is nontraditional, unorthodox, and cannot be understood in the conventional sense of patriarchal experience; thus she cannot be completely defined by the standards of orthodox tradition, whether it is a tradition of theology or literature. The mystic (particularly the anchoritic mystic, such as the apparent audience of *þe Wohunge of Ure Lauerd*) is unique (queer) within her culture because of her role as a disruptive force within it. She stands within a culture which oppresses and silences the Other, yet, because of her exchange with the Divine through her mystical experience, she will not be silenced.

Julian of Norwich, an anchoress and a mystic, again provides an illuminating example. In her work, she cannot settle on the traditional, patriarchal image of God when she seeks to describe him. She expands that image to include the masculine and the feminine:

> And so in our making, God almighty is our loving Father, and God all wisdom is our loving Mother, with the love and the goodness of the Holy Spirit, which is all one God, one Lord. And in the joining and the union he is our very true spouse and we his beloved wife and his fair maiden, with which wife he was never displeased ... I saw and understood the high might of the Trinity is our Father, and the deep wisdom of the Trinity is our Mother, and the great love of the Trinity is our Lord [*Showings, Long Text* LVIII: 2391–95, 2409–11].[9]

The love of God is both the father and the mother; Christ is her spouse, and the Christian is simultaneously his wife and a "fair maiden." Julian cannot narrow her focus to one gender or erotic category in her definition of the love of Christ any more than the mystic can be narrowed into one category (male/female, queer/heterosexual) by her audience, be it medieval or modern.

In *þe Wohunge of Ure Lauerd*, for example, the speaker identifies herself with the abject, feminized, crucified Christ and celebrates his willingness to offer his kindness and love, even in his state of abjection. Within these works, the abject (Christ's, the mystic's, even the reader's) is feminine — and that which is feminine within a culture controlled by phallic power, being Other, is always already queer. Throughout the text the speaker describes his brutalized body, emphasizing the most demoralizing and abject moments of Christ's passion. In spite of this suffering, it is his endurance of such abjection that motivates her love:

> For against all the misery and the shame that you suffered, and against all the sorrow and the painful wounds, you never opened your mouth to

complain. And still you meekly endure the shame and the misery the sinful of the world cause you every day [Savage and Watson 250].

At the same time, the speaker argues the proof of her own love is her devotion to Christ who, for the duration of the poem, is imagined during the Crucifixion:

> for often many a woman loses her honor through the love of a man of high birth. Then, sweet Jesus, upon what higher man can I set my love? Where can I choose a nobler man than you, who are the Son of the King who rules this world [Savage and Watson 250].

She takes it for granted that, as a woman, she is likely to be sexually compromised by a man; so why not choose the best of men for that compromise and seek the role of bride of Christ[10] (or perhaps, as this quotation seems to imply, sexual object of Christ): sexual contact with a great man provides her access to some of that greatness.[11] The anchoritic mystical works provide a number of powerful sexualized images of both Christ and the female speaker: images of heterosexuality which queer the text because of their excessive sensuality. Indeed, in *þe Wohunge of Ure Lauerd*, there is an image of the brutalized *queer* Christ:

> you were stripped, bound fast to the pillar, so that you could in no way flinch from the blows; there you were beaten with knitted whips for my love, so that your lovely body could be all torn and rent [Savage and Watson 245].

Christ is beaten, penetrated, and submissive to phallic power in this almost voyeuristic image described by the speaker of the poem. Indeed, the queered body of Christ in these texts has been examined elsewhere, particularly with reference to Christ's wounds and his flowing blood[12] and their symbolic resemblance to the vagina and menstrual blood.[13] This is reinforced later in the poem when the speaker reflects on Christ's wound:

> Ah! That lovely body, that hangs so pitifully, so bloody and so cold. Ah! How shall I live now? For now my love dies for me on the dear cross ... He pierces his side, cleaves that heart. And out of the wide wound comes flowing the blood that bought, the water that washed the world of strife and of sin. Ah! sweet Jesus, you open your heart to me, so that I may know it inwardly [Savage and Watson 255].

The experience of the anchoritic mystic, witnessing — in fact, as a speaker, enacting — this eroticized disempowerment of the Divine, is an example of how the Otherness of mysticism extends beyond what has traditionally been viewed as merely Other; her reflection upon Christ as her own beautiful heterosexual lover and simultaneously as a broken, bleeding (though no less beautiful) victim problematizes the nature of desire throughout these texts, making the speaker (and Christ) not merely feminine or Other in their abjection, but queer.

The paradoxical images of Christ in majesty, which the speaker summons as she looks upon the broken and bloody body of Christ as he dies upon the Cross, brings to mind the possibility that her love lifts him out of his state of abjection into his state of risen glory in the same way that his love brings her through abjection into salvation. Thus abjection, while a fairly clear characteristic of mysticism, at least in some mystical texts, seems to provide a sense of subjectivity which the mystic might otherwise not have. And because the mystic cannot otherwise have a sense of subjectivity within traditional patriarchal codes of meaning, she must be seen, at least to some degree as queer, because queerness is also characterized by exile, Otherness, and a lack of recognition and subjectivity within the Symbolic Order.[14]

Thus she is set apart from her culture intellectually and theologically, as well as physically (through her convent or anchorhold). The mystic, then, is queer, not simply because she is Other but also because her Otherness acts disruptively in the presence of the patriarchal culture that oppresses her. Her text is disruptive for a number of reasons. The text itself is also exiled, in that it exists outside of orthodox devotional writing — that is, mysticism is isolated from traditional literary genres. It is a separate genre in the same sense the mystics themselves are separate from the cultures in which they exist — in much the same way that Wittig argues that lesbians are separate from other women.[15] Thus, since it cannot be defined based on what already exists within traditional readings of medieval literature, particularly medieval poetry, then mysticism must be seen as Other, and, as I have argued, its use of language and metaphor makes it not only Other, but disruptive and unsettling. As such, the genre itself queers the canon — it stands in opposition to traditional, patriarchal notions of literature and works to subvert that tradition on many levels: its means of subversion include, for example, feminine authorship and readership, the almost exclusive use of the vernacular, and erotic and abject language and imagery. In the Katherine Group, for example, dated to approximately the same period and anchoritic audience as the Wooing Group and *Ancrene Wisse* (late twelfth century), the life of Saint Margaret is recounted. Margaret, a chaste Christian, is threatened with rape and torture by the pagan king Olibrius if she will not marry him and renounce her Christianity. In the narrative of her martyrdom, she is beaten, stabbed, strangled, drowned, burned, swallowed by a dragon, and imprisoned. She survives all of these violations, smiling and singing the praises of her true spouse, Jesus, and it is only when she is decapitated (something she requests of her torturer) that she dies. When he is threatened with violence by Olibrius, for example, she replies:

> I will submit my body to every kind of suffering that you can contrive, however hard it may be to bear or endure, as long as I may have the reward that virgins receive in heaven. God died for us, the beloved Lord, and I am not afraid to suffer any kind of death for his sake. He has set his mark on me, sealed with his seal; and neither life nor death can divide us again [*Seinte Margarete* 53].

Surely her delight in her torture on behalf of her love for Christ, her *jouissance*, reinforces the abject nature of anchoritic mysticism and the queer nature of desire in these works: Margaret rejoices in her abjection as it reveals her faith and brings her closer to her ultimate consummation with Christ, a consummation she, as a virgin, could not permit with her earthly body but which she longs for in her soul. The scholars I quoted earlier define that which is queer based on both erotic acts and sexual identity, and it is clear that the anchoritic mystics (and the audiences of their texts) are queer in just these kinds of ways — they commit queer acts, think queer thoughts, speak a queer language, and even embrace what we can now understand, perhaps, as a queer identity.

## III.

In this article I have sought to bring together two elusive concepts, queer theory and medieval mysticism in order to expose the simultaneously transcendent and transgressive nature of the mystic: earthbound and esoteric; sensual and chaste; queer and heterosexual. Mysticism is, above all else, the record of an event that is both word-less and body-less, and yet it must always (at least for the kinds of texts that I have thus far examined) be expressed using words and the body. Thus a central paradox of mysticism may not be a question of how we apply gender or theories of sexuality to its authors, speakers, or audiences. Ultimately the paradox of mysticism is how something so anti-linguistic[16] can be expressed in language at all — and that aspect of mysticism may be above all what makes it so compelling. So while I have intended to use the heterogenous nature (as defined by Dinshaw) of queer theory to understand the mystic, I must end by admitting that the mystic has ultimately helped me to understand the queer. As Karma Lochrie has pointed out, those who study both queer and medieval topics have to account for several cultures of inscription and phallogocentrism: medieval studies, critical theory, and now even the growing institutionalization of queer theory itself. She writes:

> Queer medieval scholarship might begin to question the whole grid of "heteronormativity" that we have so consistently used to delineate the queer ... the current absurdity of heterosexuality, however, calls attention to its recent "invention," and should force us to reconsider whether it is historically accurate or even wise to assume a heteronormative grid for the Middle Ages against which we define the queer [Lochrie 95].

Current critics may be limited by our own often inaccurate assumptions about the past, but, as Lochrie points out, it is important to assume that they are just that, assumptions. Instead of using such categories as queer/straight, transgressive/orthodox, female/male to define the always unknowable mystic, perhaps it is that very unknowability that we should use to inform our understanding of those categories. As Ed Cohen has argued:

> to the extent that we can transform our eccentricities into our strengths, utilizing our "off-center" positions to challenge the concrete institutional arrangements whereby the "center" is both defined and produced ... we [can] create the possibility for interrupting these defining practices even as they reiterate our specific marginalities [175].

Rather than creating (however unintentionally) an institutionalization of queer theory as a category of critical inquiry, perhaps, like the mystic, the queer theorist should speak the unspeakable and engage the unknowable in a language that only she fully recognizes, remaining aware, always, of the failure of language to fully express human desire.

## *Notes*

1. Dinshaw defines *queer history* as focusing "on *sex* as heterogenous and indeterminate, even as it recognizes and pursue's sex's irreducible interrelatedness with other cultural phenomena ... a queer history, not denying the desire for some sort of recoverable past, attempts to provide ... an account of the production of knowledge that seeks as well to account faithfully for the 'real'" (*Getting Medieval* 13-14).
2. Chewning, Susannah. "Mysticism and the Anchoritic Community: 'a time ... of veiled infinity'." *Medieval Women in their Communities*. Ed. Diane Watt. Cardiff: U of Wales P, 1997. 116-37.
3. The problematic nature of medieval virginity has been addressed recently by several critics. See *Medieval Virginities*, ed. Anke Bernau, Sarah Salih, and Ruth Evans (Wales 2003); Maud Burnett McInerney, *I Am No Woman But a Maid: The Rhetoric of Virginity from Thecla to Joan of Arc* (Palgrave 2002); Sarah Salih, *Versions of*

*Virginity* (Brewer 2001); Karen A. Winstead (ed.), *Chaste Passions: Medieval English Virgin Martyr Legends* (Cornell 2000); Cindy L. Carlson and Angela Jane Weisl, *Constructions of Widowhood and Virginity in the Middle Ages* (St. Martin's 1999); and Kathleen Coyne Kelly and Marina Leslie (eds.), *Menacing Virgins: Representing Virginity in the Middle Ages and Renaissance* (Delaware 1999). Theodora Jankowski applies queer theory to Renaissance drama in her book, *Pure Resistance: Queer Virginity in Early Modern English Drama* (Pennsylvania 2000).

4. Scholars who have recently begun to apply queer theory to Medieval Studies include Dinshaw, of course, as well as Josiah Blackmore and Gregory S. Hutcheson in *Queer Iberia: Sexualities, Cultures, and Crossings from the Middle Ages to the Renaissance* (Duke 1999), Glenn Burger and Steven Kruger in *Queering the Middle Ages* (Minnesota 2001), Glenn Burger in *Chaucer's Queer Nation* (Minnesota 2003), Jeffrey J. Cohen in *Medieval Identity Machines* (Minnesota 2003) and *Becoming Male in the Middle Ages* (co-edited with Bonnie Wheeler, Garland 1999), Michael O'Rourke (co-editor of *Love, Sex, Intimacy and Friendship Between Men, 1550-1800*, Palgrave 2003), Tison Pugh in *Queering Medieval Genres* (Palgrave 2004), and Anna Klosowka in *Queer Love in the Middle Ages* (Palgrave 2005), Karma Lochrie in *Heterosynchracies: Female Sexuality When Normal Wasn't* (Minnesota 2005). Michelle M. Sauer examines same-sex desire in connection with *A Talkyng of the Loue of God*, a later text connected to the Wooing Group in "Cross-Dressing Souls: Same-Sex Desire and the Mystic Tradition in *A Talkyng of the Loue of God." Intersections of Sexuality and the Divine in Medieval Culture: The Word Made Flesh*. Ed. Susannah Mary Chewning. Aldershot: Ashgate, 157-81.

5. Trans. Colledge and Walsh 211-12. Due to limited space, Middle English quotations will be printed in Modern English translations.

6. There is not space here to describe all the means by which the mystic expresses her desire and love for Christ in traditional heterosexual language; the nature of *brautmystik* alone has been defined and described by a number of critics and scholars in recent decades. Beginning with Bernard of Clairvaux, in fact, it was expected and encouraged for Christians, male and female, to describe their love for Christ in such terms. The co-existance, however, of such language and imagery with the queerness of the mystic within her culture makes her an appropriate subject for this study.

7. This group of texts includes *þe Wohunge of Ure Lauerd, On Ureisun of Ure Louerde, On Wel Swuðe God Ureisun of God Almihti, On Lofsong of ure Louerde, On Lofsong of Ure Lefdi*, and *þe Oreisun of Seinte Marie*. They are edited together in W. Meredith Thompson, *þe Wohunge of Ure Lauerd* (Oxford: EETS , 1958). Many of the works in the Wooing Group are also translated in *Anchoritic Spirituality*, ed. Anne Savage and Nicholas Watson. (Mahwah, NJ: Paulist P, 1991).

8. Luce Irigaray addresses the notion of this transference of subjectivity from Christ to the fallen female mystic in *Speculum of the Other Woman*, particularly in her article, "La Mystérique." See also Amy Hollywood, *Sensible Ecstasy: Mysticism, Sexual Difference, and the Demands of History*. Chicago: U of Chicago P, 2002, pp. 198-203.

9. Trans. Colledge and Walsh 293-94.

10. Denis Renevey examines the notion of mystical love and desire in his book *Language, Self, and Love: Hermeneutics in the Writings of Richard Rolle and the Commentaries on the Song of Songs*. Cardiff: U of Wales P, 2001. Renevey examines love from a variety of perspectives, emphasizing the metaphorical treatment of the erotic imagery in the Song of Songs as "carnal imagery's transference from the field of physical love to that of the spiritual" (77).

11. I expand on this notion of the wooed (the mystic) turning the tables and wooing Christ in these works elsewhere. See Carlson and Weisl, 118-21.

12. For a discussion of the penetration of Christ in related texts see Michelle M. Sauer, who writes "the many ways Christ's body can be consumed and permeated allow for multiple passionate, gratifying, and ultimately homo-erotic, unions with the Savior, unions that would be either passive or active" ("Cross-Dressing Souls" 171).

13. See Luce Irigaray, "La Mystérique": "a wound could be *sacred*? Ecstasies in that glorious cleft where she coils up as if in her residence, where she reposes as if at home- and He is in her as well. Bathing in a warm blood and purifying in his generous flood" (200). See also Amy Hollywood, who locates the relationship here between Christ's wound and "the features of the female flesh" as supporting a "specifically feminine subjectivity" (200). I would argue that rather than merely feminine here, the body of Christ is queer, while still enacting heterosexual desire and consumption.

14. See Ed Cohen, "Are We (Not) What We Are Becoming?" who recounts his own experience as a gay man and a queer theorist (in a period before the term *queer* had been applied to critical discourse), commenting that Other sexual identities "have historically been excluded from intellectual inquiry" (172).

15. Because of the time in which Monique Wittig wrote her major works, such as "The Straight Mind" and "One Is Not Born a Woman," and perhaps because of her own personal experiences, she emphasizes lesbian identity and only goes as far as that metaphor will allow her in her depiction of what we now, twenty-five years later, would call *queer*. Her position in history prevents her from using the language of queer theory, and although I find her metaphors of Otherness extremely useful in my own understanding of queer theory, I should point out here that when I read *lesbian* in her works I generally interpret it as not limited to same-sex desire among women but, rather, as queer desire.

16. As Leo Bersani writes: "We desire what nearly shatters us, and the shattering experience is, it would seem, without any specific content-which may be our only way of saying that the experience cannot be said, that it belongs to the nonlinguistic biology of human life" (40).

# *Works Cited*

Bersani, Leo. *The Freudian Body: Psychoanalysis and Art*. New York: Columbia University Press, 1986.

Burger, Glenn. *Chaucer's Queer Nation*. Minneapolis: University of Minnesota Press, 2003.

Burger, Glenn, and Steven F. Kruger. *Queering the Middle Ages*. Minneapolis: University of Minnesota Press, 2001.

Bynum, Caroline Walker. *Fragmentation and Redemption: Essays and the Human Body in Medieval Religion*. New York: Zone, 1991.

Chewning, Susannah M. "'Gladly Alone, Gladly Silent': Language, Gender, and Desire in Medieval Mysticism." In *Anchorites, Wombs, and Tombs: Intersections of Gender and Enclosure in the Middle Ages*. Ed. Liz Herbert McAvoy and Mari Hughes-Edwards. London: Boydell and Brewer, 2005. 103-15.

_____. "'Mi bodi henge / wið þi bodi': The Paradox of Sensuality in *þe Wohunge of Ure Lauerd*." In *Intersections of Sexuality and the Divine in Medieval Culture: The*

*Word Made Flesh.* Ed. Susannah Mary Chewning. Aldershot: Ashgate, 2005. 183–96.

———. "Mysticism and the Anchoritic Community: 'a time ... of veiled infinity.'" In *Medieval Women in their Communities.* Ed. Diane Watt. Cardiff: University of Wales Press. 116–137.

———. "The Paradox of Virginity within the Anchoritic Tradition: The Masculine Gaze and the Feminine Body in the *Wohunge Group.*" In *Constructions of Widowhood and Virginity in the Middle Ages.* Ed. Cindy L. Carlson and Angela Jane Weisl. New York: St. Martin's, 1999. 113–34.

Cixous, Hélène. "The Laugh of the Medusa." Trans. Keith Cohen and Paula Cohen. In *New French Feminisms: An Anthology.* Ed. Elaine Marks and Isabelle de Courtivron. New York: Schocken, 1981. 251. Originally published as "Le rire de la meduse," *L'arc* (1975): 39–54.

Cohen, Ed. "Are We (Not) What We Are Becoming? 'Gay' 'Identity,' 'Gay Studies,' and the Disciplining of Knowledge." In *Engendering Men: The Question of Male Feminist Criticism.* Ed. Joseph A. Boone and Michael Cadden. New York: Routledge, 1990. 161–75.

Dinshaw, Carolyn. *Getting Medieval: Sexualities and Communities, Pre- and Post-Modern.* Durham, NC: Duke University Press, 1999.

———. "A Kiss Is Just a Kiss: Heterosexuality and Its Consolations in *Sir Gawain and the Green Knight.*" *Diacritics* 24 (1994): 205–26.

Irigaray, Luce. "Je, tu, nous: Toward a Culture of Difference." Trans. Alison Martin. New York: Routledge, 1993. Originally published as "Je, tu, nous." Editions Grasset & Fasquelle, 1990.

———. "La Mystérique." In *The Speculum of the Other Woman.* Trans. Gilliam C. Gill. Ithaca, NY: Cornell University Press, 1985. 191–202. Originally published as *Speculum de l'autre femme.* Les Editions Minuit, 1974.

Jankowski, Theodora. *Pure Resistance: Queer Virginity in Early Modern English Drama.* Philadelphia, PA: University of Pennsylvania Press, 2000.

Julian of Norwich. *The Shewings of Julian of Norwich.* Ed. Georgia Ronan Crampton. Kalamazoo, MI: Medieval Institute Publications, 1994.

———. *Showings.* Trans. Edmund Colledge and James Walsh. Mahwah, NJ: Paulist Press, 1978.

Kristeva, Julia. "From One Identity to Another." In *Desire in Language.* Trans. Gora, Jardine, Roudiez. New York: Columbia University Press, 1980.

———. *The Powers of Horror: An Essay in Abjection.* New York: Columbia University Press, 1982.

Lochrie, Karma. *Heterosynchracies: Female Sexuality When Normal Wasn't.* Minneapolis: University of Minnesota Press, 2005.

———. "Presidential Improprieties and Medieval Categories: The Absurdity of Heterosexuality." In *Queering the Middle Ages.* Ed. Glenn Burger and Steven F Ruger. Minneapolis: University of Minnesota Press, 2001. 87–96.

Nugent, Donald C. "There Was a Feminine Mysticism." *Mystics Quarterly* 14 (1988): 135–42.

Pugh, Tison. *Queering Medieval Categories.* New York: Palgrave, 2004.

Sauer, Michelle M. "Cross-Dressing Souls: Same-Sex Desire and the Mystic Tradition in *A Talkyng of the Loue of God.*" In *Intersections of Sexuality and the Divine in Medieval Culture: The Word Made Flesh.* Ed. Susannah Mary Chewning. Aldershot: Ashgate. 157–81.

Savage, Anne, and Nicholas Watson. *Anchoritic Spirituality: Ancrene Wisse and Associated Works.* New York: Paulist Press, 1991.
*Seinte Margarete.* In *Medieval English Prose for Women from the Katherine Group and Ancrene Wisse.* Ed. and trans. Bella Millet and Jocelyn Wogan-Browne. Oxford: Oxford University Press, 1992. 44–85.
Solomon, Alisa, and Paisley Currah. "Introduction." In *Queer Ideas: The David R. Kessler Lectures in Lesbian and Gay Studies.* Ed. Alisa Solomon and Paisley Currah. New York: Feminist Press, 2003. 5–18.
Thompson, W. Meredith, ed. *_e Wohunge of Ure Lauerd.* EETS o.s. 241. London: Early English Text Society, 1958.
\_\_\_\_\_. "Response to Richard Levin's '(Re)Thinking Unthinkable Thoughts.'" *New Literary History* 28.3 (1997): 539–42.
Wittig, Monique. "One Is Not Born a Woman." *Feminist Issues* (Fall 1981): 47–54.
\_\_\_\_\_. "The Straight Mind." *Feminist Issues* (Summer 1980): 101–11.

# 4 Deviant Celibacy
## *Renouncing Dinah's Little Fetish* in Adam Bede

### KATE FABER OESTREICH

The characters of George Eliot's novel *Adam Bede* (1859) seem oddly fixated on Dinah Morris's "ugly" cap. In fact, the townspeople locate Dinah's barrier to marriage with the symbol of her celibacy — her unattractive headdress — rather than her avowal to remain unmarried. Modern critics have argued that Dinah is a paragon of chaste womanhood, but her Methodist cap is metonymic of *life-long celibacy* rather than chastity *prior to marriage*, a radical and queer — since not clearly heteronormative — choice. What at first seems to be Dinah's innocuous chastity is, within a Victorian context, dangerous and deviant celibacy, as she disrupts the inevitability of heteronormativity, an ideal that fallen Hetty Sorrel paradoxically reinforces. Female sexual transgression in the novel has typically been located in what Hetty believed was a premarital tryst with and subsequent pregnancy by Arthur Donnithorne. Dinah's fetishized cap, though, exposes her as the more sexually transgressive character. The association of Dinah's cap with death, mourning, religious asceticism, and barrenness underscores its ties to unnatural sexuality or, more specifically, Dinah's rejection of heterosexual sex and reproduction.

By refocusing attention on the way Dinah fetishizes her unconventional cap, I argue that it is Dinah's sexuality — not Hetty's — that must be recaptured and rearticulated as heteronormative prior to the narrative's resolution.

By utilizing and expanding on Sigmund Freud's theory of female fetishists, I analyze the way Dinah's celibacy is deviant sexuality instead of the feminine ideal of chastity. My reading relies on an analysis of Dinah's net Methodist cap as an overdetermined symbol that marks her as sexually unavailable. As Judith Butler famously demonstrated, gender is comprised of repetitive acts that subjects unconsciously perform. Based on these unconscious acts subjects are then recognized as properly or improperly embodying their "correct" gender. Ironically, Butler then encourages her readers to actively disrupt these hegemonic conceptions of gender by consciously performing drag, as if drag can magically erase or free subjects from others' constrictive understanding of gender. My belief is that clothing choices — be they conscious or unconscious — are as limited in signifying heteronormative desire as other "gender markers," such as hand position, directness of gaze, or the volume of one's voice. The body is a site that produces and reflects its society, where "the powers and dangers credited to social structure [are] reproduced in small on the human body" (Douglas 115). Accordingly, these gender markers are limited not only by cultural definitions of appropriateness but also by people's ability to read or understand the desire signified by the markers. What is distinctive about clothing's relationship to desire is that sartorial performances of gender can be purchased, gifted, measured, and preserved; thus, clothing may outperform other signifiers as the Rosetta Stone of queer heterosexuality.

Dinah's fetishized clothing can also be read as an anthropological fetish, a move that questions assumptions regarding the "naturalness" of Christian asceticism to a Western audience and erases the division between anthropological and sexual fetishes. On the one hand, anthropological fetishes have been historically defined as items a person overvalues due to primitive, i.e. non-Christian, religious connotations. On the other hand, sexual fetishes conjure ideas of a relationship with an object that takes *the place of* human-to-human sexuality. I argue that Dinah's cap is both an anthropological fetish and a sexual fetish because it represents her fidelity to God *and* her rejection of sexual activity. Dinah's fetish focuses our attention to both her defiance of societal rules and society's discomfort with her symbolic sexual rebellion. As Lloyd Davis reminds us, "while set up to be a subjected body, the virginal also affords a social identity under the guise of which apparently fixed social myths and institutions may be questioned, revised or even evaded. The veil works both ways" (Davis 15).

Critics who have written on *Adam Bede* and sexuality typically focus on Hetty because she is more overtly sexualized than Dinah. In part, this preoccupation with Hetty is also situated in the feminist endeavor to recover, deconstruct, and redefine the dichotomies used to categorize female literary characters of the nineteenth century: angel/demon, Madonna/whore, and old maid/fallen woman. Hetty readily fits all three of the less privileged terms. Her illegitimate pregnancy marks her as a whore, and her public trial and subsequent criminal sentence of transportation to the colonies makes her a fallen woman. Hetty is also a demon because she disrupts and lays bare the cultural paradigm laid on the "angel in the house"; she dislikes housework and children and dreams of a life of privileged ease won by her good looks, not good deeds. Nina Auerbach's seminal *Woman and the Demon* locates an autobiographical reason behind Eliot's depiction of Hetty as a fallen woman and a wannabe social climber: Eliot's own status as a fallen woman allowed her to become an artist (174). In this manner, the mirror that is typically associated with Hetty's self-admiration also becomes the mirror with which Eliot creates the narrative world in *Adam Bede*. Nevertheless, Hetty is punished for transgressing sexual norms and consequently dies, and (heteronormative) society is able to continue functioning normally. Similarly, Jill L. Matus argues that while Hetty's physical loveliness belies the internal "beauty" of motherly instinct, she is unable to develop maternal feelings *because* she must make the transition to motherhood "suddenly, alone and without support" (171), illustrating the community's portion of guilt in the death of Hetty's child. The focus on Hetty's sexuality underscores how the lesser-privileged halves of these binaries erase or suppress the unnaturalness of the privileged terms. Angels and Madonnas are constructed not only as non-sexual but also as non-interesting characters. Aside from their role as righteous women against which "bad" women are measured, angels and Madonnas are boring and therefore less likely to entice critical attention. Dinah, who is repeatedly referred to as an angel, though, is in danger of becoming an old maid. Paradoxically, Auerbach posits that artistic and narrative depictions expose the "outsider" status of fallen women and old maids, as they embodied roles outside of the nuclear family and were "defined as essential strangers in England" (153). Both under-sexualized *and* over-sexualized women disrupt heteronormative ideals for women.

Victorian novelist Charles Kingsley wrote to his wife that "a few self-conceited fools shut themselves up in a state of unnatural celibacy + [sic] morbid excitement, in order to *avoid* their duty, instead of *doing* it'" (qtd. in Maynard 103, emphasis in original). Like many people in the nineteenth century Kingsley believed that celibacy had physical as well as spiritual dangers. Celibacy was thought to make women susceptible to hysteria — a condition seen as most prevalent in unmarried and childless women. The "fools" to whom Kingsley refers are avoiding their obligation to produce the next generation of English subjects, a selfish act of self-realization before duty. And Dinah is one of these fools. She explains, "there's many of God's servants who have greater strength than I have, and find their hearts enlarged by the cares of husband and kindred. But I have not faith that it would be so with me" (511). Like chastity, celibacy is defined in relation to sexual activity. The difference is that chastity was seen as an important condition for women in relation to heterosexual marriage. Conduct manuals, like the one Wetenhall Wilkes wrote in the eighteenth century to his niece, were meant to educate young women in their *innate* femininity:

> Chastity is a suppression of all irregular desires, voluntary pollutions, sinful concupiscence, and of an immoderate use of all sensual, or carnal pleasures. Its purity consists in *abstinence* or *continence*. The first is properly attributed to virgins and widows, the other to married women. [...] Chastity is so essential and natural to your sex.... An immodest woman is a kind of monster [30, emphasis in original].

Chastity demands that women's sexual desires be constantly monitored, denied, and repressed before, during, and after marriage. Chastity was also equivalent to modern notions of monogamy, as "continence" in marriage was an integral component of chastity. Because chastity was framed within heteronormative contexts, it was sexualized and tied to fulfilling heteronormative, marital norms. Celibacy, on the other hand, is a decision to be sexually inactive for one's entire life, not simply before, during, or after a monogamous relationship. This distinction makes celibacy appear to be non-sexual; however, Dinah's celibacy is a sexual state because she consciously desires *not* to have sex. Dinah does not lack sexuality, as sexuality is defined by the mere existence of desire, not by its consummation.

Celibacy was also viewed as an act of self-indulgence rather than of self-denial in its rejection of community and seemingly life itself: duty, marriage, and children. Theodora A. Jankowski traces the history of virginity in Christian thought and argues that following the Reformation marriage became the ideal, while celibacy was increasingly viewed as unnatural. "The queer virgins...," Jankowski argues, "are those who confound the sex/gender system *not* by trying to be men, but by *not being* 'women'" (12). Indeed, the community of Hayslope in *Adam Bede* is more fixated on and concerned about Dinah's unwomanly celibacy than Hetty and Arthur's scandalous heterosexual relationship. Within heteronormative society Dinah's celibacy makes her more sexually transgressive than Hetty, and Dinah must be recovered and brought back inside the pale, not just by marriage alone but more importantly, by the physical embodiment of heteronormative sexuality: children. Hetty is transported not for producing an illegitimate child but for the unfeminine crime of abandoning that child to a lonely death. While Hetty's scandalously procreative heterosexuality demands attention, Dinah fades into the background of critical analyses under the misconception that she is the angel or Madonna that Hetty is unable to live up to. But Dinah cannot be the ideal or the narrative would have allowed her to remain a single woman dedicated to her religion.

Dinah's religious zeal is symbolized by her fetishized Methodist cap. Freud famously wrote that a fetish is "a substitute for the woman's (the mother's) penis that the little boy once believed in and ... does not want to give up" (64). Feminist scholars have rejected Freud's premise that only men can fetishize. Ultimately, so did Freud. Although Freud never published on women fetishists, minutes from a meeting of the Vienna Psychoanalytic Society illustrate Freud's view that women can and do fetishize. In fact, Freud argued that all women "must" be clothes fetishists in that by repressing their desire to be looked at, they overvalue the clothing that covers their nakedness: "All women ... are clothes fetishists. [...] It is a question of the repression of the same drive [the scopic drive], ... in the passive form of allowing oneself to be seen, which is repressed by the clothes, and on account of which, clothes are raised to a fetish" (qtd. in Rose 156). Freud implies not that all women repress their desire to be looked at but to be looked at with the *male* gaze. Freud also assumes a universal desire to be looked at that in turn requires the repression of this desire in order to appear feminine or attractive to *men*. At first it seems Freud believes all women desire heterosexual love (to be looked at and desired sexually by a man), and in order to court this look and appear feminine they must disavow the desire and project it onto the clothing. But Freud admits women can fetishize clothing in order to court unsexualized scopic attention:

> ... the most intelligent women behave defenselessly against the demands of fashion. For them, clothes take the place of parts of the body, and to wear the same clothes [as other women] means only to be able to show what the other can show, means only that one can find in her everything that one can expect from women, an assurance which the woman can give only in this form [156].

Freud's confession that women can still overvalue clothing in order to discourage male scopophilia is fascinating, in part because Freud hands out several backhanded compliments to these women. They are intelligent.

They are intentionally, awkwardly fashionable, and in being so they are not "everything that one can expect from women." In Freud's opinion a woman who intentionally and incorrectly fetishizes her clothing is not legitimately sexual, as passivity, denial, and repression define female sexuality and hence, attractiveness to men. Accordingly, these fashion victims are not entirely identifiable to Freud as women because they do not embody his model for female sexuality, which depends on a natural affinity toward "the same clothes." The unfashionable Methodist cap Dinah wears exposes her antipathy toward women's "same clothes" and connotes her intellectual attachment to a specific form of stimulation — religion, which precludes courting male desire through the male scopic drive.

The Victorian maiden, though, is specifically seen as a marketable commodity for marriage and fetishizes her clothing with the desire to make herself attractive to men. As with any package that needs a buyer — or husband — attractiveness of the package is first and foremost to both the seller and buyer. The maiden wears fashionable clothing that simultaneously cloaks and displays her sexuality to the gaze of men. So while the maiden's corporeal sexuality is physically covered by *cloth*, the *clothing* functions to highlight or accentuate her search for a marriage partner. Additionally, the maiden's clothing should be fashionable, as her "up-to-dateness" increases her market value and attractiveness to potential suitors. Examples of such clothing in the novel are lockets, earrings, cotton dresses, straw hats, and red cloaks. Eliot draws on contemporary notions of fashion, contrasting Hetty to Mrs. Poysner: "Hetty was coming downstairs, and Mrs Poyser, in her plain bonnet and shawl, was standing below. If ever a girl looked as if she had been made of roses, that girl was Hetty in her Sunday hat and frock. For her hat was trimmed with pink, and her frock had pink spots sprinkled on a white ground" (186). Mrs. Poysner and her "plain bonnet and shawl" fade into the background behind Hetty and her trendy clothing: a fashionable, patterned cotton dress and a straw hat lined with feminine pink silk.

Dinah's asceticism, on the other hand, not only signifies her ideals but also her religious profession, which — since it draws attention to her beliefs instead of her body — is an unconventional fashion objective for a woman. Her clothing signifies a denial of her body's sexual nature and heterosexuality, which paradoxically fulfills conduct literature guidelines: "That girl, who endeavours, by the artifice of dress, to attract the admiration, to stir up languishing desires, and to provoke the wanton wishes of her gay beholders, is ... guilty.... [L]et your dress always resemble the plainness and simplicity of your heart" (Wilkes 30). Although Dinah fulfills the Victorian feminine ideal of being a plain, kind Christian woman, throughout most of the text she is paradoxically viewed as an undesiring and undesirable woman *because* she wears a plain and simple black stuff dress and her Methodist cap. Dinah is deliberately out of fashion.

Since Dinah does not covet the heterosexual male gaze, she is able to be a discerning subject instead of simply a sexual object. She focuses her attention on Chad's Bess:

> Ah, poor blind child! ... think if it should happen to you as it once happened to a servant of God in the days of her vanity. SHE thought of her lace caps and saved all her money to buy 'em; she thought nothing about how she might get a clean heart and a right spirit — she only wanted to have better lace than other girls. And one day when she put her new cap on and looked in the glass, she saw a bleeding Face crowned with thorns. That face is looking at you now.... Ah, tear off those follies! [32].

Admittedly, Dinah wants Chad's Bess to "tear off" her prized pair of earrings not her cap, but Dinah uses a lace cap in order to verbally paint this allegory; the desire for a lace cap will become a crown of thorns for Chad's Bess, as her love of caps is a barrier to having a "clean heart" or a "right spirit." In contrast, while listening to Dinah preach, Chad's Bess, "had shown an unwonted quietude and fixity of attention ever since Dinah had begun to speak. Not that the matter of the discourse had arrested her at once, for she was lost in a puzzling speculation as to what pleasure and satisfaction there could be in life to a young woman who wore a cap like Dinah's" (30). The austerity of Dinah's cap is synonymous for Chad's Bess to a life without "pleasure" and "satisfaction" because it clearly articulates her desire not to be a feminine spectacle for men, not to entice heterosexual romance.

The other characters also understand Dinah's choice of caps as her unfeminine desire not to be looked at. The elderly horseman on the square feels "surprise, not so much at the feminine delicacy of her appearance, as at the total absense [sic] of self-consciousness in her demeanour" (24). Dinah is feminine aside from not acknowledging her looked-at-ness. Dinah's appearance subverts a feminine performance: "Dinah walked as simply as if she were going to market, and seemed as unconscious of her outward appearance as a little boy: there was no blush, no tremulousness, which said, 'I know you think me a pretty woman [...]'" (24). Since Dinah does not blush or act coy under the gaze of men, she is equated with a small boy. She's not manly or masculine. She is pre-sexual, a child. And not just a child but a male child. In other words, a woman who does not cringe under the (un)wanted glance of a man is not a woman. Indeed, while listening to Dinah preach, "Wiry Ben wondered how Seth had the pluck to think of courting her" (25).

Hetty's pleasure under Arthur's gaze, though, picks up on contemporary conduct literature debates whether blushing cheeks revealed chaste innocence or improper sexual knowledge. When we first see Hetty and Arthur together, she "blushed a deep rose-colour ... but it was not at all a distressed blush, for it was inwreathed with smiles and dimples" (84). The tone of the above passage underscores that Arthur's gaze would "distress" her if she did not want his attention. But instead "sparkling" eyes and "smiles" accompany Hetty's blush even while she bows her head. Nancy Anne Marck posits that "Hetty dramatizes her role as object of male desire, using the male gaze to reaffirm her power" (463), highlighting Hetty's complicity with her own objectification. "Hetty is scorned," Judith Mitchell argues, "not for assuming so readily her position as viewed object, but for being aware of this position in the first place" (93). In contrast, Mr. Irwine asks Dinah, "And you never feel any embarrassment from the sense ... that you are a lovely young woman on whom men's eyes are fixed?" (92). To which Dinah replies in the negative because she believes her corporeal body is shrouded in the light of God. This may be true but only to a point. Dinah's body is also looked at: "Adam had seen Dinah several times, but ... he was not very vividly conscious of any woman's presence except Hetty's.... But now [Dinah's] slim figure, her plain black gown ... impressed him with all the force that belongs to a reality contrasted with a preoccupying fancy" (117). Note the use of the word "fancy" to describe Adam's scopic attraction to Hetty: she is a fantasy while Dinah, physically, is "reality." Dinah's plain black gown makes her look more real than finery or false displays of attractiveness. In response to Adam's "look," "Dinah, for the first time in her life, felt a painful self-consciousness ... A faint blush came, which deepened as she wondered at it. This blush recalled Adam from his forgetfulness" (117). This moment marks Dinah's sexual awakening. She is self-conscious. She blushes. And her blush awakens Adam from his reverie. While both Hetty's and Dinah's blushes are equated with a woman's sexual awareness, it is Dinah's innocent discomfort that works to break, or disrupt, Adam's sexually charged look.

In addition to Dinah's cap in *Adam Bede*, Eliot depicts anthropological fetishes in at least two of her other novels — the iron pot and leather bags in *Silas Marner* (1861), and Maggie Tulliver's wooden baby doll in *The Mill on the Floss* (1860). Each of these fetishes is associated with phallic symbolism's under-utilized kin: yonic symbolism. The Sanskrit word *yoni* is equivalent to the English words vagina or vulva, and yonic symbols are concave (such as a lake, a pot, or a cap), symbolizing the shape of female genitals. Although Maggie's doll is not concave, it is the symbolic product of a woman's vagina. And tellingly, both Silas's leather bags and Dinah's cap are replaced by the arrival of children. Early in the novel, Silas revels in how "the guineas shone as they came pouring out of the dark leather mouths!" and he thinks "fondly of the guineas [...] as if they had been unborn children" (17). Although Silas retains his broken iron pot by propping it up on the hearth, he is heartbroken when his leather bags of gold are stolen. Soon after this theft the orphan Eppie appears in his house, underscoring that Silas's unnatural worship of the guinea vessels has been replaced with natural love for a daughter. Years later Silas reflects, "he loved the old brick hearth as he had loved his brown pot— and was it not there when he had found Eppie? The gods of the hearth exist for us still; and let all new faith be tolerant of that fetishism, lest it bruise its own roots" (Eliot, *SM* 106). Here Eliot makes a connection between fetishes, procreation, and religion, establishing a historical link between fetishism and Christianity in that primitive religious practices, such as fetishism, are the foundation and life source, or roots, of the new Christian faith.

In *The Mill on the Floss* Maggie's doll also highlights the connection between fertility, religion, and fetishes. Maggie finds release "hammer[ing ... ] nails into her wooden fetish" (367), which was shaped like a baby doll. Although Maggie dies before the end of the novel, meaning she will never have a child, her fetish, like Dinah's, is surrounded by rhetoric highlighting her (un)natural inclination *away* from the maternal:

> the trunk of a large wooden doll ... was now entirely defaced by a long career of vicarious suffering. Three nails driven into the head commemorated as many crises in Maggie's nine years of earthly struggle; that luxury of vengeance having been suggested to her by the picture of Jael destroying Sisera in the old Bible. The last nail had been driven in with a fiercer stroke than usual.... But immediately afterwards Maggie had reflected that if she drove many nails in, she would not be so well able to fancy that the head was hurt when she knocked it against the wall, nor to comfort it, and make believe to poultice it when her fury was abated... [Eliot, *MF* 78-9].

The Biblical story of the woman Jael killing Sisera, a strong male warrior, inspires Maggie's abuse of her fetish. Feminist scholars have interpreted Jael's murder of Sisera as evidence of women's strength and defiance in the face of tyrannical patriarchal social systems; therefore, the nails that

Maggie drives into her fetish not only replicate the tent stake Jael uses to kill Sisera but also mirror a woman's quest to be free of tyranny. Since girls are given dolls in order to practice being a mother, Maggie's treatment of her "fetish" illustrates the possibility that she would be as poor a parent as Hetty. Maggie's abuse of her fetish object rejects women's culturally dictated maternal duties.

Silas's pot and leather bags, Maggie's doll, and Dinah's cap each resonate with contemporary notions of anthropological fetishes. Lorraine Gamman and Merja Makinen, in *Female Fetishism*, explain that "By the nineteenth century the term 'fetishism' had entered popular language and was being used ... to refer to anything reverenced without due reason" (15). The phrase "without due reason" is especially important because until the end of the century and the rise of psychoanalysis, fetishism was understood in relation to research on non-European cultures, which effectively "othered" "savage" cultures by labeling their religious symbols as fetishes. Gammon and Makinen refute this idea and argue that "the cherishing of objects associated with those we love ... is the desire to maintain a link to an absent person.... The fetish ... becomes invested with presence, and so symbolically 'stands in' for absence or loss in the same way that the religious totem ... represents a material presence of god" (27). This explanation universalizes anthropologic fetishes as any object that replaces the physical presence of either humans or deities, slicing through cultural and religious differences. Nevertheless, nineteenth-century anthropology is typically associated with simple or rustic communities rather than sophisticated or cosmopolitan circles. It is more than a coincidence that Eliot mentions fetish objects solely in her pastoral novels written before 1864. The word fetish is used in both *Silas Marner* and *The Mill on the Floss,* and although fetish objects are not directly named in *Adam Bede*, Eliot associates Dinah's Methodism with a more primitive type of religion than Mr. Irwine's liberal Anglicanism. This distinction underscores how Eliot's pastoral novels reflect the contemporary bias that fetishes are primitive in nature and more applicable to the characters of her pastoral novels rather than her more urban or sophisticated novels.

Ultimately, though, Eliot endorses characters who embrace their responsibilities to foster and nurture children. And while parenting feminizes Silas — his masculine avarice is replaced with feminine nurturance — motherhood connects characters to each other through selfless behavior, and the plot of *Adam Bede* depends on the effect natural and surrogate mothers have on their children, especially Dinah. After her mother died Dinah's aunt raised her in the town of Snowfield. Mrs. Poyser reminisces to Dinah, "'You look th' image o' your aunt Judith, Dinah [...] when she took to the Methodists ... she talked a bit different, and wore a different sort o' cap" (78). Similar to Dinah at this point in the novel Judith was an old maid, a Methodist, and wore the same "different sort o' cap." After Aunt Judith died Dinah split her time ministering in both Hayslope and Snowfield. Thus, while the religious connection between the Methodist cap and celibacy is the same for both women, Dinah's attraction to the cap and to Snowfield shows an element of mourning for the aunt whom Dinah loved as a mother. And not until after she marries Adam is Dinah able to renounce the items associated with her aunt such as the Methodist cap, celibacy, and the barrenness of Snowfield in exchange for heterosexual love, children, and the lush growth of Hayslope.

While most critics focus on Hetty as the fallen woman who must be punished, her death is passed over so quickly it is almost a footnote to the novel. More importantly, six of the last seven chapters are dedicated to phasing out Dinah's Methodist cap, which is integral to Eliot's effort to recreate Dinah as a heterosexually procreative woman. This move erases Dinah's deviant celibacy and rearticulates it as premarital chastity, which is why the narrative doesn't end when Dinah marries Adam, according the trope of "happily ever after." Indeed, the novel cannot close until we are shown an idyllic family scene: Dinah and her son and daughter welcoming Adam home. The description of Dinah in the epilogue underscores how her new, feminine cap goes hand in hand with her procreative abilities:

> There is a figure we know well, ... shading her eyes with her hands..., for the rays that fall on her white borderless cap ... are very dazzling. [...] We can see the sweet pale face quite well now: it is scarcely at all altered — only a little fuller, to correspond to her more matronly figure, which still seems light and active enough in the plain black dress [536].

Here for the first and only time we see Dinah in a traditional, feminine white cap. Dinah's adaptation of a "white borderless cap" instead of her previous net Methodist cap corresponds with the completion of Dinah's heterosexualization, and her matronly figure is the product of two pregnancies. As a mother she now has a vested interest in the community and vice versa. As a preacher she would freely travel back and forth between barren Snowfield and fertile Hayslope, but now the deviant celibate has been confined within the pale. In the end, the novel ensures our understanding that Dinah's celibacy has been replaced by the recognizably feminine desire to wear more fashionable clothing *and* by evident progeny. Dinah's celibacy must be renounced in order to establish the primacy of heteronormativity, the "natural" state of reproductive womanhood. It is Dinah, not Hetty, who must be reclaimed and reformed by the end of the narrative. Hetty serves merely as a warning to heterosexual women, as the moral of the story is not *Do not have sex outside of marriage* but *In order to live happily ever after you must be feminine, married,* and *procreative.*

## Works Cited

Auerbach, Nina. "The Rise of the Fallen Woman." In Nina Auerbach, *Woman and the Demon: The Life of a Victorian Myth.* Cambridge: Harvard University Press, 1982. 150–184.
Buck, Anne. *Dress in Eighteenth-Century England.* New York: Holmes & Meier, 1979.
Butler, Judith. *Gender Trouble: Feminism and the Subversion of Identity.* New York: Routledge, 1989.
Davis, Lloyd. *Virginal Sexuality and Textuality in Victorian Literature.* Albany: State University of New York Press, 1993.
Douglas, Mary. *Purity and Danger: An Analysis of Concepts of Pollution and Taboo.* London: Routledge & Kegan Paul, 1978.
Eliot, George. *Adam Bede.* 1859. London: Penguin, 1985.
_____. *The Mill on the Floss.* 1860. *The Text Archive.* Peter Batke. 12 March 2004. <http://www.princeton.edu/~batke/eliot/mill/>
_____. *Silas Marner.* 1861. *George Eliot: Selected Works.* Gramercy Classics Series. New York: Random House, 1994. 1–136.
Ewing, Elizabeth. *Everyday Dress 1650–1900.* London: Batsford, 1984.
Freud, Sigmund. "Fetishism." In *Essential Papers on Object Loss.* Ed. Rita V. Frankiel. New York: New York University Press, 1994. 63–68.
Gamman, Lorraine, and Merja Makinen. *Female Fetishism.* New York: New York University Press, 1994.
Jankowski, Theodora A. *Pure Resistance: Queer Virginity in Early Modern English Drama.* Philadelphia: University of Pennsylvania Press, 2000.
Marck, Nancy Anne. "Narrative Transference and Female Narcissism: The Social Message of *Adam Bede.*" *Studies in the Novel* 35.4 (2003): 447–470.
Matus, Jill L. "'The unnaturalness of her crime': Infanticide and Maternal Instinct in *Adam Bede.*" In Jill Matus, *Unstable Bodies: Victorian Representations of Sexuality and Maternity.* Manchester: St. Martin's, 1995. 167–179.
Maynard, John. "Spirituality and Sexual Pleasure." *Sexuality.* Ed. Robert A. Nye. New York: Oxford University Press, 1999. 101–03.
Mitchell, Judith. *The Stone and the Scorpion: The Female Subject of Desire in the Novels of Charlotte Brontë, George Eliot, and Thomas Hardy.* Westport, CT: Greenwood, 1994.
Rose, Louis. "Freud and Fetishism: Previously Unpublished Minutes of the Vienna Psychoanalytic Society." *Psychoanalytic Quarterly* 57.2 (1988): 147–166.
Wilkes, Wetenhall. "From *A Letter of Genteel and Moral Advice to a Young Lady*, 1740; 8th edn 1766." In *Women in the Eighteenth Century: Constructions of Femininity.* Ed. Vivien Jones. London: Routledge, 1990. 29–35.

PART II.
THE VICTORIANS, OF COURSE

# 5 The Mark of the Brotherhood
## *Homosexual Panic and the Foreign Other in Wilkie Collins's* The Woman in White

RICHARD NEMESVARI

"This is the story of what a Woman's patience can endure, and what a Man's resolution can achieve" (Collins 9). The famous opening sentence of Wilkie Collins's *The Woman in White* (1860) quickly establishes the centrality of gender issues in the novel, and confirms its Victorian audience's assumptions about proper feminine and masculine roles. The contrast between passive womanly endurance and active manly resolve is in place before a character is introduced or a plot element developed. Yet the apparent conviction and certainty of this sentence are belied by the text that follows. *The Woman in White* is riddled with sexual and gender anxieties that are barely contained by the resolution of its sensational narrative. In particular, Collins's text obsessively explores the threat posed by improper masculinities and their resulting, illicit, homosocial bonds, which are presented as undermining not only proper personal relationships but also the very fabric of social stability. In *The History of Sexuality: An Introduction* Michel Foucault insists that "[w]e must not forget that the psychological, psychiatric, medical category of homosexuality was constituted from the moment it was characterized ... less by a type of sexual relations than by a certain quality of sexual sensibility, a certain way of inverting the masculine and the feminine in oneself" (43). Jeffrey Weeks reinforces this idea by noting that in mid-nineteenth-century Britain "[s]uch popular notions as did exist invariably associated male homosexual behavior with effeminacy" (47), and *The Woman in White* both taps into and shapes growing fears about the effeminate man and the type of individual he would increasingly come to represent.

Yet as important is the novel's prominent concentration on foreigners and foreignness. The "Colonial other" was crucial in developing a definition of Englishness that confirmed Britain's racial superiority, but what is sometimes forgotten is an even longer tradition utilizing what might be termed the "European other." That is, Victorian England often defined itself against what it saw as the moral failings, and sexual perversities, of such countries as France and, most crucially for my purposes, Italy. In *The Woman in White* Italy is presented as the source of all those forces that subvert English law and undermine British masculinity.

More particularly, *The Woman in White* provides a series of characters whose connection to foreign Italian otherness threatens true English manliness as represented by the novel's hero, Walter Hartright. The secret of these characters' improper homosociality generates a paranoid fear of infiltration and passing, yet ultimately that secret is betrayed by the various marks that they carry, both visible and hidden. Walter's acts of detection and exposure provide the reassuring fiction that such perversity is inevitably self-revealing and that it finds expression only in foreigners or those unduly under foreign influence. The novel therefore contributes to the creation of a heterosexual norm by constructing, revealing, and then neutralizing a dangerous other that serves to define proper masculinity by being its opposite. As Walter moves towards his eventual position of secure entitlement and prosperity, he encounters Professor Pesca, Frederick Fairlie, Sir Percival Glyde, and Count Isidor, Ottavio, Baldassare Fosco, each of whom is marked in varying degrees as foreign and effeminate. The precarious position from which the novel's hero starts is eventually transformed into a forcefully successful masculinity through his encounter with each of them, so that Walter becomes an embodiment of the bourgeois compulsory heterosexuality that the novel is so anxious to create and support.

The path to this resolution, however, is difficult, and one way of approaching Walter's situation is to focus on an apparently marginal figure. Professor Pesca, Walter's "worthy Italian friend" (11), appears in the first ten pages of the text and then disappears until the very end of the narrative. Yet he is crucial in initiating the novel's action, bringing about its conclusion, and establishing certain themes and motifs that run throughout the entire text. Walter's introductory description of Pesca, an expatriate Italian living in London, is striking:

> Without being actually a dwarf— for he was perfectly well-proportioned from head to foot — Pesca was, I think, the smallest human being I ever saw, out of a show-room. Remarkable anywhere, by his personal appearance, he was still further distinguished ... by the harmless eccentricity of his

## 5. The Mark of the Brotherhood (Nemesvari) 97

character. The ruling idea of his life appeared to be, that he was bound to show his gratitude to the country which had afforded him an asylum and a means of subsistence, by doing his utmost to turn himself into an Englishman. ... invariably carrying an umbrella, and invariably wearing gaiters and a white hat [11].

Pesca is presented as a comic character because his attempts to mimic being English always fail, and in fact call attention to his foreignness, while his alterity is made even more obvious by his diminutive size. This is further reinforced when he talks, for, as Walter notes, "[h]aving picked up a few of our most familiar colloquial expressions, he scattered them about over his conversation whenever they happened to occur to him, turning them, in his high relish for their sound and his general ignorance of their sense, into compound words and repetitions of his own" (15). Pesca's appearance and speech can be described as harmless eccentricity because they express an admiration for, and therefore acceptance of, England, and because they are so obviously self-defeating. The more he tries to fit in, the more he exposes himself, and as long as the foreign other is marked as easily identifiable it poses no real threat. The dangers created when that otherness is not so readily recognized, however, will become a major fixation of the novel.

As it turns out, even Pesca is not as innocuous as he seems, and a clue about what will be revealed later can be found in his relationship with Walter. Pesca also aspires to partake of English "amusements" (11), and after risky experiments with fox-hunting and cricket, he endeavours to share the enjoyments of sea-bathing with his English friend. Walter relates their swimming adventure:

> Soon after we had both struck out from shore, I stopped, finding my friend did not gain on me, and turned round to look for him. To my horror and amazement, I saw nothing between me and the beach but two little white arms which struggled for an instant above the surface of the water, and then disappeared from view. When I dived for him, the poor little man was lying quietly coiled up at the bottom, in a hollow of shingle, looking by many degrees smaller than I had ever seen him look before [12].

The key point is Pesca's reaction once Walter gets him back to the beach. We are told "his warm Southern nature broke through all artificial English restraints, in a moment. He overwhelmed me with the wildest expressions of affection — exclaim[ing] passionately, in his exaggerated Italian way, that he would hold his life, henceforth, at my disposal" (12), and that Pesca "ardently" (13) longs to show his gratitude. The bond that Pesca believes has been established between himself and the man who saved his life is clearly too passionate for Walter's comfort and hints at a foreign intensity of male relationships that cannot be acknowledged in England. Through Pesca the potential for homosocial desire is introduced early in the novel and haunts it to the very end. Ironically, however, when this small foreigner finally gets a chance to repay his English friend, he does so by informing him of a job possibility that heads Walter towards the wife who will integrate him fully and finally into heterosexual domesticity.

That Walter must rely on Pesca to discover an advantageous position for him reveals a great deal about the Englishman's status as the story begins. As a twenty-eight-year-old drawing master who must manage his "resources" (10) carefully, he should be eager to pursue Pesca's information about the lucrative job at Limmeridge House, where he is assured that "he [will] be treated ... on the footing of a gentleman" (19). But he is not eager, and the assertion that he will be given the "footing" of a gentleman provides the clue to an issue almost as galling as his pecuniary difficulties: the social role his profession forces upon him. Ann Cvetkovich argues that as a "male version of the female governess.... His professional training demands that he separate himself from his body and his feelings as though they are detachable possessions" (77). In other words, he is forced to adopt what Lyn Pykett characterizes as "the feminized role of the socially inferior artist" (18). Walter's job entails an emasculation that threatens his sense of male identity and gentlemanly privilege, and this loss of manliness is encoded in a form that will appear throughout *The Woman in White*: apprehensive nervousness.

It is no exaggeration to say that at some point in the text every one of the major characters experiences a bout of almost clinical anxiety. This endemic apprehensiveness is generated by the novel's confused gender relationships and communicates itself to the reader as a distinct uneasiness about the implications of its various liaisons. What I am calling the text's homosexual panic arises from the existence of just-about-to-be-exposed-secrets that are essential to the sensation genre, but that in *this* narrative are always clustered around representations of improper masculinity. Significantly, as D. A. Miller observes, "However general a phenomenon, nervousness is always gendered in the novel ... nervousness remains a signifier of femininity" (98). In the text's male characters, therefore, over-sensitive nerves are one of the marks that identify a weak and unstable manliness, and if we accept Eve Kosofsky Sedgwick's idea that homosexual panic centres on the *"blackmailability ...* of Western maleness through the leverage of homophobia" (89), it becomes easier to understand why so many men in the novel are nervous so much of the time. Most of them possess a problematic maleness that leaves them fearful of exposure, and blackmail is the key tool that Walter will employ to bring about justice at the text's conclusion. Collins constantly toys with revealing the secret that dare not speak its name before he pulls back to expose supposedly less scandalous truths.

As I have suggested, even the novel's hero suffers from this. Walter's radically ambiguous response to his originating encounter with the Woman in White, an encounter that is both sexually and socially charged (is she a prostitute or a lady in distress; is she a falsely imprisoned victim or a manipulative escaped lunatic?) sends him into a spiral of self-doubt that almost literally unmans him. This process is exacerbated by his experiences at Limmeridge House to the point that, when he finishes his first part of the narrative and exits the text, Vincent Gilmore, the Fairlies' family lawyer, describes his final meeting with Walter:

> If he had not been the first to greet me, I should certainly have passed him. He was so changed that I hardly knew him again.... He spoke so fast, and crowded his questions together so strangely and confusedly that I could hardly follow him....
> A momentary nervous contraction quivered about his lips and eyes....
> He looked about him. ... at the throng of strangers passing us by on either side, in a strange, suspicious manner, as if he thought that some of them might be watching us [155–56].

If Walter is not actually in a state of panic here he certainly seems on the verge of it, and we later learn that his apparent paranoia is quite well-founded, since he *is* in fact being followed and spied upon. Nonetheless, the dissolution of his character is as obvious, and to understand why such a breakdown is imminent it is necessary to look at the text's presentation of his employer, Frederick Fairlie.

Once again the opening description is important, but in this case its significance is more blatant than Pesca's. Walter informs us that Fairlie's

> [b]eardless face was thin, worn, and transparently pale.... His feet were effeminately small, and were clad in buff-coloured silk stockings, and little womanish bronze-leather slippers.... Upon the whole, he had a frail, languidly-fretful, over-refined look — something singularly and unpleasantly delicate in its association with a man, and, at the same time, something which could by no possibility have looked natural and appropriate if it had been transferred to the personal appearance of a woman [42].

When we add to this that Fairlie expresses himself through "a drowsily languid utterance" (43) we are moving towards the stereotype of homosexuality that dominated the second half of the nineteenth century. But the text also loads him with its own particular signifiers. In their first interview Fairlie informs Walter that "much of my early life has been passed abroad" (43), and in that same interview he twice refers to "'the wretched state of my nerves'" (43). Indeed, Fairlie later defines himself as "'nothing but a bundle of nerves dressed up to look like a man'" (348), but as Miller observes, "[n]o one ... is much convinced by the drag" (98).

Although it would be risky to assert that Fairlie is homosexual, Sedgwick notes that mid-Victorian, aristocratic homosexual style was associated with "effeminacy, transvestitism ... continental European culture, and the arts" (173) so that in this character the text defines the quality it reprobates: a foreign unmanliness that implies sexual perversity. Walter's forced acceptance of a subservient position under such a character, therefore, threatens both his social and sexual identity. As well, Fairlie's invalidism raises the wider question of just what effeminacy meant for the Victorians.

As Linda Dowling notes, throughout the period the effeminate male carried a political charge that early on eclipsed its sexual implications. She observes that "[t]he *effeminatus* ... is ... always a composite or protean figure, the empty or negative symbol at once of civic enfeeblement and of the monstrous self-absorption that becomes visible in a society at just the moment at which ... private interest has begun to prevail against those things that concern the public welfare" (8). And it is this that makes Fairlie so dangerous. As he concludes the section of the novel that he narrates, Fairlie goes out of his way to deny any responsibility for the dangers and disasters that beset his niece Laura and the property she inherits —"I do beg and entreat that nobody will be so very unfeeling as to lay any part of the blame of those circumstances on *me*" (356) — but it is his refusal to fulfil his duties as her male relative and protector that leaves Laura vulnerable to the machinations of the novel's villains. The obvious implication is that foreign alterity and invalidism mark not only his sexual inversion but also his unfitness to engage in the domestic and civic activities of a British citizen. *The Woman in White* thus yokes together anxieties about masculinity with anxieties about national character which subsequently find their clearest expression in Sir Percival Glyde.

One of the more sardonic moments in the novel occurs when Walter asks about Glyde's reputation and is told that he "has fought successfully two contested elections; and has come out of the ordeal unscathed.

A man who can do that, in England, is a man whose character is established" (83). This faith in the ability of English scandal-mongering to filter out undesirables will prove to be woefully inadequate, but it does reveal the menace that Glyde embodies. He manages to conceal his true corruption and therefore to infiltrate and subvert civic and domestic institutions in his positions as an MP and as Laura's husband. Unsurprisingly, we learn that Glyde "had been born abroad, and had been educated there by private tutors," and that he had only "been in England, as a young man, once or twice" (456–57) before returning to take up his estate. In other words, he is about as foreign an Englishman as it is possible to be, a foreignness that is exacerbated by Count Fosco's influence over him.

I shall be returning to Fosco in more detail later, but for now it is sufficient to note his homosocial relationship with Glyde and their ties to Italy. Fosco is Glyde's "bosom friend" (201), his most "intimate friend" (191, 239), and the dramatic nature of their first meeting explains that intimacy. Glyde has a "scar on his right hand, which ... he received years since when he was travelling in Italy" (83), and it was Fosco's "accidental presence ... on the steps of the Trinita del Monte at Rome, [which] assisted Sir Percival's escape from robbery and assassination, at the critical moment when he was wounded in the hand, and might, the next instant, have been wounded in the heart" (191). Glyde's scar is the mark that identifies the improper male bonds that affect him, and this is reinforced by the parallelism that the scene establishes between the pairings of Fosco/Glyde and Walter/Pesca. In the one case an Englishman saves an Italian's life, and in the other an Italian saves an Englishman's life, with the clear implication that some kind of transference takes place. Walter's rescue of Pesca establishes the Italian's commitment to his friend's influence, and Fosco's rescue of Glyde achieves the same thing, but the values involved are represented as opposed. Walter restrains Pesca's impetuous attempt to establish an intense homosocial bond, but it becomes clear that it is just such a bond that unites Fosco and Glyde. The Count's "extraordinary power" (246) over Glyde is constantly emphasized, and at one point Laura says of Fosco that "[p]erhaps, I dislike him because he has so much more power over my husband than I have" (228). This un-English, Continental male-male relationship seriously undercuts their marriage, and its subsequent failure is used to introduce the secrets that will propel the rest of the story.

This being the case, Glyde is yet another character who is overwhelmed by nervousness. Marian Halcombe takes especial note of the "incessant restlessness and excitability" (188) that characterize him before his wedding. These qualities grow even more extreme after the marriage and his return to England, and Glyde has a particularly revealing way of attempting to deal with his constant sense of apprehension. Once again Marian acts as reporter for the reader:

> It seems to be part of his restless disposition always to separate himself from his companions ... and always to occupy himself, when he is alone, in cutting new walking-sticks for his own use. The mere act of cutting and lopping, at hazard, appears to please him. He has filled the house with walking-sticks of his own making, not one of which he ever takes up for a second time. When they have been once used, his interest in them is all exhausted [229–30].

This compulsive behaviour, combining as it does the castrative act of "cutting and lopping" with the creation of a series of new phallic objects, each of which proves to be ultimately unsatisfactory, clearly represents sexual insecurity. The pleasure Glyde derives from the manufacture of walking sticks is a kind of compensation for his own sense of emasculation, which is embodied both in his subservient position with Fosco and in the related failure of his marriage with Laura.

As the text proceeds he becomes increasingly desperate. Later one of the servants says of Glyde, "Almost all the afternoon and evening, he had been walking about the house and grounds in an unsettled, excitable manner ... his voice calling loudly and angrily.... The gardener ... declared that his master was quite out of his senses — not through the excitement of drink, as I had supposed, but through a kind of panic or frenzy of mind, for which it was impossible to account" (396). It may be impossible for the gardener to "account" for his master's "panic," but the reader has some very real suspicions. Glyde's foreign background, his intimate friendship with the Italian Fosco, his lack of intimacy with his English wife, and the extreme anxiety that he experiences, all suggest a looming same sex scandal of the type that punctuated the nineteenth century, from the Vere Street brothel case of 1810 to the Wilde trials of 1895.

In the end, however, Collins does not explicitly speak what he has been implying about this character, partly because overt recognition of homosexuality is still a fictional taboo, and partly because finally Glyde *is* an Englishman. He has been tainted as un-English in his values and conduct, but the novel is not willing to demonize him completely as degenerate. So when Walter reappears in the narrative, with the express purpose of learning Glyde's secret in order to "force him from his position of security ... [and] drag him and his villainy into the face of day" (450), the crimes that he discovers are fraud and illegitimacy, not sodomy. Because his parents did not marry, Glyde has no claim on the baronetcy that he holds or to the social position that it provides him. Walter, acting as the novel's agent, successfully pursues and indirectly destroys his rival and thus cleanses English society of his pernicious influence. With Glyde dead, however, Walter loses the leverage that knowing his secret temporarily gave him, and he is left with only one other way of regaining Laura's stolen identity: confronting the considerably more formidable figure of Glyde's mentor, Count Fosco.

If Pesca is the comic, unthreatening foreigner, then Fosco is his opposite in practically every way. Certainly they are different in size, for whereas it is Pesca's smallness that characterizes him, we are told that Fosco is "immensely fat" (217). This serves to mark him in the same way that Pesca's physical distinctiveness does, but there is another major difference between the two. Marian observes of Fosco that

> his unusual command of the English language necessarily helps him. ... until I saw Count Fosco, I had never supposed it possible that any foreigner could have spoken English as he speaks it. There are times when it is almost impossible to detect, by his accent, that he is not a countryman of our own [219].

Fosco's skill with English makes him dangerous because it camouflages his truly foreign morality. His ability to infiltrate England successfully, through his connection with Glyde and through his ability to mimic being English, invokes the fear of the enemy within that has always been a powerful element of both homophobia and xenophobia. It is predictable, therefore, that the novel also chooses to mark him as its most flagrant example of effeminate, illegitimate homosociality.

The list of qualities suggesting that Fosco possesses stereotypically unmanly characteristics is so extensive as to be almost embarrassing. Marian tells us that he "devours pastry as I have never yet seen it devoured by any human beings but girls at boarding-schools" (223). Connected to this, he "is as fond of fine clothes as the veriest fool in existence" (221) and at one point appears in the following outfit: "A blue blouse, with profuse white fancy-work over the bosom ... girt about the place where his waist might once have been, with a broad scarlet leather belt. Nankeen trousers, displaying more white fancy-work over the ankles, and purple morocco slippers" (227). While parading about in this exotic ensemble Fosco looks, Marian informs us, "like a fat St. Cecilia masquerading in male attire" (227). This direct comment on his grotesque androgyny comes as close as the text is willing to describing Fosco's inversion, although it is further reinforced with Marian's observation that "[h]e is as noiseless in a room as any of us women; and, more than that ... he is as nervously sensitive as the weakest of us. He starts at chance noises as inveterately as Laura herself" (219). As it turns out, Fosco has a serious reason to be nervous, but this also fits him into the discourse of effeminacy that the novel has developed. Understandably Glyde often chafes under Fosco's control, for to be subservient to a womanly foreigner is to be all but fully emasculated, yet the Italian "puts the rudest remarks Sir Percival can make on his effeminate tastes ... quietly away from him ... smiling at him with the calmest superiority; patting him on the shoulder; and bearing with him benignantly" (222). The relationship thus established encapsulates the danger of both the foreign other and improper homosocial bonds; it places an Englishman under an Italian's domination, subverts true masculinity, and leads to a series of crimes against inheritance and property. Fosco therefore embodies, as the self-described "wily Italian" (242), the novel's most overt threat to social and gender stability. Finally, though, he leaves himself vulnerable when he meets his ironic nemesis in an equally gender-ambivalent character: Marian herself.

Most of what we learn about the Count comes from Marian's perspective, and she has attracted a great deal of critical attention, for in a novel filled with womanly men she is the opposite: a manly woman. Marian's intense attachment to Laura early in the text is presented as problematically erotic and possessive. In contemplating Laura's marriage to Glyde, Marian can barely contain her despair: "Before another month is over our heads, she will be *his* Laura instead of mine! *His* Laura! I am as little able to realise the idea which those two words convey — my mind feels almost as dulled and stunned by it — as if writing of her marriage were like writing of her death" (185). Marian's eventual willingness to accept Walter as an appropriate husband for Laura demonstrates her movement away from the questionable connection to Laura suggested by comments such as this, and because she ultimately accepts this relationship, she is not punished for her transgressive feelings. Before this transformation takes place, however, her ambiguous presentation makes her a perfect match for the Count.

Walter's first impression of Marian focusses on the discrepancy between her attractive feminine figure and her ugly masculine face. We are told that "[t]he lady's complexion was almost swarthy, and the dark down on her upper lip was almost a moustache," and that she has "a large, firm, masculine mouth and jaw" (35). Walter's reaction is "to be almost repelled by the masculine form and masculine look of the features in which the perfectly shaped figure ended" (35), but Fosco's response is very different. He apostrophizes her as a "'grand creature'" and proclaims, "'I admire [her] with all my soul'" (324). And when he has Walter, Marian, and Laura at a complete disadvantage and could remove the danger that they pose to him by exposing their hiding place, he does not because of what Marian calls "the horrible admiration he feels for *me*" (547). Fosco himself puts it in a characteristically dramatic way:

> I have to assert, with the whole force of my conviction, that the one weak place in my scheme would never have been found out, if the one weak place in my heart had not been discovered first.... Behold the cause, in my Heart — behold, in the image of Marian Halcombe, the first and last weakness of Fosco's life! [611].

Marian's masculine appearance and vigour, which repulse men such as Walter, have the ability to evoke a queerly heterosexual passion in Fosco's heart that is certainly unmatched by what he feels for his thoroughly cowed wife. His marriage to the former Eleanor Fairlie, an Englishwoman whose frigidity is encapsulated in the description of her sitting silent and "frozen up" for "hours together" (216) at the Glyde estate, is transparently a cover which gains him the veneer of propriety necessary for access to English society. Fosco shows no passion for this woman, but he does evince it for Marian, a man-in-a-woman's body, and in doing so he both reveals his perverse foreign desires and brings about his own destruction.

Walter, given a second chance but still completely unable to formulate a plan of attack on Fosco, looks for help. And where else should he turn but to Pesca, "the only Italian with whom [he is] intimately acquainted" (564)? Having discovered that Fosco intends to go to the opera, Walter arranges for him and Pesca to get tickets in the pit in order to show his enemy to his friend. Astonishingly Walter learns that there is a connection between them, for although Pesca does not recognize Fosco, Fosco recognizes Pesca and shows every sign of terror at seeing him. Thus Walter and the reader are introduced to the secret existence of "The Brotherhood," to which both Pesca and Fosco belong. Each member carries a mark that identifies him as belonging to the group, and Pesca, showing Walter the inner side of his upper arm, reveals "a brand deeply burnt in the flesh and stained of a bright blood-red colour" (577).

Once having received the mark and entered the Brotherhood, one is never allowed to leave, and to betray it is to become the target of inescapable assassination. Pesca regrets his membership but he cannot escape it now. Fosco, as it turns out, has radically altered his appearance because he also bears the mark of the Brotherhood, but having attempted to leave its ranks he is liable to be murdered if discovered. Walter has therefore received the information that he needs to blackmail the Count and to extort from him a letter confessing his schemes against Laura in exchange for not informing on him, and for allowing him to leave the country.

Within the novel, therefore, the Brotherhood, with its exclusively male membership that must remain secret and that creates a bond that marks the individual in a way that can never be erased, is an encoded representation and encapsulation of all the illicit homosocial and queer heterosexual relationships that have permeated the text. Walter's use of Fosco's membership to blackmail him can be seen as a classic expression of homophobia and a manipulation of the homosexual panic that comes with it. The Brotherhood's Italian origin suggests comfortingly, if inaccurately, that homosexuality is alien to England, and Pesca's efforts to turn himself *into* an Englishman represent his attempts to leave such influences behind. But as he says, "I try to forget them — and they will not forget *me*!" (622). Further, the clue about him has been there from the start. When we first meet Pesca, we are told that he is teaching Dante's *Inferno* in an English household and that he hears about the position at Limmeridge House while translating a passage from "the Seventh Circle" (16). Although we are not told which ring of the circle he is reading, that the Seventh Circle contains the Sodomites is an overt enough indication of what we need to know about him, Fosco, and the Brotherhood.

Although the Count manages to flee England successfully, he cannot flee the Brotherhood. At the opera in London he was also being observed by what Walter describes as "a mild gentlemanlike man, looking like a foreigner," who also happens to have a "scar on his cheek" (571). This is the last marked man in the text, and although we never learn his name, it becomes obvious to what foreign group he belongs. When next we see Fosco it is as a naked corpse on display in the Paris morgue, where Walter and Pesca discover him by chance. Walter informs us that "[t]he wound that had killed him had been struck with a knife or dagger exactly over his heart. No other traces of violence appeared about the body, except on the left arm; and there, exactly in the place where I had seen the brand on Pesca's arm, were two deep cuts in the shape of the letter T, which entirely obliterated the mark of the Brotherhood" (623–24). He also tells us that the T on Fosco's arm "signified the Italian word, 'Traditore', and showed that justice had been done by the Brotherhood on a traitor" (624). But in what does the novel suggest that Fosco has been a traitor? How else but in his love for Marian? Miller argues that "[t]he wound struck 'exactly over his heart' hints broadly at the 'passional' nature of the crime in which — for which — Fosco is murdered" (122), and the Count's earlier claim that Marian is "inscribed on [his] heart" (599) provides the reason that the Brotherhood erases that inscription by plunging a knife into the traitor organ. Manly-woman or not, to the Brotherhood Marian is an illegitimate object of desire, and Fosco cannot be allowed to survive the betrayal represented by his feelings for her.

Thus, although technically Walter kills neither Glyde nor Fosco, it is no exaggeration to say that his relentless hounding of them is the direct cause of their deaths. His role as detective is scarcely differentiated from that of a hunter, and in the end he brings down his prey. Walter's masculinity is confirmed/created by a direct confrontation with a foreign alterity that threatens England, and in the end he eradicates that threat. True English manliness is proven to be superior to European effeminacy, and the heterosexual, domestic bliss that Walter achieves with Laura replaces the illegitimate homosocial bonds that had initially surrounded and overwhelmed them.

*The Woman in White*, like most sensation fiction, is structured so as to create in the reader a *frisson* of shared dread through its plots and characters. It is perfectly positioned to generate anxieties that it can then alleviate by imposing resolutions that, at best, only partly disguise the ideological imperatives behind them. The texts combination of encoded homophobia and xenophobia is just overt enough to make their eventual suppression a satisfactory confirmation of British masculine normalcy. But the fact that the text is required to do this is revealing. From 1860 on, as the Victorians expanded and consolidated their empire, the perils of alterity became harder to avoid, for as a world power the English were forced into more and more contact with foreign otherness, both European and Colonial. Such engagements were profoundly disturbing, and although the novel does its best to elide the implications it raises, it cannot be fully successful. Walter Hartright is victorious, but just barely. *The Woman in White* illustrates the kinds of containment strategies that become increasingly necessary as the period advances, while at the same time it suggests precisely how precarious such strategies can be; finally, in its nervous acknowledgement of secrets that cannot be fully named, it reveals what it is trying to hide and foreshadows the collapse of the authority that it is struggling so hard to create.

## Acknowledgment

A longer version of this essay first appeared in *English Studies in Canada* 28.4 (December 2002). "The Mark of the Brotherhood: The Foreign Other and Homosexual Panic in *The Woman in White*" is reproduced with the permission of *English Studies in Canada*.

## Works Cited

Collins, Wilkie. *The Woman in White*. Ed. Matthew Sweet. Harmondsworth: Penguin, 1999.
Cvetkovich, Ann. *Mixed Feelings: Feminism, Mass Culture, and Victorian Sensationalism*. New Brunswick, NJ: Rutgers University Press, 1992.
Dowling, Linda. *Hellenism and Homosexuality in Victorian Oxford*. Ithaca, NY: Cornell University Press, 1994.
Foucault, Michel. *The History of Sexuality Volume I: An Introduction*. Trans. Robert Hurley. New York: Vintage, 1990.
Miller, D. A. "*Cage aux Folies*: Sensation and Gender in Wilkie Collins's *The Woman in White*." In *The Nineteenth-Century British Novel*. Ed. Jeremy Hawthorn. London: Edward Arnold, 1986. 95–124.
Pykett, Lyn. *The Sensation Novel from* The Woman in White *to* The Moonstone. Plymouth: Northcote House, 1994.
Sedgwick, Eve Kosofsky. *Between Men: English Literature and Male Homosocial Desire*. New York: Columbia University Press, 1985.
Weeks, Jeffrey. "The Construction of Homosexuality." In *Queer Theory/Sociology*. Ed. Steven Seidman. Cambridge: Blackwell, 1996. 41–63.

# 6 "A rod of flexible steel in that little hand"
## Female Dominance and Male Masochism in Mary Elizabeth Braddon's Aurora Floyd

DENISE HUNTER GRAVATT

Victorian sensation novelist Mary Elizabeth Braddon established her career, as well as her notorious reputation as an author of domestic scandal, with her creation of Lucy Audley, the "fair-haired demon" of *Lady Audley's Secret* (1862). She incited further critical outrage with the "unnatural" and sexually aggressive heroine of her subsequent novel, *Aurora Floyd* (1863). Critics of sensation fiction chastised Braddon for her favorable delineations of "fast young ladies," and for her portrayal of female characters who failed to comply with the Victorian ideal of womanhood.[1] Reviewers upbraided Braddon for her (mis)representation of femininity, and, significantly, quoted at length the same erotically charged passage in which the heroine passionately horsewhips a stable hand:

> Aurora sprang upon him like a beautiful tigress ... her cheeks white with rage, her eyes flashing in her passion.... She disengaged her right hand from his collar and rained a shower of blows upon his clumsy shoulders with her slender whip [...] stinging like a rod of flexible steel in that little hand [193].[2]

Margaret Oliphant, one of Braddon's harshest contemporary critics, castigated the author for modeling her lusty female characters after men, and found Braddon's characterizations of dominant females particularly "repulsive" because they were the creation of a woman writer.[3] The censorious reaction to Aurora Floyd's sexually assertive and masculine behavior suggests that Braddon's critique of "angelic" femininity not only highlighted the restrictive nature of gendered roles for Victorian women, but it also simultaneously exposed the cultural anxieties regarding the fragility of traditional Victorian masculinity. Braddon debunked both "ideals" as fabrications contingent upon clearly demarcated roles between the sexes.

Feminist scholars have revived Braddon's fiction for its representation of female power and assertiveness, and others have considered her treatment of questionable masculinities within the context of male same-sex relations.[4] However, little critical consideration has been given to her depictions of gender "deviance" within the context of heterosexual relations — particularly those depictions that disrupt traditional power relations and re-articulate them into female dominance and male submission. Inasmuch as Braddon's valorization of her unconventional heroine reveals female resistance to the patriarchal structures underpinning middle-class gender dualities, her commentary on the fluidity of power dynamics, and the possible pleasures that emerge from gender role reversals, also represents counterhegemonic forms of heterosexual desire.

The recent emergence of critical inquiries that consider non-normative sexual relations between the sexes, what has been labeled "Queer Heterosexuality" in gender theory, informs my reading of Braddon's radical reconfiguring of the erotic valences of conventional femininity and masculinity. Despite concerns that appropriation of the word *queer* by non-normative heterosexual critics, or "straight queers," will neutralize the term's ability to denaturalize gendered identities and sexual practices, and hence weaken its capacity to radically critique heterosexual privilege, I adhere to Michael Warner's assertion that "'queer' gets a critical edge by defining itself against the normal rather than the heterosexual" (xxvi). According to Annette Schlichter, Warner's observation "creates a space for heterosexuals with an interest in critiquing and subverting the practices of heteronormative normalization" (547). This space of resistance enables critical work that moves beyond merely analyzing sex or gender in terms of sexual object choice, to considering the normativizing constraints regulating sexual and social power relations between the sexes. For Schlichter, theoretical attempts to "rethink (straight) identity ... offer a perspective on the potential reconfiguration of sociocultural relations and the creation of antinormative forms of sociality" (550). Braddon's narrative, subversively working within and against mid-Victorian sociocultural constructions of gender and sexuality, exposes the conflations of femininity/passivity and masculinity/activity as unnatural and proffers "antinormative forms of sociality," through its positive portrayal of male characters whose erotic predilections involve sexual submission to a dominant woman. Braddon's Victorian representation of queer heterosexual relations proleptically participates in what Schlichter calls the "antinormative" cultural project in the "resistance against heteronormativity," at an important cultural moment that presaged both the literary discourses that popularized male masochistic heterosexual desire, as well as the works by late nineteenth century sexologists that refashioned such desire into a psychosexual pathology (556).

*Aurora Floyd* (1863) predates Leopold Von Sacher-Masoch's literary depictions of male masochistic desire and the dominant woman in *Venus in Furs* (1870), what has been called the Ur text of masochism. The term *masochism* was coined in 1886 by Richard von Krafft-Ebing, in an effort to classify erotically driven heterosexual male submission — epitomized in much of Sacher-Masoch's work — as indicative of "perverse" desire. In *Psychopathia Sexualis*, Krafft-Ebing examined the sexual inclinations of Sacher-Masoch and men like him, and crystallized male sexual passivity into a categorical perversion:

> By masochism I understand a particular perversion of the psychical sexual life in which the individual affected, in sexual feeling and thought, is controlled by the idea of being completely and unconditionally subject to the will of a person of the *opposite sex*; of being treated by this person as a master — humiliated and abused [emphasis added 119].

Kraft-Ebing discusses masochism as a phenomenon occurring almost exclusively in men, and as a perverse reversal of sexual hierarchies strictly within heterosexual relations. By the end of the nineteenth century, Freudian psychoanalysis — conflating male masochistic desire with feminine passivity — categorized men with these "aberrant" sexual desires as "effeminate," and thus solidified its transmutation into delitescent homosexual desire. Freud's hypothesis remained the predominant theory of male sexual submission, eclipsing other views, until as recently as Gilles Deleuze's re-examination of Sacher-Masoch's masochistic narrative in *Sacher-Masoch: An Interpretation* (1967). Refuting Freud's postulation that male submissive desire masks an unresolved, homoerotically charged Oedipal interest in the Father, Deleuze suggests male masochists desire alliance with the Mother against the Father, to punish him and nullify paternal "law."[5] By reinstating a female as central to the masochistic narrative, Deleuze's work not only recontextualizes male masochism within a heterosexual framework, it also points to masochism's resistance to the [hetero]normativizing law of the Father (77).

In "Sex in Public," Lauren Berlant and Michael Warner define heteronormativity as "the institutions, structures of understanding, and practical orientations that make heterosexuality seem not only coherent — that is, organized as a sexuality — but also privileged." Furthermore Berlant and Warner make a distinction between heteronormativity and heterosexuality in their claim that even in heterosexual relations, "forms of sex between men and women might not be heteronormative" (548n2). This distinction becomes significant when attempting to unite queers (both straight and gay) against the hegemony of heteronormativity, which legitimizes itself by defining not only what it deems as normative at any given cultural moment, but also in denying cultural legibility to what it deems as non-normative or perverse. As Jonathon Dollimore observes, the term *perversion* was linked with "the wayward, assertive woman, the woman on top," as it were, before it became a designation connected to homosexuality (3). Just as homosexual relations have been denied cultural legitimacy, analogously non-normative heterosexual relations that failed to correspond to gendered codes of behavior, such as female dominance and male masochism, have similarly been pathologized and thus marginalized. According to Richard Fantina, this stigmatization of both homosexuality and heterosexual male masochism as perversions "should be common ground among gay men and masochistic heterosexual men in their common resistance to prevailing stereotypes of masculinity" (44). Male masochism disavows a masculinity predicated on phallic mastery, and hence becomes a strategic site for queer heterosexual resistance to heteronormativity.

In an effort to render heterosexuality compatible with feminist goals, in *Male Masochism*, Carol Siegel links male masochistic desire with romantic love in its ability to "reverse the hierarchies of misogyny" inherent in patriarchal power structures (167). Siegel's analysis resists synchronic interpretations of literary texts and shifts emphasis entirely away from the psychoanalytic models of both Freud and Deleuze, who she reads as complicit in "the erasure of female agency and presence" (51). Siegel claims that representations of "active, heroic masculine love" expressed through the "articulation of desires to fall down in worship at the feet of the beloved, to be teased, or even struck by her"— saliently recur throughout literary history (10). Characterizations of willful male subservience emerge in novels by prominent Victorian women writers, in characters such as George Eliot's Ladislaw of *Middlemarch*, and Olive Schriener's Gregory Rose of *Story of an African Farm*. Siegel contends that these female authors were participating in an established literary tradition that depicted "helpless submission to love as an attribute of true manliness" (12). For Siegel, the reconfiguration of the "traditional, sacrificial male lover [into] an unmasculine pervert" and the pathologization of heterosexual masochistic desire were late-nineteenth century inventions constructed to undermine women's literary and political advancements (11).

Siegel's progressive theoretical framework provides a useful paradigm within which to consider Braddon's representation of alternative heterosexual relations between the powerful woman and the submissive man.[6] Braddon's novel merges love and eroticism, and exemplifies Siegel's view that male masochism functions to simultaneously empower the woman and provide pleasurable possibilities for both sexes. What is absent in Siegel's Victorian examples of submissive male desire, but overtly present in Braddon's narrative, is the sheer corporeality of the dominant woman; her physicality is evoked when the heroine's "little hand" utilizes "the rod of flexible steel" in a display of eroticized female sexual power over men. Braddon's auspicious depictions of the dominant female and submissive male characters, and the immense popularity of *Aurora Floyd* among readers of both sexes, suggests that while Victorian middle-class readers appeared, at least ideologically, to endorse the rigid gender distinctions, they were nonetheless titillated by the possibility of vicariously transgressing those boundaries. Braddon's literary depiction of alternative heterosexual relations intimates that male masochism was not an exclusively male-gendered cultural fantasy, but rather one that appealed equally to women.

The eponymous heroine of *Aurora Floyd* is the motherless daughter of a wealthy banker. Aurora is "unwomanly," fallen, and embodies the characteristics of the dominant and thus dangerous woman. Embedded in the explicit sensational plot of Aurora's secret, her unintentional bigamy, the novel's subplot of female dominance is energized by her sexual aggression. Aurora inaugurates her transgression of Victorian morality when she elopes with James Conyers, her father's groom, in what Oliphant called "a fit of sensual passion" (602). Within the first year of her marriage, Aurora discovers that Conyers is a rampallion, flees the exploitive relationship, and returns to her father's home. Aurora then rejects marriage proposals from two suitors, Talbot Bulstrode and John Mellish, in the same day. Upon receiving a report that Conyers is dead, Aurora accepts Talbot's offer the following day, and when the relationship with Talbot dissolves during their engagement, she marries John within the year.

While Aurora may appear to be a capricious young woman who "play[s] fast and loose with the male sex" (181), the narrative is less concerned with reproving female inconstancy in love, or resolving the "crisis" of female dominance, then in evaluating male devotion and finding an apt partner for the desirable and dominant heroine. In *Aurora Floyd,* male submission functions as the ideal by which the desires and suitability of the male characters are measured. Braddon disciplines her male characters according to their response to Aurora's dominating presence, by punishing those who either deny their masochistic desires or respond with sadistic fantasies of their own, and rewarding the submissive man who compliments her strong woman.

## *Aurora Floyd: The Dominant Woman*

According to Victorian standards, Aurora's decidedly unfeminine nature is apparent even "before [she] emerged from the nursery," as she "evidenced a very decided tendency to become what is called 'fast'" (62). Aurora's equestrian interests — she chooses a rocking-horse over a doll as a young child and as an adolescent favors horse-riding — take precedence over the conventional education that would have made her "the most refined and elegant, the most perfect and accomplished of her sex" (63). The unfeminine characteristics of Aurora's wild nature are the result of being both motherless and spoiled by an indulgent and inept father who could not "govern or direct that impetuous nature" (63). Left to define and navigate her sexuality on her own, Aurora develops into a beautiful, frank, fearless girl, who "said what she pleased; thought, spoke, acted as she pleased [and] learned what she pleased" (61). The self-possession of the adolescent heroine sets the stage for her sexual adventurousness and self-assertiveness as a young woman, and drives the plot forward in anticipation of an appropriate male counterpart.

At seventeen, Aurora is sent to a Parisian finishing school as punishment and corrective after a six-hour horse ride with the handsome young groom hired by her father to be her companion. Horse-riding, according to Lyn Pykett in *The Improper Feminine,* represents Aurora's "masculinised interest[s]" (86), and the sexual symbolization of her as a "horsey girl" reveals her defiance of feminine sexual passivity. Margaret Oliphant equated "horsey novels," written by Braddon and other sensation authors, with female sexual latitude and immorality (Casey 77). Aurora's "unchaperoned riding," with the young man, coupled "together with the contemporary slang meaning of 'ride' to indicate sexual intercourse," according to Nemsevari and Surridge, signifies the heroine's "sexual permissiveness," and would have signaled to the Victorian reader that sexual impropriety, during her long afternoon with the groom, is the reason why she is sent away (21).

In addition to her masculine interests and activities, nineteen-year-old Aurora is further encoded as a dominant woman in the narrator's description of her physical beauty: "a phrenologist would have declared her head to be a 'noble one' and a sculptor would have added that it was set upon the throat of a Cleopatra" (62). For the Victorian reader, Aurora's identification with Cleopatra, in both physical appearance and mannerisms, immediately conjured up distinct images of a highly erotic, and potentially dangerous, "unwomanly" woman. In discussing popular response to Shakespeare's Cleopatra, Camille Paglia writes: "her sexual libertinism and volatility led to Victorian and post-Victorian vilification" of her as "the archetypal femme fatale" (213). Braddon's narrative describes Aurora as a "Cleopatra ... with a taste for horseflesh" (80), an "imperious creature, this Cleopatra" (78), whose "thick plaits of her black hair made a great diadem ... and crowned her an Eastern Empress" (87); Aurora is "like Cleopatra sailing down the Cydnus ... like everything that is beautiful, and strange, and wicked and unwomanly, and bewitching" (93). Lisa Starks identifies Shakepeare's Cleopatra as a precursor to Sacher-Masoch's dominatrix, Wanda, and claims she is "the male masochist's ideal woman: a domineering yet sentimental female despot to who he submits himself and for whom he yearns to suffer" (59). Although Cleopatra and Wanda are male literary representations of dominant women, the similarities between them and Braddon's Aurora, suggests that the dominant woman was also an appealing alternate "ideal" for women.

Paglia describes Cleopatra as "robustly half-masculine" and asserts that she "appropriates the powers and prerogatives of both sexes more lavishly than any other character in literature" (216). Similarly, Aurora's temperament and physicality are identified as masculine. Linking Aurora's unladylike outburst of whipping a stable hand for kicking her dog to aggressive sexuality, Natalie Schroeder observes that Victorian critics "considered self-assertive or masculine female behavior as much a threat to Victorian society as unchastity"; when Aurora brandishes the horsewhip, she exerts female sexual dominance and power (87, 96). Although flagellation was a form of pedagogical correction for Victorian boys who, perhaps more than girls, were whipped by schoolmasters, this scene of heteroerotic flagellation, of an adult woman whipping an adult man, transgresses the gender-specific roles central to hegemonic power relations between the sexes. When Aurora's slender whip, "a mere toy with emeralds set in its gold head," is transformed into a "rod of flexible steel" (193), the scene becomes strikingly similar to the erotic confrontations popularized in Victorian flagellation literature.[7]

## Male Masochism: A Menace to Traditional Masculinity

Captain Talbot Bulstrode, an aristocratic descendent of Sir Walter Raleigh, and Aurora's first legitimate suitor, is a thirty-two year old bachelor whose masculinity is predicated on clearly demarcated gender distinctions and male domination. In *A Man's Place*, John Tosh observes that for the mid-Victorians, "the association of masculinity with reason, authority and resolve was consolidated, together with their dissociation from the feminine" (47). Talbot's masculinity relies on autonomy and mastery, over both the self and others, to shore up his patriarchal position, and hence his erotic desire for Aurora threatens to dismantle his traditional masculine identity that depends on female passivity for its formation. Braddon strategically employs two signifiers to represent Talbot's masculinity: attitudinal (his penetrating gaze) and philosophical (his Cartesian-based male subjectivity). These signs also function to complicate the signification of masculinity in the narrative because they serve to construct, and then conversely to undermine, Talbot's "manliness." Although Talbot's penetrating gaze and coherent subjectivity initially appear to signify phallic mastery and manly autonomy, Braddon deploys masochistic desire to deconstruct these signs and destabilize conventional masculinity.

From the privileged position of eligible bachelor and evaluating subject, Talbot scrutinizes female bodies under his phallocentric gaze, searching for virginal purity and on guard against the femme fatale. In spite of his indifference to other women, his first reaction upon seeing Aurora is tinged with masochistic desire; conflating visual pleasure with pain, he describes her as "A divinity! ... painfully dazzling to look upon, intoxicatingly brilliant to behold" (77). As the dominant woman, Aurora's powerful sex appeal incites desire comingled with dread and results in Talbot's simultaneous fascination and repulsion towards this "horrible woman" (79), with "unfeminine tastes and mysterious propensities" (95).

Talbot interprets Aurora's body as sexual and therefore dangerous: "A woman with a head and throat like hers could scarcely fail to be ambitious — ambitious and revengeful" (90). However, the text undermines the certitude of Talbot's phallocentric and objectifying gaze, which links female sexuality to moral corruption, and resists dichotomizing Aurora as either angelic/virginal or demonic/sexual. Instead, Braddon proposes an alternate female ideal in the dominant woman — an ideal constructed by the confluence of overt sexual passion and moral goodness. Talbot's association of female dominance with sexual immorality causes him to initially demonize Aurora; however, despite his own rationality, "the more he protested against her [and] argued with himself upon the folly of loving her ... the more he grew the veriest *slave* of the *lovely vision*" (emphasis added 102). In a temporary abdication of his dominant position in the heterosexual relationship, Talbot "abandon[s] himself to the spell of the siren" (123), and proposes to Aurora.

Talbot's domestic economy, centered on male mastery, is irreconcilable to the masochistic libidinal economy that idealizes male subordination. His internal struggle is evinced in his first lover's quarrel with Aurora. Exerting her dominant position, Aurora defiantly refuses to be interrogated: "I will not submit to be called to account for my actions — even by you" (138). Fearing he has been unmanned by his vulnerability and the intensity of his love for her, he asks Aurora: "tell me ... that I have no need to despise myself for having loved you with an intensity which has scarcely been manly" (156). As a result of Aurora's refusal to disclose her secret, Talbot renounces masochistic love, and dissolves their engagement. In his attempts to assuage his heartache over the failed relationship, Talbot considers the costliness of his love for Aurora, and determines that it would have ultimately resulted in the loss of his masculine subjectivity:

> she might have been his, this beautiful creature; but at what price? At the price of honour; at the price of every principle of his mind.... *Forbid it manhood!* He might have weakly yielded; he might have been happy, with the blind happiness of the lotus-eater, but not the reasonable bliss of a Christian [emphasis added 14].

Talbot's turn from the dark-eyed siren, Aurora, to her blue-eyed cousin, Lucy Floyd, for solace, is actually a return to his domestic ideal, which Lucy embodies, and for which he chooses her "calmly and dispassionately" for his wife (221). The angelic Lucy, the narrator assures, "knew no abnormal tendencies [and] had none of the eccentric predilections which had been so fatal to her cousin" (426). The contrast between the two women moves beyond their contrary physiques or manners to the distinction in the kind of love they inspire in Talbot. Whereas he "had loved Aurora for her beauty and her fascination; he was going to marry Lucy ... because he believed her to be all that a woman should be" (221). Yet, through Talbot's equivocal happiness with Lucy, Braddon subverts the presumption that marital bliss is ensured by adherence to patriarchal authority and female submission.

## John Mellish: A "Cruelly Henpecked" Husband and a "Happy Slave"

If Aurora is the female ideal of the dominant woman, then her husband John Mellish, the "hearty sporting squire," is the ideal masochistic man. Like Talbot, John is also attracted to Aurora's Cleopatra-like regality and domineering persona, and both men invoke transvestism to describe her masculine propensities. In Talbot's initial observations of Aurora, he recalls the legend of the female Pope Joan, who ascended to the papal position by masquerading as a man (80n4). Imagining that Aurora could likewise be a "female 'Napoleon of the turf,'" he links female ambition to political tyranny and foreshadows his own later struggle against the disruptive desire she engenders. Conversely, John's adulation of Aurora as "that beautiful black-eyed creature ... who looks at you with two flashes of lightning and rides like young Challenor [a male jockey who rode in women's clothes] in a cloth habit" suggests that her male-identified interests and behavior, far from threatening John, serve to augment his romantic interest in her (142n3).

Talbot's agony over his unnerving erotic attraction to a dominant woman contrasts to John's unflinchingly acceptance of his masochistic desire and Aurora's benevolent despoticism: he "did not even debate the point." In his marriage proposal John insists that he doesn't expect her to love him: "I don't ask that. I only ask you to let me love you, to let me worship you, as people ... in the churches here worship their saints" (177). Accordingly, John "loved [Aurora] and he laid himself down to be trampled upon by her gracious feet" (200), and "submit[ed] to the pretty tyrant with a quiet smile of resignation" (197). A reproving look from Aurora's flashing eyes translates to John: "Slave, obey and tremble ... [and he] follow[s] her meekly wonderingly, fearfully" (275). The narrative eroticizes mastery and submission by employing the words "slave" and "obey" to describe John's subservience to Aurora in their romantic relationship and to solidify the power dynamic into Aurora's dominance and John's submission. Referring to her husband as "my darling boy" (215), "that ridiculous old John" (221), and "laugh[ing] at his embarrassment" (231), Aurora establishes her supremacy in the marriage by making "sentimental declarations" one minute, only to "alternately ridicule, lecture, and tyrannize over him for the rest of the day" (200). Unlike Talbot, who is nearly divested of his masculine identity by his masochistic desire, John accepts Aurora's humiliation of him and "submerged his very identity into the woman that he loved" (411). The narrator preemptively contests possible doubts of John's manliness that might arise because of his submissive desires and instructs the reader not "to despise [John], for his very weaknesses were manly"; further, he insists that Aurora's dominance is in fact magnified by her rule over such a man (200).

John's contentment as a happy subject of Aurora's "petticoat government" (197) inspires him to consider the positive social effects that his domestic arrangements with Aurora, defined by her assertive sexuality, could have on English society if extended and embraced by other couples. John muses on the conjugal benefits that would result if social sanctions prohibiting women from enjoying the turf with their spouses were lifted:

> I think the good old sport of English gentleman was meant to be shared by their wives ... I think our British wives and mothers might have the battle in their own hands, and win the victory for themselves and their daughters if they were a little braver in standing their ground; if they were not quite so tenderly indulgent to the sins of eligible young nobleman [262].

Despite his insistence that the state of Victorian heterosexual affairs makes it a "sad world ... one that [he] is not going to set ... right" (262), John advocates female sexual authority and male discipline — employing militaristic terminology — battle, victory, bravery — as both a prescription for marital contentment and a solution to the social crisis of men seeking sexual satisfaction and erotic discipline through extra-marital outlets, such as brothels, where erotic flagellation was a popular practice.[8] John's joking remark to Aurora about "whether solemn Talbot beats [Lucy] in the silence of the matrimonial chamber" (261), underscores his opinion that whoever dominates the marriage, undoubtedly does so in the conjugal bed, and Aurora's firm grasp on the whip implies that her tyranny over the Mellish household and over John also extends to or even perhaps originates in the bedroom.

In her complex social commentary on masculinity and male submissive desire, Braddon privileges the "henpecked husband" John Mellish, whose masochistic, sacrificial love is rewarded with marital sexual fulfillment. On the other hand, female exploitation and sadistic male violence are punished through Braddon's treatment of James Conyers and

Steeve Hargraves. Aurora's first husband, Conyers, by his own admission, was never a physical match for her, even on his best days (322). His motive for blackmailing Aurora — "the tiger-cat, whose claws ... left a mark" (270) permanently scaring his forehead — stems more from his desire to avenge himself for the physical attack than from greed. The sensation plot hinges on Aurora's reputation as a woman capable of inflicting physical pain on a man, for when Conyers is murdered shortly after a heated discussion with her, she is suspected of the crime, even by her husband.

The real murderer, Steeve Hargraves, the "Softy," is the stable hand "a bit touched in the upper-story" (190), whose identity becomes enmeshed with the eroticized whipping scene from the moment in the narrative when he is flogged by Aurora. Subsequent appearances of the "Softy" are often followed by direct references to the incident of Aurora's horsewhipping him. The connection between name and identity is significant in Victorian literary discourse, and if (as Marlene Tromp suggests) Steeve Hargraves acts as James Conyers's double, then Aurora's punishment of the "Softy" — whose *sobriquet* covertly connotes sexual impuissance — signifies both a physical manifestation of the heroine's dominant characteristics as well as potentially latent frustrations harbored against those who are neither intellectually nor sexually her equal. For Braddon to have written explicitly on female sexuality was to breach one level of Victorian propriety, but for her to openly disclose female sexual discontent within the marital relationship would have been unpardonable. By encoding male sexual inadequacy into a nick-name, and displacing the source of Aurora's frustration from her husband to the stable hand, Braddon is able to provocatively, albeit covertly, insinuate female sexual dissatisfaction, while maintaining narrative discretion.[9]

Male performance anxieties and fears of sexual incompetence are reinforced in Hargraves' description of his erotically charged fantasies of murdering Aurora by cutting her throat:

> I've seen her in my dreams ... with her beautiful white throat laid open, and streaming oceans of blood; but for all that, she's always had the broken whip in her hand, and she's always laughed at me. I've had many a dream about her; but I've never seen her dead or quiet; and I've never seen her without the whip [253].

Softy muses thus while he "grasped something in the loose pocket of his trousers" (253), presumably the knife he would like to use on Aurora. However, the ambiguity of what is signified by the "something ... in his trousers," connects the masculine fear of impotence with the humiliation of public exposure and the potential shame in being dominated by a woman. Fears of female mastery and emasculation engender Hargraves's sadistic dreams of Aurora as larger than life, with her throat slit open, holding the *broken whip* in her hand, still laughing and far from reticent. At the novel's end, the "Softy" is found to be the murderer of Conyers, exonerating Aurora of the crime on the level of narration and extra-narratively, punishing the man who responds sadistically to female dominance.

While Nemesvari and Surridge assert that the whip is restored to male control at the end of the narrative, as Aurora seemingly gives up her "taste for horseflesh," for maternity (30), I contend that we cannot so readily accept the heroine's recuperation into domesticity as a reinstatement of phallic power. Despite the seemingly conservative plot line that reinscribes Aurora to domesticity through maternity — a conventional narrative closure that some feminist critics read as punishment or incarceration — female sexual dominance, embodied by the indomitable heroine, does not disqualify her from being a "good" woman and mother. As Nemesevari and Surridge agree: "Braddon goes some way towards suggesting that [Aurora] will make a better wife and mother than her blonde chaste cousin Lucy who is the very embodiment of the Victorian angel" (22). Inasmuch as the fictive Aurora yields the horse-whip to rock the cradle at the novel's end, the male characters have been measured according to their level of investment in masochistic love for a dominant woman and have been disciplined and punished by the pen-whip of the living version of Aurora, Braddon herself.[10]

Braddon's contemporary William Fraser Rae asked, "[H]ave we found her a creator of new types, a copyist of living personages or a creator of unnatural monstrosities?" (589). Considering other literary representations of dominant women who share Aurora's "eccentric predilections"— Shakespeare's Cleopatra, and Sacher-Masoch's Wanda — it's clear that Braddon's powerful woman is a recurring heroine. However, what distinguishes Braddon's representation of gender-inverted heterosexual relationships is its extreme optimism. Shakespeare's play ends in the tragic death of both Antony and Cleopatra, and *Venus in Furs* concludes with a reinstatement, albeit sardonic, of male mastery. Conversely, Braddon's novel ends in domestic bliss and offers the re-negotiation of gendered roles, through male masochism and female dominance, as a prescription for mutual conjugal contentment.

*Aurora Floyd* is a seminal novel, exemplifying a radical reconfiguring of "femininity" and "masculinity" by resisting the heteronormativity of gendered roles in marriage, and by promoting romantic and erotic possibilities available to both sexes through non-normative heterosexual relations. As queer theory's attempts to destabilize both sexual and gender identities are succeeding in liberating both alternative heterosexualities and homosexuality from their categorical status as perversions, revisiting Braddon's Victorian fiction as a rendering of non-normative heterosexual practice broadens the discursive history of what has become only recently, either affectionately, problematically or both, termed queer heterosexuality.

## Notes

1. For contemporary reviews of Braddon's fiction, see Appendix B: Reviews and Responses in *Aurora Floyd* eds. Richard Nemesvari and Lisa Surridge (573–630). Also see Marlene Tromp (103–6).
2. All narrative references from *Aurora Floyd*. eds. Richard Nemesvari and Lisa Surridge. Peterborough, Ontario: Broadview Press, 1998.
3. See Oliphant's unsigned review in Nemesvari and Surridge (599).
4. For feminist discussions of Braddon see Elaine Showalter, Winifred Hughes, Marlene Tromp, and Lyn Pykett. On male homoeroticism, see Richard Nemesvari's "Robert Audley's Secret: Male Homosocial Desire and 'Going Straight' in *Lady Audley's Secret*" *Straight With A Twist: Queer Theory And The Subject Of Heterosexuality*. ed. Calvin Thomas. Urbana: University of Illinois Press, 2000. 109–121; and Jennifer S. Kushnier's "Educating Boys to Be Queer: Braddon's *Lady Audley's Secret*" *Victorian Literature and Culture* (2002), 61–75.
5. See Deleuze (53, 59).
6. I recognize that deploying the term *masochism* to describe the libidinal economy operating in Braddon's text is anachronistic; however, I think it aptly delineates — to a post-psychoanalytic audience — the theme of female dominance and male submission that emerges in her work.
7. See Marcus (257–262).
8. In 1885, W.T Stead published a series of articles in the *Pall Mall Gazette* entitled "The Maiden Tribute of Modern Babylon," addressing social evils such as erotic flagellation he insists "goes on regularly" in London brothels. See also Marcus (158, 255).
9. According to Robert Woolf, Braddon portrayed "male sexual inadequacy" for the first time in *John Marchmont's Legacy* (1863); however, I see this theme emerging earlier that year in *Aurora Floyd* (160).
10. Braddon was nicknamed "Miss Aurora" by George Sala (Woolf 116).

## Works Cited

Berlant, Lauren, and Warner, Micheal. "Sex in Public (Intimacy)." *Critical Inquiry* 24.2 (1998): 547–567.
Braddon, Mary Elizabeth. *Aurora Floyd*. Eds. Richard Nemesvari and Lisa Surridge. Peterborough, Ontario: Broadview, 1998.

Casey, Ellen Miller. "Other People's Prudery: Mary Elizabeth Braddon." *Sexuality and Victorian Literature*. Ed. Don Richard Cox. *Tennessee Studies in Literature* 27 (1984):72–82.
Deleuze, Gilles. *Sacher-Masoch: An Interpretation*. Trans. Jean McNeil. London: Faber and Faber, 1967.
Dollimore, Jonathon. "The Cultural Politics of Perversion: Augustine, Shakespeare, Freud, Foucault." *Genders* 8 (Summer 1990): 1–16.
Fantina, Richard. *Ernest Hemingway: Machismo and Masochism*. New York: Palgrave Macmillan, 2005.
Hughes, Winifred. *Maniac in the Cellar: Sensation Novels of the 1860s*. Princeton: Princeton University Press, 1980.
Krafft-Ebing, Richard Von. *Psychopathia Sexualis, with Especial Reference to the Antipathetic Sexual Instinct; a Medico-Forensic Study*. Trans. from the 12th German edition. New York: Stein and Day, 1965.
Marcus, Steven. *The Other Victorians*. New York: Basic, 1964.
Nemesvari, Richard. "Robert Audley's Secret: Male Homosocial Desire and 'Going Straight' in *Lady Audley's Secret*." In *Straight with a Twist: Queer Theory and the Subject of Heterosexuality*. Ed. Calvin Thomas. Urbana: University of Illinois Press, 2000. 109–121.
_____, and Lisa Surridge. "Introduction." In Mary Elizabeth Braddon, *Aurora Floyd*. Eds. Richard Nemesvari and Lisa Surridge. Peterborough, Ontario: Broadview, 1998.
Oliphant, Margaret. "Novels (No. II)." *Blackwood's Edinburgh Magazine* 102 (September 1867): 257–80. In Mary Elizabeth Braddon, *Aurora Floyd*. Eds. Richard Nemesvari and Lisa Surridge. Peterborough, Ontario: Broadview, 1998. 599–607.
Paglia, Camille. *Sexual Personae: Art and Decadence from Nefertiti to Emily Dickinson*. New York: Vintage, 1991.
Pykett, Lyn. *The 'Improper' Feminine: The Women's Sensation Novel and the New Woman Writing*. London: Routledge, 1992.
Rae, W. Fraser. "Sensation Novelists: Miss Braddon." *North British Review* 43 (1865): 180–204. In Mary Elizabeth Braddon, *Aurora Floyd*. Eds. Richard Nemesvari and Lisa Surridge. Peterborough, Ontario: Broadview, 1998. 583–592.
Schlichter, Annette. "Queer at Last? Straight Intellectuals and the Desire for Transgression." *GLQ: A Journal of Lesbian and Gay Studies* 10.4 (2004): 543–564.
Schroeder, Natalie. "Feminine Sensationalism, Eroticism, and Self-Assertion: M.E. Braddon and Ouida." *Tulsa Studies in Women's Literature* 7.1 (1988): 87–103.
Showalter, Elaine. *A Literature of Their Own: British Women Novelists from Brontë to Lessing*. Princeton: Princeton University Press, 1977.
Siegel, Carol. *Male Masochism: Modern Revisions of the Story of Love*. Bloomington: Indiana University Press, 1995.
Tosh, John. *A Man's Place: Masculinity and the Middle-Class Home in Victorian England*. New Haven: Yale University Press, 1999.
Tromp, Marlene. *The Private Rod: Marital Violence, Sensation, and the Law in Victorian Britain*. Charlottesville: University Press of Virginia, 2000.
Warner, Micheal, ed. Introduction. In *Fear of a Queer Planet: Queer Politics and Social Theory*. Minneapolis: University of Minnesota Press, 1993.
Woolf, Robert. *Sensational Victorian: The Life and Fiction of Mary Elizabeth Braddon*. New York: Garland, 1979.

# 7 "Was ever hero in this fashion won?"
## Alternative Sexualities in the Novels of George Meredith

MELISSA SHIELDS JENKINS

George Meredith's novels feature no open homosexuals and only a few recognizable specimens of the stereotypical "dandy." Instead, his novels undermine sex and gender conventions within depictions of heterosexual unions. More specifically, in novels such as *Diana of the Crossways*, *The Egoist*, and *The Amazing Marriage*, male characters channel seemingly homoerotic desires through attractions to masculine women, and women gain social and sexual freedom by adopting masculine traits. I begin here with Meredith's first full-length novel, 1859's *The Ordeal of Richard Feverel*, which moves so far beyond the comfort zone of what his narrator disparagingly calls "the virtuous ... English book-buying public" (22) that it was banned by England's largest circulating library for its "generic unorthodoxy" (Roberts 868). The *Saturday Review* declared, "It is quite right that there should be men's novels, if only it is understood at the outset that they are only meant for men ... *The Ordeal of Richard Feverel* is entirely a man's book" (74–75), implying that the content was too explicitly and unconventionally sexual for delicate female readers. These days, George Meredith has been rediscovered by critics interested in unconventional narrative practice, but not yet by those interested in unconventional sexualities. In addition, generations of critics who read the 1875 or 1896 revisions of *Feverel*, in which Meredith edited out the more controversial content, missed many hints of his original intentions.

The story Meredith tells centers around Sir Austin Feverel, an author of a book of aphorisms called "The Pilgrim's Scrip," who, taking a page from Sterne's Walter Shandy, decides to raise his son Richard based on a written plan. His son, however, seeks to push the boundaries between the writing of sex and the living of it. Since Sir Austin's plan doesn't allow for sexual maturity until Richard's twenty-fifth year (121), the book and the boy break ranks when he reaches puberty. Richard's rebellion from his father's plan involves living out all of the clichés of texts that do center around romantic entanglements between young people: he marries a poor farm girl against his father's will (courting her in a chapter, "Ferdinand and Miranda," that pastiches the idealized lovers in Shakespeare's *The Tempest*), commits adultery, fights a duel, and goes mad when his wife dies of brain fever. The young hero's homosocial attractions, freely alluded to throughout the novel, are summed up most succinctly by an early entry in his disappointed cousin's diary, "Richard was not sorry to lose me. He only loves boys and men" (444). Not surprisingly, then, when Sir Austin tries to write his son into a classic eighteenth-century didactic novel, Richardson's *Sir Charles Grandison,* by marrying him to a supposed female descendant of the fictional hero, Richard is drawn only to the youngest daughter, a tomboy who asks Richard to call her Carl.

Meredith's early readers then had to contend with Bella Mount, the androgynous temptress who draws Richard away from his bride Lucy with her "man-like conversation" (397). The double meaning of "conversation" here — discourse and sexual intercourse — becomes clear when Bella takes on the persona of a male character she calls "Sir Julius" in order to capture Richard's attention sexually. Meredith's contemporary reviewers did not know what to make of this unconventional love interest. The *Saturday Review* simply called her a "much naughtier woman" than Richard's wife (72), and *The Critic* deemed her a "temptress and an enchantress" and chastised Meredith lightly for the warmth of the seduction scene that "betrays a fondness for gloating over what had better be only hinted at" (65). Samuel Lucas's review in *The Times* gets closest to the expected objection about the sexually subversive nature of the pairing. His statement — "the winning of the hero under such circumstances revolts our notions of consistency and drags us from the sphere of harmonious art into the chaos of caprice" — registers Meredith's subversion of both literary expectations and societal norms. Yet, Lucas still phrases the objection in literary rather than literal terms. The seduction seems wrong "in an artistic sense" and violates the doctrines of "harmonious art" (5). The review does not try to explain "Sir Julius" or Richard's attraction to him. In eliding Bella's status as a masculinized woman, and focusing instead on her disruption of the fabric of a literary representation, these reviewers begin the transference of Bella Mount from social to artistic problem.

Without the intervention of queer theory, modern critics differ about what is most shocking about the sexuality in *Feverel* — the open depiction of sexual desire in women, the forgiving attitude of the narrator toward sexual indiscretion, or, writes Neil Roberts, "perhaps the cross-dressing episode, an example of behaviour practiced widely enough, historians knew, but not admitted" (86). These critics continue the transformation of Bella Mount from sexual reality to social metaphor. Mervyn Jones looks at Bella Mount and sees not literal androgyny, but "frank female sexuality" (157), and Richard Stevenson finds in the feminized Sir Austin a search for a "fully integrated male personality" (60). Lewis Horne interprets Bella's statement to Richard that he is "as tempting as a girl" (*Feverel* 469) as evidence of Bella's lesbian identity (43). This reading puts the sexual difference, the divergence from the "norm," at Bella's door. Finally, Bella becomes an object for feminist readings that neutralize her as a reflection on Richard's ambiguous sexual status. In these readings, making a woman like a man is a political statement, not a biological one.

Queer theory reminds us, though, that "lesbian" is an insufficient term for someone like Bella, especially in the nineteenth century climate where, as Judith Halberstam writes, the terms "romantic friendship," "androgyne," "female husband," and "masculine woman" all carry significantly different valences (50–1, 57–9). Martha Vicinus notes the "extraordinary attachment to male or androgynous nicknames" in the history of lesbianism, but also the *political* valences of such namings — that they "not only implied woman-to-woman intimacy, but also the creation of a self-sufficient world where masculinity could be assumed with the ease of a change in clothing or naming" ("Gift of Love" 249). Marjorie Garber discusses the need to distinguish between the androgyne and the transvestite, especially in pre–twentieth century cultures, and between drag performance and transgender identity (124–131; 151–2). She adds that popular literature for women (and, for that matter, instruction manuals for male crossdressers) reflect society's continual "concept of woman as artifact, assembled from a collection of parts" (49). Bella uses the constructed nature of female identity to her advantage, turning her physical sex into a persona that can be easily discarded or partially assumed when useful. Without "Sir Julius," the wholly female Bella could not have pursued or attracted Richard, and in turn could not have escaped the disapproving gaze of the neglectful Lord Mountfalcon. But the same goes for Sir Julius' dependence on Bella. While assumed, Bella's double identity translates itself into both sexual and social leverage. She moves out of two isolated spheres of influence — male and female — to create her own.

As with Bella Mount's "man-like conversation," in Meredith's later literary forays into gender politics, sexual identity is steeped in questions of language and performance. As his career continues, however, Meredith becomes increasingly accepting of more permanent forms of androgyny in his heroines, but makes the middle ground inaccessible for later heroes. In his poem "Marian," the speaker praises his heroine by noting that she can "talk the talk of men" (Jones 49), but in *The Egoist*, Sir Willoughby Patterne becomes ridiculous and undesirable due to his mastery of "ladies' language." Meredith's heroines charm men and women through a gender flexibility in social situations that matches their middle status in economic terms. In "The Tale of Chloe" (1894), the title character is an intermediary between the lower classes and the aristocracy (she is a formerly wealthy women who has become the paid companion of a duchess), between the old and the young, and also between men and women. The narrator writes that Chloe was "like a well-mannered sparkling boy ... her sex's deputy, to tell the coarser where they could meet, as on a bridge above the torrent separating them" (41). Here, Meredith employs a character who contains both sexes as his agent to teach heterosexual couples how to productively relate to one another.

Most famously, in the novel *Diana of the Crossways*, often looked to as the most proto-feminist of Meredith's works, he provides his heroine — a woman who, as with Bella Mount and Marian, had "caught a trick of 'using men's phrases'" (157) — with a female friendship that steers quite close to lesbianism. Diana herself is hard to pin down. Her best friend's husband calls Diana both a "man and woman in brains" (298), and her admirer Dacier concludes that she "was dear past computation, womanly, yet quite unlike the womanish woman, unlike the semi-males courteously called dashing" (288). Diana, or "Tony," as she prefers to be called, emerges from a deep depression through the love of Emma, a female friend who shares her bed during her convalescence. It is hard to miss the homoerotic undertones in passages such as "'I am with my darling.' Tony moaned. The warmth and the love were bringing back her anguish" or "Emma strained to her ... There was a faint convulsion in the body ... 'You are in Emmy's arms, my beloved'" (411). Emma and Tony emphasize their relationship as unique *because* it is between two women; the two "had often talked of the possibility of a classic friendship between women, the alliance of a mutual devotedness men choose to doubt of" (87). "Classic" as a term to describe this friendship evokes the Platonic ideal of non-sexual love between two people, but at the same time may recall the more open acceptance of intimate same-sex relations in some ancient civilizations. A third interpretation of the term "classic" is "legendary," which would signal the relative absence of strong female friendships in secular history and myth. Indeed, other characters in *Crossways* can only comfortably describe this relation as if it were between men. One character calls Diana and Emma "the Damon and Pythias of women" (183), alluding to the fourth century story of legendary male friends who are rewarded for their willingness to die for each other.

Meredith's goal in these early passages is to depict an alternative love affair that lies in stark opposition to the worlds of male homosociality and male-female love (Beer 150–151). However, by the end of the novel, as Roberts notes (222, 224), Meredith balances Diana's masculinity and romantic friendship by "hypermasculinizing" her victorious suitor, Redworth, into a "stormy man" (473) whose every breath is "hugely masculine" (483). Readers learn little about Redworth in the body of the novel; he emerges as a character near the end to refeminize Diana. Earlier in the novel, the narrator describes Diana's skill in "wooing" women into friendship and allegiance (148). The most charmed, Emma, cries near the end of the novel, "Tony, do you love me? But don't answer: give me your hand. You have rejected him!" (474). A few pages later, however, Emma is dressing Tony, now Diana, for her "marriage with the man of men" (491).

How does one "learn" heterosexuality? In *Diana of the Crossways*, as with *Richard Feverel*, Meredith's protagonist achieves heterosexual union after experimenting with homosexual attractions. Emma's nocturnal attentions do not prevent Diana from heterosexual marriage, but instead facilitate it. Similarly, Richard's child-bride in *The Ordeal of Richard Feverel* allows Mrs. Berry in her bed only temporarily, to comfort her during Richard's parallel dalliances with Mrs. Bella Mount. Mrs. Berry, regarding the young Lucy in bed, "eyed her roguishly, saying, 'I never see ye like this, but I'm half in love with you myself, you blushin' beauty'" (430). Yet, several aspects of the scene eventually pull this union into the realm of the "female husband," a known Victorian practice that is not, says Halberstam, "easily assimilated into modern notions of lesbian sexual practice." Halberstam defines the female husband as a woman role-playing in the part of a husband to compensate for, rather than replace, the absent or neglectful male (66–67). A related term, the Sapphic romance or the Sapphic fairy tale, is adopted by Martha Vicinus and Elaine Marks to describe the phenomenon in which an older woman steps in temporarily to prepare a younger woman for a mature sexual life ("Wonder" 476).

Mrs. Berry explains to Lucy, recalling her own experiences after being abandoned by Mr. Berry, "It don't somehow seem nat'ral after Matrimony — a woman in yer bed! I was 'bliged t' ave somebody, for the cold sheets do give ye the creeps when you've been used to that that's different'" (430). As with numerous real-life affairs between Victorian women, Lucy and Mrs. Berry's night in bed together is additionally explained via a mixture of the sacred and the erotic (Vicinus "Gift" 242–3). The narrator describes how they "cooed, and kissed, and undressed by the fire, and knelt at the bedside, with their arms about each other, praying" (430). Finally, a third presence in the bed, Richard's unborn son, reminds the reader that the husband's return is imminent.

What messages lie behind Meredith's creation of Bella/Sir Julius, Carola/Carl, and Diana/Tony? With beautiful understatement that again turns self-consciously to literary convention, the narrator, adapting *Richard III* (I.ii.229–30), asks upon Richard's seduction by Bella/Sir Julius, "Was ever hero in this fashion won?" (416). Not in *Sir Charles Grandison*, not in *The Tempest*, not in clichés of chivalric romances, but in a less canonical, but no less useful, literary form. When Adrian calls Mrs. Bella Mount "a sister to Miss Random" (369), he links her to a pornographic text that, earlier in the novel, facilitated the heterosexual awakening of Richard's first male playmate, a young boy named Ripton. In the pivotal "unmasking" of Richard's approach to sexual maturity, his concealment of the *Adventures of Miss Random* within a heraldry manual, which is itself hidden deep in his desk behind law textbooks, reminds the reader of the griffin and wheatsheaves crest that opens Sir Austin's didactic "Pilgrim's Scrip." Meredith invites readers to investigate similarities between the contents of the two imaginary texts, as well as the covers. The passage draws attention to the similarity between literature that seeks to define socially acceptable sexual conduct and literature that uncovers the details of illicit sexual practice. In the process, *Feverel* raises the question of whether traditional sexual education (the cold details of conduct books) is as effective as more explicit forms of writing about sex.

*The Ordeal of Richard Feverel* centers around questions of how words should direct a young man's education in sexual practice — whether pornography is "a necessary Establishment" (330), or whether boys should write poetry as a "safety-valve" (123) to curb sexual urges. Eventually, though, Meredith's quest to loosen gender conventions fades into a frustrated indictment of genre conventions. As with Sir Austin's overly prescriptive "Pilgrim's Scrip," the literary systems at hand proved to be too inflexible to hold all alternative sexualities. In making the sexual textual, an author is likely to disrupt the way readers think about bodies, which can become a mode of erasure when convention forces him to leave things out. In *Feverel*, Adrian Harley criticizes the way that Richard's poems, and cavalier poetry in general, renders the object of affection as only partial: "Lips, eyes, bosom, legs — legs?" he says, "I don't think you gave her any legs. No legs and no nose. That appears to be the poetic taste of the day" (235). Words can erase the woman's body if there are literally no words for her, as Mrs. Berry remarks of her status as an abandoned wife, a "widow and not a widow," that they "haven't got a name for what she is an any Dixionary ... Johnson haven't got a name for me!" (272). In Mrs. Berry's melancholy allusion to Samuel Johnson's *Dictionary* (the same book that Thackeray's Becky Sharp throws out of the carriage window), Meredith again looks to, and rejects, an eighteenth-century model of social definition and control through writing. If Johnson has no name for an abandoned woman, he certainly has no terms for a masculine one.

"The reason why men and women are mysterious to us, and prove disappointing," says Sir Austin in "The Pilgrim's Scrip," "is, that we will read them from our own book: just as we are perplexed by reading ourselves from theirs" (287). Critics read these lines, and in general read the failure of marriage in the novel, as an indictment of heterosexual discourse, but have not yet allowed for the hints Meredith lays down about the virtues of homo-socialization. Characters repeatedly describe the feminine nature of Richard's father; Sir Austin's sister explains, "Austin is not like other men ... He is just like a woman" (367), and Mrs. Berry adds that Sir Austin "makes ye think you're dealin' with a man of iron, and all the while there's a woman underneath. And a man that's like a woman he's the puzzle o' life!" (396). Sir Austin is "a man that's like a woman" in temperament, but also profession, writing conduct books during decades in which the genre was dominated by female writers and readers (Warhol vii). As Alan Sinfield discusses in *Cultural Politics — Queer Reading*, the progression toward effeminacy was a real consideration of Victorian professional authors, as writing was increasingly described as a feminine counterpart to masculine industry (32–34).

In the opening chapters of the 1859 edition of the novel, in which a court of female admirers and critics surround Sir Austin Feverel, we are told that Sir Austin "was melting to Woman. Woman appreciated his Aphorisms, and Man did not" (15). "Melting to Woman" means both that he is warming to their company, and that he is shifting his own shape to match theirs. The Griffin crest on Sir Austin's title page leads the women to call him a "double animal," and the woman writer is described as "the long-nosed, the literary," and "the half-man" (13, 154). In these chapters, all authors are defined as hermaphroditic. As novelist Severo Sarduy writes when exploring the slippery connections between language and identity, "Transvestism ... is probably the best metaphor for what writing really is" (Sarduy 33; Garber 150).

We find in Meredith's early novel an experiment with a different kind of narration, one that would live out Coleridge's statement that "a great mind must be androgynous" (188). In his 1877 "Essay on the Idea of Comedy," Meredith claims strongly that comedy, and thus society, cannot exist where men and woman are not equal (15, 31). In *Diana of the Crossways*, a novel about a woman novelist who proofs her manuscript as she faces charges of adultery, close-minded narration is the obstacle that stands between the heroine and sexual freedom. Her social isolation begins when she makes the same objections as Bella Mount, speaking out about the "misfortune of her not having been born a man" (186). When Bella Mount says in *Feverel*, "Wasn't it a shame to make a woman of me when I was born to be a man?" (398), she registers sex based on the degree of assertiveness that is culturally acceptable in either gender. The shaping power, the ability to "make a woman" or a man of someone, is given to the "author" of perceptions rather than to his object. Writes Diana, "We women are the verbs passive of the alliance ... We are to run on lines, like the steam-trains, or we come to no station, dash to fragments. I have the misfortune to know I was born an active" (75–76). Diana's misfortune of being an active verb trapped in a passive construction — in other words, her status within a written text — parallels her laments about her gender status as a man's soul in a woman's body. In this passage, Meredith uses his writer-heroine to reflect upon the relationship between gender, narration, and power. As Judith Butler writes in *Gender Trouble*, woman represents absence in any "phallogocentric language" (14), but once we move beyond the categories of male and female, gender is no longer "a static cultural marker" but "an incessant and repeated action of some sort," an active verb (143).

Meredith was not shy about connecting Diana's situation as a stifled author with his own, or her sensibilities as a woman author with his as a man. In a 1907 letter to D.H. Anders, he writes, "In *Diana of the Crossways* my critics own that a breathing woman is produced, and I felt that she was in me as I wrote," and that he has "treated [his] books of prose as the mother bird her fledglings" (197). Good authorship, for Meredith, is not even gender neutral, but rather an intentional mixture of genders. Meredith begins his career with a novel about a spectacularly failed heterosexual union, poorly plotted by a father's conduct book and the conventions of multiple outdated literary genres. In his last work, *The Amazing Marriage*, the union is similarly ill-fated, but the heroine gains strength through her capacity to contain both man and woman. Carinthia, deemed one of Meredith's "triumphant androgynes, a wonderful girl with a man's heart" by a contemporary reviewer ("Method" 842), finds guidance when she crosses gender lines to consult her dead father's *Maxims for Men*. Meredith's narration attempts the same feat, as the novel alternates between the voices of a restrained male narrator and a chatty woman nicknamed "Dame Gossip."

It is especially useful to look to Meredith when thinking about the transition from Victorianism to modernism. Meredith's frustrations with the gender categories imposed by all kinds of literature, categories that demand that exteriors directly correlate with interiors (that the contents of books match their covers), lead him to break down what he himself constructs in words. As we look forward into modern experiments in relating sex, text, and authorship, we should ask why Sir Austin's aphorism against sentimentalism — "the sentimentalist is he who would enjoy without incurring the immense debtorship for a thing done" — is quoted by James Joyce in chapter nine of *Ulysses*, as the characters convene in the National Library to talk about the relationship between Shakespeare's personal life and his literary creations (199). The "ordeal" of reading human sexuality in Meredith's works brings out all of his hopes that art may someday truly imitate life. As his speaker muses in Sonnet 25 of "Modern Love," responding to his auditor's objection to sexually frank literature, "Unnatural? My dear, these things are life, / And life, some think, is worthy of the muse" (13–14).

## *Works Cited*

Beer, Gillian. *Meredith: A Change of Masks*. London: Athlone, 1970.
Butler, Judith. *Gender Trouble: Feminism and the Subversion of Identity*. New York and London: Routledge, 1999.
Coleridge, Samuel Taylor. *Table Talk*. London: John Murray, 1836.
Garber, Marjorie. *Vested Interests: Cross-Dressing and Cultural Anxiety*. New York and London: Routledge, 1992.
Halberstam, Judith. *Female Masculinity*. Durham, NC, and London: Duke University Press, 1998.
Horne, Lewis. "Sir Austin, His Devil, and the Well-Designed World." *Studies in the Novel* 24.1 (Spring 1992): 35–47.
Jones, Mervyn. *The Amazing Victorian: A Life of George Meredith*. London: Constable, 1999.

Joyce, James. *Ulysses*. New York: Vintage, 1990.
Lucas, Samuel. Review of *The Ordeal of Richard Feverel. The Times* (14 Oct. 1859): 5.
Meredith, George. *Diana of the Crossways*. New York: Russell & Russell, 1968.
\_\_\_\_\_. "Essay on the Idea of Comedy." In George Meredith, *Collected Works. Vol. 23: Miscellaneous Prose*. New York: Russell and Russell, 1968. 3–58.
\_\_\_\_\_. "Modern Love." In George Meredith, *The Poetical Works of George Meredith*. London: Constable and Company, 1912. 144.
\_\_\_\_\_. *The Ordeal of Richard Feverel*. Ed. Edward Mendelson. New York: Penguin, 1999.
\_\_\_\_\_."The Tale of Chloe." In George Meredith, *George Meredith's 1895 Collection of Three Stories*. Ed. Elizabeth J. Deis. Lewiston, ME: Edwin Mellen, 1997. 3–76.
"The Method of George Meredith." *Saturday Review* 80 (Dec 21, 1895): 842–843.
Review of *The Ordeal of Richard Feverel. Saturday Review* 8 (9 July 1859). In *George Meredith: The Critical Heritage*. Ed. Ioan Williams. London and New York: Routledge, 1995. 71–76.
Review of *The Ordeal of Richard Feverel. The Critic* 19 (2 July 1859). In *George Meredith: The Critical Heritage*. Ed. Ioan Williams. London and New York: Routledge, 1995. 63–67.
Roberts, Neil. *Meredith and the Novel*. New York: St. Martin's, 1997.
Sarduy, Severo. "Writing/Transvestism." Trans. Alfred Mac Adam. *Review* 9 (Fall 1973): 31–33.
Sinfield, Alan. *Cultural Politics—Queer Reading*. 2nd ed. London: Routledge, 2005.
Stevenson, Richard C. *The Experimental Impulse in George Meredith's Fiction*. Lewisburg, PA: Bucknell University Press, 2004.
Vicinus, Martha. "'The Gift of Love': Nineteenth Century Religion and Lesbian Passion." *Nineteenth Century Contexts* 23 (2001): 241–64.
\_\_\_\_\_. "They Wonder to Which Sex I Belong: The Historical Roots of the Modern Lesbian Identity." *Feminist Studies* 18.3 (Autumn 1992): 467–497.
Warhol, Robyn. *Gendered Interventions: Narrative Discourse in the Victorian Novel*. New Brunswick, NJ, and London: Rutgers University Press, 1989.

# 8 She
## *Rider Haggard's Queer Adventures*
### SHANNON YOUNG

Rider Haggard's *She* (1887) opens up a world of queer possibilities: dominatrix fantasies, same-sex desire, orgies lighted by flaming embalmed bodies, and polymorphous sexual tastes enacted upon the outered African topography. This is curious material in view of Haggard's sanctimonious admonition in his essay "About Fiction," published the same year as *She*, that criticized the French Naturalist school for its attention to prurient material, rendered "in full and luscious detail," that irresponsibly calls "attention to erotic matters" (176–77). Lindy Steibel observes that Haggard seemed wholly unconscious of the sexual nature of his narratives, and this apparent obliviousness extended to the reading public. Steibel quotes one contemporary reviewer who found Haggard's adventure stories: "wholesome ... in no page of which is there anything of a degrading or unmanly tendency" (80). It would fall to the next century with its greater attention to the frequently unconscious, convoluted nature of desire to penetrate into the buried eroticism, or what Rebecca Stott would graphically call "the landscape of pornographic fantasies and sexual terrors" in Haggard's African tales.

Were the Victorians so sexually constrained as to seriously undermine their ability to acknowledge erotic material? The nineteenth century in England was a period of extreme sexual regulation. The bourgeois crusade to enthrone the family and defend against forces perceived to be undermining the fundamental bond between a man and a woman resulted in increasingly vigilant attention to sexual matters with an eye to restraining lasciviousness. In 1892, as noted by David Halperin, the terms "homosexual" and "heterosexual" first appeared in the *Oxford English Dictionary*, indicating the society's determination to define normal and abnormal sexual practices. Individuals had to locate themselves within a strict binarism between the new heterosexual and homosexual camps (26). This pressure to conform to heteronormative rules extended to criminalizing homosexual behavior. The Criminal Law Amendment Act of 1885 outlawed homosexual activity between men (but curiously neglected female same-sex acts), culminating during the 1890s in the highly publicized trial and imprisonment of Oscar Wilde. This increased scrutiny around sexual issues resulted in the Victorians imposing, as many have noted, a false break in the continuum of sexual desire, and consequently individuals were compelled to adopt a mindset of greater self-consciousness over their sexual expression.

This chapter explores the implications of this mindset in the work of Rider Haggard. Biographers note that a dualism characterized his life arising on the one hand from his fervent devotion to the social standards such as marrying and raising a family, devoting one's self to civic life, and advancing the cause of the Empire. On the other hand, he produced a prolific body of weird fiction that expressed his socially taboo sexual desires via the anarchic, primitive realm of his imaginatively constructed Africa.[1] Henry Miller was astounded by the bizarre tales that emerged from this "earthbound ... conventional ... orthodox" specimen of an Englishman, and theorized that Haggard's manner of writing his romances "at full speed" enabled him "to tap his unconscious with freedom and depth" and thereby reveal a "hidden nature" (93). *She*, which D.S. Higgins characterizes as Haggard's "most creative work, in which were integrated his nightmares, repressed desires, and fantasies" (90–1), was written, as Haggard discloses, "at white heat," and reveals sexual fantasies decidedly outside the pale of acceptable heterosexuality: desire for the dominating, forbidden woman, preoedipal desires for his mother, and, most disturbingly, same-sex desires which grew out of the convolutions of his heterosexual desire (*Days*, I, 245). In effect, *She* reveals how tenuous the veil between heterosexual and homosexual desire can be, and how untenable it is to impose such a divide on human sexuality. It reveals the delicacy of each person's erotic itinerary and the strangely contorted routes that sexual expression can take. Diana Fuss observes how "rigid ... cultural binaries" can interfere with the "complexity of sexual identity formations" (392). Haggard's fiction provided him with a subversively creative escape from the sexual rigidity of his heteronormative culture, but he also internalized his society's sexual mores, leading him to sublimate his queer sexual desires.

*She* begins with a description of insular male bonds that exclude women. The narrator of the adventure, Holly, is a professor at all male Cambridge. He lives with his ward, Leo, and a manservant, Job, chosen specifically because Holly did not want a woman in his home who "would steal [Leo's] affections" from him (19). Holly describes himself as hideously ugly, even gorilla-like, and, like Cain, an outcast. His tie with Leo helps to counteract Holly's feelings of inadequacy, for Leo is beautiful, and his family line is "one of the most ancient" (10). When the adventure in Africa beckons and Leo determines to search out the legendary African queen Ayesha, Holly possessively declares that he would never let Leo go without him: "Leo was all the world to me—brother, child, and friend—and until he wearied of me, where he went there I should go too" (46). Ironically, the search for this extraordinary woman propels this story that begins in an aversion to women.

After passing through life-threatening challenges, Holly and Leo arrive at the remote African region ruled by Ayesha, known by her subjects as She-who-must-be-obeyed. Ayesha is a two thousand-year-old ravishingly beautiful and seductive virgin, in spite of her quasi-sexual encounter two millennia earlier with the male-gendered "pillar of fire" in the "womb of the earth." This combination of male and female sexual symbols is a recurring motif in Haggard's *She* saga, representative of the author's desire to blur male and female distinctions. In a late sequel to *She,* the novel *Wisdom's Daughter* (1923), Ayesha portrays her encounter with the pillar in sexual terms: "it seemed to take the shape of a mighty man" with "green eyes of emerald ... [and] blood-red, splendid arms that stretched themselves toward me as though to clasp me to that burning breast ... The Fire possessed me, I was the Fire's, and in a dread communion, the Fire was mine" (352). After this union, she possesses supernatural powers and Medusa-like qualities—a gaze that overwhelms her male spectators, and persistent snake-like imagery that conveys both her threatening and beguiling nature.

These alternately desirable and terrible characteristics are evident to Holly during their first encounter. Ayesha usually keeps herself veiled so as to not be wearied with the attentions of her admirers, but when it suits her purposes she unveils herself to men she wishes to bewitch and manipulate. She unveils before Holly with a "serpent-like grace," and he is captivated (155). But not long afterwards Ayesha sees a signet ring on Holly's hand that provokes a distressing memory, and she suddenly becomes enraged: "The lovely face grew rigid, and the gracious willowy form seemed to erect itself. 'Man!' she half whispered, half hissed, throwing back her head like a snake about to strike" (156). Ayesha's erection turns her into a phallic woman who unmans Holly who falls to the ground before her babbling in terror. When he summons the courage to look into her eyes, he is "bewildered and half-blinded" by a current that passes between them. He observes that her face bore the stamp of "unutterable experience, and of deep acquaintance with grief and passion," and concludes for no definitive reason that her "awful loveliness and purity was *evil*" (155). Sandra Gilbert and Susan Gubar state that *She* addresses "the problem of female power" (7), specifically because, like a variety of other vexing Victorian heroines, Moneta, Morgan La Faye, Cleopatra, Lilith, her "mystical powers deprive man of *his* powers" (8). Such is the nature of the male dominated social order that empowers men to establish the terms of the encounter so as to delimit and condemn powerful women.

Paradoxically, although Ayesha has an emasculating effect upon both Holly and Leo, both men are irresistibly drawn to her. As Holly observes, "we could no more have left her than a moth can leave the light that destroys it" (241). Holly experiences in her presence a release from his inhibitions, as well as an enlarged awareness of his sexual desires that are apparently actuated through a dominant, phallic woman. Regina Barreca develops the thesis that Ayesha is most remarkable and alluring, both for her male author and her largely male audience, because of her capacity to represent all that "men long for, project onto, desire, and are appalled by in women" (vii). Ayesha bears this overwhelming burden and is treated in an alternately rapturous and punishing way as a result. As Barreca notes, through Ayesha Holly taps into "aspects of his personality that he had repressed for most of his adult life," such as "the importance of his earlier unhappy relationships with women," and "his fierce, if not actually homoerotic, attachment to Leo and subsequent fear of being in a sexual rivalry with him" (xiii). However, the erotic possibilities of the triangular relationships that quickly develop between these three central characters are augmented by the queer nature of each of the individuals. First, Ayesha's phallic capacity infuses the interaction with a polymorphous sexual dynamic. Second, in view of Eve Kosofsky Sedgwick's theory about male homosocial desire and the instrumentality of the woman in both legitimating and advancing that desire, Holly's desire for Ayesha enhances his bond with Leo (*Between* Men 50). In fact, since Holly knows that Leo is Ayesha's destined mate, his sexual attraction for her may indirectly express his attraction for Leo. When Leo first embraces Ayesha, Holly observes that he was rent with "mad and furious jealousy," and "could have flown at him" (229). Judith Butler theorizes that when a man loves a woman who, in turn, is loving another man, the rage the first man feels might just as well be "compounded by an inability to avow same-sex desire" (112). Therefore, Holly's jealousy as he imagines Ayesha and Leo together sexually could be not only about his desire for her, but his sublimated desire for him. Butler notes that the desire passes along the circuit of all the actors in the scene, "thus confounding the identificatory positions" of each, that, in fact, profoundly and inescapably "heterosexuality and homosexuality are defined through one another" (112). Moreover, as Holly subsequently puts his suit for Ayesha aside, removing any impediment to Leo's bond with her, he simultaneously enables his circuitous homosexual expression for Leo that, as we will see, arises through Holly's desire for and identification with Ayesha. This does not defuse the intensity of Holly's erotic desire for Ayesha, but reveals the complex, multivalent ways that desire can be experienced, for "apparently heterosexual persons and object choices are strongly marked by same-sex influences and desires, and vice versa" (Butler 117). Herein lies the essence of the queer experience, which addresses "such moments of productive undecidability" (Butler 114). Male, female; heterosexual, homosexual: queer sexuality rejects the divisiveness of these categories, and consequently queer desire yields paradoxical and provocative results.

The denouement of the novel reveals more clearly the continuum between heterosexual and homosexual desire that Haggard explores through the triangular relationship of his three main characters. Ayesha takes Holly and Leo on a journey to visit the womb of the earth so that Leo, preparatory to their marriage, can likewise bathe in the pillar of fire and receive the boon of enhanced beauty, life, and knowledge that She has possessed for two thousand years. The topography they traverse to arrive at the womb is significant. They cross over a "mighty chasm ... jagged, torn, and splintered ... by some awful convulsion of Nature, as though it had been cleft by stroke upon stroke of the lightning" (271). This chasm, as Steibel likewise notes, symbolizes sexual difference. On one side of the chasm is a huge spur of rock that juts out into the void of the chasm, while on the other side of the chasm, the feminized side, is a flat rocking stone fronting the entrance to the "womb of the earth." The placement and description of this rocking stone suggests the clitoris[2]: "Within eleven or twelve feet of the tip of the tongue-like rock whereon we stood ... rested a tremendous flat ... rocking stone, accurately balanced upon the edge of the cone or miniature crater" (274). The tongue-like phallic rock pointing to the clitoris-like rocking stone is itself a powerful representation of heterosexual desire, whereas the womb that contains the phallic pillar of fire combines traditionally male and female sexual characteristics. As Holly, Leo and Ayesha stand within the chasm symbolic of sexual difference, Ayesha undergoes a transfiguration. While poised upon the phallic spur, the wind buffeting around her, a beam from the setting sun lights upon her, "illumining Ayesha's lovely form with an unearthly splendour" (273). This illumination of Ayesha as she stands on the spur jutting out into the chasm symbolizes her instrumentality in the expression of Haggard's sexual fantasies.

Ayesha and the Englishmen traverse the chasm by extending a plank "so that one end of it rested on the rocking stone, the other remaining on the extremity of the trembling spur," then slide down the surface of the rocking stone and arrive at the tunnel conducting to the womb. The entrance into the womb suggests a determination to merge with the maternal figure that is problematic, particularly within a patriarchal culture that pressures men to eschew feminine identifications. The entering of the womb can also be read as an act of penetration, but one that engulfs the penetrator and therefore threatens like the vagina dentata. Because Haggard, as a child, was very close to his mother, the Englishmen's encounter with Ayesha in the "womb of the earth" also suggests the child's desire for symbiotic union with the mother, and yet the experience is a threatening one. Steibel notes that this is the case in all of the womb enclosures that enter into Haggard's stories (76).

Holly, Leo, and Ayesha advance along the passageway and arrive at a spacious, beautiful cavern suffused with a rosy glow as they become "sensible of a wild and splendid exhilaration" (288). This area takes on erotic significance as Ayesha undresses and prepares to join with the pillar of fire. Before she does so, however, she clasps Leo around the neck and kisses him on the forehead, and Holly observes: "It was like a mother's kiss" (291). This action confirms Ayesha in her role of the maternal figure as erotic object. She then steps into the path of the flame. As the novel's two most significant topographical symbols of feminine and masculine potency commingle, Holly describes Ayesha as "the very Spirit of the Flame," and exclaims upon her ethereal beauty, observing, "Even now my heart faints before the recollection of it" (292). Ayesha is at this point a complex array of symbols: the quintessential mother figure, an overwhelmingly seductive sexual object, and a powerfully phallic female. Haggard's complex sexual desire requires her to perform this mutating function within his fantasy as he moves through the transitions in his subjectivity to the point of identification with the maternal figure, so as to then consummate the fantasized sexual act. This climactic scene represents the moment Holly identifies with the maternal figure, and from this position of psychic union his relationship with Leo becomes more manifestly sexual, particularly following Ayesha's subsequent startling demise. Despite her powers, Ayesha was unaware that a second bathing in the "pillar of fire" is fatal. She comes to an ignominious end as in a matter of minutes the weight of her two thousand years falls upon her. She shrivels up and falls to the ground shrieking in an agony of death. Holly's description of the change Ayesha undergoes is noteworthy, for he uses the same adjectives to describe her that had also been used to describe him, "hideous," and like a "baboon."[3] As Ayesha assumes Holly's characteristics, Holly takes her place.

The events following Ayesha's demise are rife with sexual overtones. The two men, devastated by Ayesha's death, make their way back to the chasm. But the plank that had conducted them from the tip of the spur to the rocking stone has fallen within the chasm, so they are trapped on the feminized side. They decide they must attempt the leap to the spur. Before they do, however, Holly turns to Leo and kisses him on the forehead, just as Ayesha had. As the men leap to the spur, the force of their jump causes the rocking stone to topple inside the crater, "for ever sealing the passage that leads to the Place of Life" (305). In the earlier movement from the spur to the rocking stone, there is a bridging of sexual characteristics. But this later movement back to the spur castrates the female topography. The previous need for female intervention is now dramatically reconfigured. The fantasized consummation occurs following the two men's treacherous leap, as they lie for half an hour upon the spur which "sprang out like a spike from a wall ... panting side by side, trembling like leaves, with the cold perspiration of terror pouring from [their] skins" (306). They have exchanged the pillar within the womb for the phallic spur located on the male topography. Furthermore, subsequently they traverse a tunnel opening off of the base of the spur suggesting anal intercourse.[4] However, the exhausting experience of groping along this passage is one of "despair" (307).

The "terror" and "despair" of the sexual experience rest in the perilous nature of the queer sexuality Haggard expresses in *She*. Haggard's identity combined male and female, heterosexual and homosexual characteristics. The bridging of the male and female topography in *She* signifies this attempt at reconciliation of the two. The imaginative intensity of Haggard's creation of Ayesha expresses the fecundity of the queer sexual experience, as well as his need to challenge his culture's sexual programming. Lauren Berlant and Michael Warner note that intimacy in queer culture is particularly powerful because it is more imaginative and daring,

"Not confined within the narrow limits of institutionalized sexuality ... neither hetero nor homo, nor sutured to any axis of social legitimation" (561, 565). However, in *She,* the punishing end to Ayesha and the castration of the female topography are symptomatic of Haggard's conflicting need to force divisions through eschewing psychosexual tendencies that problematize his place in his male dominated culture. Speaking with the voice of the patriarchy, Holly declares after She's death, "Thus she opposed herself against the eternal Law and ... by it was swept back to nothingness — swept back with shame and hideous mockery!" (295). In spite of his fascination, love, and attraction for the unbridled Ayesha, he nevertheless feels compelled to condemn her brazen and transgressive presence.

And yet, the male protagonists are emotionally devastated by Ayesha's sudden and gruesome death, indicating an empathic engagement with her. Leo ages twenty years at the sight of her destruction, and his golden hair turns white. Holly has stamped upon his face ever after "a wild look where with a startled person wakes from deep sleep" (308). Holly's identification with Ayesha is, therefore, not one of mastery, but one that increases his vulnerability. Fuss observes that the process of identification "is the detour through the other that defines a self" so as to potentially create mutually vulnerable and fertile alliances rather than oppressive bonds (387). Such vulnerability is among the foundational experiences of queer identity, for the queer person feels alienated from institutionalized sexuality that strips sexual expression of its "fragile and ephemeral" qualities (Berlant and Warner 561). Haggard's society rigidly maintained the heteronormative culture, as it did such other oppressive institutions as imperialism, racism, and sexism. According to Berlant and Warner, "oppressions and sublimations around sex and sexuality" correspond with other systems of violence and exploitation that form the "national culture" (347). The various mechanisms for oppression work synergistically to safeguard the national mission, which may account for Haggard's imperial fervor.

The dualism of Haggard's identity gradually became untenable as heteronormative societal pressures eroded the imaginative energy of his fantasy life and thoroughly indoctrinated him in the socially controlling emotions of sin and shame. His autobiography concluded upon some telling reflections about sin, which he defined as going against society's rules: "If we go against the rules of the game as they are laid down for us by the creed we serve in that part of the world in which we have been born, even when those rules seem unnatural to us, we err, and what is more we injure others, which is surely the essence of sin" (*Days,* II, 255). Haggard resignedly bowed before his society's rigid ideas of sexual expression, even though those ideas "seem unnatural." He wrote further that one must choose to serve God rather than "Nature," for if Nature, designated "She," prevails, one is overwhelmed by remorse:

> See where She stands with longing arms and lips that murmur love....
> "Touch not ..." answers the cold stern Law.
> Often enough it is Nature that prevails and, having eaten of the apple that She, our Mother, gives us ... we see and bewail our wickedness [256].

Haggard came to repudiate the fruit that She holds out to him — in the form of sexual expressions in violation of his society's rigid standards. Haggard's later novel, *Wisdom's Daughter*, published two years before his death, makes a direct tie between Ayesha and the Nature that leads one to sin. When Haggard composed *She* thirty-six years earlier, he was more susceptible to these natural temptations. *She* presents Ayesha more as a figure of wish fulfillment for Haggard's sexual fantasies, whereas *Wisdom's Daughter* represents Haggard's eventual submission to his society's relentless advocacy of appropriate sexual conduct that severely curtails the desires of the flesh, as Haggard fervently explained to Rudyard Kipling: "In that book is my philosophy ... the Eternal War between the Flesh and the Spirit, the Eternal loneliness and Search for Unity" (qtd. in Ellis 1). *Wisdom's Daughter* is his mea culpa response to the sexual desires he unleashed in *She*.

Sedgwick observes that a "susceptibility to shame" arises from "the terrifying powerlessness of gender-dissonant or otherwise stigmatized childhood," and notes that "far from being capable of being detached from the childhood scene of shame, it cleaves to that scene as a near-inexhaustible source of transformational energy" ("Queer Performativity" 4). Haggard's identification with his queer childhood self is a manifestation of his shame, as well as a source of sustaining and fanciful release from the severely constraining experience of adulthood. Through *She* Haggard expresses his escapist fascination for outered states, symptomatic, I believe, of his queer identity that he did not feel free to realize. During one bizarre scene of revelry in Ayesha's realm, the night is illuminated by flaming torches of the embalmed dead set ablaze by the native revelers. Holly notes that the embalming fluid "rendered them so inflammable that the flames would literally spout out of the ears and mouth in tongues of fire a foot or more in length" (218). This macabre scene symbolizes both a violent sexualization of bodily orifices and a frenzied desire to speak what cannot be articulated, because the language is too strange, or the ears cannot hear. It foreshadows the traumatic demise of Ayesha so significant for Haggard because She is an eroticized, maternal figure instrumental in the expression of his most intimate, distinctive childhood self. Her destruction represents his shame, and his attempts at conformity that involved a denial of his essential nature, alive in childhood, undergoing repression in adulthood — except through a fantasy life that attempts to commemorate this loss. Tragically, Haggard's shame would come to punitively overwhelm his fantasy life and eventually stilt his fiction.

## *Notes*

1. Biographers speculate that, as a young man living in Africa, Haggard may have had an affair with a native woman (Higgins 35), and even fathered a child who died in infancy (Steibel 24). Sexual relationships between the white adventurer and a native woman occur frequently in Haggard's African romances. In *She*, Leo becomes sexually involved with the native woman, Ustane.
2. Steibel also refers to this "clitoral" stone (87).
3. Haggard's fiction makes frequent, curious reference to baboons in the context of sexual license. In *Allan's Wife* (1889) the term indicates same-sex relationships. Hendrika, the baboon-woman, competes with Allan Quatermain for the love of Stella, and tells him that women love women better than men love women. Quatermain agrees that same-sex desire can be stronger (107–8). Moreover, the book is dedicated to Haggard's very close friend, Arthur Cochrane, with whom he lived for six months in Africa, and refers to their "long past romance," and Cochrane's experience "with the baboons," suggesting that Haggard's relationship with Cochrane may have been sexual.
4. Haggard's *King Solomon's Mines* also describes an experience involving an anal cavity, as noted by Steibel: "The escape route from the caves is an anal back passage- predictably in 'the bowels of the mountain'" (84).

## *Works Cited*

Barreca, Regina. Introduction to Rider Haggard, *She*. New York: Signet Classics, 1994.
Berlant, Lauren, and Michael Warner. "Guest Column: What Does Queer Theory Teach Us About X?" *PMLA* 110, (1995): 343–49.
\_\_\_\_, and \_\_\_\_. "Sex in Public." *Critical Inquiry* 24 (1998): 547–66.
Butler, Judith. "Capacity." In *Regarding Sedgwick: Essays on Queer Culture and Critical Theory*. Ed. Stephen Barber and David Clark. London and New York: Routledge, 2002. 109–19.
Fuss, Diana. "Look Who's Talking, or If Looks Could Kill." *Critical Inquiry* 22 (1996): 383–92.
Gilbert, Sandra, and Susan Gubar. *No Man's Land: The Place of the Woman Writer in the Twentieth Century*. Vol. 2, *Sexchanges*. New Haven and London: Yale University Press, 1989.

Haggard, Rider. "About Fiction." *Contemporary Review* 50 (1887): 172–180.
_____. *Days of My Life: An Autobiography*. London: Longmans and Green, 1926.
_____. *She*. New York: Signet Classic, 1994.
_____. *Wisdom's Daughter*. New York: Doubleday, 1923.
Halperin, David. *One Hundred Years of Homosexuality: and Other Essays on Greek Love*. New York: Routledge, 1990.
Higgins, D.S. *Rider Haggard: A Biography*. New York: Stein and Day, 1983.
Miller, Henry. *The Books in My Life*. London: P. Owens, 1952.
Sedgwick, Eve Kosofsky. *Between Men: English Literature and Male Homosocial Desire*. New York: Columbia University Press, 1985.
_____. "Queer Performativity: Henry James's *The Art of the Novel*." *GLQ* 1 (1993): 1–16.
Steibel, Lindy. *Imagining Africa: Landscape in H. Rider Haggard's African Romances*. West Port, Connecticut: Greenwood Press, 2001.
Stott, Rebecca. "The Dark Continent: Africa as Female Body in Haggard's African Fiction." *Feminist Review* 32 (1989): 68–89.

## PART III.
## THE INCOMMENSURABILITY OF SEX/GENDER/DESIRE

# 9 Strange Anatomy, Strange Sexuality
## *The Queer Body in Jeffrey Eugenides' Middlesex*

ZACHARY SIFUENTES

If feminist and queer scholars are right, that anatomy has produced a ritualistic cultural anxiety regarding sexuality, then perhaps there has been no anatomy stranger, and no corresponding anxiety more acute, than that of the hermaphrodite. The social life of such a body reifies the conjecture of "mimetic biologism,"[1] in which indeterminate anatomy spells out a corresponding uncertain social identity and, more importantly, an ambiguous sexuality. The material fact of the intersexed body, often inaccurately believed to be carrying the physiology of both man and woman, directly questions current definitions of sexuality in psychological, cultural, and legal terminology. *Heterosexual, homosexual, bisexual*— such identities expose their own limits for accommodation when it comes to intersexed people or intersexuals, especially when they refuse "corrective" surgery, or are medically "discovered" to be a sex different from the one assigned at birth. Whether in biological or performative ways, a hermaphrodite's sexual practice jeopardizes dominant and radical visions of sexuality alike, in which the sustained ambiguity of the body unseats the very concept of sexual orientation, regardless if it is based on gender, sex, or some complex of the two. Still, amid such uncertainty, one consistent extrapolation, whether from medical, legal, or literary narratives by and about intersexuals, grounds itself squarely on the notion that mimetic biologism, derived from cultural apprehension over the grotesque body, is itself a grotesque practice that produces equally mishappen definitions of that body's sexuality. As Alice Domurat Dregger puts it: "strange anatomy, strange sexuality" (126–127).

Such is the case for Calliope Stephanides, the narrator of Jeffrey Eugenides' *Middlesex*, who was born a girl, reached puberty as a boy, and now, as an adult man on the verge of consummating his first serious relationship with a woman, feels "another birth coming on" (3). The story of these beginnings, delicately and poetically told through the intersecting histories of recessive genes, racial wars, and cultural exile, places a near singular scrutiny on Callie's, and later Cal's, sexual orientation. As Callie, the young daughter of a Greek orthodox family, she discovers her proclivity for other girls, and as Cal, running from a medical industry that wants to cut him up, he reaffirms his sexual philogyny. In so doing, Cal avails himself to what can only be called a very queer sexuality — one decidedly *hetero* in outward appearance but evidently strange behind the closed door and in the dimmed lights of the bedroom. In terms of his developing biological identity and evolving sexual orientation, the consequence of Cal's *bildungsroman* for contemporary discussions surrounding what Judith Butler called "The Compulsory Order of Sex/Gender/Desire" (*GT* 6) seems best enunciated by Calliope's physician, Dr. Luce: "It's a very rare condition.... Exceedingly rare. But in terms of research, its importance can't be overstated" (421).

Because the significance of Calliope's condition straddles both biological developments and social deployments of sex, gender, and sexuality, Dr. Luce's medical proclamation bears particular relevance to current work on gender and sexuality, one that enables the rather thorny and ironic marriage of *queer* and *heterosexuality*. Dr. Luce treats Calliope, after all, at his Sexual Disorders and Gender Identity Clinic, where the comforting bifurcation of nature and nurture was, in Callie's 1974 meeting with the doctor, then beginning to overlap in unsettling ways. As Suzanne L. Kessler has noted, "social constructivism" was regarded at that time as "an 'alternative' perspective" in gender formation (4), one that since has gone on to become an underlying principle in contemporary gender debates within academia and, to a large extent, popular culture as well. Indeed, in terms of research on identity and sexuality, the importance of *Middlesex*, even as a work of fiction, simply cannot be overstated. In reiterating and troubling scientific and cultural engagements with sex, gender, and desire, *Middlesex* purports to transcend what have become, according to Cal's informed narration, overdetermined theories of gender and sexuality. "My psychological makeup doesn't accord with the essentialism popular in the intersex movement," says Cal, declaring that "a strange new possibility is arising. Compromised, indefinite, sketchy, but not entirely obliterated: free will is making a comeback. Biology gives you a brain. Life turns it into a mind" (479).

Of course, *Middlesex*'s critique of the culturally validated logic of sex/gender/desire already had been articulated convincingly by Butler, who expended ample energy in *Gender Trouble* on the difficult identity of Herculine Barbin, perhaps the most famous hermaphrodite in academia thanks to Michel Foucault's introduction. By title alone, Butler's most recent enterprise, *Undoing Gender*, indicates that the logic of sex/gender/desire continues unabated some fourteen years after *Gender Trouble*. In other words, she is still issuing her critique — a reminder that "[a]lthough being a certain gender does not imply that one will desire a certain way, there is nevertheless a desire that is constitutive of gender itself and, as a result, no quick or easy way to separate the life of gender from the life of desire" (*UG* 1–2). In her view, this compulsory logic continues unmitigated because gender, as the fulcrum of this formula, has not been sufficiently troubled and identity not sufficiently subverted. For Butler, the body's "biological intractability" creates a necessary "solidarity of identity" (*GT* 6) among feminists, and in this sense feminism has problematized gender while shoring up "sex" as a biologically determined, "politically neutral" category, often without acknowledging that "sex itself is a gendered category" (*GT* 7). While the notion of "gender performance" has become vested in academic discourse, and has made significant inroads into popular parlance, the compulsory but false logic of sex remains largely intact. As Judith Halberstam has commented, the near "universal concurrence" with Butler's theories of gender fluidity has not met corresponding concurrence with the fluidity of sex: "very few people," says Halberstam, "[seem] to be noticing or thinking through the material effects of disassociating sex and gender" (2). These "material effects" potentially reassert that the body, as a physical locus of theory, defines the limits of contemporary notions of identity because these notions cannot fully accommodate anatomical phenomena — a point that Butler has conceded, writing that "[a]nything that might be said against" sexual difference only serves as an "oblique proof that it structures what we say" (*UG* 177).

Queer interrogations of hegemonic identity regulation have likewise sought to shore up the category of sex in the effort to consolidate identity, even if queer theory is, as Butler notes, "opposed to the unwanted legislation of identity" (*UG* 7). In the still fervent climate of identity politics, queer scholars continue to articulate ways in which sexualities implicate knowable anatomical differences; queer projects, in other words, deploy terms (like "gay" and "lesbian") that necessarily point to stable sexual identities in order to stay politically and ethically relevant. Such concerns over political and ethical relevancy nearly always point to what Annette Schlichter, in her framing of the "queer straight" individual, terms "the material realities of sexual minorities" (547). It is possible, in contemplating a queer theoretical project, to forgo or forget the bludgeoned body of Matthew Sheppard, but it is unconsciable to do so. This is not to suggest that queer studies must reiterate the body as a site for ethical scholarship to emerge, but scholars have issued calls for remembering that queer scholarship "could not exist without the identity politics of sexual minorities inside and outside the academy" (Schlichter 554). David Halperin's recent academic and pedagogical work, in this regard, has attempted to steer his scholarship and his students toward an "intimate engagement with the sensibilities of gay men," therefore forcing readers to "engage with queer culture" (343) in an effort to rescue queer theory from becoming utterly detached from the lived, material experiences of the gay body. Queer and feminist projects, in other words, aim at keeping discourse immediately tied to the culture of the body. Thus have both feminist and queer projects historically made necessary assumptions of the body based on a knowable, readily accessible, and stable category of sex — an invocation that should not only be expected but allowed, especially given the climate of cultural and legal hostility toward minorities.

This reification of the body through stable sexual identities has continued largely uncontested because, unlike gender, anatomical differences remain nearly invisible. Where the trouble with gender can express itself in socially — and therefore publicly — disruptive behaviors like crossdressing and metrosexuality, the possibility for biological indeterminacy stays cloaked under clothes, behind bedroom doors, and, since the advent of chromosomal and hormonal managements of sex and gender, even under microscopes. As Kessler has noted, "in the everyday world gender attributions are made without access to genital inspection" (90). In terms of anatomy, in other words, sexual difference easily remains hidden, while in terms of chromosomes and hormones, only medical technology and expert physicians can determine it (and thus make sexual difference "real"). Chromosomes and hormones, in other words, remain invisible to the "naked," untrained eye of popular culture; *out of sight* really remains *out of mind*. Although a fluid gender identity now seems culturally possible, an equally fluid biological identity can only be permitted as long as it remains a discreet invisibility — as a hormonal or chromosomal possibility that cannot be directly seen. The results of such tests, translated into bar graphs and other symbolic indicators, often retroactively explain some long held, unsettling, and nebulous pathology that something, in fact, just wasn't right. Because the invisibility of a fluid sexual identity persists, and test results can only indicate microscopic medical "facts," accepting a corresponding fluid biological continuum, in which no one is fully male or female, can only be envisioned metaphorically, produced symbolically, and understood allegorically. It can permit the rhetoric of the figurative, but not the figure itself.

This is where intersexuals usher in another possibility for disrupting the compulsory and still contemporary logic of sex/gender/desire: despite all efforts to the contrary, it is difficult to deny that Cal continually gestures past the fictional fact of his character and toward the material body and lived experiences of intersexuals themselves. He collapses feminist and queer discourse into the indeterminacy of his body, even if he decides to maintain a stable social identity as a man. And even as a man in an apparently straight relationship, Cal continually reasserts the queerness of his sexuality — not only in Dreger's "strange anatomy, strange sexuality" formulation, but in what Butler describes as the aspiration of queer theory to seek "a utopian life beyond gender" (*UG* 184). There is nothing Cal wants more than to move beyond the debate of gender, but he also seeks a life beyond the sexed body. He does this while keeping his natural body intact; oddly enough, what is natural for Cal is abnormal, and he therefore constantly reminds us of the material consequence of being queer. In a fictional narrative like *Middlesex*, one that seeks to expose the biological rampages and social survival of an intersexed body, Cal's body constantly threatens to eclipse the figurative, to put materiality in the place of the imaginary, and to push the book past the imperceptible lines of its own fiction and into an arena of ethical and political relevance.

This is to say that Cal, in deciding to maintain his natural body, confounds the discourses of sexuality from both queer and radically conservative groups alike. No matter how sexuality is defined, Calliope's decision to maintain an "uncorrected" body but change her gender exposes the degree to which sex and gender assumptions are embedded in sexuality as the fictional conditions for sexuality to emerge. Such assumptions are anchored firmly if neatly in historical and contemporary research from both medical and psychological points of view, evidence that Eugenides did his research in constructing Cal's narrative. Dreger, for instance, claims that sexuality in the medical community "constantly still make[s] reference to anatomy" (127). This genital culture, as it were, provides the setting for *Middlesex*, in which sexuality is confused so regularly and problematically with anatomy that it dictates nearly every turn in the book. In organizing Cal's narrative, this confusion also structures the book's fiction, and in so doing, the conflation of sexuality with anatomy also manages its own fiction, its own means of occulting and exposing its compulsion and construction. This becomes most apparent when Calliope runs away from a medical industry that seeks literally to cut her into a female form, and, in assuming a male identity, Cal inaugurates both a new narrative and a new tone. Calliope had fled largely because, as a teenager, she had had sexual relations with another girl, and in lying to her doctor about the orientation of her desire, Calliope feels his conclusion about her gender was based on her deliberate misinformation.

The real story, though, rests in Cal's narrative as a forty-one-year-old man now coming to terms with the social compulsion of sex/gender/desire. While working for the State Department in Germany, he initiates a relationship with Julie, an ex-patriot photographer, but he also enters a familiar cycle of drawing her close and then pushing her away as the stigma of his genitals exercises its control. In the upswing of such a cycle, though, he allows himself to approach Julie for a kiss:

> When the kiss was over she opened her eyes very wide. "I thought you were gay when we met," she said.
> "Must have been the suit."
> "My gay-dar went off completely." Julie was shaking her head. "I'm always suspicious, being the last stop."
> "The last what?"
> "Haven't you heard of that? Asian chicks are the last stop. If a guy's in the closet, he goes for an Asian because their bodies are more like boys'."
> "Your body's not like a boy's," I said [184].

Julie's initial instinct about Cal's sexual orientation simultaneously points to how off course and yet how close she is to figuring him out. There is something obviously queer about Cal, but Julie's experience has conditioned her to concentrate on the wrong part of the equation. Cal's gender and desire position him squarely within an apparent heteronormativity, but as his chiseled, masculinized body exemplifies, deceptions often come wrapped in appearances; their kiss, then, marks the initiation of an apparent heterosexuality queered on the basis of anatomy alone. The irony, of course, is that Julie, in being so close to identifying what is "strange" about him, also couldn't be more wrong: Cal, as well as Callie, never showed any real interest in men.

The supposition that creates nearly all the tension and drama of Cal's narrative — that anxieties surrounding sexual orientation determine the gender and sex of the body in an effort to conform it to heteronormative practice — reiterates historical research on the subject. Christina Matta, for instance, declares that it is no coincidence that the emergence of "homosexual" in the late nineteenth century met near simultaneous technological advances in "corrective" surgery for hermaphrodites, nor that there was an acute rise in the number of such surgeries once doctors pathologized non-normative desire. She attests that medical reports, at an implicit and rhetorical level, indicate that surgeons "tacitly agreed that surgery was a potential means of correcting sexual ambiguity while also preventing sexual depravity" (78), adding that "physicians had a moral obligation to correct their patients' bodies to forestall inevitable tendencies towards sexual deviance" (79). Apparently, the obsession with anatomy as a site of cultural anxiety was obvious. Ambiguous genitalia did not in turn create ambiguous medical standards; on that the medical industry was clear.

What remain unclear, however, are the statistics of intersexed births. The official line at the Intersex Society of North America, an organization founded in 1993 "to end shame, secrecy, and unwanted genital surgeries" (ISNA), stipulates that statistics vary widely based on how intersexuality is defined (an argument Dreger herself has advanced). A collective research effort by scientists in Brown University's Department of Molecular and Cell Biology and Biochemistry concluded that "the frequency of deviation from the ideal male or female," including chromosomal anomalies, idiopathic occurrence, and phenotypical ambiguity, "may be as high as 2% of live births" (Blackless 151). These statistics derive from a survey of the medical literature since 1955, contextualizing the medical climate and frequency of intersexuality for Cal's fictional world — a postmodern world over which the medical and cultural attitudes of the nineteenth century have prevailed. This is to say that nineteenth-century anxieties with the emerging pathology of sexual deviance continued unabated, bridging a society then beginning its modernity to a society fully vested in the aftermath of modernity itself.

In Cal's narrative, these late nineteenth century medical standards continue to thrive at a more pervasive and holistic cultural level, in which moral suppositions concerning hermaphrodites and their latent sexuality have acquired scientific "factuality." *Middlesex*, in this sense, is a novel set in part in the aftermath of the breakdown of objective scientific practice, in which morality, cultural norms, and pervasive anxiety over anatomical indeterminacy and sexuality had shaped medical standards for nearly a century. As far as intersexuals are concerned, doctors have deployed science

## 152   III. The Incommensurability of Sex/Gender/Desire

for cultural rather than medical goals. "[I]nfant genital surgery," remarks Anne Fausto-Sterling, "is cosmetic surgery performed to achieve a social result — reshaping a sexually ambiguous body so that it conforms to our two-sex system" (80). *Middlesex*'s implicit critique of "moral" surgeries under the guise of medical necessity is encapsulated by a parallel construction: Julie's comment that Asians constitute the "last stop" for closeted gay men because Asian bodies approximate the bodies of boys. The idea that race could ever gender and sex an individual in any way other than in metaphorically ludicrous terminology is a meta-narrative meant to comment on the parallel impossibility for sexuality to make similar claims on the body's sexual identity. This is to say that one problem with defining sexuality, and therefore a possible non-normative or queer heterosexuality, rests in the discordant but persistent logic that the body's desire can contribute in any meaningful way to its sociology and biology. The same holds in the reverse: anatomy simply has no viable bearing, except as a purely cultural construction, on that body's gender or sexuality.

Asserting that sexuality is confused regularly and problematically with anatomy throughout *Middlesex* is to say that Cal, in narrating his story, seeks to undo the stigma this confusion has created for him without forgoing the various identities he has assumed. Those male, straight identities, however personally stable for him, create tensions within a larger "heterosexual matrix" (Butler, *GT* 5) while allowing supposedly normative sexual practices to continue their masquerade of hegemony. Knowing full well that the problem with his body rests squarely on society and its anxiety regarding sexual desire, Cal nevertheless seeks to become comfortable within a gender not entirely his own. In other words, it might have been easier for Cal, upon recognizing the compulsory but false logic of sex/gender/desire, to return to the feminine mannerisms and dress he had already mastered as a child and as an adolescent, but that would do little to help him become a woman, on the one hand, or a lesbian, on the other. Such identities have their own independent learning curves, and at forty-one, even with a woman willing to accept the anomaly of his anatomy, it is an education that simply no longer matters to Cal. As he quips to Julie, "I might be your last stop, too" (514).

This is not to suggest that Cal's sexuality becomes queer only when he becomes comfortable with his identity as an intersexed, straight man; there are a host of earlier sexual experiences that open up ways for articulating how sexuality for Cal was queer even before becoming Cal, and, by extrapolation, for articulating ways in which sexuality is itself already queer, regardless of its various (and variously grotesque) prefixes. He reflects throughout *Middlesex*, for instance, that his interest in women began early, when he was still a girl going by the name of Callie. Her experiences at an all girls' school, for instance, reveal that its exclusive sociology of women allowed crushes and even ritualized an "intimate atmosphere" among them, even if "the ethos of the school remained militantly heterosexual" (327) — in other words, the school neatly reiterates a gendered inversion of Eve Kosofsky Sedgwick's prescription of "homosocial desire" among men (1). Callie's already "troubled" sexuality (she had an earlier tryst with a neighborhood girlfriend) cannot easily conform to this kind of ethos, however, and she ultimately crosses the invisible yet firmly imposed line separating being with girls and being *with* them.

The girl she falls for is named only "the Object," a so-identified anachronism from Luis Buñuel's *That Obscure Object of Desire* meant to revisit Cal's lingering nostalgia for her and to shore up his desire "to protect her identity" (325). Their teenage courtship is long and unacknowledged, and when they finally consummate their attraction, it is done under the guise of unconscious activity in their sleep. "Over the course of ten minutes," Callie slides "nearer and nearer" to the Object's seemingly sleeping body. Then another long pause, some more nudging, a finger hooking into her underwear. "Just then," Cal remembers, "the Object lifted her hips, very slightly, to make it easier for me. This was her only contribution" (384). In other words, despite being outwardly lesbian and therefore apparently "queer," their "unconscious" activity assumes the very normal postures and conditions of many incursions into teenage sexuality: it is motivated largely by nervous excitement, incremental escalation, and the implicit promise not to discuss what happened.

This consummation, however, is preceded by another sexual experience, one that simultaneously occults and exposes its own queer context. Vacationing at the country home of the Object's parents, Callie and her friend, accompanied by the Object's brother Jerome and his friend Rex, explore an old shack in the woods. Marijuana and alcohol make several rounds, and before Callie knows it, the narrative has the couples separated and intimate, heteronormatively speaking, but still close to one another. The scene physically encapsulates Butler's assertion that gender performance "is a practice of improvisation within a scene of constraint" and that "one does not 'do' one's gender alone" but always "with or for another" (*UG* 1). The incursions in the cabin, in other words, contextually assert Calliope's identity as unambiguously female, even if their collective exploration into sexuality begins to take a very strange turn:

## III. The Incommensurability of Sex/Gender/Desire

> High for the first time, drunk for the first time, I felt myself dissolving, turning to vapor. Like the incense at church my soul rose toward the dome of my skull — and then broke through. I drifted over the plank floor. I floated above the little camp stove. Passing by the bourbon bottles, I hover over the other cot, looking down at the Object. And then, because I suddenly knew that I could, I slipped into the body of Rex Reese. I entered him like a god so that it was me, and not Rex, who kissed her [374].

Calliope's dissolution in the cabin prefigures her later dissolution of gender, and her desire to be with the Object transposes her into the body of Rex Reese so that she can take on the figure of being the man while allowing another man to explore her own body. Her identification with Rex, and her later decision to run away and become a male-identified intersexual, is due to circumstance rather than an internal, "natural" sense of gender as a differentiated category of identity. That is, Calliope bases her decision largely on happenstance — a default, heteronormative coincidence. Rex simply "happens" to be in the position she coveted as much as the Object simply "happens" to be complying with heteronormative practice. Her desire to become a man later in the narrative, then, reveals itself to be neatly convenient, but it also exposes itself as a misinformed, compulsory participation in the logic of sex/gender/desire. She specifically identifies first becoming the body of Rex Reese and then kissing the Object, and this differentiation creates multiple possibilities for pleasure that in turn produces corresponding possibilities for chiasmus: not only does desire cross from one body to another, but gender and anatomy transpose themselves across the bodies of the four teenagers as well. Calliope's dance from one sexual partner to another, as well as her assumption of the male role and the male anatomy, differentiates the categories of sex, gender and sexual orientation while simultaneously conflating them.

Calliope, meanwhile, is pushed further sexually with Jerome, a realization brought suddenly home by the advent of intense pain, one that reminds her of her feminized body: "It spread up my belly all the way to my nipples. I gasped; I opened my eyes; I looked up and saw Jerome looking down at me" (376). The ability of pain to straighten out the queer logic of the cabin becomes an irony: it may pull Calliope back into her body, but it is also the moment in which she suddenly becomes aware "for the first time ... that I wasn't a girl but something in between" (376). Jerome had penetrated the intersexual Calliope, whose hypospadias allowed them to simulate heterosexual sex not through a vagina but through the small opening of what is, in fact, her male urethra. As Dreger notes, "[s]ome hermaphrodites' anatomy allows for relations resembling vaginal intercourse, so that, as far as the partners were concerned, nothing about their relationship was bothersome" (120). But it is also, as far as a critical reading is concerned, decidedly *queer*.

Calliope's sudden awareness of her anomalous anatomy is accompanied by an understandable anxiety that Jerome knew as well, a conclusion Calliope reaches because of "the shocked expression on Jerome's face" (376). This shocked expression, however, is mistaken for what it really was: the expression of orgasm. Thus what appears, by all accounts, to be an alienating experience for Calliope is lost on Jerome. Inside the dilapidated cabin, under the dark night, and in the midst of the woods, Jerome has no idea just how "unnaturally" he engaged his desires; he has no idea just how queer his experience really was. This is to say that Eugenides sets these sexual encounters, in both real and symbolic ways, within a naturalized context. The rundown cabin, as a cultural and culturally neglected construction, indicates that the nature of the woods is, nevertheless, merely a fictional setting in a larger work of fiction, and the hypospadic sex, as a queer act, suggests that sexuality is, however defined, already queer. Eugenides quickly replicates this predicament when Jerome discovers Calliope and the Object caressing one another on a hammock. "Most guys wouldn't be so happy to find out that they'd been two-timed by a lesbian with their sister," Jerome mockingly asserts (392). What is lost on Jerome, even upon catching them, is that their collective experience only days earlier in the woods, in which brother and sister had sex in each other's company, was already queer, already abnormal, already taboo. In this way, Jerome and the Object had approximated incest literally in spirit, in which Calliope's transposition linked brother and sister in chiasmic fashion.

Jerome's discovery of Calliope's sexual orientation immediately prefigures the medical discovery of her body, a chronology in the book that suggests the degree to which the crisis over sexuality culturally determines (and is determined by) the crisis over anatomy. Calliope fights Jerome, spits on him, and then runs away from the hammock, through the woods, and into a tractor. She lays unconscious on the ground, bleeding, as Jerome and his sister call an ambulance that transports her to an emergency room where a doctor unveils the strange physiology of her genitals. This odd but strictly chronological circumstance of discovery is, itself, decidedly strange: it occurs at the climax of a book that relentlessly relies on a decidedly post-modern conception of time, in which Cal interlaces 250 years of familial, cultural, and chromosomal history with his present crisis with Julie. That is, a strict chronology surrounds the climax of a book that favors a post-modern present, in which Cal shuffles the past, present and future into a conglomerate story. In terms of the craft of fiction, Eugenides highlights chronology only at the moment when it most matters: at the book's climax. The development of the narrative, in other words, rarely follows a chronology that begins in the past and proceeds to the present, but the book maintains a fiction of order — the story of "a single gene through time" (4) — by subverting its own post-modern tendencies.

Conflating these various issues — time, form, anatomy — is one way to understand Cal's alienation within a modern society governed by moral science, fictional facts, and social surgery. His decision to maintain an "uncorrected" body while choosing a gender reflects, historically speaking, a decidedly pre-modern approach to the problem of hermaphrodites, in which they were sanctioned to choose, as adults, their preferred gender. As Foucault notes in his "Abnormal" lectures at the Collège de France, during the seventeenth century, "hermaphrodites were asked to choose their sex, their dominant sex, and to conduct themselves accordingly, especially by wearing the appropriate clothes. They were subject to criminal law and could be convicted for sodomy only if they made use of their additional sex" (67). Such a choice, then, came tightly wrapped in regulations that then determined the orientation of their desire in order to uphold the hegemony of heterosexuality. Still, the differences between pre- and post-surgical advancement in the arena of genital "correction" could not be starker: choice, such as the one exercised by Cal, was once an acceptable solution to the strange possibilities of nature, but the possibility for choosing has since capitulated to the culture of cosmetics and surgery. And while one of the themes of *Middlesex* may be the fiction of science, a close cousin would also be the fiction of normal sexual practices and normal genitalia. For Cal, who describes the penis as "the feed bag, the dry tuber, the snail that had lost its shell" (452), there is no sexuality and no anatomy that is not already strange. His decision to forgo surgery highlights the difficulty of classifying sexuality according to pat and convenient prefixes, because his ambiguous genitalia forces the acknowledgement that sexuality continues to refer to specific and knowable anatomies. As Butler has asked, "[i]f we cannot refer unambiguously to gender in such cases, do we have the point of reference for making claims about sexuality?" (*UG* 142). In the case of Cal and in the material fact of intersexuality itself, however rare and however remedied by social surgery, making knowable, stable claims about sexuality is not so much impossible as it is irrelevant. An identity as suggested by *queer heterosexuality* may be the only available means to capture rhetorically the difficult paradox of his body.

## Notes

1. Maureen Quilligan uses this phrase to describe the utter strangeness of gendered rhyme in the English language, in which a woman's supposedly soft and weak nature gets rhetorically inflected in the softness and weakness of feminine rhyme. Gendered rhyme for Quilligan "seems motivated by the most direct appeal to the physical differences between male and female bodies," and therefore "seems immediately grounded on a mimetic biologism that is innocent of larger, social constructions" (311).

## Works Cited

Blackless, Melanie, et al. "How Sexually Dimorphic Are We? Review and Synthesis." *American Journal of Human Biology* 12 (2000): 151–166.
Butler, Judith. *Gender Trouble: Feminism and the Subversion of Identity.* New York: Routledge, 1990.
———. *Undoing Gender.* New York: Routledge, 2004.
Dreger, Alice Domurat. *Hermaphrodites and the Medical Invention of Sex.* Cambridge, MA: Harvard University Press, 1998.
Eugenides, Jeffrey. *Middlesex.* New York: Picador; Farrar, Straus and Giroux, 2002.
Fausto-Sterling, Anne. *Sexing the Body: Gender Politics and the Construction of Sexuality.* New York: Basic Books, 2000.
Foucault, Michel. *Abnormal: Lectures at the Collège de France, 1974–1975.* New York: Picador, 1999.
Halberstam, Judith. "Masculinity without Men." Interview. *Genders* 29 (1999). http://genders.org/g29/g29_hulberstam.html [July 25, 2005]
Halperin, David M. "The Normalization of Queer Theory." *Journal of Homosexuality* 45 (2003): 339–343.
Intersex Society of North America. *Mission Statement.* http://www.isna.org/node/ 728 [September 5, 2005]
Kessler, S.J. *Lessons from the Intersexed.* New Brunswick, NJ: Rutgers University Press, 1998.
Matta, Christina. "Ambiguous Bodies and Deviant Sexualities: Hermaphrodites, Homosexuality, and Surgery in the United States, 1850–1904." *Perspectives in Biology and Medicine* 48 (2005): 74–83.
Quilligan, Maureen. "Feminine Endings: The Sexual Politics of Sidney's and Spenser's Rhyming." In *The Renaissance Englishwoman in Print: Counterbalancing the Canon.* Ed. Anne M. Haselkorn and Betty S. Travitsky. Amherst, MA: The University of Massachusetts Press, 1990: 311–326.
Schlichter, Annette. "Queer at Last? Straight Intellectuals and the Desire for Transgression." *GLQ* 10 (2004): 543–564.
Sedgwick, Eve Kosofsky. *Between Men: English Literature and Male Homosocial Desire.* New York: Columbia University Press, 1985.

# 10 Freudian Foreplay
## *Lesbian Failure and Freud's Desire in "The Psychogenesis of a Case of Homosexuality in a Woman"*

ASHLEY T. SHELDEN

Of all the characters in modern literature, the one least recognizable *as* a character may well be the queerest of all. This figure is none other than the analyst in psychoanalysis, but more specifically, Sigmund Freud-as-analyst. And in "The Psychogenesis of a Case of Homosexuality in a Woman" (1920), this figure makes decidedly clear that the structure of the analyst's desire is glaringly *queer*. More than a few queer and feminist critics have been interested in this case history because of its explicit inquiry into feminine sexuality and gender. After all, this piece — Freud's most sustained engagement with the question of female homosexuality since *Dora: An Analysis of a Case of Hysteria* (1905) — foregrounds the lesbian desire that Freud's prior work simply relegates to a footnote late in the text. But what garners by far the most critical interest in the "Case of Homosexuality in a Woman," almost without exception, is Freud's failure: to inspire positive transference, to follow through with the analysis, to achieve his aim to convert "one variety of the genital organization into the other," and crucially, to provide a clear psychoanalytic understanding of lesbian desire ("Psychogenesis" 150,151). What few critics *do* notice, however, is the way in which such failures implicate Freud in the girl's queer, or perverse, sexuality. Freud's famously troubled relationship to his homosexual analysands becomes most troubled, and most compelling, where Freud's own desire *becomes* the desire he cannot theorize; where Freud, in other words, enacts the desire *of*, rather than the desire for, the lesbian.

Since Freud cannot assimilate female homosexuality into the logic of psychoanalysis, most critics suggest that this study bespeaks a certain resistance — desiring, political, and ethical — which belongs specifically to the lesbian subject. Such critical interventions make visible a gap within the epistemological scope of psychoanalysis, so that even as Freud attempts to take account, and develop a theory, of female homosexual desire, his Oedipal model cannot make such desire legible as something other than a pathology.[1] However, homosexuality in women, as Freud represents it, does not seem too recalcitrant to, or too distant from, psychoanalysis so that the former resists and renders futile the epistemological project of the latter. Rather, Freud's figuration of the lesbian actually appears to be too close to psychoanalysis, too structurally similar for comfort. Indeed, the fantasmatic logics through which psychoanalysis and lesbian sexuality establish their relation to each other have everything to do with the *discomfort of similarity and proximity*. Just as Freud's work on female homosexuality, and sexuality in general, encounters his inability satisfactorily to conclude his analyses,[2] so too does Freud's representation of lesbian desire in the "Psychogenesis" fail finally to satisfy. Such desire enacts the trajectory of Freud's work itself, posing the female homosexual as a figure for, rather than simply an obstacle to, the analyst's enterprise. And Freud's representation of the homosexual girl is at all points bound up with the desire of psychoanalysis, which turns out not to aim towards a totalizing theory of sexuality, but aims always to miss this aim. It aims, that is, to fail.

Certain critics ground arguments for the homosexual girl's counter-hegemonic resistance on what Diana Fuss calls Freud's "often incoherent writings on female homosexuality" (Fuss 66). John H. Gagnon, for instance, suggests that "profoundly digressive and incoherent" currents of Freud's narrative prohibit access to the "behavioral facts of the case" (Gagnon 78). And more commonly, both Freud and many of his critics suggest that analytic "incoherence" locates the greatest obstacle to this case at the level of the transference. Freud's inability either to inspire or to read the transference of the homosexual girl not only suggests the limitations of Freud's position as "master" of psychoanalysis, but also opens up possibilities for political, as well as epistemological, defiance. Mandy Merck follows Judith Roof's work, in which she argues that the threat of female homosexuality is its impossible registration as desire within a male-centered, Oedipal model. As a result, lesbian desire stands in for, and consistently eludes, knowledge itself, so that Freud must represent female homosexuality as a "mask" for other more readable desires such as heterosexuality and male homosexuality.³ Following from these arguments, Brenda Wineapple maintains "that for Freud female homosexuality still remains illegible, elusive, unknown ... [and] therefore, it cannot be represented" (Wineapple 91).

To be sure, both critics and Freud have great difficulty establishing the "facts" of this case. Neither does the girl experience a "seduction fantasy," as Dora does, nor can Freud "uncover," through analytic construction, an unconscious seduction fantasy that subtends the girl's homosexuality. Freud writes, "She did not remember any sexual traumas in early life, nor were any discovered by the analysis," which explicitly introduces the problem the girl poses for Freud's analytic schema: she offers no fantasmatic representation of her desire ("Psychogenesis" 155). This absence of a seduction fantasy may exacerbate the epistemological instability centered on the homosexual girl, but contrary to Wineapple's argument, such instability does not render impossible any representation of her desire. Rather, insofar as this fantasy is absent, it becomes imperative that Freud construct, *through the very text of this case history*, his own fantasy of what seduces in the girl's sexuality. Fundamentally at stake in the "Psychogenesis" is Freud's representation of lesbian desire in relation to his own *analytic desire*. After all, homosexuality in women not only submits to the demands of representation, but also becomes legible through an explicitly formulaic sexual model. This formula by which lesbian desire becomes legible — becomes precisely a representation — is nothing other than the structure of medieval courtly love.⁴ Slavoj Žižek points out that in courtly love, "the knight's relationship to the Lady" dramatizes "the idealization of the Lady, her elevation to a spiritual, ethereal ideal" (Žižek 90). This keeps the lady always at a distance from her lover, "valoriz[ing]," as Jacques Lacan argues, "the preliminary stages of the act of love" (*Sem. VII* 152). Similarly, the girl of the "Psychogenesis" loves with what Freud characterizes as, "humility and the sublime overvaluation of the sexual object so characteristic of the male lover," while "insisting on the purity of her love and her physical repulsion against the idea of sexual intercourse" ("Psychogenesis" 154, 153). The girl acts towards the lady as though she were "far above" herself, feeling "bliss" merely being allowed "to accompany the lady a little way and to kiss her hand on parting" ("Psychogenesis" 160). Thus, the girl's courtly love does not simply maintain her distance from the object of desire, but it also becomes *a representation of seduction*, albeit an unsuccessful one. To the extent that the girl feels "bliss" by simply accompanying her lady, eschewing all possibility of "sexual intercourse," the girl, as in Lacan's characterization of courtly love, "valorizes" her perpetually enacting a certain fantasy of seduction, which Freud reports, is curiously absent from this case.

Faced with this lesbian seduction, Freud ostensibly directs his analytic efforts not towards the aim of "resolving a neurotic conflict" (because the girl has no hysterical symptoms and is "not in any way ill") but rather towards the aim of "converting one variety of genital organization into the other" ("Psychogenesis" 150–151). Freud acknowledges that this goal might well be doomed from the outset because the analysand does not "complain of her condition" and her parents bring her to analysis against her will ("Psychogenesis" 150). Freud actually spends three full pages detailing all the reasons why this case is not going to succeed, admitting, "for these reasons I refrained altogether from holding out to the parents any prospect of their wish being fulfilled" ("Psychogenesis" 151–152). But for all of Freud's admissions of the inevitable failure of the case, other questions arise with regard to Freud's desire to change the girl's genital organization, especially in light of her courtly love for the lady. In the *Ethics of Psychoanalysis*, Lacan suggests that in courtly love, "the object involved, the feminine object, is introduced oddly enough through the door of privation or of inaccessibility ... the inaccessibility of the object is posited as a point of departure" (*Sem. VII* 149). Not unlike Freud's position at the outset of the analysis, the relation between the lover and beloved does not *eventually* accede to the impossibility of the lover's achieving her goal, but rather takes this "privation" as a "point of departure." Similarly, the girl's love is predicated upon such privation; Freud recounts that "the lady used to recommend [to] the girl every time they met to withdraw her affection from herself" rather than welcoming her advances ("Psychogenesis" 153). The girl, then, never consummates her love with the lady, and, as Freud reports, "with none of the objects of her adoration [does] the patient enjoy ... anything beyond a few kisses and embraces" ("Psychogenesis" 153). Thus, as Freud says, the girl's "genital chastity, if one may use such a phrase, had remained intact" ("Psychogenesis" 153). And throughout the text, Freud emphasizes almost compulsively the fact that the girl's "genital chastity" remains unperturbed. He writes, "the lady ... received her [the girl's] advances coldly," and that the girl "had avoided sexual adventures for herself, and ... regarded coarsely sensual satisfactions as unaesthetic" ("Psychogenesis" 148, 161). Considering all these iterations of the girl's non-genital desire, one might want to question why precisely Freud's aim in this case is to convert the girl's genital sexuality. Freud establishes, without a doubt, that genitals have almost nothing to do with the girl's desire for her lady. In fact, this impossible genital relation seems precisely to drive the girl's consistent and unreciprocated pursuit. Thus, if this version of homosexual desire satisfies the girl to the extent that she does not "complain of her condition," then this is a version of sexual satisfaction that has *nothing at all to do with satisfaction*. That is, the girl's taking pleasure in her lady depends upon the absolute absence of conventional sexual pleasure. Freud's aim to convert the girl's genital sexuality turns out to be a ruse, a cover, a false object of his analytic desire; there is no genital organization to correct, no pleasure to reroute.

Lacan argues that the "paradox" of courtly love is precisely that it refuses the appeal of the pleasure principle by pursuing perpetual "foreplay," and "it is only insofar as the pleasure of desiring, or, more precisely, the pleasure of experiencing unpleasure, is sustained that we can speak of the sexual valorization of the preliminary stages of the act of love" (*Sem. VII* 152). Indeed, for Lacan, the "paradox" of courtly love is that it lets the lover get off by persistently *avoiding* sex. Counter-intuitively, then, the homosexual girl is satisfied precisely to the extent that she is unsatisfied. Such a representation may well partake of a phobic understanding of lesbian sexuality, which figures lesbian sex as simply foreplay and not as "actual" sex. And considering Slavoj Žižek's suggestion that "the libidinal economy of courtly love" becomes legible through the "emergence of masochism," Freud potentially associates his figure of the lesbian with a certain masochistic pathology (Žižek 89). It might, therefore, be slightly naïve and politically problematic to valorize Freud's figure of the homosexual girl as somehow resisting conventional paradigms of gendered and sexual subjectivity. Freud may well fail to inspire positive transference and to complete the analysis, but he also manages to reinscribe the girl's desire in paradigms of female masochism and phobic sexuality. Nonetheless, the girl *does* pose an obstacle to Freud's analytic project, and it turns out that what threatens most about lesbian sexuality is *not* the possibility of taking pleasure in unpleasure, of moving, as it were, "beyond the pleasure principle." Rather, what threatens more is Freud's own implication in this unsatisfying insistence of desire always already doomed to fail, as he enacts his own *per*-version of a certain never-ending, masochistic, epistemological foreplay.

Such Freudian foreplay draws us in not because it provides the "facts" of the case, not because it produces the "truth" of female homosexuality, but rather because it shatters the solid ground on which Freud's theoretical claims might stand, seducing us through this act of un-grounding. Nowhere does this become more apparent than in the moment in which Freud's foreplay should ultimately climax: the case's failure. Teresa de

Lauretis argues that Freud's case history unravels because of his disingenuous "imposition of a structuring narrative, or a structuring fantasy, onto the 'material' of the case history" ("Unknown Woman" 45). As a result, she aims to create a new model "of perverse desire ... that is non-Oedipal and nonreproductive," which could account for the fact of lesbian desire ("Unknown Woman" 47). But lesbian sexuality devolves into incoherence not simply because Freud's narrative imposition does not suffice to explain it. Rather, here, lesbian sexuality quite crucially resists narrative in general, resists the narratological and sexual logic of *climax* itself. Freud admits that "linear presentation is not ... very adequate," suggesting that both Freud and de Lauretis would be hard pressed to create any "lesbian" narrative at all ("Psychogenesis" 160–167).[5]

Nonetheless, Freud elaborates the girl's Oedipal trajectory by which "she changed into a man and took her mother in place of her father as the object of her love" ("Psychogenesis" 158). This moment is interesting less because of its reduction of desire to a psychic sex-change operation than because of the footnote Freud offers following it:

> It is by no means rare for a love-relation *to be broken off* through a process of identification on the part of the lover with the loved object, a process equivalent to a kind of regression to narcissism. After this has been accomplished, it is easy in making a fresh choice of object to direct the libido to a member of the sex opposite to that of the earlier choice ["Psychogenesis" 158; emphasis added].[6]

On the one hand, Freud argues in this passage that the girl's love for her father is so excessive that she identifies with him. On the other hand, in the very moment that Freud locates the "origin" of the girl's homosexual desire, he also echoes his failure in the "Psychogenesis" as a whole. The girl's love for her father is "broken off" and directed towards her mother, just as Freud himself states that this "analysis was *broken off*" as well ("Psychogenesis" 155; emphasis added). In other words, Freud explicitly aligns the girl's homosexual desire with what should be the climax of this case history: the need to end the analysis. But Freud fails even to articulate properly this failure: "breaking off" the analysis becomes an end, a "point of departure," *and* the interim between the two. Which is to say, Freud repeats — indeed, repeats compulsively — this "end" throughout the text. What should be the climax of his narrative, like the climax of the girl's sexual desire, is hardly climactic at all; the end of the analysis is no end, and becomes instead the structuring principle of the text as a whole.

These repetitions form the fabric of Freud's lesbian "seduction fantasy," but this fantasy reads less like a standard Freudian seduction and more like the masochistic beating fantasy that Freud details in "A Child is Being Beaten."[7] And in so doing, Freud aligns himself not only with the homosexual girl, but also with one of the figures that he uses to illustrate the frequent failures of homosexual conversion. Of this exemplary homosexual who cannot be "convinced" to change Freud writes: "One then soon discovers his secret plan, namely, to obtain from the striking failure of his attempt a feeling of satisfaction that he has done everything possible against his abnormality, to which he can now resign himself with an easy conscience" ("Psychogenesis" 151). This imaginary homosexual's "striking failure" from which he can "obtain ... a feeling of satisfaction" reverberates throughout the "Psychogenesis." That is to say, Freud's articulations of his own "*striking* failure" seem to produce just such "satisfaction," especially when considered in relation to the child's masochistic fantasy of *being struck*. The beating fantasy, according to Freud, develops through three phases, and the differences between these stages hinge upon variations in syntax, which reorganize the positions of subject and object. In the first phase, the subject fantasizes, "My father is beating the child"; in the second, "I am being beaten by my father"; and in the third, "My father is beating the child, he loves only me" ("Child" 164, 165, 169). These phases are by no means directly analogous to the three phases of what might be called Freud's "failure fantasy," but the former nonetheless shed some light on the repetitions, marked by curious differences, that Freud articulates in the latter.

Freud first refers to the failure of this analysis in a benignly passive construction, "it was not continued" ("Psychogenesis" 152). Neither Freud nor the girl occupy the positions of subject or object in this iteration, and Freud has not yet introduced the idiom of "breaking off" to characterize the abrupt end of the girl's analysis. Not unlike the child in the first phase of the beating fantasy, the subject who articulates the fantasy stands at a distance from the scene in view ("Child" 164). That is to say, in this first stage of Freud's failure fantasy, it remains unclear why the analysis ends and who ends it, suggesting that the case is completely out of Freud's control. "It was not continued," and through this vague construction, Freud appears to be passively subject to the disturbance instantiated by the girl's desire. However, this is not simply the case. Just as in first stage of the beating fantasy Freud questions whether the satisfactions involved are "masochistic," "sadistic," or if the fantasy provides any satisfaction at all, so too does Freud force us to doubt the sexual valence of his construction here ("Child" 164). Insofar as Freud is not present in this articulation — wholly distancing himself not only from the case, but also from the girl's desire — he remains in control, actively absenting himself from the failure of this analysis. The first stage of the beating fantasy, like the first stage of this failure fantasy, appears to be neither masochistic nor sadistic, affording neither mastery nor submission, to the extent that Freud syntactically erases himself and the girl from the scene of the analytic discontinuation. Here, the analysis might well spontaneously discontinue itself.

But the second iteration of Freud's failure alters the force of analytic termination, so that the dynamics of passivity and activity, marked in both Freud's syntax and the syntax of the beating fantasies, shift considerably. With reference this time to the unconscious seduction fantasy, which neither the girl remembers nor Freud uncovers, Freud elaborates: "As I have already said, the analysis *was broken off* after a short time, and therefore yielded an anamnesis not much more reliable than the other anamneses of homosexuals, which there is good cause to question" ("Psychogenesis" 155; emphasis added). In this repetition, Freud preserves the passive structure of the first instance, introducing the violence of "breaking off," which resonates with the violence of the beating fantasy's masochistic scene. And here such violence is crucially yoked to the anxiety that centers on the question of memory. After all, fundamentally at issue is the fact that neither the girl nor Freud can produce the representation of a fantasy, and the girl, because she is "unreliably homosexual," cannot remember anything herself. And indeed, the fact that "the analysis was broken off after a short time" has everything to do with these "anamneses ... which there is good cause to question." Thus, in this iteration of the case's failure, Freud remains uninvolved with ceasing the analysis, as in the first passive construction. However, the homosexual girl comes explicitly into view, so that she seems, through her unreliable memory, actually to cause the analysis to stop. As long as Freud stands in the place of the one upon whom the girl acts, through her inability to remember reliably, Freud can come to the end of the analysis satisfied not with *his* failure, but rather the "striking failure" of the homosexual girl.

However, this displacement onto the girl's bad memory is not wholly salutary for Freud, and cannot produce the ease of self-satisfaction to the extent that the question of unreliable memory is itself anxious-making. Not only the girl, but also potentially Freud's readership, suffers from undependable "anamneses," motivating Freud to style this repetition of the case's failure as a *favor* to his readers. "As I have said already," Freud reminds us lest we forget, "the analysis was broken off," which aligns his

### III. The Incommensurability of Sex/Gender/Desire

audience, through its potentially faulty memory, with the homosexual girl herself. The passive reiteration in this passage, then, carries with it at least a two-fold sexual charge. On the one hand, insofar as the girl's unreliable recollections displace the failure of this case from Freud onto the girl, the passive construction produces satisfaction and reduces textual tension. On the other hand, however, unreliable memory also threatens the integrity of the text where Freud's readership is involved, exacerbating tension, so that Freud is forced to reiterate and repeat his "satisfaction" with the girl's failure, providing no proper pleasure at all. This alignment also positions both the girl and Freud's readers as those who stand in positions of control, subjecting Freud to the failure of the case. That is to say, it is not Freud who breaks off the analysis; rather, the girl and potentially even Freud's audience force the analysis to end, making Freud's position analogous to the subject in the beating fantasy who is being beaten rather than doing the beating himself. But such passivity does not divest Freud of his power, and instead serves to reconsolidate his mastery to the extent that the girl and his readers, rather than Freud, endanger the success of the analysis.

The challenge that the homosexual girl poses to Freud's mastery becomes explicit in the third and final repetition of Freud's failure where the issue of the girl's negative transference comes to the fore. Freud diagnoses this final obstacle as the

> reality [that] she transferred to me the sweeping repudiation of men... As soon, therefore, as I recognized the girl's attitude to her father, *I broke off* the treatment and advised her parents that if they set store by thetherapeutic procedure it should be continued by a woman doctor ["Psychogenesis" 164; emphasis added].

In this passage, Freud identifies, as he sees it, the greatest shortcoming of this analysis: the girl refuses to transfer positively onto Freud because of the "sweeping repudiation of men." This "discovery" allows Freud to establish a causal relationship between the negative transference and the failure of the case so that he writes, "as soon ... as I recognized the girl's attitude to her father, I broke off the treatment." To be sure, the homosexual girl disrupts the logic of Freud's analytic method at the level of the transference; nonetheless, this obstacle also allows Freud to ground his claims, more than anywhere else in the text, in the domain of certainty. A far cry from the iteration preceding this one, neither the girl nor Freud's readers threaten the integrity of this case with bad memories, enforcing the need for repetition. Indeed, here, just as in the third stage of the beating fantasy, the subject (Freud) produces a structure in which he actively engages. "I broke off the treatment," Freud writes, suggesting that this stage of the failure fantasy, as in the beating fantasy, "seems to have become sadistic" ("Child" 169). But also like the third phase of the beating fantasy, as Freud writes in "A Child Is Being Beaten," "only the *form* of this fantasy is sadistic; the satisfaction which is derived from it is masochistic" ("Child" 169). That is, in the very moment where Freud seems most like the master of psychoanalysis, he is nonetheless mastered by the analysis itself; Freud produces himself as an "I" only in order to *disappear altogether*. In the guise of mastery, Freud masochistically obliterates himself. After all, immediately after he writes that he "broke off the treatment," another figure takes his place. The "woman doctor" who Freud suggests should "continue" the "therapeutic procedure" effectively usurps Freud's position. This moment thus establishes the end of the treatment as not simply an end, but also a beginning. And this beginning is not just any beginning, but is very specifically the beginning of this case; the woman doctor's "continuation" echoes the *dis*continuation of the first iteration of failure. Thus, Freud breaks off the treatment only to return to the place where the treatment begins, effectively drawing the text of the analysis back onto itself. Freud's textual relation to the girl's homosexual desire becomes, then, not only "digressive" or "incoherent," but also crucially, circular, driving the development of the text — potentially without end — around the girl's baffling courtly love for her lady, drawing the reader as well into a vertiginous circuit of this insatiable analytic desire.

It may well be the case, then, that the difficulty of the "Psychogenesis" is not, as Lacan argues, that Freud fails "to formulate correctly ... the object of the female homosexual's desire," but rather Freud fails to recognize the object of his *own* queer desire (*Sem. XI* 38). That is to say, the repetitions of the end of this analysis suggest that Freud does not desire the homosexual girl, but rather desires *like* her, taking the analysis as its own object, which turns out to be no object at all. Desiring without a "proper" aim, Freud not only aligns himself *with* the homosexual girl but also adds to this structure a little twist of his own, effectively queering the girl's already-queer desire. Freud's position in the "Psychogenesis" thus becomes at least doubly perverse. In Jacques-Alain Miller's, "On Perversion," in which he discusses Lacan's theory of perverse sexualities, Miller, without a hint of irony, asks, "Is that to say that the analyst is a pervert?" and answers unequivocally, "Certainly not" (318). But the "Psychogenesis" suggests otherwise and provides us with the irony we need to read Miller's question. Where *lesbian failure* determines the trajectory of *Freud's desire*, this case history invites a chiastic reversal of the terms, making "failure" and "desire" interchangeable. Lesbian failure and Freud's desire, lesbian desire and Freud's failure become inextricably linked to each other in the movement of continuous reversals. Constituting nothing other than the seductive "foreplay" of and as this text, such a movement teases us to see the enigma of the lesbian's desire as Freud's own. In response, therefore, to Miller's question — *is* the analyst a pervert?— we must now answer, along with Freud, "Certainly, of course."

## Notes

1. See Teresa de Lauretis' *The Practice of Love: Lesbian Sexuality and Perverse Desire* (Indiana UP, 1994).
2. See Freud's *Three Essays on The Theory of Sexuality* for an enactment of this critical tendency (Basic Books, 2000).
3. See Mandy Merck's *Perversions* (Routledge, 1993), Judith Roof's *A Lure of Knowledge: Lesbian Sexuality and Theory* (Columbia UP, 1991).
4. See Mary Jacobus', "'Russian Tactics': Freud's 'Case of Homosexuality in a Woman" in *Freud and the Passions* (Penn. State UP, 1996) and H.N. Lukes' "Unrequited Love: Lesbian Transference and Revenge in Psychoanalysis," in *Homosexuality and Psychoanalysis* (U Chicago Press, 2001).
5. See Leo Bersani's, *The Freudian Body* (Columbia UP, 1986) for a discussion of such "nonnarativity."
6. In her brilliant and incisive critique of this case, Diana Fuss persuasively argues that this footnote enacts the collapse of the classic psychoanalytic distinction between identification and desire (Fuss 69).
7. See Freud's " 'A Child Is Being Beaten': A Contribution to the Study of the Origin of the Sexual Perversions," in *Essential Papers on Masochism* (New York UP, 1995).

## Works Cited

Bersani, Leo. *The Freudian Body*. New York: Columbia University Press, 1986.
De Lauretis, Teresa. "Letter to an Unknown Woman." In *That Obscure Subject of Desire: Freud's Female Homosexual Revisited*. Ed. Ronnie C. Lesser and Erica Schoenberg. New York: Routledge, 1999.
_____. *The Practice of Love: Lesbian Sexuality and Perverse Desire*. Bloomington: Indiana Univerity Press, 1994.
Freud, Sigmund. " 'A Child is Being Beaten': A Contribution to the Study of the Origin of Sexual Perversions." In *Essential Papers on Masochism*. Ed. Margaret Ann Fitzpatric Hanly. New York: New York University Press, 1995.
_____. *Dora: An Analysis of a Case of Hysteria*. New York: Touchstone, 1995.
_____. "Psychogenesis of a Case of Homosexuality in a Woman." In *Standard Edition of the Complete Psychological Works of Sigmund Freud* (1901–905). Ed. and trans. James Strachey, with Anna Freud. 24 vols. London: Hogarth, 1953.

\_\_\_\_\_. *Three Essays on the Theory of Sexuality*. Trans. and Ed. James Strachey. New York: Basic Books, 2000.
Fuss, Diana. *Identification Papers*. New York: Routledge, 1995.
Gagnon, John H. "Who Was That Girl?" In *That Obscure Subject of Desire: Freud's Female Homosexual Revisited*. Ed. Ronnie C. Lesser and Erica Schoenberg. New York: Routledge, 1999.
Jacobus, Mary. " 'Russian Tactics': Freud's 'Case of Homosexuality in a Woman.'" In *Freud and the Passions*. Ed. John O'Neil. University Park: Pennsylvania University Press, 1996.
Lacan, Jacques. *The Ethics of Psychoanalysis, 1959–1969: The Seminar of Jacques Lacan Book VII*. Trans. Dennis Porter. New York: W.W. Norton and Company, 1992.
\_\_\_\_\_. *The Four Fundamentals of Psychoanalysis: The Seminar of Jacques Lacan Book XI*. Trans. Alan Sheridan. Ed. Jacques-Alain Miller. New York: W.W. Norton and Company, 1981.
Lukes, H.N. "Unrequited Love: Lesbian Transference and Revenge in Psychoanalysis." In *Homosexuality and Psychoanalysis*. Ed. Tim Dean and Christopher Lane. Chicago: University of Chicago Press, 2001.
Merck, Mandy. *Perversions*. New York: Routledge, 1993.
Miller, Jacques-Alain. "On Perversion." In *Reading Seminars I and II: Lacan's Return to Freud*. Ed. Richard Feldstein, Bruce Fink, and Marie Janus. Albany: State University of New York Press, 1996.
Roof, Judith. *A Lure of Knowledge: Lesbian Sexuality and Theory*. New York: Columbia University Press, 1991.
Wineapple, Brenda. "Lying Dreams." In *That Obscure Subject of Desire: Freud's Female Homosexual Revisited*. Ed. Ronnie C. Lesser and Erica Schoenberg. New York: Routledge, 1999.
Žižek, Slavoj. *The Metastases of Enjoyment: Six Essays on Woman and Causality*. London: Verso Press, 1994.

# 11 Latent Lesbians and Heterosexual Narrative
## Tracing a Queer Poetics in Fay Weldon's Fiction

LORENA RUSSELL

This article explores the fiction of contemporary British writer Fay Weldon through the notion of "queer heterosexuality."1 My approach considers what this category allows for opening theoretical space between queer and feminist theories alongside considerations of the inherent risks the notion carries. Judith Butler has formulated an important argument "against proper objects," and I will follow her lead in my position on the topic of queer heterosexuality. I argue that it is important to retain a certain elasticity in applying queer theory, one that would allow for considerations of heterosexuality as potentially distinct from heteronormativity. For me, such a distinction opens the possibility for considering potentially radicalizing formulations of "queer heterosexuality."

It is queer theory's flexibility around issues of sexual identity that allows such a stretch, and it is in these outlying spaces that I feel one can in some ways best understand differences and continuities between those tentative yet potent categories of "gay" and "straight."2 Yet I remain concerned that the paradoxical space of queer heterosexuality that Weldon's fiction allows holds as much potential for normalizing constriction as it does for queer expansion.3 It is here in this uncertain territory that the fiction of Fay Weldon operates in its most radical way: to elude any neat distinction between conservative and radical, straight and queer, feminist and sexist. At the same time, I am aware of the risks such blurring allows. While I fully support the creative impulses central to the proliferation of new categories like "queer heterosexuality," I am simultaneously aware of the risks such categories entail.[4] My approach to Weldon thus seeks to balance the tendency towards proliferating identities with a careful consideration of what such queering might perform in terms of its potential collusion with homophobic discourse. For me, queer theorizing demands such a tightrope walk. While anti-homophobic theorizing must remain a central ideal for any queer project, one must balance this goal with a pragmatic eye to the need for accommodation. The category of queer heterosexuality illustrates one way that queer theory might become less about patrolling the boundaries of homophobic thinking and more about risking accommodation.

Fay Weldon is a prolific popular author of over twenty-five novels who invites an ambivalent response from her feminist readers. On the one hand, her consistent focus on gender inequality and her repeated plot line of the disenfranchised woman places her squarely in the camp of feminist authors. On the other hand, her mockery of radical forms of feminism and her irreverent treatment of many feminist themes has distanced her from others. One of her most famous novels, *The Life and Loves of a She Devil*,[5] ends with the title character undergoing massive plastic surgery in an attempt to "become" her estranged husband's sexy lover. While Ruth Pradgett's surgery is clearly exaggerated through fictional excesses, Weldon remains unapologetic in her defense of cosmetic surgical choices for women, and in doing so has alienated numerous feminist readers. This ambivalence within her feminism is part of what has attracted me to Weldon. As someone with equal interests in feminist and queer theory, I consider such ambivalence potentially useful in mapping shared positions between the two inquiries.

In an earlier article "Dog-Women and She Devils: The Queering Field of Monstrous Women" I consider how Weldon, alongside Jeanette Winterson and Angela Carter, recasts female heterosexuality through portraits of monstrosity to create the potentially radical category of queer heterosexuality. I trace how these three authors craft their characters through various "queering fields" of Bakhtinian excesses, pornography, and S/M. I conclude that those resulting monstrous bodies open spaces for a queer configuration of female heterosexuality, one useful for mapping intersections between feminist and queer inquiries. In this article, I retain my interest in understanding overlaps between feminist and queer impulses. But here I am less interested in tracing the bodily contours of queer heterosexuality, and want to focus instead on the shifts in Weldon's narratives between queer and straight possibility. While my previous work focused on characterizations and practices, in this essay I consider the sexual poetics of Weldon's narratives and what this poetics offers for framing queer heterosexuality.

The heterosexual impulses of Fay Weldon's fiction at times erase or obscure lesbian possibilities.[6] Weldon repeatedly offers lesbianism as a possible "solution" for her troubled heterosexual protagonists only to reject it for a reasserted heterosexuality. Despite this normalizing potential, I am arguing here that the work of Weldon functions as both feminist *and* queer. I am willing to tolerate a certain doubleness or ambivalence in my analysis as to what constitutes "feminist" and what constitutes "queer": to allow that the homophobic can coexist with the anti-homophobic, the sexist alongside the anti-sexist.

In part, this ambivalence emerges through Weldon's concern with the barriers and limitations society offers heterosexual women. Lesbianism would seem one option for Weldon's characters given the grim treatment she affords women in heterosexual relationships. Most Weldon women find themselves victims of unworthy men, unsatisfied at best, but more often sorely injured by male infidelity and betrayal. One might think that lesbian relationships could offer some relief, and her plots do occasionally swerve towards this possibility. After laying bare the miseries of marriage, her stories frequently involve the dissatisfied wife in some lesbian subplot. But ultimately, Weldon does not seem very interested in exploring the possibilities of life without men. Her heroines experiment with lesbian relationships before returning to heterosexual unions. The overdetermined force of these heteronormative conclusions demonstrates what a difficult balancing act it is between normative female heterosexuality and lesbian possibility.[7]

However, even given the seemingly rigid parameters of the heterosexual framework, Weldon's fiction still works to undermine any stable notion of heterosexual identity, troubling sexual difference. In *Big Women* Nancy, who leaves her boyfriend at the beginning of the novel, happily reunites with him after 20 years, leaving her feminist community behind.[8] The novel thus ends with the resolution implying that men are a necessity, and feminism, especially radical feminism with its separatist tendencies, has somewhat misplaced goals given the women's propensity towards heterosexuality. Yet within the framework of what seems at best a homophobic, heteronormative conclusion, readers are given the threads of queering. Here, Weldon offers her usual critique of separatist feminism, but the remnants of male authority in this reconfigured straight world are oddly diminished:

[Feminists] had got things wrong, personally and politically, but who ever got everything right? They had wept, screamed, shouted, protested, loved and laughed more than most. If the separatists had won over the socialists and the radicals, if young women everywhere assumed men were an optional extra, a decoration not a necessity, not essential to their well-being, or survival, that too in time would shift and change, and become more merciful. Men are people too. Gender, like the state in Marxist aspiration, might in the end wither away, and be relevant only in bed and the approach to it, and the aftermath. There is no harm in living in hope [338].

Despite the liberal strain allowing that "men are people too," Weldon describes a radical feminist Utopia where gender may become irrelevant. Even more interesting in terms of queering is the metonymic association between her use of the terms of gender and the phallus. When she likens the ideological force of gender within feminism to the position of the state in Marxism, her choice of words has a strong phallic overtone: one might substitute the penis as something that "might in the end wither away" and "be relevant only in the bed and the approach to it, and the aftermath." This metonymic chain of associations further implies that the penis is in fact irrelevant ("a decoration not a necessity"), effectively rendering the penis "an optional extra," something akin to an unnecessary but potentially useful dildo. Even as she critiques separatist feminism, her words seem to imply a radical alternative to heterosexuality.

Weldon's lesbian figures are often marginal, located to the side of the protagonist. In her perceptive work on Weldon, Patricia Smith describes how her lesbians tend to work in critical ways despite their apparent marginalization: "While never central figures, Weldon's lesbian characters invariably play crucial and provocative roles, providing her put-upon heterosexual protagonists with foils, role models, experimental sexual encounters, or objects upon which to focus their all-pervading anxieties" (Smith 125). Encounters with these marginal women are often an important formative experience for the Weldon heroine.

In *Remember Me*,[9] Madelaine's lesbian neighbor Renee is one of the more positive characters in the novel who bounces on the scene like a proverbial breath of fresh air:

Renee is a delicate, wide-eyed young woman, fresh, long-legged and clear-complexioned, like some outdoor girl on an old-fashioned chocolate box. Renee has two equally pretty little daughters, sometimes with her. Renee claims to be bitter; Renee was abandoned by her father, and then abandoned her husband. Renee has, she says, renounced men. Renee has girl-friends instead, from whom, physically and emotionally, she extracts comfort, company and solace. From time to time Renee kindly offers the same to Madeleine, in the shape of a warm and companionable bed, but Madeleine is too conscious of her own raggedy body and troubled mind to be able to offer herself on such simple terms. Although, as Renee complains, she seems perfectly well able to offer herself to any passing man [51–52].

Smith argues that this positive depiction of Renee helps to counter narratives of lesbians as sick and perverted, thereby it "reverses conventional expectations of the relative happiness and sanity of lesbians" (127). On the other hand, Renee's characterization still carries some damaging and rather unimaginative implications. As is so often the case, Weldon's lesbians come to their position as a reaction to failed relationships with men. Such an assumption retains heterosexuality as the default position, making lesbianism a kind of "second best." It further contributes to the notion that lesbians are "man-haters," an association continued by Weldon's repeated association of lesbians with the 1970's style of radical feminist separatism, a political position that Weldon categorizes as laughably impractical.

Renee will later offer her companionship to Margot, who has begun to lose sexual interest in her husband. Margot's reflections on Renee's advances leads to one of the more conflicted passages on lesbianism in any Weldon novel:

> But if her own body is so forbidden, always was, to touch, to see, to know — how much more forbidden must another woman's be? No, no; she could not, must not. To feel soft female lips against her own? There is too much danger in it. If sensuous pleasure is so easily come by after all; if sexual fulfillment can be so gracefully, privately, gently arrived at, between women and women; if love can be without war, without struggle, without the conflict of non-identical interests — this sly, primrose path to happiness is so dangerous, so monstrous, the very sun might hide its face in horror, and the light of the world go out [186].

Here Margot's imagination swerves from a sensuous engagement with lesbian possibility to an overstated, homophobic rejection of Sapphic pleasures. The potential sweetness of the individual encounter is eclipsed by her panicked fear of apocalyptic repercussions, a sense of a love so monstrous that it could shift the heavens. Lesbianism is offered as one tantalizing possibility, but as is so often the case in Weldon, heterosexuality is ultimately reasserted as the preferred order. In typical Weldon fashion, *Remember Me* will conclude through the superficial reinstatement of the nuclear family, as Margot takes Madeleine's daughter into her home, and happiness is restored by that most commonplace of heterosexual plot devices, the concluding reunited family. Yet the happiness in this conclusion is partial at best. Intimacy between Margot and Phillip is never regained, and the sexual energy engendered by Margot's encounter with Renee remains unresolved. It through such unresolved elements that Weldon's category of queer heterosexuality comes to be developed, as these narrative strands produce a current of uncertainty that upset the seeming stability of the heterosexual conclusion.

Other novels present similar tensions between heterosexual and queer possibilities. In *The Life and Loves of a She-Devil,* the wronged Ruth Pradgett sleeps with Nurse Hopkins, an affair that might be read as a Machiavellian move in Ruth's grand revenge scheme. The lesbian sex does, after all, serve to establish an intimacy that in turn enables Ruth to fund an employment agency, Vesta Rose. This agency is instrumental in masterminding the financial ruin of her wayward husband, Bobbo. We learn that Ruth's plan to embezzle her husband's money demands that she plant a seductive secretary in his office. In order to have such control over a secretary, Ruth establishes Vesta Rose, which in turn requires funding. To get access to Nurse Hopkins' sizeable savings, Ruth needs to endear herself, a move which is accomplished by suggesting that they sleep side-by-side: "Nurse Hopkins agreed. The beds were moved, and there was much cuddling, kissing and sexual experimentation between the two women" (117). Ruth might be said to have simply used Hopkins to advance her revenge, and the novel seems to imply as much.

To read the affair solely in the darkest of Machiavellian terms is not quite just, however, as Nurse Hopkins (like so many who come in contact with Ruth) ultimately ends up a benefactor. It is not at Nurse Hopkins' expense that Ruth maneuvers the affair. As Ruth anticipates, the affair heightens intimacy and trust between the two women, but it also has a "tonic effect" on Nurse Hopkins: "her menstrual cycle became regular, her eyes brightened, she lost weight, divested herself of many layers of woollies and moved briskly around the hospital" (118). They leave the rather grim work at the hospital for the criminally insane, and co-found the Vesta Rose Employment Agency together. When Ruth's embezzlement scheme is complete, she leaves Hopkins with a viable business and an adopted son, telling her: "These two legacies will keep you busy enough, especially the latter: too busy for you to grieve for me much" (128). This "tonic effect" becomes a pattern throughout the novel, as Ruth manages to improve any number of lives. While Ruth's grand revenge ultimately destroys Bobbo and his mistress Mary Fisher, others along the way, like

Nurse Hopkins, benefit from her machinations, and experience some form of improved conditions in her wake.

The affair with Nurse Hopkins does not, of course, represent any permanent sexual identity for Ruth, but neither does her engagement as a sex slave for the sadistic Judge Bissop, or her stint on a commune with separatist feminists. This fluidity of identity is part of what makes Ruth Pradgett queer, even though we may understand her primary sexuality as heterosexual. In the end, though, we might do best to consider her as "posthuman," for when she takes up the role of Mary Fisher, looking every bit the perfect woman, she is in fact completely shed of her humanity, a true she-devil.[10] The normalizing implications of this conclusion, like those of *Puffball* and *Big Women*, seems to counter the more radical tones that her stories establish. Ultimately, though, I conclude "it is the very ambiguity of the ending that allows for the novel's social critique of heterosexual normativity, a normativity implicated in constructions of materiality" (191). Weldon's use of satire, parody and excess allows for such doubleness. Even while the "resolution" of *She-Devil* may on some level disappoint, it is through satire that her fiction functions politically.

This doubleness in Weldon's fiction is not attributable to satire alone. In tracing the outlines of what one might consider a queer poetic, readers must also consider the various tensions and resolutions of the narrative itself. Another reason that Weldon's novels conclude in unsatisfying ways for her queer readers relates to their simultaneous avoidance of and insistence on lesbian possibility. The lesbian "solution" would tie things together too neatly. It is a bit too much like changing the rules of the game. But at the same time her novels seem to beg for such relationships. It is not as though the men or the women ever really change. Some hope is posited through generational evolution, as in *Down Among the Women*, but for the most part, things just "keep on keeping on," and heterosexuality is part of that status quo. But despite the stable structure such plots imply, the narrative tension her stories produce counters normalization. In short, Weldon's plots establish so much dissatisfaction with heterosexuality, that lesbianism remains a possibility, even though it is seldom realized. And it is here, on the level of narrative tension, that Weldon's fiction produces another level of queer heterosexuality.

One way of reading such tension is to understand lesbianism as a repressed term in Weldon's fiction, an element which might help to satisfy some of the unresolved tensions around heteronormativity which her plots put into play. In *Reading for the Plot*, Peter Brooks writes: "As readers we know that there has been created in the text an intensive level of energy that cannot be discharged through these official plots" (Brooks 122). What Brooks says about heterosexual incest in Victorian fiction applies as well to lesbianism in Weldon: "Throughout the Romantic tradition, it is perhaps most notably the image of incest (of the fraternal-sororal variety) that hovers as the sign of a passion interdicted because its fulfillment would be too perfect, a discharge indistinguishable from death, the very cessation of narrative movement" (109).[11] Like Brooks's characterization of incest, lesbianism in Weldon would signal a level of fulfillment that might grind the plot to a halt, yet remains a tantalizing latent possibility.

In short, when taken against the radical potentials of her characters and themes, Weldon's conservative plots engender outrage in the reader, which creates a kind of energy/desire/drive that works beyond her conventional heteronormative conclusions. This rather overwrought dynamic is part of what I proffer as a "queer poetic." Even though her plots often resolve in traditional ways, readers are ill-prepared for the return to normalcy that her more traditional conclusions imply. Even though most of her novels keep gay and lesbian issues well to the side of their heterosexual focus, the *potential* for lesbianism is both asserted and denied in very queer ways.

Another Weldon novel where lesbianism both asserts and evades its potentiality is *The Heart of the Country*. Here Natalie Harris finds herself abandoned by her husband, who has run off with a local carnival queen. An intimacy develops between the narrator, Sonia, and the recently-divorced Natalie.[12] In some ways, this attraction between the women would make lesbianism quite important and central. But despite her desire, Sonia herself does not identify as a lesbian, keeping the question of sexual identity in play. Although she loves Natalie from afar, Sonia falls short of lesbian identity, and can't imagine kissing or actually making love to Natalie, let alone self-identifying as "lesbian." Yet the narrative is in some ways dependent on her position as a lesbian, or on its "lesbian-like" markers.[13] It is, after all, Sonia's feminism, a radical feminism inspired by her rejection of men that provides the point-of-view in the novel. And it is also Sonia's separatist position that educates Natalie and powers the plot, which culminates in Sonia's vengeful burning of the "happy housewives" carnival float. Like Ruth Pradgett's burning of her home in *The Life and Loves of a She-Devil*, this moment of violent destruction becomes a point of release for feminist outrage, a classic moment of resistance that opens space for queering. And despite the fact that Sonia and Natalie never consummate their relationship, they are nonetheless perceived as lesbians by others, a perception that fuels homophobia in the small town, exemplifying the ideological link between homophobia and sexism. *The Heart of the Country*, in much the same way as *Down Among the Women*, builds its feminist sensibility as it chronicles levels of women's oppression under patriarchy, an oppression signaled largely by Sonia's homophobically-inspired social alienation.

By the end of the novel, however, Sonia seems on the verge of pairing with her male psychiatrist — a pragmatic, survivalist shift that will get her out of the mental institution where she was placed, but also one that reasserts the heterosexual role as the final choice for the Weldon woman, dashing any hopes for feminist solidarity that the novel's story might have inspired. The release of political energy is expressed by the novel's carnival scene when Sonia burns the float. But for Sonia, the act of arson results in an unforeseen death, and the potential power of the moment is cut short with regret. The sobering turn makes an additional point about the limitations of carnival as resistance. As Angela Carter asserts: "Things don't change because a girl puts on trousers or a chap slips on a frock, you know. Masters were masters again the day after Saturnalia ended; after the holiday from gender, it was back to the old grind ..." (389). As is so often the case for both Carter and Weldon, utopian or idealist impulses, including those congregating around homoeroticism, are cut short by a pragmatist turn, a normalizing gesture inspired by a recognition of the limits of material reality.

In *Contemporary Women's Fiction*, Paulina Palmer links the lack of feminist solidarity in Weldon's (and Carter's, Margaret Atwood's and others') writing to the lack of lesbian themes: "[F]ar from stressing community and collectivity, [they] present the relationship which the central character experiences with other women as one of alienation and even antagonism...." Palmer goes on to take issue with "their strongly heterosexual and, in certain cases, heterosexist, bias. Motifs of woman-identification and erotic female relations are, on the whole, absent" (38). I agree that lesbians themes are sparse in these novels, but am not sure that I want to cast such scarcity in terms of heterosexist bias.[14] Rather, my point is that Weldon's commitment to a feminist heterosexuality leads to some radical re-phrasing of that identification, reformulations towards thinking queer heterosexuality. Moreover, the kinds of mobility such readings demand, the dialectic tensions that the plots establish between actualized heteronormativity and lesbian possibility, become characteristic of what I am terming a queer poetics.

The position of lesbianism in Weldon is not unlike what Teresa de

Lauretis describes as "space-off," a film term referencing "the space not visible in the frame but inferable from what the frame makes visible" (De Lauretis 26). Weldon's fiction resists resolving the impossibility of heterosexual relationships through a fixed resolution of those relationships, effectively keeping lesbian possibility enticingly off-frame. For de Lauretis, this off-frame represents a space of non-representation constructed in the margins of hegemonic discourse. The movement between the hegemonic (representational) space and the marginal (unrepresented) space "is not that of a dialectic, of integration, of a combinatory or of *difference*, but it is the tension of contradiction, multiplicity, and heteronomy" (26). Such a lack of commitment signals a mobility in many ways consistent with queer theory: a gesture towards identity without the reification that a stronger representation might imply. Weldon's evasive treatment of lesbianism, its positioning "on the side," effectively keeps such tensions in play.

Even writers like Jeanette Winterson, who deal more explicitly with lesbian possibility, work such tensions productively in their fiction. In her useful study, *Heterosexual Plots and Lesbian Narratives*, Marilyn Farwell describes ways that heterosexual plots engage transgressively with lesbian possibility. She cites Winterson's characters Dog-Woman of *Sexing the Cherry* and Louise in *Written on the Body* as "female bodies in excess, lesbian subjects as grotesque bodies" (Farwell 22). She acknowledges, however, that "[t]heir literal sexuality is problematic..." and reads their lesbianism as arising from a narrative space that "undermines gender opposition and hierarchy" rather than explicitly constructing homosexual identity (23).

What Farwell reads as lesbian, I am reading as a formulation of a queer heterosexuality. In positing this queer heterosexuality, my intention is not to foreclose lesbian possibility through what Farwell calls "erasure of the lesbian" (19). Rather, it is the opening of lesbian possibility as described by Farwell that marks all of these Weldon texts, an opening that allows in part for a queering of normative heterosexuality, a paradoxical space based more on potentiality than certainty, and one that may, by its very nature, risk normalizing spaces alongside the transgressive.

# *Notes*

1. This article is drawn in part from a book-length manuscript entitled "Queering the Pulpit: Feminist Metafiction in Weldon, Winterson and Carter."
2. Other theorists who have extended the term "queer" to include modes of heterosexuality include Pamela Robertson, "What Makes the Feminist Camp?" *Camp:*

## III. The Incommensurability of Sex/Gender/Desire

*Queer Asethetics and the Performing Subject*, ed. Fabio Cleto (Ann Arbor: University of Michigan Press, 1999).; Cathy J. Cohen, "Punks, Bulldaggers, and Welfare Queens," *GLQ* 3 (1997).; Calvin Thomas, ed., *Straight with a Twist: Queer Theory and the Subject of Heterosexuality* (Urbana and Chicago: U of Illinois P, 2000).; and Fabio Cleto, "Introduction: Queering the Camp," *Camp: Queer Asethetics and the Performing Subject*, ed. Fabio Cleto (Ann Arbor: University of Michigan Press, 1999).

3. I am reminded here of Terry Castle's call to beware of criticism that contributes to the closeting of lesbianism. Terry Castle, *The Apparitional Lesbian: Female Homosexuality and Modern Culture* (New York: Columbia UP, 1993).

4. I am drawing here from Eve Kosofsky Sedgwick and Judith Halberstam, each of whom proposes the strategic creation of taxonomies to counter the limitations of traditional identities and categories. For a discussion of these so-called "nonce categories" and their usefulness in formulating a queer methodology see Judith Halberstam, *Female Masculinity* (Durham, NC: Duke UP, 1998), Eve Kosofsky Sedgwick, *Epistemology of the Closet* (Berkeley: University of California Press, 1990). I consider "female masculinity" a nonce category in the sense offered by Halberstam and Sedgwick.

5. Fay Weldon, *The Life and Loves of a She-Devil* (London: Hodder and Stoughton, 1983).

6. It is worth noting here the dynamics of "lesbian panic" outlined by Patricia Juliana Smith, and how such narrative moments contribute to normalizing as well as anti-homophobic impulses. Patricia Juliana Smith, *Lesbian Panic: Homoeroticism in Modern British Women's Fiction*, Between Women-between Men: Lesbian and Gay Studies, eds. Lillian Faderman and Larry Gross (New York: Columbia UP, 1997).

7. I define heteronormativity as a system of social and cultural forces that work to maintain heterosexuality as the dominant and natural form of sexuality. I am using the term *normative* in the philosophical sense, as a language of "good" and "bad," of "oughts" and "shoulds." This is the language of ethical statements, and by extension, of political positioning and praxis. In my use of the terms *normalizing* or *normativity*, I am signaling the Foucauldian notion of interrelated strands of cultural, social, economical and political effects that produce common-sensical beliefs and inform normative values.

8. Fay Weldon, *Big Women* (London: Flamingo, 1997).

9. Fay Weldon, *Remember Me*, 1st American ed. (New York: Random House, 1976).

10. For a discussion of the relationship between the categories of posthuman and queer, see Judith Halberstam and Ira Livingston, *Posthuman Bodies*, Unnatural Acts (Bloomington: Indiana University Press, 1995).

11. Brooks's language betrays his masculinist bias. As Sally Robinson points out, Brooks's reading of narrative progress is closely modeled on male sexuality (116). To get around the Freudian phallic logic of drive/tension/discharge/death that Brooks claims, one might posit some of Weldon's themes of multiplicity and afterlife. Her fiction is filled with characters whose splittings create multiple plots (Joanna May in *The Cloning of Joanna May*, Ruth's personas in *The Life and Loves of a She-Devil*, Angelica's personalities in *Splitting*, Praxis's incarnations in *Praxis*). Could Weldon be countering Brooks' "one shot plot" with something more womanly?

12. Fay Weldon, *The Heart of the Country* (London: Hutchinson, 1987).

13. See Judith Bennett, "'Lesbian-Like' and the Social History of Lesbianisms," *Journal of the History of Sexuality* 9.1-2 (2000).

14. In her essay on feminist shortcomings in Carter's revisionary fairy tales, Patricia Duncker makes a similar point to Palmer's, citing Carter's evasion of lesbianism to a failure of imagination: "Some things are unthinkable. She could never imagine Cinderella in bed with the Fairy Godmother" (8). I'd argue that it is Duncker's rigid imagining of a feminist politics (drawn from Andrea Dworkin) that limits her reading of Carter's subversive potential. See Patricia Duncker, "Re-Imagining the Fairy Tales: Angela Carter's Bloody Chambers," *Literature and history* 10.1 (1984).

## Works Cited

Bennett, Judith. "'Lesbian-Like' and the Social History of Lesbianisms." *Journal of the History of Sexuality* 9 (2000): 1–24.
Brooks, Peter. *Reading for the Plot: Design and Intention in Narrative*. Cambridge, MA: Harvard University Press, 1984.
Carter, Angela. "In Pantoland." In *Burning Your Boats: The Collected Short Stories*. New York: Penguin, 1997. 382–89.
Castle, Terry. *The Apparitional Lesbian: Female Homosexuality and Modern Culture*. New York: Columbia University Press, 1993.
Cleto, Fabio. Introduction to *Camp: Queer Aesthetics and the Performing Subject*. Ed. Fabio Cleto. Ann Arbor: University of Michigan Press, 1999.
Cohen, Cathy J. "Punks, Bulldaggers, and Welfare Queens." *GLQ* 3 (1997): 437–65.
De Lauretis, Teresa. *Technologies of Gender: Essays on Theory, Film, and Fiction (Theories of Representation and Difference)*. Bloomington: Indiana University Press, 1987.
Duncker, Patricia. "Re-Imagining the Fairy Tales: Angela Carter's Bloody Chambers." *Literature and History* 10 (1984): 1–14.
Farwell, Marilyn R. *Heterosexual Plots and Lesbian Narratives*. New York: New York University Press, 1996.
Halberstam, Judith. *Female Masculinity*. Durham, NC: Duke University Press, 1998.
\_\_\_\_\_, and Ira Livingston. *Posthuman Bodies. (Unnatural Acts)*. Bloomington: Indiana University Press, 1995.
Palmer, Pauline. *Contemporary Women's Fiction: Narrative Practice and Feminist Theory*. Jackson: University Press of Mississippi, 1989.
Robertson, Pamela. "What Makes the Feminist Camp?" In *Camp: Queer Aesthetics and the Performing Subject*. Ed. Fabio Cleto. Ann Arbor: University of Michigan Press, 1999. 266–82.
Russell, Lorena. "Dog-Women and She-Devils: The Queering Field of Monstrous Women." *International Journal of Sexuality and Gender Studies* 5 (2000): 177–93.
Sedgwick, Eve Kosofsky. *Epistemology of the Closet*. Berkeley: University of California Press, 1990.
Smith, Patricia Juliana. "Lesbian Panic: Homoeroticism in Modern British Women's Fiction." In *Between Women—Between Men: Lesbian and Gay Studies*. Eds. Lillian Faderman and Larry Gross. New York: Columbia University Press, 1997.
\_\_\_\_\_. "'Women Like Us Must Learn to Stick Together': Lesbians in the Novels of Fay Weldon." In *British Women Writing Fiction*. Ed. Abby H. P. Werlock. Tuscaloosa: University of Alabama Press, 2000. 125–47.

Thomas, Calvin, ed. *Straight with a Twist: Queer Theory and the Subject of Heterosexuality*. Urbana and Chicago: University of Illinois Press, 2000.
Weldon, Fay. *Big Women*. London: Flamingo, 1997.
\_\_\_\_\_. *The Heart of the Country*. London: Hutchinson, 1987.
\_\_\_\_\_. *The Life and Loves of a She-Devil*. London: Hodder and Stoughton, 1983.
\_\_\_\_\_. *Remember Me*. 1st American ed. New York: Random House, 1976.

# 12  Stepping into the Same River Twice

## *The Tragic Sexual Mulatto and Subversion of the Inside/Outside Dialectic in the Novels of E. Lynn Harris and Alice Walker*

GRACE SIKORSKI

As Eve Sedgwick has argued so persuasively, the "epistemology of the closet" does indeed seem to structure modern concepts of sexual identity formation. But another aspect of the inside/out dialectic seems to occupy the margins of many bisexual texts — the dialectic of race. In Ernest Hemingway's *The Garden of Eden*, Catherine's bisexuality seems at its height when she role-plays David's African girlfriend and eroticizes her suntan, wishing to be the darkest that she can be. Then she introduces David to Marita, who is darker still, and who cuts her hair to resemble David's African girlfriend as well. In Carson McCullers' *The Member of the Wedding*, Frankie notices that Honey, a paradigmatic mulatto, appears to be a half-made boy to the other characters because of his lavender skin and his alternating use of high and low diction. And even other texts which thematize the problems in representing bisexuality (Nella Larsen's *Passing*, James Baldwin's *Another Country* and *Tell Me How Long the Train's Been Gone*, E. Lynn Harris's *Invisible Life* trilogy, among others), seem to gesture toward a common epistemological puzzle in the representation of bi-racial identity.

Keith Boykin's recent book, *One More River to Cross: Black and Gay in America*, offers a relevant discussion of the connections between concepts of sexual identity and concepts of racial identity. Not only does the rhetoric surrounding race and sexuality intersect on issues such as visibility, authenticity, and passing, but Boykin also observes an insistence on partitioning racial and sexual identities when he writes:

> When we ask multiracial people to self-identify in our bipolar racial dyad, we are asking them to choose which part of themselves is most important ... to box themselves into neatly wrapped categories that make our worlds easier to understand [35].

In other words, the inside/outside dialectic is operative in the formation of communities and the placement of individuals within collectives.

Just as racial distinctions require the division between inside/outside, sexual distinctions often operate on the assumption that homosexuality and heterosexuality are separate, discreet, and pure categories. Due to various political and social forces, a hierarchy of heterosexuality over homosexuality has been established and perpetuated. Homosexuality is an ever-present threat to the purity of heterosexuality. Therefore, one drop, one instance, one impulse of same-sex desire taints the subject so totally that it is coded homosexual. The division between inside (staying in the closet, hiding, or repressing same-sex desire) and outside (being out of the closet, declaring an identity, or acting out same- sex desire) has conceptually dominated the field of sexual identification so much so that any sexuality other than heterosexuality is by default classified as homosexual.

This "one drop rule" is a metaphor borrowed from discourses on racial identities. As Fritz Klein has observed:

> Many people in this country, especially in the South, consider a person with "one drop" of African-American blood to be "black." Why is this person not seen as white at least in degree? The answer is as simple as it is profane. A threat is best dealt with if it is dismissable. In the world of sexual choice the homosexual is the black [10].

That is to say, any degree or frequency of same-sex desire damages the purity of a heterosexual identity because it represents latency or repression, just as one drop of African-American blood tinges an otherwise homogeneous white identity. Even as recently as 1986, Boykin states, the "U. S. Supreme Court let stand a lower court's ruling that a visibly white Louisiana woman was actually black because her great-great-great-great-grandmother had been a black slave in the eighteenth century" (34).

Elizabeth Grosz explains this phenomenon more generally in *Volatile Bodies*:

Dichotomous thinking necessarily hierarchizes and ranks the two polarized terms so that one becomes the privileged term and the other is the suppressed, subordinated, negative counterpart. The subordinated term is merely the negation or denial, the absence or privation of the primary term, its fall from grace; the primary term defines itself by expelling its other and in this process established its own boundaries and borders to create an identity for itself [3].

The process of identity formation, then, requires an I/Thou, subject/object division and the degradation and repression of the identity that threatens the purity of the dominant subjectivity. Or, as Kate Millett comments in her autobiography, *Flying*, "one queer drop queers it all" (433). This accounts for the phenomenon of identity formations based on the divisions and hierarchies of man/woman, adult/child, mind/body, homosexuality/heterosexuality, etc., and the anxiety that is generated when the thin membrane between the two presumably mutually exclusive identities is revealed to be porous, leaky, and perhaps even saturated.

E. Lynn Harris's first novel, *Invisible Life*, is an excellent example of how AIDS rhetoric, coming-out narrative structures, and the genre of the passing novel intersect to reinforce the conception of bisexuality as a threat to homosexual purity and health. Raymond, a young aspiring African-American, struggles not only to define his sexuality, but also his masculinity. As an undergraduate student at a Southern "lily white university" (4), he is torn between his love for his cheerleader girlfriend, Sela, and his football star boyfriend, Kelvin. Haunted by the stereotypes which tell him that he is a "sissy" (14), driven by a "sinful sexual longing" (16), Raymond is filled with fear, shame, and self-loathing because of his bisexuality. After graduation, Raymond moves north to New York City to attend Columbia Law School and begin his career as a sports and entertainment lawyer. Repeating the pattern of the first part of the narrative, he falls in love with Nicole, an understudy for *Dreamgirls*, who is "a porcelain Barbie doll dipped in chocolate" (123) and Quinn, a rich stockbroker who is "a black Adonis" (199). Although he acknowledges his bisexuality at this later point in his life, Raymond still torments himself with his own need to choose between Nicole and Quinn, between a heterosexual identity and a homosexual identity.

The critical point of this narrative is when Raymond discovers that his college lover, Kelvin, has infected a young woman, Candance, with HIV. When she dies, Raymond is consumed with guilt for being bisexual like Kelvin, the alleged conduit for HIV between the straight and gay communities. Raymond reflects:

> I was overcome with a tremendous amount of guilt regarding Candance's death. I was part of a secret society that was endangering black women like Candance to protect our secret desires. Would this have happened if society had allowed Kelvin and I to live a life free from ridicule? Was it our fault for hiding behind these women to protect out futures and reputations? ... Many of us passed in and out of their worlds [253–254].

Raymond regards his bisexuality as an unavoidably duplicitous state of being, torn between two discreet worlds, experiencing a sexual double consciousness, and ultimately destructive in his deception and his ability to pass.

These themes are continued in *Just as I Am*, Harris's sequel to *Invisible Life*. Raymond opens the novel bemoaning his fate in an "imperfect world" (4), calling himself a "sexual mulatto" (4), invoking the literary figure of the "tragic" racial mulatto. The turning point in *Just as I Am* occurs when Nicole and Raymond's mutual friend, Kyle, admits that he is actively dying of AIDS. Kyle teaches Nicole and Raymond the importance of honesty and faith. The novel closes with all of the other main characters uniting to set up an AIDS foundation in Kyle's name, and the reader is reassured of the redemptive powers of family, friends, faith, and honesty. The moral of the story is more than apparent: bisexuality is O.K. as long as everyone knows that you are bisexual.

In her essay, "Invisible Sissy: The Politics of Masculinity in African American Bisexual Narrative," Traci Carroll observes that Harris uses the conventions of the passing novel employed in works such as James Weldon Johnson's *Autobiography of an Ex-Colored Man*, William Faulkner's *Light in August*, Frances Ellen Watkins Harper's *Iola Leroy*, Pauline E. Hopkins's *Contending Forces*, and Charles Chesnutt's *The Wife of His Youth*. Not only in his title's allusion to Ralph Ellison's *Invisible Man*, but also in the frequent references to skin color and mulattos, Harris reveals how bisexuality and biracial identity both challenge "the notion of a fundamental, unitary identity, a truth whose denial offers myriad social benefits at the cost of political compromise and constant fear of exposure" (181). Harris alludes to W. E. B. DuBois's concept of double consciousness:

> It is a peculiar sensation, this double-consciousness, this sense of always looking at one's soul by the tape of a world that looks on in amused contempt and pity. One ever feels his two-ness — an American, a Negro; two souls, two thoughts, two unreconciled strivings; two warring ideals in one dark body, whose dogged strength alone keeps it from being torn asunder.

In some interesting ways, just as homosexuality is the closet to heterosexuality, black is the closet of white. It is that which must be kept hidden to preserve the purity of the dominant classification. According to this equation, homosexuality and black-ness must be repressed and denied; they belong to the unconscious which emphasizes the mulatto's duty to maintain allegiance to a black identity instead of passing for white. Raymond sees it as his duty to pass as heterosexual; he feels that in order to be truly black, he must pass as straight. And, as Carroll observes, "Raymond initially represents bi men as a threat to straight African American women and to the black family, the cause of generational rifts between African American men, and the instigators of a sexual tension that forecloses real emotional intimacy between male friends" (183). Passing threatens the survival of the race, just as it threatens the health and well-being of and marriage of Candance. This casts bisexual men in the role of contagion to women and the African American community. Not only has Raymond's duplicitous sexual nature betrayed a female friend in his refusal to out Kelvin to her which perhaps would have saved her life, he has also lied and betrayed his lovers, his family, his friends, his fraternity, and his coworkers. In alluding to Raymond's conflicts as those of the tragic mulatto, Harris inadvertently reinscribes the dichotomies and hierarchies of race, gender, and sexuality.

Alice Walker demonstrates a significantly different sensitivity to this field of identification, which is structured according to such exclusive and hierarchical categories, when reflecting on the years of her early career in 1987:

> My adult awareness of homosexuality comes from my own feelings of attraction to other women as well as to men (and to yellow people, red people, brown, and white people, in addition to the prescribed black ones). But these feelings toward women, as toward people of other races, were buried very deep, so deep in fact, that I was friends for many years with a woman with whom I discussed everything, who actually had women lovers, but we never discussed that. It was my fault, I'm sure, that we didn't. I was married. I was obviously attracted to men. For that is one of the things, for a woman, that marriage is supposed to "prove." I never spoke of women sexually. It never even occurred to me. Saying the word "lesbian" caused me to stammer ["All the Bearded Irises of Life: Confessions of a Homospiritualist," *Living by the Word* 164].

Walker's anxiety over using the word "lesbian" to name herself reflects not necessarily a degree of homophobia, but perhaps a sense of the inaccuracy of the term. She seems to be negotiating between on the one hand the available vocabulary and conceptual frameworks for sexual identity which presuppose monogamy and monosexuality and on the other hand her experience of loving men and women of various races which implies a plurality of desire and bisexuality.

In the same vein, her well-known definition of "womanist" articulates a philosophy of identity focused on diversity, variability, and acceptance. Part of Walker's definition of "womanist" is most relevant here:

> A woman who loves other women, sexually and/or nonsexually. Appreciates and prefers women's culture, women's emotional flexibility (values tears as natural counterbalance of laughter), and women's strength. Sometimes loves individual men, sexually and/or nonsexually. Committed to survival and wholeness of entire people, male and female. Not a separatist, except periodically, for health [*In Search of Our Mother's Gardens* xi].

Critics have commented that Walker's concept of "womanism," obviously based on a plural and flexible matrix of identification, reflects her feminist woman-identification and her racial pride, but they rarely prioritize her celebration of the bisexual impulse. Bisexuality, the permeability of sexual boundaries, celebration of excess beyond traditional limits, and the logical collapse of the inside/outside dialectic are all necessary aspects of womanism.

Walker demonstrates the potential for deconstructing the categories and boundaries of identification, brings them to the point of collapse, and suggests the potential to reconstruct the terminology used to describe identity. In coining a new term, Walker is engaged in a struggle to create new categories for self-identification from the ruins of the old, new ways of being a body within the cultural field, and new languages of description, a struggle toward agency which she plays out both in her autobiographical and fictional texts.

In *The Same River Twice* (1996), Walker addresses her bisexuality more directly. She explains that, early in her career, her bisexuality caused both her and her male partner "a degree of anxiety." She writes, "At times my deep love of and reverence for women felt like ambivalence to both of us" (27), as if loving men foreclosed the possibility of loving women. However, with the separation from her male lover, her initiation into sexual relationships with women, and her return to health after a prolonged depression and illness, Walker entered a new stage in her writing career. She characterizes this turning point as an "initiation into the next, more mature, phase of life" (32) and a loss of attachment to the "images others might have" (33) of her. In *The Same River Twice*, Walker reveals how she identifies with her character Shug from *The Color Purple* (1982) in her "completely unapologetic self-acceptance as outlaw, renegade, rebel, and pagan; her zest in loving both women and men, younger and older" (35) and the "concept that what is holy is the whole thing" (35). She explains that this shift was like growing a "new skin":

> [W]orking with women, loving and being partners with women, but also recognizing, loving and honoring men who can "see" and affirm women, men who can write true songs about women and attempt to make true movies, is much of the new skin [40].

Significantly, Walker uses skin to signify the semi-permeable boundary between inside and outside, between soul and flesh, between infinite and finite, and between potential and actuality. Skin embodies some of the contradictions and paradoxes of human identity: it at once keeps its shape as a protective layer in order to distinguish between inside and outside, offering an illusion of fixity and permanence, while at the same time stretching or shedding occasionally to grow or regenerate. Skin is the barrier and point of contact between self and other, same and different, individual and collective, and essence and culture that can on occasion bleed into one another. E. Grosz explains:

> The surface of the body, the skin, moreover provides the ground for the articulation of orifices, erotogenic rims, cuts on the body's surface, loci of exchange between the inside and the outside, points of conversion for the outside into the body, and of the inside out of the body. These are sites not only for the reception and transmission of information but also for bodily secretions ..., ongoing processes of sensory stimulation which require some form of signification and sociocultural and psychical representation [36].

Marks, scars, and other imprints can be read on the skin as traces of past events. Skin is also the obvious location of many racial markers and sexual markers. For Walker, skin is a temporary container of a more elusive spirit that ultimately complicates representation and transcends the corporeal matter of the body and its cultural context. Skin is a membrane that is at once inside and outside, at once fixed and ever changing, at once intensely individual and extremely cultural. In relation to representations of sexual and racial identities, this metaphor is highly significant.

One particular character in Walker's later novel *The Temple of My Familiar* serves as an example of how a virtual oversignification of a single body (one character) effects a short circuit in the machinery of monosexual epistemologies and their attendant aesthetics and interpretive strategies. This character is not only a representation of bisexuality's deconstructive potential, but also a representation of postmodern conceptions of racial identity. Through what regulatory norms are sexuality and race materialized? What is the link between sexual bodies and textual bodies? And finally, questions borrowed from Judith Butler that are pertinent to this investigation: "What is left when the body, rendered incoherent through the category of sex, is desegregated, rendered chaotic? Can this body be re-membered, be put back together again? Are there possibilities of agency that do not require the coherent reassembling of this construct?" (*Gender Trouble* 127).

The main narrative of *Temple* involves a young man named Suwelo, whose name we are told is a rune for wholeness, who inherits an old Victorian house in Baltimore when his Uncle Rafe dies. In his uncle's house, Suwelo feels "suspended" (33), not only because he has temporarily put his life on hold, but also because Hal and Lissie, two old friends of his uncle who visit him, tell him their life stories. Suwelo is an American History scholar and professor who prides himself on presenting an even and fair account of history to his students, although he overlooks and belittles the significance of alternative histories, cross-cultural perspectives, and especially women's roles. For the first time in his life, he finds himself reading occasional "scribbled" reactions to events and people, which his uncle had left him "in margins, on notepads and even on some of his medicine-bottle labels" (33). However, his Uncle Rafe is not the character who really catches Suwelo's attention and curiosity. Another marginal figure begins to emerge. Suwelo looks at Rafe's photos hanging on the walls. "They all look like they're trying to speak, but without their names, I can't seem to hear them" (38). Suwelo's worldview is obviously limited by this need to name and define images around him; however, he gradually comes to notice "light oval and square spots where pictures had once hung on the walls. Someone had taken them down" (40). The opening of Suwelo's narrative indicates to the reader that this young man will, in the course of the novel, discover what is missing and learn a new way to interpret and appreciate not only written words, but people they so inadequately represent.

The missing photographs, Suwelo discovers, are of Lissie, who Hal explains is "a lot of women" (38), and whom he calls "our wife" (39). As a child, he says,

> She ruled over the boys, the same way she did over the girls, and she would fight at the drop of a hat. I mean fight like the very devil. She had these big white teeth, and when she got in a fight with anybody she just chopped away at them. She bit a boy's ear near about off that tried to beat up on her, and after that she was like a queen. She'd speak and the waters parted [43].

Lissie is also described as a trickster figure: "There never was enough going on to suit her, so she tended to look on people's lives as if they was plays. She was always moving people around" (43).

Since she can recall all of her past lives, and indeed, all of her past lovers of all genders and races, Lissie's character reveals the potential of one subject to possess or enact plural desires without contradiction. Just as when she was a witch who had a mystical connections to "all three planes — past, present, future — of life" (196), Lissie claims that her hindsight and infinite regression to past lives is a natural human capacity: "it is the nature of the eye to have seen forever, and the nature of the mind to recall anything that was ever known" (65). However, she observes that written representations tend to limit this talent. When "man started to put things on paper" (65) the dynamic and performative aspects of oral delivery were lost. Lissie recognizes the limitations of narrativity and temporality because they reinforce unified subjectivity, linearity, repression, and closure — all of which seem to be contrary to the plural, boundless, expansive nature of memory and spirit.

Therefore, Lissie's relationship with media such as written language, audio recording, photography, and painting is a strained one because representational art, both written and visual, imposes a limited, frozen view of complex reality because it attempts to represent a fragmented and complex subject as a coherent *Gestalt*. Like Hemingway and McCullers, Walker's fiction offers a metafictional commentary on the relationship between life and art as well as writing and reading processes.

Lissie's narrative subjectivity and her very identity is a shifting cipher as meaning is revealed to be impermanent, and interpretation unreliable. Even Lissie's self-portrait reflects a complex attitude toward self-representation. Lissie and Hal paint each other's self-portraits, leaving a blank outlined form where they can each fill in their images: "On the back of Lissie Lyles' self-portrait were the words, in emerald lettering, 'Painted by Hal Jenkins.' On Hal's self-portrait, in bright red, were the words, 'Painted by Lissie Lyles'" (193). In effect, they have constructed the frame, the background, and the context for each other's self-portrait, in a mode reflecting how even self-representation is merely a way of inserting yourself into another's context. The image you attempt to create for yourself is at all times already framed by someone else. Such an image reinforces the concept of permeable membranes between subject positions and the non–Western concepts of inter-being and ego-less-ness.

In these various representations of Lissie, the tension between what is visible and invisible, between personal agency and the imposition of interpretation, and the fixity of image and playful multiplicity reflect in many ways the dynamic between body and soul, which Lissie's character dramatizes, and which comment directly on representations and conceptualizations of bisexuality and multiple racial identities.

Walker seems to be suggesting that claims to the exclusively essential nature of race and sexuality are fallacious not only because race and sexuality are complex categories, but also because identity is linked to the spirit as well as to the body. One is born into a field of signification made up of cultural, social, political, and discursive conventions which identify a body (particularly through language) as a particular race according to skin color (typically white or black) just as it seems to determine the significance of your sexual behaviors and code them either homosexual or heterosexual, through a process of differentiation. However, spirit, which is not corporeal and therefore not identifiable according to its race, sex, sexuality, etc., transcends these categories. Furthermore, if one considers the possibility of reincarnation, the spirit represents wholeness while the body represents only a trace of the whole. And, in Walker's text, spirit is always potentially bisexual and multiply racial, while the body, which is merely a representation of the spirit, is potentially monosexual and singularly racial. Because the body, the penultimate signifier, occupies the time of the present, it is fragmented and incomplete. Lissie explains: "The times of today are nothing, nothing, like the times of old. The time of writing is so different from the so much longer time of no writing" (366). Memory, however, has the potential to reveal wholeness because unlike the body and the "time of writing" or the linearity of narrative, spirit occupies past, present and future simultaneously.

Identities based on hierarchies of difference such as heterosexual/homosexual and white/black are revealed in Walker's text to be artificial, constructed, and at times violent ways of regulating the potential of the human spirit. Identity is based on the superficial appearance of the body more often than it is on the elusive nature of the spirit. Therefore, according to Walker, it requires repression and selection. In contrast, movement toward wholeness and health in Walker's text involves memory excavation of the sort Lissie engages in as well as acceptance of human complexity. Suwelo is led to such wholeness and health when he understands why his wife Fanny falls in love with spirits regardless of their race and sex and how his experience is "Human, the same as woman" (322).

Walker's text is positioned within the matrix of both sexual and racial "regulatory regimes." Her text is concerned with the configuration of bodies that subvert not only sexual categories but racial categories as well. How is sexuality shaped by race and conversely, how is race shaped by sexuality? The binaries of sexual and racial identities are unsettled, dynamic, and relational and sexual identity is positioned complexly within a matrix of racial discourses. Walker attends to the borderlines between and the spaces among these categories in order to call into question the very assumptions of such systems of taxonomy or categorization. She does not assume that all oppressions are congruent, but that they are differently structured, and intersect in complex embodiments. Walker suggests that the only viable subversive potential within the field of sexuality is a multiple, dynamic, fluctuating sexuality that disrupts dichotomies and boundaries of not only sexual identity, but racial identity, and the division between self and other as well. This aberrant sexual identity does not necessarily transcend the conventional discursive field of sexuality, but stimulates anxiety, ambiguity, and crisis, and renders taxonomies of identity problematic.

A textual body, much like a sexual body, is the effect of a dynamic of power, indissociable from the regulatory norms that govern the materialization and the signification of those material effects. In short, the materialization of a sexed human body and the materialization of a sexed textual body are events subject to similar proscriptions, and can be understood as bodies which have the potential to maintain or subvert certain horizons of expectations. Walker's text characterizes in Lissie the potential for what Butler identifies as qualities that have been "foreclosed from the proper domain of 'sex'—where that domain is secured through a heterosexualizing imperative ... an enabling disruption, the occasion for a radical rearticulation of the symbolic horizon in which bodies come to matter at all" (*Bodies That Matter* 23). Walker's characterization of sexual and textual bodies deprives hegemonic culture the claim of essentialist constructions of gender. She does, in effect, "expose the phantasmic effect of abiding identity as a politically tenuous construction" (141).

Through a comparison of Walker's and Harris's texts, one observes two gestures toward bisexuality. Harris characterizes it as a sexual double-consciousness that implies a compromise between two unavoidably different points of view—one true sight and one false consciousness. This formulation of the tragic sexual mulatto reinforces the dichotomies of gender and sexuality and the logic of the "one drop" rule. However, Walker's characterization of bisexuality as one within a complex web of sexual desires which can be and sometimes are enacted by a singular psychological subject who is also paradoxically a plural physical subject collapses the divisions between identity and behavior, between heterosexuality and homosexuality, and between self and other. The very mechanisms of identity formation and textual representation are subverted in the character of Lissie. Perhaps such a speculative and fictive characterization of sexuality forecasts future conceptualizations of desire and identity.

## *Acknowledgment*

© 2002 by The Haworth Press, Inc. All rights reserved.
"Stepping into the Same River Twice: Internal/External Subversion of the Inside/Outside Dialectic in Alice Walker's *The Temple of My Familiar*." Sikorski, Grace. Co-published simultaneously in *Journal of Bisexuality* (Harrington Park Press, an imprint of The Haworth Press, Inc.) Vol. 2, No. 2/3, 2002, pp. 53-71; and: *Bisexual Women in the Twenty-First Century* (ed: Dawn Atkins) Harrington Park Press, an imprint of The Haworth Press, Inc., 2002, pp. 53-71. Article copies available for a fee from The Haworth Document Delivery Service 1-800-HAWORTH; docdelivery@haworthpress.com.

## *Works Cited*

Baldwin, James. *Giovanni's Room*. New York: Dell, 1956.
\_\_\_\_\_. *Tell Me How Long the Train's Been Gone*. London: Joseph Press, 1968.
Boykin, Keith. *One More River to Cross: Black and Gay in America*. New York: Anchor Books, 1996.
Butler, Judith. *Bodies That Matter: On the Discursive Limits of "Sex."* New York: Routledge, 1993.
\_\_\_\_\_. *Gender Trouble: Feminism and the Subversion of Identity*. New York: Routledge, 1990.
Carroll, Traci. "Invisible Sissy: The Politics of Masculinity in African American Bisexual Narrative." In *RePresenting Bisexualities: Subjects and Cultures of Fluid Desire*. Ed. Donald E. Hall and Maria Pramaggiore. New York: New York University Press, 1996. 180-206.
Chesnutt, Charles. *The Wife of His Youth and Other Stories*. Ridgewood, NJ: Gregg Press, 1967.
Faulkner, William. *Light in August*. London: Chatto & Windus, 1933.
DuBois, W. E. B. *The Souls of Black Folk*. Chicago: A. C. McClurg, 1903.
Grosz, Elizabeth. *Volatile Bodies: Toward a Corporeal Feminism*. Bloomington and Indianapolis: Indiana University Press, 1994.
Harper, Frances Ellen Watkins. *Iola Leroy*. Boston: James E. Earl Press, 1892.
Harris, E. Lynn. *Invisible Life*. New York: Anchor, 1994.
\_\_\_\_\_. *Just as I Am*. New York: Doubleday, 1994.
Hemingway, Ernest. *The Garden of Eden*. Ed. Tom Jenks. New York: Scribner's, 1986.
Hopkins, Pauline. *Contending Forces*. Miama: Mnemosyne Press, 1899.
Johnson, James Weldon. *Autobiography of an Ex-Colored Man*. Reprint, New York: Hilland Wang, 1991.
Klein, Fritz and Tim J. Wolf, eds. *Two Lives to Lead: Bisexuality in Men and Women*. New York: Harrington Park Press, 1985.

Larsen, Nella. *Quicksand* and *Passing*. New Brunswick, NJ: Rutgers University Press, 1986.
McCullers, Carson. *The Member of the Wedding*. Boston: Houghton Mifflin, 1946.
Millett, Kate. *Flying*. New York: Knopf, 1974.
Richard, Harriette. "Review of *Invisible Life*." *Journal of African-American Psychology* 21(1995) : 206–210.
Sedgwick, Eve. *Epistemology of the Closet*. Berkeley: University of California Press, 1990.
Walker, Alice. *The Color Purple*. New York: Harcourt Brace Jovanovich, 1982.
_____. *In Search of Our Mother's Gardens*. San Diego: Harcourt Brace Jovanovich, 1983.
_____. *Living by the Word*. San Diego: Harcourt Brace Jovanovich, 1988.
_____. *The Same River Twice*. New York: Scribner, 1996.
_____. *The Temple of My Familiar*. San Diego: Harcourt Brace Jovanovich, 1989.
_____, and Pratibha Parmar. *Warrior Marks*. New York: Harcourt Brace, 1993.

# 13 "Beautiful, or thick, or right, or complicated"
## Queer Heterosexuality in the Young Adult Works of Cynthia Voigt and Francesca Lia Block

DEBORAH KAPLAN AND REBECCA RABINOWITZ

While some have written about what Alexander Doty calls "the queerness of and in straights and straight cultures" (xv), even conventional queer theory (if such a thing exists!) raises hackles when applied to children's literature. Gay characters in children's books are becoming more common, but critical exploration of nonexplicit queerness is still new. How much stranger, then, to apply queer theory to children's books in search of specifically heterosexual queerness. But children's literature is not sexless, and is ripe for exploration of alternative sexualities. While the genre has, of course, less explicit sex than adult literature, it does have some. Moreover, even in the absence of explicit sex, children's literature has sexuality. Queer reading strategies can reveal nuances and dimensions of sexuality in children's as well as in adult literature. Queer theory's interrogatory tools unsettle paradigms of sexuality and gender and bring to light a multiplicity of sexualities — including heterosexuality — that might otherwise be mistaken for a few simple or stable categories. Books which, when viewed with more traditional theoretical lenses, might be seen as exhibiting feminism, alternate forms of manhood, or offbeat relationship structures, reveal powerfully subversive interpretations when viewed through a queer lens. Both the conventional and the queer readings can be equally valid, equally important; separately or together, they both bring something new and important to the text.

Exploring queerness and heterosexuality together offers a multitude of benefits: it brings complexity into the otherwise undifferentiated concept of "heterosexuality"; it defines queerness on it own terms, rather than as radical other existing only in opposition to patriarchal heteronormativity; it allows exploration of various sexual identities and practices among opposite-sex partners; and it acknowledges the richness of human and literary sexuality. However, using queer theory to analyze heterosexuality walks a potentially dangerous line. It enriches both discourses but potentially colonizes the radicalism of queer theory. Cherrie Moraga explores this quandary, ultimately choosing neither side as completely correct. As Moraga says, the overuse of "queer" can dilute its radical potential. On the other hand, human sexuality encompasses a "whole spectrum ... [because] human beings do not conveniently fit within those strict categories of homosexual or heterosexual" (66). She concludes, "queer [i]s a good term to incorporate all those identities" (66). While it is important to identify and minimize the potential pitfalls of applying queer theory to heterosexuality, such application can free heterosexuality from its traditional state of mythic non-complexity, preventing what Annamarie Jagose calls the inappropriate maintenance of "heterosexuality and homosexuality as radically and demonstrably distinct from each other" (18).

Cynthia Voigt's young adult novel *Orfe* is a modernized retelling of the Orpheus story. Narrator Enny (who could be seen as a representation of Ennius, father of Roman literature) tells of her best friend, the singer Orfe. Orfe falls in love with recovering addict Yuri, and she marries him. At their wedding, Yuri is slipped drugs by his addict friends, and returns to their drug-filled house, which (like Eurydice in Hades) he can never leave. Orfe goes into his drug house to sing him out but walks out alone. Yuri plays the role of Eurydice, the twice-killed bride, and Orfe takes on the role of world-class singer Orpheus — though unlike Ovid's Orpheus, she does not mourn the second death of Yuri by retiring for several years of pedophilic gay sex.

Despite the gender swap (and the mythological Orpheus's place as he who introduced gay sex to Thrace), *Orfe* is a heterosexual love story. The primary love story here, as in the Orpheus myth, is that of Orfe and Yuri. The basic narrative is Enny's story of her friend Orfe's love, from meeting Yuri, to marrying him, to losing him and dying in her grief. As Enny tells us, "there was never any question: Yuri was for Orfe, Orfe for Yuri." (75) When Yuri is lost, Orfe's story is ready to end.

Surrounding Orfe and Yuri's relationship are a multitude of other heterosexual relationships. Enny is serially monogamous, dating a series of boyfriends who deserve mention only in passing: "my boyfriend of the time ... Zach" (43); "my boyfriend of the time, whose name was Tommy" (84); "my then-new boyfriend Michael" (63). Even in grade school, Enny has a boyfriend, Leo. Though she dates other men, Enny is obsessed physically and sexually with Yuri. Her descriptions of him are thoroughly sensual, focusing on his hair, "tightly curled ... like the tendrils of grapevines". (78) When she thinks he is going to kiss her at his own wedding to Orfe, the thought brings "an eager swelling of the heart, a longing upward." (98) Yuri has also been solidly heterosexual: "There had always been girls for Yuri. He'd always been there for the girls too.... Girls, women, females — he thought they were wonderful..."(75). The peripheral characters, too, are overwhelmingly heterosexual. By the story's end, Michael has paired off with Enny, and band members Willie Grace and Raygrace (female and male, respectively) are a couple.

Beyond the inherent problematization of heterosexuality caused by the gender swap of Orfe for Orpheus and Yuri for Eurydice, heterosexual relationships transmogrify. Yuri's relationships with Orfe and Enny are complicated by the love triangle among the three of them. Enny desires Yuri, but never considers wanting him enough to take him from Orfe. Despite her attraction and his inaccessibility, Yuri and Enny have an unusually close relationship, one that could be mistaken for dating at first glance. Enny is physically and romantically interested in Yuri, but since she intends to remain loyal to Orfe, one might expect her relationship with Yuri to stay safely distant. However, when Enny first explains her relationship with Yuri, she mentions in passing — strangely casually — that they have been going to movies together. While Enny and Yuri are just friends, they have been participating in this courtship ritual with Orfe's full knowledge and presumed approval. Enny, as narrator, has not bothered to mention it. Does this mean that this traditional heterosexual courtship activity, performed by a couple whose romantic entanglement would have problematic consequences, is insignificant? Or does it, instead, open up a whole queer space of uncertainty? What other significant yet cryptic acts of sexuality could be going on without the reader's knowledge?

Living arrangements are also indicative of fluid gender and sexuality relationships. Orfe never consistently lives with Yuri, but shares time between Yuri's apartment, Enny's room, and her studio. After the wedding, Enny moves into Orfe and Yuri's apartment, sleeping in their bed and paying their bills. Despite her crush, Enny never comes between Orfe and Yuri, but she is an essential part of their relationship, complicating it.

While Orfe sleeps primarily in her studio, Enny beds down in Orfe's apartment by herself. The studio — where she makes her music — is yet another player in this complicated love story. Music fills some of the roles of sex throughout the book. For example, music is how Orfe realizes that she is in love with Yuri:

> She didn't know if she could ask him to kiss her (and she wrote a song). She thought that if she didn't find out, she would waste away with wondering (and she wrote a song). She thought that if she found out what she didn't want to know, she would drown in grief (and she wrote a song) [82].

Atypically, it is the woman, Orfe, who wants to rush into sexual activity while Yuri urges her to wait. Orfe's intertwining of music and sexuality is such that she doesn't understand she's in love with Yuri until she realizes "that there's nothing that doesn't get turned into a song, into music, inside [her]" (82). For Enny, too, Orfe's music is closely tied to sex. At the wedding, Orfe's songs "made you want to go somewhere private and make generous love, but you didn't because you wanted to stay to hear the song." (64). Although the song provokes sexuality, it also acts as a stand-in, making sex itself unnecessary or less relevant. Orfe's final song is similarly complicated, with Enny explaining that she "called [it] a love song, even though ... it never had the word in it." (112). But though the music is complicatedly sexual, it still ultimately contributes to the heterosexuality, leading Enny to desire consummation of her relationship with Michael, and Orfe to understand her love for Yuri. It stands as an odd member of the complicated love triangle, or square — after all, it is not just Yuri's apartment and Enny's dorm room where Orfe spends her time, but also her musical studio with neither of them. Orfe's music is an unorthodox, untraditional element of sexuality and passion that never compromises the characters' underlying heterosexuality.

In addition to sexualized music, the novel is full of queer implications and strange gender roles beyond those inherent in the mythological retellings. When Enny first becomes friends with Orfe, she offers her boyfriend to her, because she would rather have Orfe then Leo. But Orfe shows Enny that "he was dumb, I was dumb, the whole setup was dumb, and Orfe was right not to want to take any part in it" (7). The girls are bound to each other, queerly both opposites and similar simultaneously: Orfe is both "everything [Enny] wasn't" (5) and "more like [Orfe] than anyone" (16). It is Orfe who encourages Enny to throw off her childhood submission to classroom boys, a feeling Enny describes as if she emerged out of "a little closet ... and broken myself free" (19). As an adult, Enny encounters Orfe singing with a band. At the band's concert, Enny is "taken to the girlfriends' table" (27), where she, as Orfe's female friend, sits with the girlfriends of the band members. When Enny worries that she will no longer be Orfe's manager, she is afraid that "she'd dump [her]" (47). Consistently, the terminology of Orfe and Enny's specifically nonsexual friendship is that of a sexual relationship. Perhaps Orfe even recognizes the troubling implications. When one night Enny allows the overly tired Orfe to sleep in her bed, Orfe tells her not to "give me your bed. If you do that, I'll have to move out" (35).

It is more complicated, though, than implied homosexuality between Enny and Orfe. Different sexualities, beyond the either/or of homo/hetero, pervade the book. Even as children, when they play Red Rover — a game in which children must stand on one side or the other — Orfe breaks the rules. She would dart "toward one section, then feint to another side, run backward, or simply run down around the end of the long line, and the line would pull itself sideways like a drunken snake to try to keep Orfe in the game" (12). This is not a direct metaphor for sexuality but it offers a new nonbinary theoretical model: more sides exist than the traditional two. It also defines Orfe as someone who does not take simple sides. It is Orfe who says, when as an adult she is thinking about forming her own band, "there will never be only one center stage" (52). She sets the scene for shifting circles of focus and passions that lean in multiple directions. Her music, acting almost as a sexual partner, is yet another element of her sexuality which is more complicated than a simple homo/hetero distinction.

Even their friends, paired off into heterosexual partnerships, contribute to the strangeness. Michael feels like he should be jealous of Yuri and Enny's feelings for him, but he is not. Enny, while admiring Yuri's masculinity, notices how his body "relaxed into curves" (78), even though curves are traditionally feminine markers. And "Yuri could have had anybody, and he picked Orfe" (80) — but does "anybody" include both men and women? Willie Grace, a woman with a man's first name, is fierce and aggressive. Raygrace is gentle and reasonable, and even incorporates the female name "Grace" into his male name "Ray" when it seems like Orfe's band (female-only until that point) will reject him without the assimilating name change. These two form a seemingly stable heterosexual partnership. They are not simply gender role swapping; as their bi-gendered names suggest, their relationship is more complex.

A different version of the same novel could have been a frustrated lesbian novel. Orfe and Enny, that story could have gone, are destined for each other, but society will only allow them to show their feelings through friendship, shared heterosexuality, and music. But that is not this story. There is no potential for homosexual relationships in the world of *Orfe*, but only because that is not what this book is about. This is not a repressed world but a world of great and varying passion and fluidity. Everyone is heterosexual, from repulsive boyfriend Tommy with his nuclear, heteronormative, and misogynistic vision of marriage; to Enny with her string of boyfriends; to Yuri, who is found beautiful by everyone, even by Enny's otherwise-heterosexual boyfriend Michael. The most explicitly complicated sexuality in the novel is the polyamory that Yuri finds in his Hades, surrounded by drug addicted girls from whom Orfe cannot win him free. But the heterosexual characters and their relationships are infused with queerness, from Enny and Orfe's friendship, to their sexualized music, to their bizarre love triangles.

Cynthia Voigt creates a different kind of heterosexual queerness in *Seventeen Against the Dealer*, the last book in her Tillerman Cycle, a series of seven books about the Tillerman family and their friends. Dicey Tillerman, who began the series at age thirteen, is now 21. Having tried college and decided it is not for her, Dicey returns home to Crisfield, Maryland, to live with her grandmother and siblings. What she wants more than anything is to build boats. *Seventeen Against the Dealer* concerns Dicey's attempt to form a boat business from the ground up while juggling her relationship with her boyfriend and her care for her family.

Dicey, like everyone else in this cycle of novels, is heterosexual. Though the novel subverts heteronormativity, heterosexuality is never questioned; no other options are possible in this world. Dicey's boyfriend, Jeff, lives nearby but spends the majority of the story conveniently away at college. As in *Orfe*, the heteronormativity of their relationship is immediately problematized by a gender role reversal and then further by Dicey's fierce, soul-driven relationship with her boat business. Dicey is, however, thoroughly heterosexual.

There is no doubt that Dicey loves Jeff. His voice, over the phone from college, goes "into her heart" (249). When she thinks about him, it is "like the sun coming out after days and days of rain" (239–40); planning to call him feels "like the promise of sunrise held out at the end of darkness," something that fills her time and actions with "lightness" (247). When she can not locate him, she feels "an empty hollowness locked inside her rib cage. Like an empty house" (287). She calls him "'the man I love'" (8). He is "woven into her life ... the warp threads and the woof threads, all the colors and the intricate design.... Even the texture wouldn't be what it was without Jeff" (9). She loves him physically and sensually, as well as with her heart: she thinks of "[t]he silky feel of his hair, and his strong young shoulders — the clean smell of him and the distant beating of his heart from deep inside his body" (13). He certainly returns her love, and she knows it. Although Voigt is never sexually explicit, Jeff and Dicey do sit in a darkened car where Jeff "gather[s] her into his arms" (13). The heterosexuality also extends to their probable future of marriage and to the total dearth of Dicey's interest in anyone else, ever. In the whole Tillerman cycle, Dicey never considers any romantic or sexual relationship with anyone except Jeff, and once she has accepted Jeff as a partner, she never questions her desire.

Nonetheless, heterosexuality is problematized. Dicey's grandmother worries that Dicey and Jeff "don't ... spend half-enough time necking" (16), which implies a slightly distant or only mildly sexual relationship. Dicey says that even if she never marries Jeff she does not think she would ever marry anybody else. Dicey is more Jeffsexual than classically heterosexual. Finally, despite this implied mildness of desire, Dicey would have sex with Jeff if only he would agree — but Jeff will not before marriage. This male insistence on waiting hearkens back to *Orfe*, where Yuri insists on waiting before sex in defiance of Orfe's initial desire.

Yuri and Jeff, less sexually-driven their female partners, perform their genders queerly. Judith Butler's theory of performative gender holds that gender must be understood not as a "stable identity" but rather as "the mundane way in which bodily gestures, movements, and styles of various kinds constitute the illusion of an abiding gendered self" (179). Gender is not an innate quality that predetermines the actions an individual will take in life. Instead, gender is acted out as a complex role whose performance (both conscious and unconscious) is the result of those "gestures, movements, and styles" — and also major life choices and tendencies. Dicey and Jeff, like Orfe and Yuri, frequently perform gender by acting in ways traditionally associated with the opposite sex. Their attitudes towards sexual activity, in which each character expresses preferences associated with both sexes, brings a multiplicity of genders into their bedroom attitudes.

When Jeff goes off to college — where he remains for almost the entire story — Dicey ignores him for so long that she almost loses him. She does not ignore him intentionally; she is simply too wrapped up in her boat business to remember how much time is passing without her returning his calls. When she does remember him, she resents the time commitment a telephone call requires. Jeff, though beloved, is not her highest priority. Preoccupation with business at the expense of a romantic relationship reverses traditional gender roles; stereotypically it is the man who ranks work over romance and contact.

But this gender reversal also reveals a queerness in sexuality, because Dicey's boat business plays the role of a lover in her life. Boats are what she dreams about and describes with an unusual sensual affection:

> She wanted to build a boat with a carved rudder to guide it by and the long, varnished tiller under your hand. Not plywood either. Dicey Tillerman had an idea about a slender, soft-bellied boat built out of planks of wood fitted together so close it was as if they'd grown that way, sturdy enough for heavy winds but light enough so the slightest breeze would fill the sails and move it across the water [2].

Unlike Orfe, who has room in her life for both music and Yuri, monogamous Dicey has room in her life for only one or the other — business or boyfriend. Everything she does requires full absorption, full dedication, and full passion. She almost loses Jeff while trying to get the business off the ground. Dicey's feelings towards her boats are all-encompassing, all-important, her soul's deepest desire. The opening scene sets up this structure: the first chapter's first word is Jeff calling Dicey's name; "[s]he heard him, but didn't hear him"(1); she contemplates her boat business plans for two full pages; he says her name again; and she contemplates her boat business for two more pages before she answers. The boat business provides a reverie for her, while Jeff— the boyfriend she really does love — must fight to penetrate her focus. When she returns to Jeff after the business fails, she offers to give up any further idea of a boat business in order to marry. Jeff, unthreatened by Dicey's quasi-adulterous relationship with boats, is offended by the offer and insists she keep her other love as well. Eve Kosofsky Sedgwick says that queerness exists whenever "the constituent elements of anyone's gender, of anyone's sexuality aren't made (or *can't be* made) to signify monolithically" (8). Such lack of monolithic signification can also reveal queerness in particular moments and particular acts, as it does here with Jeff's refusal of Dicey's offer.

The couple's debate following Dicey's offer is infused with such fluid signifiers. Jeff does not accept her agreement to get married until she explains her reasoning; it is not enough for him that she has come back to him in lieu of the boat business. The answer he does accept, which she could not come up with earlier in the book, is this: "She couldn't explain. She couldn't even begin to explain. There were too many reasons, all too woven tight together into a cloth that was too ... beautiful, or thick, or right, or complicated, she didn't know what — she only knew what its value was" (334). Things that can not be explained and do not fit neatly into definitions are the core of queerness — and are the only answers that satisfy Jeff. Jeff points out, "'There's no need for you to have to choose, Dicey'" (331), asking her "'besides me, what are you going to do?'" (337). By proposing that Dicey learn boat-building in a course or an apprenticeship, Jeff gives her back her other love — boats — and overrides her assumption of being allowed only one passion. Like Orfe and Yuri, who did not reject either music or Enny when they chose one another, there will be room for third parties in their heterosexual, monogamous marriage. Their relationship, finally, is both perfectly heterosexual (including an upcoming wedding) and queer.

When it is settled that they will be together, it feels to Dicey "like the wind rising to fill the sails of a boat" (335). Their togetherness is called "right" (335) and the sudden resurrection of her boat-building plan is also called "'right'" (337), linking Dicey's two kinds of love. Dicey's feeling as the book closes is of happiness, gratitude, and the need for courage from "the heart, or the stomach, or wherever courage came from" (338). But there is no need to know where it comes from, and there is no doubt that a love that is "beautiful, or thick, or right, or complicated" (334) is perfect for Dicey and Jeff.

The sexualities that queer theory reveals in *Seventeen Against the Dealer* and *Orfe* would be seen under other lenses as forms of gender politics, feminism, alternate masculinity, or simply unusual — but not extreme — heterosocial and homosocial relationships. Doty points out that even when queerness in texts is not an "essential, waiting-to-be-discovered property," it is not "any less real than the straightness others would claim the same texts" (xi). This lens disturbs boundaries and reveals powerful and powerfully subversive social constructions in the seemingly most innocent of texts. Although we focus on the misleadingly innocent world of children's literature, these subtle subversive sexualities are nowhere near as extreme as children's literature allows. Francesca Lia Block's critically acclaimed young adult novel *Weetzie Bat*, written in 1989 and oddly noncontroversial, provides one example.

Weetzie is a loving teen in Los Angeles. With her "bleach-blonde flat-top" (4) and homemade hipster dresses, she roams LA with her best friend, Dirk. Dirk is "the best-looking guy at school" (4), but when he tells Weetzie he is gay, she reassures him that it "doesn't matter one bit" (9). Moreover, when Dirk comes out to Weetzie, he tells her that she is "a beautiful, sexy girl" (9). Sex appeal and attractiveness are not exclusive to potential romantic partners. Weetzie and Dirk go out every night looking for romance, but instead find a string of worthless men, including one who (probably) date rapes Weetzie. At last Dirk finds his boyfriend Duck, a sweet boy with a "blonde flat-top" (29) — a hairstyle just like Weetzie's, but natural instead of bleached. But Weetzie, who "ha[s] been mistaken for a boy before" (34), has not been a mere temporary stand-in for Dirk's partner, to be rejected when he finds love. The three teenagers move into a house together, a perfect little family: "They were a threesome. A foursome if you counted Slinkster Dog" (30). The sexualized language of "threesome ... foursome" is repeated later in the paragraph, and followed up with Weetzie trying not to listen to the boys' sex through her bedroom wall. This family, described in magical realist, fairytale terms, is explicitly sexual.

The decidedly odd sexuality of Weetzie's little family only increases after she finds her own romantic partner. The allegorically named My Secret Agent Lover Man is exactly what Weetzie had explicitly wished for. Alas, Weetzie wants to perfect her non-conventional family in a conventional manner: with a baby. MSALM refuses to participate, and Dirk and Duck step in. Weetzie joins with two gay men acting as surrogate partners to father her child. In a pseudo-romantic interlude, they order sushi, reaffirm their love for one another, and have sex (multiple times, a fact dropped casually, as almost unworthy of mention). The incident is treated by the narrative as naive and well-meaning but unhealthy, though not because Weetzie is using two otherwise fully homosexual young men to father her child. Rather, the dysfunction is rooted in deceiving MSALM. There is nothing that the narrative voice finds wrong with the thoroughly queer sexual act of a heterosexual woman having intercourse with a pair of partnered gay men.

Ironically, in later books in the Weetzie Bat series, Weetzie's daughter Cherokee Bat — eventually adopted by MSALM — is well adjusted and as wholly normal as any daughter of Weetzie's could possibly be, although she was conceived in an act of thoroughly queer heterosexuality. The dysfunctional child of the series is Witch Baby, MSALM's daughter who was conceived in a heterosexual affair he has in his anger over Weetzie's deception. Witch Baby — conceived heterosexually but in anger — grows up bitter, surreal, and depressive, unlike the lovely and lighthearted Cherokee.

Weetzie's triangle of het girl, gay boy, gay boy is an overtly queer heterosexuality. Cherokee's conception is heterosexual, yet there are many other aspects to the sex act which leave it queer: the homosexual young men who sleep with a woman for love; the polyamory of the threesome; the implied recurrence of the act; and the deliberate, loving friendship surrounding the act, in stark contrast to Weetzie's incense- and massage-filled romantic interludes with MSALM just a few pages previously. Cherokee is born as an initially ungendered baby. Contrary to popular American practice of announcing the gender simultaneously with the birth, Cherokee has been in existence for many paragraphs before she is identified as female. Additionally, the foursome delight in finding similar features in the baby's face to her mother and her three fathers. She is a girl-child in Weetzie's model: "a girl love-warrior" (54) in a "pink fringed coat" (72). Weetzie's queer family is finally complete when Witch Baby arrives. "[W]elcome to the family" (63), MSALM tells his daughter. Dirk and Duck return home from coping with an AIDS death to find

> Weetzie and MSALM and Cherokee and Witch Baby and Slinkster Dog and Go-Go Girl and the puppies Pee Wee, We Wee, Teenie Wee, Tiki Tee, and Tee Pee were waiting on the front porch drinking lemonade and listening to Iggy Pop's "Lust for Life" as the sky darkened and the barbecue summer smells filled the air.... Then all six of them held on to one another in a football huddle and the dogs slunk around their feet [87].

Here is their household: a girl; an allegorically named lover; two gay boys; a baby with one mother and three fathers, conceived in a queer threesome; a witchy love child, adopted lovingly by the betrayed partner; and seven dogs; living together as a family in a little house. It is not clear how old these teenagers are; the book begins in high school, with no clear time stream in the magical realistic narrative. But whether they are older teens or young adults, they are perfectly content with their postmodern family. They have a mom, dads, kids, dogs, even a car. Their family forms a portrait by a queer Norman Rockwell outlined in glitter, an alternative American dream.

Nothing in *Seventeen Against the Dealer* or *Orfe* is as starkly queer as even the most mainstream of Francisca Lia Block's books. The wide range of explicit queerness in *Weetzie Bat* does not, however, diminish the potential queerness of the Cynthia Voigt books. Instead, the books together reveal several new points on the complex and infinite web of queer possibilities. Sedgwick describes some of her work as directed "not at reconfirming the self-evidence and 'naturalness' of heterosexual identity and desire, but rather at rendering those culturally central, apparently monolithic constructions newly accessible to analysis and interrogation" (9). We have aimed in this paper to render both queerness and heterosexuality more accessible to analysis and interrogation, while also questioning the presumed simplicity of children's sexuality. Are these books straight? Yes. Are these books queer? Yes. As Doty recognizes, "texts and people's responses to them are more sexually transmutable than any one category could signify — excepting, perhaps, that of 'queer'" (xix). Queer theory reveals the beautiful, thick, right, and extremely complicated range of possibility in literature and in life.

## Works Cited

Block, Francesca Lia. *Weetzie Bat.* New York: HarperCollins, 1989.
Boone, Joseph A. et al,. eds. *Queer Frontiers: Millennial Geographies, Genders, and Generations.* Madison, WI: University of Wisconsin Press, 2000.
Butler, Judith. *Gender Trouble: Feminism and the Subversion of Identity.* New York: Routledge, 1990.
Doty, Alexander. *Making Things Perfectly Queer: Interpreting Mass Culture.* Minneapolis, MN: University of Minnesota Press, 1993.
Jagose, Annamarie. *Queer Theory: An Introduction.* New York: New York University Press, 1996.
Moraga, Cherrie. "An Interview with Cherrie Moraga: Queer Reservations, or, Art, Identity, and Politics in the 1990s." By Rosemary Witherspoon. In Boone et al. 64–83.
Sedgwick, Eve Kosofsky. *Tendencies.* Durham, NC: Duke University Press, 1993.
Voigt, Cynthia. *Orfe.* New York: Atheneum, 1992.
_____. *Seventeen Against the Dealer.* New York: Simon Pulse, 1989.

# PART IV.
## INSTABILITIES AND WAYWARD SUBVERSIONS

# 14 Nom de Guerre
## Homosociality in Timothy Findley's The Wars

SHELTON WALDREP

"His wounds are poems." — *The Wars*, 49

Through poetic images, fictitious tape recorded monologues, and an unusually successful use of the second-person singular point-of-view, Timothy Findley's novel *The Wars* (1977) accurately recreates a delicate time in history.[1] The reader manages to feel the First World War for what it really was: the boredom of semi-isolated groups of men attempting little jobs at great odds; officers who felt abandoned; infantry nearly paralyzed with fear or longing; and the tragic underestimation of modern technology and the ruthlessness that this created. The Great War, as Findley demonstrates, was the last war in which men could claim the innocence of boys at play, of a past that can be explained using the same old stories. Though World War I dominates the novel's theme, it must share some of its room with protagonist Robert Ross, a character who is both transparent and opaque. One feels intimate with him and yet the novel is an attempt to mend fragments and create him out of the past and out of the reader's mind. On the surface, Ross is a nineteen-year-old Ontario native who leaves his comfortable home to endure the horrors of the Western Front. Metaphorically Ross is an observer in an age filled with people always on stage. He stands in for Robbie Ross, the literary executor and first male lover of Oscar Wilde. Ross was the friend who saw Wilde through the pain, and often boredom, of his relationship with young Lord Alfred "Bosie" Douglas and who stood by Wilde through the fatal fall of his trial. Ross outlived Wilde to write perhaps the best early critical work on him and to compile the first complete edition of his writings. In Findley's novel, Ross is the observer of two such relationships: the brotherly relationship between Clive and Michael, and the overtly homoerotic relationship between Clive and Jamie Villiers. Ross learns of the latter as a child when he hears his sister Barbara refer to the couple as Wilde and Bosie. The narrator notes that Clive "was one of the Cambridge poets whose best-known work — like that of Sassoon and Rupert Brooke — had its roots in the war" (103).

The character of Ross connects the era of Wilde with the dawning of early modernism and the great homoerotic poets of the First World War — Robert Graves, Siegfried Sassoon, Brooke, and perhaps especially, Wilfred Owen. An important key to an understanding of *The Wars* lies in the link between the sexuality of the novel and the homoerotic sensuousness that is evident in their poetry. In *The Great War and Modern Memory*, Paul Fussell delineates the major themes and nodes of the thinly closeted connection between the fragility of male physical beauty and the near defenselessness this beauty, these bodies, encounter at the front — "flesh menaced by hurtling iron," as Fussell terms it. The description that Fussell paints of Owen and the soldier boy most admired in his poetry could, in fact, easily apply to the character Ross: "faunlike good looks, innocence, vulnerability, and 'charm'" (272); "athleticism ... heroic readiness ... for 'sacrifice'" (278); "conscientious, efficient, and sympathetic" (289). Ross's own love takes its strongest form in his devotion to fellow soldier Harris. But this love occurs at a hospital when it is too late to be anything but pure and chaste. The dying Harris is also allowed to symbolize all of the generation of sensitive British poets who were cut down with machine gun fire at the battle of the Somme. In the hospital, Harris occasionally regains consciousness to mumble snatches of subconsciously created poetry and then look deeply into the eyes of Ross who spends every day by his friend's bedside, but is confused by his desire to do so: "The hours were made worthwhile whenever Harris woke and smiled and sometimes Robert had to look away because he was confused by what he felt" (95). Harris's dreams often include underwater fantasies in which he imagines himself swimming with fish because "they accept you there" (95). After Harris's death, Ross steals his gloves and blue scarf and wears them the entire time he is at the Western Front. Along with Harris, Ross occupies the position of both subject and object, lover and loved, as did the real heroes of the poetry of the Great War.

Certainly the masculine image as developed through Ross and his fellow soldiers would be considered odd by heterosexist standards. Ross is "sensitive" and not at all keen on killing. He refuses to kill his sister's pet rabbits after she dies even though his mother orders him to. Similarly, he is almost unable to comply with the dictates of rank when ordered to kill a horse that has broken its leg. Ross's devotion to the "feminine" as much as to the "masculine" side of himself imbues his character with a kind of gender ambivalence that is heightened by the book's wartime setting, though some of what may be taken as Ross's gender ambiguity may also be an aspect of Findley's acknowledgment of a Canadian masculinity. Though working in medium of film, Lee Parpart's notion of a "colonial masculinity" pertains to Ross's situation as well. Parpart notes that "chronic political and economic uncertainty and exposure to heterogeneous influences from within — may have contributed to a spectrum of masculine/Canadian performative styles that are in some cases milder, more respectful of marginality and less invested in symbolic shows of phallic authority than those in other parts of the world" (176). A Canadian hero-/anti-hero such as Ross must be "soft around the edges" to be convincing. However, Findley frames the question of male gender in general as constructed, changeable, and difficult ever to pin down. In considering the particularly Canadian aspect of masculinity, the critic Jay Scott concludes:

> Americans routinely condition their males to swagger with a strut that is rare in Canada, so rare that a gay friend of mine on his first business trip to Toronto was stupefied. "Every man in this town seems gay to me," he swooned. "They're all so effeminate." It's merely that Canadian male children grow up softer around the edges — less assertive, less demanding, less butch — than their American cousins [46].

Findley's creation of Ross supplies his country with another kind of hero and at the same time questions the very nature of what a Canadian hero should be. By using the archetype of the poet of the Great War, Findley creates an alternate model of male gender construction: out of war, the most masculine of enterprises, comes a specific kind of androgynous awareness.

Ross's sexual and gender identities are shaped by his experience of sex as violent and always ambivalent in terms of identity. As a mere recruit, Ross is shocked to see Taffler, his country's greatest living war hero, get his rocks off playing horsy with a tongueless Swede in the brothel where Ross is expected to lose his virginity.[2] This scene may come a little late to have Oedipal ramifications, but it is still significant to Ross's psychic makeup since his job, as an officer, is to emulate Taffler. Several critics

(Brydon among them) have noted that Ross's life parallels Taffler's: both men are in their physical prime; both have ambivalent sexualities; both sleep with the same woman; both end up horribly wounded. They appear to be, in some ways, Gothic doubles. Ross goes on to have the standard male heterosexual experiences, though he remains a bachelor. Significantly, Ross's bachelorhood is supported by his mother. In Canada he is pursued by hometown girls, but refuses their advances: "Robert turned away, annoyed and confused. He was shy of girls, just now — distrusting them and wondering why they had to look at you and make you think you wanted them" (18). As E.K. Sedgwick postulates about James and his characters: "To refuse sexual choice, in a society where sexual choice for men is both compulsory and always self-contradictory, seems, at least for educated men, still often to involve invoking the precedent of this nineteenth-century persona — not Mr. Batchelor himself perhaps, but generically, the self-centered and at the same time self-marginalizing bachelor he represents" ("Beast" 160). When Ross finally does have a heterosexual experience, it is set within an overdetermined Gothic framework.

Ross visits the convalescent hospital that is run by the parents of the d'Orsey daughters on the grounds of their country estate where he subsequently has an affair with Lady Barbara d'Orsey. While at the house, Juliet and Barbara's gay brother, Clive, who refuses to go to war, entertain "all his pacifist friends" (148), including Taffler, who tries to commit suicide by rubbing the stumps of his arms against the wall of his room. Ross is given a guest room that the twelve-year old future Lady Juliet says is haunted by "Lady Sorrel's ghost" and that Ross should "expect her every night at two but not to wait up for her since she isn't really all that exciting" (145). The reader learns that the ghost lights candles to "keep her vigil" for her husband, the Earl of Bath, who perished against Cromwell's army as a Royalist (150). Young Lady Juliet decides to frighten Ross by dressing as Lady Sorrel's ghost, entering his bedroom while he is asleep, and lighting a candle on the mantle. However, when she opens his door, she is the one who is frightened by what she sees:

> Two people hurting one another. That's what I thought. I knew in a cool, clear way at the back of my mind that this was "making love" — but the shape confused me. The shape and the violence. Barbara was lying on the bed, so her head hung down and I thought that Robert must be trying to kill her. They were both quite naked. He was lying on top of her and shaking her with his whole body.... Robert's neck was full of blood and his veins stood out. He hated her. And Barbara's hand was in her mouth [156].

Once again, as with the scene between Taffler and "the Swede," sex is linked to the appearance of violence — specifically, a tableau in which Ross is poised like a vampire. Though Ross appears to be in the dominant position, it is Lady Barbara who seems to suck men dry: she loves and abandons Jamie, Taffler, and Ross, each after they are wounded, and dumps a current beau as soon as Ross arrives and she realizes he is available. As Mary K. Patterson Thomburg observes, the Gothic myth creates the polarities of masculine and feminine, often as two sides to one person, but also as two characters: the ultra-manly villain and the ultra-feminine heroine/victim. The myth conventionalizes these aspects into what she terms the "sentimental." Ross's ambivalence corresponds to Thomburg's definition of a Gothic character: "The fragmentation of characters implied in the Gothic complexity of motive begins in the sentimental side of the myth, with the behavioral ambiguity that suggests deeply conflicting motives within characters who are otherwise presented as more or less singly, if not simplistically, motivated" (52–53). The novel's Gothic characteristics emphasize the sexual tensions that function within the world of the war: a decentered, horrified, Gothic world in is own right.

The most disturbing manifestation of these tensions occurs toward the end of the novel when Ross is sexually assaulted in a public bath run at an insane asylum. Ross believes he is overpowered by four strong, and he thinks, retarded men; however, the narrator relates that the men are four soldiers — possibly his own. Some critics (McKenzie and Brydon, for instance) have viewed this scene simply as a metaphor for the violence of war. However, every encounter with sex that Ross has had in the novel has been either violent, "perverse," and/or guilt-ridden. The first of these occurs when as a teenager Ross is "making love to his pillows" while his invalid sister, Rowena, falls from her wheelchair and dies (21). Ross is supposed to be her protector and is normally never away from her. The next encounter is in the bordello where he has a premature ejaculation and, with the prostitute, he spies on Taffler engaging in his sado-masochistic homosexual activity. The next event is the vampiric encounter with Lady Barbara. The penultimate is when Ross masturbates himself to sleep after looking at himself in the mirror: "He made a fist around his penis. He thought how small it was. He drew his knees up" (163).[3] The last is the rape scene.

While the rape is clearly described as an act of violence toward Ross, we are also told that the rapists caress him, lie under him and on top of him, and attempt to give him oral sex. The scene is significantly set in "the baths." The description of the asylum is one of separate "cells," now serving as changing rooms, and one large common bathing area. Towels are left for the clients in the cells; the water is illuminated by a large skylight. The ambiguity of the connection between sex and violence is brought together in a setting reminiscent both of a contemporary gay bathhouse and the steely horror of a prison. The physical and mental violence of war interconnect in an ambivalent montage to create one of the book's major binaries: wanting, and not wanting. Going to the Western Front to die, but not wanting to be killed. While Findley does not, of course, condone rape or war, he sees their ultimate driving mechanisms as being, perhaps, one of the locations for both homosexual and heterosexual male sexual desire.

War as rape blurs the line between violence and sexuality and complicates the novel's portrait of masculinity by making literal the male body as the site of struggle in war. The setting of a common bath area underlines the novel's particular concern with and framing of Ross's body. Early in the book, Ross's mother notices bruises that he received from attempting to stop the hired-hand from murdering Rowena's rabbits: "'There's such a large blue mark just above your shoulder blades,' she said with a smile. 'You look as if you'd gone to sea and had yourself tattooed'" (26). He is also described as being popular because "no one could dislike a man who blushed" (29). Later, he is given sick leave for falling down in the hold of the ship; he is uninjured, but the bruises alarm his commanding officer. Finally, his body burns in a scene that is described mythically and heroically: "But just as the walls began to fall in on top of the fifty horses — all of them standing in their places while they burned — Robert turned the mare and she leapt thorough the flames — already falling — with Robert on her back on fire" (186). Ross's easily bruised, fragile, blushing body is itself a locus of desire on the part of the reader and the narrator/Findley. This framing of Ross's body as fragile is connected to two aspects of the novel as a whole: Fragility functions as a metaphor for the book's structure, its fragmentation into tape recordings, diary entries, photographs, narration, etc. Simone Vauthier describes the "overall narrative" as "a mosaic of fragments" (25). The metaphor for fragility also extends to the fragile sanity of the characters in the novel: Mrs. Ross slowly goes insane; Bonnycastle commits suicide; one of Ross's men goes insane during the gas attack; Taffler attempts suicide; Ross describes Leather as insane; Ross is considered officially insane after he frees the horses, etc. And literally, the metaphor is embodied in the stained glass door to the dugout that Ross shares with Devlin, a soldier who collects antiques and has a "devotion to fragility," and with the other members of the dugout: one of whom collects wild animals and the other books. The devotion, then, is widespread. The devotion to Ross's body as an object of lust is shared by the Ladies Juliet and Barbara d'Orsey, the prostitute, Rowena, his mother, the rapists, Harris, and, probably, Taffler, not to mention various fellow soldiers such as the young "bugler" who Ross befriends, along with many horses and dogs, during his travels. Ross's body, its sensual and sensuous tangibility, is constantly foregrounded by the book and is metaphoric of its main structure and theme.

\* \* \*

"There is no good picture of this except the one you can make in your mind."—*The Wars*, 71.

Though the book gives us a rich background of muddy trenches, meetings of the Bloomsbury Group, and brilliant stories by the Lady Juliet d'Orsey, it also provides a dissertation on perception: the twentieth-century obsession with language and consciousness of which the book's own words and structure become the literal and metaphoric example. Findley constantly confronts the reader with questions concerning the interpretation of the novel's events. The reader becomes conscious of her own belief in the abstract objectivity of the past tense, the assuming of the persona of the barely etched archivist, and her own role of reader as reader. This last is brought about by the novel's shifting point-of-view, choice of detail, and self-conscious style of writing that is woven together with an artistry that manages almost always to sidestep awkwardness. Process and self-conscious artistic enjoyment are modeled with shades of the detective and biographical genres. It is not accidental that *The Turn of the Screw* and *The Picture of Dorian Gray* are mentioned by Lady Juliet as her favorite childhood books (154).

However, Findley primarily develops the novel's tensions between point-of-view and presentation, and not between plot and expected novel convention. Almost every critic who has written on *The Wars* has found it necessary to discuss the novel's modernist structure, something that for Sedgwick, is connected directly to the homo/hetero binary and the dictates of the closet:

> The public rhetoric of the "empty secret" ... the cluster of aperçus and intuitions that seems distinctively to signify "modernism" (at least, male high modernism), delineates a space bounded by hollowness, a self-reference that refers

back to — though it differs from — nineteenth-century paranoid solipsism, and a split between content or thematics on the one hand and structure on the other that is stressed in favor of structure and at the expense of thematics. [T]his rhetoric of male modernism serves a purpose of universalizing, naturalizing, and thus substantively voiding — depriving of content — elements of a specifically and historically male homosexual rhetoric. But just as the gay male rhetoric is itself already marked and structured and indeed necessitated and propelled by the historical shapes of homophobia, for instance ... of the highly permeable closet, so it is also true that homophobic male modernism bears the structuring fossil-marks of and in fact spreads and reproduces the specificity of desire that it exists to deny [*Closet* 165].

When Robert Ross deserts the army, a peculiar event occurs at the Ross family's house in Canada: "In the drawing room, sitting in its silver frame, Robert's picture started to fade. It got completely dark" (180). Ross's fate becomes that of Dorian's. He loses his beauty in the fire, yet he is allowed to live for a few more years. The novel's moral, however, does not need to follow quite so homophobic a paradigm as Wilde's. There is at least a suggestion that Ross might have survived in another time and place. The period, the coming of modernism, is one in which it is impossible to avoid the pressure related to the invention of homosexuality. The break that occurs with past history includes a new definition of sexuality, sex acts, and gender. The character of Ross typifies the problem of defining these new identities by differing with oneself and with others. The allo/autosexuality that characterizes him throughout the novel is parallel to the inability to separate the feminine and masculine within one person's psyche. While naming, labeling becomes difficult and silence as a discourse can seem to dominate, the book struggles to make visible and to complicate the erotics of the homosocial via the display of the male body, the trajectories of the various relationships — especially those between men — and the existence of gay characters. The novel's fragmentation and search for the picture of an event are part of the epistemological problems involved in the construction of a theory of gay writing.[4] The book sets up various binaries that attempt to form and reform axes of investigation: marriage/sexuality; gay/straight; sentimental/demonic; individual/collective; national/international; sickness/health, etc. However, as Foucault analyzes the beginning of the century: "Henceforth social differentiation would be affirmed, not by the 'sexual' quality of the body, but by the intensity of its repression" (129). *The Wars* provides a view of both the repression and the beauty of the sexual.

# Notes

1. For a detailed synopsis of *The Wars*, see Diana Brydon's "'It could not be told:' Making Meaning in Timothy Findley's *The Wars*." The novel's complex structure does not present events chronologically: As Brydon notes: "[W]e are entirely dependent for the telling on the teller — the anonymous researcher working in the archives, sorting through the debris of the past in an effort to discover a pattern that makes sense for him. The archives, a combination library and museum, provides the framing space in which the telling of this story takes place" (65). Many articles, some of which will be referenced in this paper, have dealt with the technical artistry involved in constructing the novel's form.

2. There is much more to say about the idea of the hero that is at work in the novel than I can mention here. Much of Ross's conception of the hero comes from his meetings and images of Taffler. Associated with these are horses, which are also used as metaphors for sexual acts as in Peter Shaffer's *Equus*, and the subgenre of boy's literature: Conrad, Chums, etc. At the same time that Ross is becoming a hero and dealing with Taffler's image, his younger brother is also falling under the influence of the heroic soldier ideal: a perverse influence seen as popular during wartime.

3. Mirrors are mentioned throughout the book. Ross breaks the mirror in the room in the bordello after he sees Taffler. Lady Juliet remembers catching her brother Michael masturbating before a mirror. Pirie notices yet others: "When Lewis Carroll's Alice leaves behind one identity, she exchanges it for a looking-glass reflection of herself, mirros and pictures that alter identity.... Similarly, Robert looks down into a puddle which foreshadows the watery world of the trenches but is also a mirror that shows his new military identity.... The decisive moment arrives when he steps into the puddle and stands there. Identity-distorting mirrors appear again, along with pictures, in that other place of initiation, the brothel: 'Directly opposite the door, there was a wall that was covered with paintings of Odalisques and mirrors, so the first thing you saw was yourself, intermingled with a lot of pink arms and pale breasts'" (77).

4. The novel's ultimate refusal to mend the fragments of heterosexuality (or homosexuality) into a stable whole are not unlike the reading that Guy Davidson provides of William Friedkin's controversial film *Cruising*. Davidson argues that much gay literature post-Stonewall actually "restores the homo/hetero divide" by recreating, at the level of narrative structure, "the reification of gay identity." In Friedkin's film, by contrast, "the radical failure or disruption of the conventional protocols of narrative closure emphasizes a blurring of straight and gay categorization and, collaterally, points up the fluidity of identity that is the flip side of commodified identity in contemporary consumer capitalism." The film, therefore, "refuses teleological revelation, instead positing at its close an enigma that leaves open the possibility of a deconstruction of the paranoid heterosexual subject..." (54).

# Works Cited

Brydon, Diana. "A Devotion to Fragility: Timothy Findley's *The Wars*." *World Literature Written in English* 26 (1986): 75–84.

\_\_\_\_\_. "'It Could Not Be Told:' Making Meaning in Timothy Findley's *The Wars*." *The Journal of Commonwealth Literature* 21. (1986): 62–79.

Davidson, Guy. "'Contagious Relations': Simulation, Paranoia, and the Postmodern Condition in William Friedkin's *Cruising* and Felice Picano's *The Lure*." *GLQ* 11 (2005): 23–64.
Findley, Timothy. *The Wars*. New York: Penguin Books, 1977.
Foucault, Michel. *The History of Sexuality, Volume I: An Introduction*. Trans. Robert Hurley. New York: Vintage Books, 1978.
Fussell, Paul. *The Great War and Modern Memory*. New York: Oxford University Press, 1975.
McKenzie, Sister M. L. "Memories of the Great War: Graves, Sasson, and Findley." *University of Toronto Quarterly: A Canadian Journal of the Humanities* 55 (1986): 395–411.
Parpart, Lee. "The Nation and the Nude: Colonial Masculinity and the Spectacle of the Male Body in Recent Canadian Cinema(s)." In *Masculinity: Bodies, Movies, Culture*. Ed. Peter Lehman. New York: Routledge, 2001. 167–192.
Pirie, Bruce. "The Dragon in the Fog: 'Displaced Mythology' in 'The Wars.'" *Canadian Literature* 91 (1981): 70–79.
Scott, Jay. "Girls Make Passes at Boys Who Wear Dresses: The Cross-Dressing Comedy of the Kids in the Hall." *The Village Voice*, 12 Dec. 1989: 43–47.
Sedgwick, Eve Kosofsky. "The Beast in the Closet: James and the Writing of Homosexual Panic." In *Sex, Politics, and Science in the Nineteenth-Century Novel*. Ed. Ruth Bernard Yeazell. Baltimore: The Johns Hopkins University Press, 1986.
_____. *Epistemology of the Closet*. Berkeley: University of California Press, 1990.
Thomburg, Mary K. Patterson. *The Monster in the Mirror: Gender and the Sentimental/Gothic Myth in* Frankenstein. Ann Arbor: UMI Research Press, 1987.
Vauthier, Simone. "The Dubious Battle of Storytelling: Narrative Strategies in Timothy Findley's *The Wars*." In *Gaining Ground: European Critics on Canadian Literature*. Ed. Robert Kroetsch and Reingard M. Nischik. Edmonton: NeWest Press, 1985. 11–39.

# 15 Granville Barker's Effeminate Heterosexuals

## *The New Drama's New Men*

### ANNE STILES

But what is vitally important to the play ... is the balance of sympathy in [Amy's] case. We must feel that beside Trebell's future career ... she is a *worthless little thing*; but we must also feel enough pity for her fate to understand why Trebell ... shoots himself [Harley Granville Barker to Nicholas Hannen, 11 October 1936].

In this striking letter to Nicholas Hannen, Edwardian playwright, producer and director Harley Granville Barker explains the meaning of his drama *Waste*, which the state had censored in 1907 on the grounds that its allusions to a terminated pregnancy were morally offensive. Clearly, Granville Barker wished to make one thing plain to Hannen, who played the part of the philandering protagonist, Henry Trebell, in the production that took place in 1936 when the ban on *Waste* was finally lifted. The playwright emphasizes that the drama's leading lady, Trebell's mistress, Mrs. Amy O'Connell, should in no way eclipse Trebell as an object of audience attention and sympathy. Granville Barker evidently wanted his cast to know that *Waste* is unequivocally a drama about male affairs and the male-dominated arena of politics, not about the "worthless" heroine whose seduction and botched abortion dominate the first two acts. The vehemence of the language he uses to convey this point suggests doubt about whether Trebell's character could, in fact, carry "four solid acts ... on his shoulders"—in short, whether the audience would acknowledge Trebell as the play's dramatic center (Granville Barker to Hannen, 17 September 1936).

Certainly, Henry Trebell is an unlikely hero for an Edwardian political drama. While first act of the play depicts Trebell as a "hard-bitten, brainy" and emphatically masculine hero, he ends up an effeminate emotional wreck (*Waste*, 231).¹ Before committing suicide to atone for the death of his unborn child, Trebell identifies with his deceased mistress and her terminated fetus, undergoing a symbolic pregnancy: "The man bears the child in his soul as the woman carries it in her body" (336). While effeminate male behavior in *fin-de-siècle* British drama is not unheard of—one thinks of Wilde's insouciant, overdressed dandies, for example—Trebell's desire to usurp female reproductive functions is something else altogether. Although Trebell appears resolutely heterosexual, his effeminacy and gestation fantasies queer his role within the drama. This essay will explore how Henry Trebell and Edward Voysey, the protagonist of Granville Barker's earlier play, *The Voysey Inheritance* (1905), embody a queer heterosexuality that is ultimately a reactionary response to the presence of the New Woman on the late-Victorian and Edwardian stage.

Granville Barker's anxiety about whether Trebell could sway the "balance of sympathy" in his favor and "carry the play" reflects the upsurge of interest in various polemical forms of femininity at the *fin de siècle*. New Women, odd women, and the "woman with a past" pervaded plays of this period, sometimes relegating men to peripheral onstage roles. Simultaneously, female actors, theater managers, and playwrights gained increased prominence, alarming some male rivals. Important *fin-de-siècle* women in theatre include actress and playwright Elizabeth Robins, actress-manageress Mrs. Patrick Campbell, and Granville Barker's first spouse, actress Lillah McCarthy. Opportunities for women in theater widened significantly between 1885 and 1910, the decades during which Henrik Ibsen, Oscar Wilde, Arthur Wing Pinero, George Bernard Shaw, and other dramatists initiated the cult of the heroine on the Victorian and Edwardian stage.

While the degree to which these prominent women actually undermined male dominance of the theatrical world remains questionable, male playwrights grumbled about this growing feminine influence. The most notable example is Shaw, who, like his friend Granville Barker, was a member of the reformist-socialist Fabian Society and an advocate of women's suffrage. Nonetheless, he memorably complained in 1894 that women were taking over contemporary drama both onstage and behind the scenes:

> We cannot but see that the time is ripe for the advent of the actress-manageress, and that we are on the verge of something like a struggle

between the sexes for the dominion of the London theatres, a struggle which ... must in the long run end disastrously for the side which is furthest behind the times. And that side is at present the men's side [xxix-xxx].

Shaw describes turn-of-the-century British theatre as a battle of the sexes, indicating that he saw the actress-manageress as part of a broader feminist social upheaval.

Another friend of Granville Barker, prominent theatre critic William Archer, likewise regretted what he saw as late Victorian playwrights' failure to achieve a "virile" or "potent" English drama, partly due to foreign and female influences on the stage. In "Drama in the Doldrums" (1892), Archer denounces the "intellectual impotence" of "native drama," suggesting that modern British drama had become effete or emasculated (150). Meanwhile, in "The Free Stage and the New Drama" (1891), Archer eagerly anticipates "the new English drama — the vigorous, accomplished, virile stage-literature of the future" (663).

Granville Barker sympathized with Archer's views, putting them into practice during his management of the Court Theatre from 1904 to 1907. Indeed, Granville Barker's lifelong effort to create a British national theater (realized thirty years after his death, in 1976) was partially an attempt to find a suitable venue for the virile national drama Archer imagined. In 1904, the two authors jointly penned *A National Theatre: Scheme and Estimates* (published in 1907), where they proposed to establish a British National Theatre to rival the Théâtre Français in Paris or the German Court Theatres. In this work, they envisioned a "vitalised English drama" that would "restore the English drama to that honourable place among the intellectual achievements of the race which it has so long forfeited" (xi, 9). While *A National Theatre* tones down the misogynist rhetoric of Archer's earlier work, replacing "virile" with "vitalized," the proposal still contains masculine overtones. The National Theatre must aggressively "bulk large in the social and intellectual life of London" and "impose itself on public notice" (xvii).

The writings of Granville Barker, Shaw, and Archer thus bear out Rebecca Walkowitz's observation that progressive *fin-de-siècle* males could support "the advanced New Woman in the abstract" while simultaneously being "terrified by and disoriented by any signs of female sexual agency in the flesh" (qtd. in Showalter, *Sexual Anarchy*, 52). In contrast to Shaw and Archer, however, Granville Barker responded to female influence not with polemic but with two male-centered dramas, *The Voysey Inheritance* and *Waste*. These dramas attempt to come to terms with the New Woman, and create a dramatic New Man who could compete with her on the Edwardian stage.

## Granville Barker and the New Woman

Granville Barker's male-centered dramas needed male protagonists who could "carry a play" by demonstrating the same emotional range and dramatic appeal of contemporary onstage women. In investing male characters with breadth and depth, Granville Barker consciously or unconsciously modeled his male protagonists after popular female characters of the period. As a result, Granville Barker's male heroes seem effeminate, even queer, with their melodramatic posturing and emotional display, and their deviant wish to usurp feminine roles more generally (exemplified by Trebell's imaginary pregnancy). In fact, Edward Voysey and Henry Trebell closely resemble heroines of dramas in preceding decades, specifically, the New Women and the "woman with a past." Like Paula Tanqueray of Pinero's *The Second Mrs. Tanqueray* (1893) or Vivie Warren of Shaw's *Mrs. Warren's Profession* (1894), the heroes of these New Dramas monopolize audience attention and sympathy, demonstrating physical legibility and emotional lability that abruptly depart from stereotypes of stoic Victorian manliness.

Granville Barker's emotive male protagonists also diverge from the well-known figure of the Wildean dandy. Alan Sinfield describes the Wildean dandy as "effete, camp, leisured or aspiring to be, aesthetic, amoral, witty, insouciant, charming, spiteful, dandified" (vi). By contrast, Granville Barker's heroes are usually prudish upper-middle-class professionals. Moreover, Wilde's dandies in plays like *Lady Windemere's Fan* (1892), *A Woman of No Importance* (1893), and *The Importance of Being Earnest* (1895) are flippant and humorous flâneurs, rarely tragic or serious figures like Edward Voysey and Henry Trebell.

There is another important difference between Granville Barker's heterosexual protagonists and Wilde's sexually ambiguous dandies. Twentieth-century critics often assume that Wilde's dandies are implicitly homosexual, although Sinfield reminds us that dandies are "generally pursuing women characters" (vi). One might even argue that dandies lack passion towards either sex. For instance, Joseph Bristow has described Lord Illingworth in *A Woman of No Importance* as one of those "dandies [who] are for the most part libertines who seem to have little interest in whether their objects of desire or sexual exploitation are male or female" (letter to the author, 22 March 2005).

Nonetheless, Bristow suggests that the word "effeminate," which could be applied to both Granville Barker's and Wilde's protagonists, has been "firmly, if not exclusively — linked to male homosexuality [ever since] Oscar Wilde was tried for 'gross indecency' in 1895" ("Effeminacy," 269). It would apparently follow that if Granville Barker's protagonists exhibit effeminate behaviors like emotional expressiveness and aesthetic display, then they must necessarily be homosexual. I would join Lisa Hamilton in cautioning readers against "over-read[ing] effeminacy as a stable signifier of homosexuality in the works of the nineteenth-century and earlier periods" (232). Moreover, I would extend her warning to some early twentieth-century texts (like Granville Barker's) whose characters display effeminate behaviors that differ markedly from Wilde's audacious fictional and public personae.

Given Granville Barker's dream of a "virile" English drama, why did he create this somewhat humorless, emotional, and insistently effeminate type of male character? Probably Granville Barker promoted these effeminate male protagonists to better utilize the talents of the male actors in his troupe — himself included. Granville Barker occasionally played Edward Voysey and Henry Trebell, albeit only "when there was no more suitable player available" (Morgan, xviii). In such a role, Granville Barker and others could demonstrate dramatic flexibility that would prove harder to achieve with a stoic, traditionally masculine hero. Ironically, then, an effeminate hero promoted masculine theatrical dominance by stealing attention away from female leads.

Granville Barker's effeminate protagonists are not just a reactionary bid for male domination of the British stage, however. They are also (paradoxically) a response to feminist demands for male virtue. As a Fabianist and sometime champion of women's causes, Granville Barker surely knew of the virtuous "New Men" advocated by New Women as the antithesis to domineering, vice-ridden Victorian patriarchs. *Fin-de-siècle* feminists coined the term "New Man" to denote a type of effeminate heterosexual who could serve as an appropriate love interest for a New Woman. Olive Schreiner, for example, vividly contrasts the old-fashioned "fox-hunting, hard-drinking, high-playing, recklessly loose-living country squire, clergyman, lawyer and politician who headed the social organism of the past," with the virtuous New Man, who "find[s] in woman active companionship and cooperation rather than passive submission" (118).

An earlier influential description of New Men comes from novelist Sarah Grand, whose 1894 articles in *North American Review* oppose the virtuous "man of the future" to the degenerate "man of the moment," a "weak-willed, inconsistent creature" whose "low tone about women is a sign of a degenerated gentleman ... [and] a decaying nation" ("Man of the Moment," 622). The sexual incontinence of the "man of the moment" leads to venereal disease and makes him an undesirable spouse. By contrast, the man of the future demonstrates high moral standards, intelligence, courtesy and sexual continence — in short, "the truth, the affection, the earnest purpose, the plain living, high thinking, and noble self-sacrifice that make a man" ("New Aspect of the Woman Question," 275).

Grand's theoretical prototype of the virtuous New Man finds fictional embodiment in her own novels and in influential works by New Woman writers like George Egerton and Charlotte Perkins Gilman. These fictional New Men share certain traits with their New Women counterparts, like artistic sensibilities, intellectual rigor, bohemian lifestyles, sexual frigidity, as well as androgynous appearances and mannerisms. Unlike the New Woman, however, the New Man appears passive and childlike. In *fin-de-siècle* feminist narratives, the heroine often rescues her male love interest. While Beth Maclure of Sarah Grand's *The Beth Book* (1897) nurses Arthur Brock back to health during a long illness, the heroine of George Egerton's "The Regeneration of Two" (1893) saves her New Man from hypothermia in the icy Norwegian forest. Such male helplessness echoes Grand's statement that "man morally is in his infancy ... now woman holds out a strong hand to the child-man, and insists, but with infinite tenderness and pity, upon helping him up" ("New Aspect of the Woman Question," 273).

While one might read Granville Barker's effeminate protagonists as sexual dissidents, then, their effeminacy also makes them suitable partners for New Women. Edward Voysey and Henry Trebell resemble the New Men of 1890s feminist fiction in several significant respects, being intellectual, emotionally vulnerable, and dependent upon women. Moreover, both characters occasionally adopt passive or feminine roles: while Trebell undergoes a symbolic pregnancy, Edward Voysey accepts a New Woman's marriage proposal. Henry Trebell is particularly interesting because his character resembles that stock character of late-nineteenth-century drama, the "woman with a past."

Granville Barker innovatively refashioned such effeminate, emotive characters into dramatic heroes rather than sidelined love interests in feminist fiction. The playwright's effeminate protagonists simultaneously fill his need for an emotionally expressive onstage presence to "carry a play," accommodate feminist demands for male purity, and acknowledge Archer's call for a virile national drama that would privilege masculine concerns.

## Edward Voysey: The New Man

*The Voysey Inheritance*, Granville Barker's first acclaimed play, centers on the corrupt business dealings of Edward's father, Mr. Voysey, an unscrupulous solicitor who embezzles his clients' money. When Edward Voysey discovers the family firm's dirty secrets, he threatens to quit, but ultimately remains in order to help his father pay back stolen funds. Mr. Voysey dies shortly thereafter, forcing Edward to inform his family about the father's crimes. The anticlimactic ending reveals that the family members know about Mr. Voysey's "mismanagement" but do not wish to repay their ill-gotten gains. Edward nobly resolves to tidy up the Voyseys' financial mess on his own, living on a reduced salary. Meanwhile, he accepts the marriage proposal of his New Woman love interest, Alice Maitland.

The play's first act contrasts Edward's understated manliness with his father's overbearing traditional masculinity. Mr. Voysey is "masterful" (83); by contrast, Edward appears "refined but self-conscious" (85)."[2] Edward's interests in philosophy, agnosticism, and ethics signal his deviation from mainstream Edwardian manliness. George Booth, Mr. Voysey's close friend, complains that Edward is "no use. Too many principles ... men have confidence in a personality, not in principles" (122). Contemporary reviewers of the play evidently took their cue from such passages. For instance, Max Beerbohm wrote in 1905 that Edward "is a prig, and has steeped himself in various ethical systems" (519). Such critiques fulfilled Granville Barker's own prediction that Edward Voysey would be misread because of "the superstition that a good man on stage must always be a strong one, and that a sensitively weak character cannot be interesting" (Letter to Archer, 8 November 1905).

Another indication of Edward's non-traditional masculinity is his relationship to the aggressive New Woman, Alice. Alice Maitland is introduced by the ever-present stage directions as "a young lady of any age to thirty. Nor need her appearance alter for the next fifteen years ... She possesses indeed the sort of athletic chastity which is a characteristic charm of northern spinsterhood" (109–110). Alice's agelessness, her "athletic chastity" (which suggests, perhaps, her New Woman-like muscular celibacy), and her authoritative demeanor contrast with Edward's youth and passivity, indicating gender role reversal.

The drama circles playfully around Alice's dominating, even emasculating behavior, sometimes resorting to off-color humor to get the point across. For instance, in Act II Edward cracks nuts for Alice, which she then ravenously devours, and Alice mischievously offers Booth a cigar cutter. Clearly, this castrating New Woman is a threat to her New Man as well as a potential helpmeet. Alice even questions Edward's fitness for his job: "A business life is not healthy for you, Edward. You look more like a half-baked pie crust than usual" (114). With her condescending concern for Edward's well-being, Alice becomes a phallic mother figure, while the unresisting Edward becomes "like a child with her" (155). The exchanges between Alice and Edward thus reflect anxieties about castration and infantilization of the patriarch.

Paradoxically, Edward's future marriage also holds forth redemptive possibilities. This union would make Edward head of his own domestic sphere, reinforcing his masculinity. If Alice rescues Edward, in effect, then this story could read like a fairy tale in reverse, where a courageous New Woman redeems a passive New Man (not an unusual scenario in feminist fiction, as we have seen). Archer seemed to favor this reading of the play, recommending that Granville Barker close with Alice and Edward's handclasp part-way through the final scene, instead of extending the drama another few minutes. Granville Barker responded that he stood by the drama in its original form, since he did not wish to emphasize Edward and Alice's relationship: "I won't, won't bring the curtain down on the handclasp at the end ... the last bit is a necessary finish to the play which has been about Edward's Inheritance and not about his love for the girl" (Letter to Archer, 8 November 1905). Granville Barker's reply emphasizes the dramatic importance of the male protagonist and the relative contingency of the woman he intends to marry.

Perhaps Granville Barker refused to end the play with the blissful union of New Man and New Woman because he was not entirely confident that "sensitively weak" Edward Voysey could carry *The Voysey Inheritance* all by himself. By concluding the play with the unresolved inheritance plot, rather than the resolved marriage plot, Granville Barker symbolically preserves the male domain of financial affairs from the encroachment of the New Woman. Evidently, Granville Barker perceived the New Woman as a dramatic threat whose onstage presence must be minimized and contained.

## *Henry Trebell: The Man with a Past*

Granville Barker's controversial *Waste* recycles many elements of the earlier drama: the action focuses on the plight of aspiring politician Henry Trebell against the backdrop of a tightly-knit, all-male homosocial group (not unlike the abundant, mostly male Voysey clan). Secondary characters include a thoroughly dispensable New Woman who serves as a catalyst for the play's main events. Despite these familiar elements, *Waste* departs from its predecessor by introducing the "man with a past" or fallen man, a protagonist who is severely punished within the drama for his sexual transgressions. He is, of course, a variation of the fallen woman character so common in period drama. As Sos Eltis notes, "the epithet 'fallen' could be applied to any woman who had indulged in sex outside the legal and moral bonds of marriage, whether as a seduced virgin, adulterous wife, or professional prostitute" (223). While novelistic incarnations of the fallen woman include the eponymous heroines of *Lady Audley's Secret* (1862), *Tess of the D'Urbervilles* (1891), and *Ruth* (1853), the fallen woman could also be found onstage in plays by Ibsen, Shaw, Wilde, and Pinero.[3] Like a typical fallen woman, Trebell is alternately seducer and seduced, sinner and penitent. More importantly, Trebell's sexual past destroys his hopes for a viable future. In a period in which so many dramas focused on fallen women of one sort or another, centering a play on a fallen man defied conventional double standards for male and female sexual behavior.

As Eltis observes, the categories of fallen woman and the New Woman often overlap. In Pinero's *The Notorious Mrs. Ebbsmith* (1895), for example, New Woman Agnes Ebbsmith's tragic fate demonstrates that, in Eltis' words, "the new woman [is] the fallen woman in a different frock" (232). The categories of New Man and fallen man likewise overlap, so that Trebell fits fairly well within both. In contrast to Edward Voysey, Trebell outwardly displays a stoic, rugged manliness that belies his emotional volatility. But this traditionally masculine exterior hides a morbidly sensitive interior. By the play's conclusion, the audience can literally read Trebell's emotional turmoil in his gestures and facial expression. Granville Barker achieves Trebell's dramatic catharsis at the expense of Amy, the play's female lead, who gets shoved ungraciously offstage as soon as she presents serious competition for audience attention.

The complicated plot of *Waste* centers on Trebell's political maneuvering as he tries to form alliances with his rivals in Parliament. Early in the play, he sleeps with and impregnates Mrs. Amy O'Connell, a married woman separated from her husband. When she asks him to recommend a competent abortionist, Trebell urges her to have the child; when she refuses, he turns her away in disgust. Soon after, Amy dies as a result of a botched operation, a preventable tragedy since Trebell knows of capable and willing physicians. Her death takes place offstage, however, and

Act III opens upon politicians deciding how best to hide Trebell's disgraceful sexual affair from the public. The remainder of the play focuses on Trebell's political downfall, as his peers decide it is too risky to work alongside a politician tainted by this scandal.

The play's treatment of the fallen man may be one of the reasons *Waste* was banned from public performance for many years. The censor's official objections to the play included "extremely outspoken references to sexual relations" and "reference to a criminal operation [i.e., abortion]" (qtd. in Kennedy, 84). Earlier that year, however, the censor had condoned Robins' *Votes for Women!* (1907), which also contained overt references to abortion. Dennis Kennedy speculates that *Waste* was more controversial because the drama highlights negative consequences of a man's sexual transgressions. While censors passed numerous light bedroom farces, a drama like *Waste* went too far because, as a reviewer for the *Observer* stated in 1912, "You may show a flagrant and cheery adulterer so long as you do not suggest that any harm can come to him" (qtd. in Kennedy, 96). *Waste* thus breaks down sexual double-standards by introducing a male character who suffers and dies as a result of a disastrous love affair.

The striking manner in which the drama focuses on men's reactions to a woman's tragedy, culminating in a tragedy in a man's life, presents an intriguing dilemma. If *Waste* were a traditional drama of a fallen woman, then the play would focus on Amy's emotional turmoil and tragic death, rather than the reactions of politicians who barely know her. Amy's contingency is underscored by the fact that her tragedy occurs relatively early in the drama, and entirely offstage. Moreover, the politicians who later discuss Amy's death seem devoid of sentimentality or sympathy. One of them insensitively remarks, "Since Mrs. O'Connell is dead what is the excuse for a scandal?" (280). Trebell himself cruelly dismisses the subject of Amy's death: "Well...? We can stop thinking of this dead woman, can't we? It's a waste of time" (299).

Amy fades from view as the play decidedly shifts the focus onto Trebell. The last two acts depict Trebell's emotional turmoil leading to his suicide, as well as his surprising transformation from manly womanizer to emotive, effeminate hero. As the drama's conclusion approaches, sometime philanderer Trebell increasingly adopts demonstrative behavior and physical posturing appropriate for melodrama. For instance, in a heart-to-heart conversation with his sister just before his suicide, Trebell becomes increasingly emotional, speaking first "in deep anger" (325), then with "his voice strangled in his throat" (330), finally "helpless, almost like a deserted child" (332). Trebell starts exhibiting tell-tale symptoms of that stereotypically feminine disease, hysteria, including his strangulating sensation, which resembles the *"globus hystericus"* that Elaine Showalter describes as "the sensation that a ball was rising in the esophagus, producing a feeling of choking or suffocation" (*The Female Malady*, 130).

If Trebell's position as the play's dramatic focus were not clear enough from the stage directions, Granville Barker's correspondence would remove any lingering doubts. In a letter to Hannen, the playwright emphasizes the centrality of the hero's role: "Trebell has to carry [the play] on his own shoulders ... *four solid acts to carry on his shoulders. And we must be glad to see him when he comes on in the fourth!*" (Letter to Hannen, 17 September 1936). A subsequent letter to Hannen, cited in the introduction to this essay, describes Amy as a "worthless little thing" in comparison to Trebell's political career. While the audience might be tempted to identify with Amy, the playwright and his hero seem utterly uninterested in her, despite her marked resemblance to Trebell; after all, both characters flaunt traditional gender binaries and demonstrate the slippage between "New" vs. "fallen" manhood and womanhood.

Although Granville Barker vehemently protests that Amy cannot be the focal point of the drama, it is uncertain whether the play actually manages to move "the balance of sympathy" entirely away from her. Amy's dramatic presence lingers long after her demise. She ultimately achieves her dramatic revenge as her misfortune poisons Trebell's chances for happiness. Like Amy's terminated pregnancy, Trebell's symbolic gestation ends in a stillbirth or abortion; he refers to "some feeling ... some power which should be the beginning of new strength. But it has been killed in me unborn" (335). His failed symbolic pregnancy can be interpreted in three ways: the death of his unborn child, the end of his promising political career, and his own suicide, all indirect results of Amy's tragic fate. Granville Barker's desire to have his effeminized hero "carry the play" and wrest attention away from its "worthless" heroine ultimately fail, as Amy haunts the play's conclusion despite the playwright's efforts to banish her memory.

The play's ambivalent conclusion leaves us with a paradox of sorts. In evaluating Granville Barker's dramas, one must weigh in the balance both his innovative development of male roles and his reactionary plots, which deliberately sideline female characters. One must further consider the contrast between Granville Barker's apparently progressive dramatic achievements and their conservative motivations. On the one hand, Granville Barker's New Men brought excitement and depth to Edwardian theatre, where duller, more static male characters predominated. Further, these New Men introduce a fascinating type of deviant heterosexuality to the Edwardian stage.

On the other hand, one must remember that the dramatic triumph of the New Man in Barker's plays is achieved at the cost of the New Woman. Even if Granville Barker's heroes embody attributes of the New Man described in the visions of Grand and Schreiner, it remains the case that his New Men are most decisively not the democratic companions whom these New Women so ardently sought. Instead, Granville Barker's effeminate protagonists are dramatic competitors for the cultural space that New Women had come to occupy in 1890s drama. By stealing the limelight away from their female counterparts, Granville Barker's New Men upstage whatever political gains the New Woman might have achieved in progressive venues such as the Court Theatre. The misogynist origins of Granville Barker's sensitive New Men should remind us that queer forms of heterosexuality do not imply a progressive outlook, but may indeed stem from conservative or even reactionary cultural trends.

## Notes

1. There are two published versions of *Waste*, one written in 1907 and the other in 1927. Though most of the characters remain the same, the dialogue has been significantly changed in the revised version. Because of my focus on the Edwardian period, I will refer to the 1907 version.

2. Because I focus on Granville Barker's Edwardian literary productions, I cite this out-of-print, earlier version of *The Voysey Inheritance* rather than the slightly revised 1912 version reprinted in Dennis Kennedy, ed., *Plays by Harley Granville Barker* (New York: Cambridge UP, 1987).

3. For a fairly extensive list of popular English *fin-de-siècle* plays featuring fallen women, see Eltis, 227.

## Works Cited

Archer, William. "The Drama in the Doldrums." *The Fortnightly Review* 52 (1892): 146–167.

\_\_\_\_\_. "The Free Stage and the New Drama." *The Fortnightly Review* 50 (1891): 663–672.

\_\_\_\_\_, and Harley Granville Barker. *Scheme and Estimates for a National Theatre.* London: Duckworth, 1907.

Beerbohm, Max. *Around Theatres.* New York: Knopf, 1930.

Bristow, Joseph. "Effeminacy." *Gay History and Cultures: An Encyclopedia.* Ed. George Haggerty. New York: Garland, 2000. 268–270.

\_\_\_\_\_. Letter to the author. 22 March 2005.
Eltis, Sos. "The Fallen Woman on Stage: Maidens, Magdalens, and the Emancipated Female." In *The Cambridge Companion to Victorian and Edwardian Theatre*. Ed. Kerry Powell. Cambridge: Cambridge University Press, 2004. 222–236.
Grand, Sarah. "The Man of the Moment." *North American Review* 158 (1894): 620–628.
\_\_\_\_\_. "The New Aspect of the Woman Question." *North American Review* 158 (1894): 270–277.
Granville Barker, Harley. "The Voysey Inheritance." In *Three Plays by Harley Granville Barker*. London: Sidgwick and Jackson, 1909. 83–210.
\_\_\_\_\_. "Waste." In *Three Plays by Harley Granville Barker*. London: Sidgwick and Jackson, 1909. 213–342.
Hamilton, Lisa. "Oscar Wilde, New Women, and the Rhetoric of Effeminacy." In *Wilde Writings: Contextual Conditions*. Ed. Joseph Bristow. Toronto: University of Toronto Press, 2003. 230–253.
Kennedy, Dennis. *Granville Barker and the Dream of Theatre*. New York: Cambridge University Press, 1985.
Morgan, Margery. Introduction to Harley Granville Barker *The Madras House: A Comedy in Four Acts*. London: Methuen, 1977.
Salmon, Eric, ed. *Granville Barker and his Correspondents: A Selection of Letters by Him and to Him*. Detroit: Wayne State University Press, 1986.
\_\_\_\_\_ Harley Granville Barker to William Archer, 8 November 1905. Salmon, 46–47.
\_\_\_\_\_ Harley Granville Barker to Nicholas Hannen, 17 September 1936. Salmon, 471.
\_\_\_\_\_ Harley Granville Barker to Nicholas Hannen, 11 October 1936. Salmon, 475.
Schreiner, Olive. *Woman and Labour*. Johannesburg: Cosmos Publications, 1975.
Shaw, George Bernard. Preface to William Archer *The Theatrical "World" of 1894*. London: Scott, 1895.
Showalter, Elaine. *The Female Malady: Women, Madness, and English Culture, 1830–1980*. New York: Pantheon, 1985.
Showalter, Elaine. *Sexual Anarchy: Gender and Culture at the Fin de Siècle*. New York: Penguin, 1990.
Sinfield, Alan. *The Wilde Century: Effeminacy, Oscar Wilde, and the Queer Moment*. New York: Columbia University Press, 1994.

# 16 "The most primeval of passions"
## Incest in the Service of Women in Angela Carter's The Magic Toyshop

MADELEINE MONSON-ROSEN

In "Notes from the Front Line," Angela Carter writes,

> I become mildly irritated (I'm sorry!) when people [...] ask me about the "mythic quality" of work I've written lately. Because I believe that all myths are products of the human mind and reflect aspects of material human practice. I'm in the demythologizing business. [...] I'm interested in myths — though I'm much more interested in folklore — just because they *are* extraordinary lies designed to make people unfree [38].

Carter combines two separate ideas of myth: as fantastical etiological narrative and as operative ideology that naturalizes inequalities between people. The two are not entirely discrete, however. Both kinds of myth are composed of "extraordinary lies." Carter's political project is to unmask the harm that myth, as ideological smokescreen, does to women. Her fiction asserts, I argue, that narratives of conventional heterosexual romantic love *always* conform to a patriarchal standard. Her feminist answer is not to reverse the patriarchal paradigm, which would follow the historical lead of conventional Western feminism, but to pervert and profane it. This process offers a challenge to the structure of patriarchally-mandated heterosexuality while acknowledging that an overt opposition is not possible. Instead, Carter adopts the alphabet that the patriarchal tradition has left her, and systematically and deliberately contaminates it by means of perverse and profane elements.

In *The Magic Toyshop* (1967), Carter perverts the ideal of romantic heterosexual love as she profanes the narrative of that love. She does this by introducing incest into the novel's gothic romance plot. For Carter, incest offers a challenge to patriarchal narrative and ideology both by presenting a model of heterosexual love that does not accord with that sanctioned by patriarchy and by violating the most primeval of taboos. She takes the motif of incest even farther than perversion and profanation, however. She uses it as a way of turning heterosexual practice against the normative and hegemonic operation of patriarchally-authored heterosexual-romantic narrative. She puts incest in the service of women by envisioning a version of heterosexual sexual behavior, and heterosexual romance, that is conceived in terms other than those sanctioned by conventional heterosexuality. In Carter's fiction, incest becomes a form of heterosexual practice that can be deployed within a radical feminist politics.

In the novel, Carter employs both versions of myth, the ideological and the etiological: the first appears in the novel's romantic structure, the second in its allegorized depiction of patriarchy. Critics have accused Carter of utilizing myths in the first sense, and thereby perpetuating myths in the second sense, while she herself continued to insist upon her demythologizing project.[1] In this paper, I want to read *The Magic Toyshop* alongside Carter's own polemical nonfiction to determine if the politics implicit in the former are matched by the politics explicitly expressed in the latter.

My central question is whether Carter's fiction reflects the feminist materialist politics she espoused in her nonfictional writings. This question is relevant to Carter because although her politics were openly radical, her literary writing employs multiple textual allusions, drawn from fairy tales and folklore, mythological narratives, and the Western literary canon. Carter's textual borrowing and recycling raises this question: Does such use of the canon and classical mythology serve to reinscribe the value of such narratives as it critiques them? Or does she take those myths apart, defuse their ideological power, by means of a radical deployment? In "Notes from the Front Line," Carter asserts, "I'm all for putting new wine in old bottles, especially if it makes those bottles explode" ( 37). In reading *The Magic Toyshop* through the politicized lens that Carter's nonfiction works offer, we can see a model for a treatment of the literary canon that acknowledges the pleasure Carter as writer and reader takes in it, while at the same time we see a political operation in which Carter deliberately and systematically profanes the canon.

Carter continues to state her case against myth in her "Polemical Preface" to *The Sadeian Woman*: "Myth deals in false universals, to dull the pain of particular circumstances. In no area is this more true than that of relations between the sexes" (5–6). While *The Sadeian Woman* is primarily concerned with the reductive quality of pornography, Carter also holds the narrative of conventional heterosexual romance culpable in perpetuating false and damaging notions about love and sex: "Pornography, like marriage and the fictions of romantic love, assists the process of false universalizing. Its excesses belong to that timeless, locationless area outside history, where fascist art is born" (*SW* 12). That area outside history is the realm of myth. She continues, "The notion of a universality of human experience is a confidence trick and the notion of a universality of female experience is a clever confidence trick" (*SW* 12). For Carter, the universalizing impulse of fictions of romantic love, the myth that love conquers all, necessarily harms women. Against this myth of universality of experience Carter opposes lived experience — that is, history.

Carter is invested in creating romantic narratives that do not conform to the universalizing or mythologizing model, and it is in incest that we see Carter's fiction offering us one example of a queer heterosexual love. That is to say that, for Carter, the conventional narrative of heterosexual romance *always* works to reinforce the patriarchal social arrangement, but the possibility for a non-normative heterosexuality resides in narratives that are perverse or profane. Carter's narratives of incest are queer because they offer models for heterosexual relationships that are both non-normative and liberatory. I argue that Carter's incest narratives fall under the rubric of queer heterosexuality because they are conceived as practices that are unsanctioned, unmandated, and unapproved by patriarchal institutions such as the Church, the State, and the family.[2]

For Carter, a patriarchal order necessitates conventional heterosexual relationships such as those leading to marriage. As Roland Barthes writes, "myth consists in turning culture into nature, or at least turning the social, the cultural, the ideological, the historical into the 'natural'" (1989, 65). The version of heterosexuality that Carter's strategy of profanation and perversion works to challenge pretends to express a natural order, but is in reality patriarchal ideology in action. Incest in Carter's fiction represents her specific brand of feminism by accounting for heterosexual love: it projects a model for a way in which such a queer heterosexuality might work. But it also shakes the foundations on which the paradigmatic patriarchal structure is built. If *The Magic Toyshop*'s tyrannically ruled house is an allegory of patriarchy, then incest literally tears that house down.

*The Magic Toyshop* realizes the myth of patriarchy in the hyperbolic microcosm of the Flower home. Uncle Philip, the family patriarch, has a presence that "brooding and oppressive, filled the house" (92). He rules his home as a living image of the God that Carter describes in *The Sadeian Woman*: "In the Kingdom of God, man is made in the image of God and therefore a ravenous, cannibalistic, vicious, egocentric tyrant" (140). The family relationship described in the novel both reflects and generates the notion of patriarchy as a natural order. Carter perverts and profanes that order by introducing an element that contaminates both structures. That element is incest.

Uncle Philip's household is comprised of two families: the Flowers and the Jowles. Philip's orphaned niece Melanie is the novel's protagonist. The household also includes Philip's mute wife, Margaret, and her two brothers: Finn and Francie Jowle. *The Magic Toyshop* in fact includes two narratives of incestuous love. The first is a relationship between Melanie and Finn. Their relationship becomes incestuous because they can only realize their love after Melanie has been incorporated into his family.

Two pivotal scenes demonstrate Melanie's introduction into the Jowle family. In the first, Melanie hallucinates the severed hand of a young girl in the silverware drawer of the kitchen. She faints, and is found by Francie, Finn's older brother. He revives her, and the three Jowle siblings put her to bed. Finn sits by her into the night. After this experience, Melanie assigns all her love and loyalty to the Jowle family, who, she realizes, are all in bondage to Philip. At the moment when Melanie "threw in her lot with the Jowles" (123), she makes herself a part of their family, allied with them against Philip. Also on the night of the severed hand, she imagines Finn as her "phantom bridegroom" (123). He admits his love for her, and she acknowledges her love for him, not as an imagined ideal of romance, as she pictured an earlier kiss between them, but as a love born out of mutual alliance, out of familiarity. This is itself a challenge to the conventional resolution of romance. Love does not entail rescue. Instead, it grows out of shared circumstances, even mutual enemies. "[W]e'll christen the first one Proximity," Finn says to Melanie (183), in a joke about their imagined future children.

For Jean Wyatt, proximity suggests a sibling bond between Melanie and Finn: "Melanie forms a romantic alliance with Finn, her counterpart in age, status, and subordination to the father — her 'brother,' in a word" (561). Wyatt's reading recognizes Carter's positing of a post-patriarchal heterosexuality, yet she fails to account for the effects of such a relationship in the still-patriarchal world. At the end of the novel, the consequence of incest is revealed to be the utter destruction of this patriarchal microcosm. Incest tears the house down.

Judith Butler's reading of Levi-Strauss shows that the incest taboo mandates the exogamous exchange of women that in turn solidifies the homoerotic bonds upon which a patriarchal social organization is founded (52–55). In subverting this exogamous exchange, Carter depicts a heterosexual love that undermines patriarchal authority instead of consolidating it. Butler notes that Levi-Strauss's incest taboo, via Lacan's interpretation, works to reproduce culture. This reproduced culture functions in the kinship relations that are realized by means of the incest taboo's libidinal displacements. In Butler's formulation, therefore, patriarchy, crystallized in the always-patriarchal family, depends on the incest taboo. To violate this taboo is to shake the foundation on which patriarchy rests. For Butler, the incest prohibition is a primal example of patriarchy's investment in separating sexual practice into licit and illicit categories. The incest model then serves to inscribe a heterosexual love that is outside the realm of the interwoven structures of societal patriarchy, heterosexual hegemony, and conventional romance. Carter offers a model for a relationship conceived outside of naturalizing patriarchal law, and, in violating that most primal of laws, she shakes the myth of patriarchy at its very core.

Wyatt opens her essay on Carter with the same "demythologizing" quote with which I began, yet her reading suggests that Carter engages in a sort of *re*mythologizing: "The best defense against a social myth is, perhaps, another myth" (549). This suggestion flies in the face of Carter's own assertions about myth. Wyatt goes on to say, "Carter both points up the age-old patriarchal preference for certain kinds of heroines — passive, inert — and sets an alternative model of womanhood in the place of the old" (549). However, Wyatt finds an "alternative womanhood" only in its relation to masculinity. She writes that Carter's "revisions are liberatory not just because of their 'demythologizing' effect: they also suggest alternative forms of masculinity — and therewith, since gender is a relational term, the possibility of revising notions of femininity as well" (565). But gender is not relational in the sense that an alternate masculinity necessarily means an alternate femininity. Indeed, to say that the one follows from the other is to repeat the gender binarism that Carter tries to overcome, to admit that the only possibilities that exist are hetero- as normative and homo- as non-normative, masculine as empowered and feminine as powerless. *The Magic Toyshop*'s incestuous love opens up the possibility of a heterosexuality that is queer, in that it challenges the history of relational normativity. Furthermore, Wyatt's dismissive reading of Carter's demythologizing project suggests that her essay remains in the epistemological binarism that Carter's writing works to challenge. Carter in no way tries to replace one myth with another. Rather she works to reveal the mythical narrative, any myth, as a container for ideologies that work in support of those in power.

Demythologizing for Carter means exposing "social fictions" and the ways in which they are "palmed off on me as the real thing" ("Notes" 38). Carter's project is not, as Wyatt suggests, to substitute one myth for another, in this case a system in which femininity is valued over masculinity. Again in *The Sadeian Woman*, Carter writes:

> All the mythic versions of women from the myth of the redeeming purity of the virgin to that of the healing, reconciling mother, are consolatory non-senses; and consolatory nonsense seems to me a fair definition of myth, anyway. Mother goddesses are just as silly a notion as father gods. If a revival of the myths of these cults gives women emotional satisfaction, it does so at the price of obscuring the real conditions of life. This is why they were invented in the first place [5].

Carter by no means invents new myths with which to replace the old. She admits that, while gender, as "social fiction," occupies the space of myth, "real conditions," those which conventionally fall under the rubric of class, and which fit into her definition of history, stand in opposition to myth. Carter then exposes the old myths, profanes them, and explodes them.

So Carter explodes the bottle of the conventional romantic narrative by profaning that narrative. She not only *suggests* an incestuous love in Finn and Melanie's relationship, she also offers an example of a sexual relationship that is *literally* incestuous. The second incestuous relationship depicted in the novel takes place between Margaret and Francie Jowle. One night when Philip is away, the rest of the family has an impromptu party, and all become slightly intoxicated by food, Guinness, and the music the Jowle family plays. Melanie sees Francie and Margaret embracing: "It was a lover's embrace, annihilating the world, as if taking place at midnight on the crest of a hill, with a tearing wind beating the branches above them. The brother and sister knelt" (193–4). Incest is an effective profanation of patriarchal narrative because it violates the primary taboo; that is, it violates both the "natural" and "cultural" laws that govern sexual relationships. It transgresses, not only the laws that govern sexual behavior, but also the foundations of the entire patriarchal social arrangement. It threatens to break down the primary patriarchal institution: the family. In addition, the language in which Carter describes Francie and

Margaret's relationship foregrounds, and foreshadows, the destruction wreaked by incest upon the patriarchal-heterosexual family structure.

After they witness Francie and Margaret's embrace, Finn and Melanie retreat to his room. "'This is our secret,' said Finn [...] 'You know our heart's core, now, the thing that makes us different from other people, Francie, Maggie, and I'" (195). He includes himself in the incestuous relationship, and Melanie, as a member of their family, is now included too: "Incest, invoked downstairs on the worn rug, invoked upstairs in the quiet bedroom" (195). If we read the Flower household as a metaphor for patriarchal domination in the world, then Francie and Margaret's incestuous *and adulterous* love first undermines the foundations of that house, and eventually destroys it. The image of the incestuous embrace, "Francie and Aunt Margaret locked together in the most primeval of passions" (195), drives Philip to his final act of violence, by which he destroys himself as well as his house.

But Carter is not simply interested in offering a model for heterosexual love outside the mythical operation of patriarchal heterosexuality. There is a second level upon which her demythologizing works, and it rests upon her deployment of literary language itself. There is a relationship between Carter's demythologizing project and her persistent use of canonical text and imagery. *The Magic Toyshop* opens with a line from John Donne and ends with a line from John Keats. Carter reconciles her use of, and love of, the literary canon by profaning it. Just as she profanes overarching mythologies, like that of romantic love, she profanes these canonical texts by their context and by using them as descriptive shorthand for events and actions that lie well outside the realm of meaning into which they have been received. These lines embody the "old bottle." Carter's project is to account for it and to explode it.

Audre Lorde famously said, "*the master's tools will never dismantle the master's house.* They may allow us to temporarily beat him at his own game, but they will never enable us to bring about genuine change" (112). And yet Carter consistently used "the master's tools" in both her fiction and non-fiction, and it is undeniable that she wanted "genuine change." Lorde, perhaps, is unable to see that the house itself is a fiction, a fantasy, a myth. To extend the house conceit for a moment (because it is one Carter uses), let us say that the Flower house is the master's house. The master's tools, the master's house, in the Barthesian formulation of myth, are impotent. Myth is not a structure, but a system. Carter calls the "official past [...] a vast repository of outmoded lies, where you can check out what lies used to be à la mode and find the old lies on which new lies have been based" ("Notes" 41). Lorna Sage names this "[t]he house of fiction's heritage" (*Flesh*, 6), and she writes of *The Magic Toyshop*: "in this house [...] there are no mirrors, *because it is a world you find in books and mirrors*, the region of copies and images and representations" (*Angela Carter*, 15). So Carter's project is not to dismantle the house, but to highlight the illusions and lies on which it is built.

Carter's critique, in opposing history to myth, introduces history, "material condition" as a corrective to myth-as-ideology. Barthes writes, "Myth deprives the object of which it speaks of all history," and goes on to quote Marx: "...we must pay attention to this history, since ideology boils down to either an erroneous conception of this history, *or to a complete abstraction from it*" (1985, 151). When Carter writes, "Our flesh arrives to us out of history" (*SW* 9), she echoes Marx, but specifically with respect to that abstraction of sexual intercourse that is pictured as romantic love. In many of her feminist arguments, Carter posits history as an antidote to myth. Carter's fictions historicize myth. In so doing, she releases narratives from the mythic register. They can no longer pretend to eternality. Her fiction reveals the pretence of the ideological to the natural.

The second pivotal moment in the novel is a dramatic performance of the myth of Leda and the Swan. It is essentially a performance of Yeats' version of the myth, which depicts Leda's encounter with Zeus as explicitly violent, and which links the act of sexual violence to the large-scale violence of the Trojan war. In this episode, Carter uses a myth to demonstrate the institutionalized violence against women that Philip's house stands for. Philip, who on special occasions offers dramatic performances by his puppets for the audience of his family, casts Melanie as Leda opposite his own puppet swan. Although initially Melanie wants to laugh at the "mocked up" swan, as it performs the rape, she becomes truly frightened: "She thought of the horse of Troy, also made of hollow wood; if she did not act her part well, a trapdoor in the swan's side might open and an armed host of pigmy Uncle Philips, all clockwork, might rush out and savage her. The possibility seemed real and awful. All her laughter was snuffed out" (166). The episode is disturbing, not just because it relates an eroticized act of violence, but because it reveals that Philip can wield his power through something so flimsy and ephemeral as his puppet swan.

Although Philip certainly wants to do Melanie harm, his clutches are not exclusively (or even primarily) lecherous. In separating the desire for domination from erotic desire, Carter realizes the point she argues in *The Sadeian Woman*: that erotic violence stands for institutional violence. She foregrounds an act of erotic violence and uses it as shorthand for the whole patriarchal operation. Philip finds that he prefers his puppets to Melanie: "You were melodramatic. Puppets don't overact" (167). Finn, who, according to the convention of romance, should rescue Melanie, is as immobilized by Philip's creation as she is. Carter de-eroticizes the patriarchal power-relationship. She challenges Yeats' vision of the Leda myth, and she reveals the eroticism of pornography, romance, and rape as veils for the institutionalized violence of patriarchy.

Nicole Ward Jouve discusses the Leda episode, but argues the opposite: "Rape of a mortal woman has nothing to do with political violence. The trope is a patriarchal power trip. Uncle Philip's swan has neither knowledge nor power. He is all cardboard, and creaking machinery. Only Melanie's fear makes him overwhelming" (154). For Carter, however, rape has *everything* to do with political violence. Carter works to reveal that patriarchy, and its attendant violence, *is* mythological in that it is ideological; it depends on the individual's, the victim's, always-already subjected state. Only when Melanie sees Philip in the swan does she begin to be afraid. Violence, the stylized violence of myth, is powerful only when its victims are frightened. The fantasy of patriarchy exists inasmuch as its subjects believe it. In *The Sadeian Woman*, Carter asserts that erotic violence shows most clearly "that violence has always been the method by which institutions demonstrate their superiority" (23). Contrary to Jouve's assertion that rape is not an act of political violence, I argue that Carter purposely uses the trope of erotic violence as an emblem for institutionalized violence.

In her deployment of mythological imagery, Carter reveals the very emptiness of mythical narratives. She neither reinscribes myth in its own language, nor rewrites myth while continuing to use its form. She demythologizes by means of myth. The Leda episode becomes a revelatory narrative as it displays the emptiness of myth. Sarah Gamble responds to the criticism that Carter focuses too much on the world as invented by patriarchal ideologies, and addresses Carter's relationship to myth: "herein perhaps lies Carter's clue to the deconstruction of patriarchy — its greatest horror and its greatest weakness is that it is sustained by the force of its subject's belief. Cease to believe, and it becomes nothing more than a masquerade or a puppet show in the simplest, most obvious sense: theatrics" (72). Carter reveals patriarchy, as ideological myth, as only so much masquerade. Ideology is necessarily artifice because mythological language is a lie.

In *The Sadeian Woman*, Carter offers a possibility for a "moral" pornography, which bears on Carter's treatment of both canonical text and myth:

The moral pornographer would be an artist who uses pornographic material as part of the acceptance of the logic of a world of absolute sexual license for all the genders, and projects a model of the way such a world might work. [...] Such a pornographer would not be the enemy of women, perhaps because he might begin to penetrate to the heart of the contempt for women that distorts our culture even as he entered the realms of true obscenity as he described it [19–20].

Carter provides a model for her own moral pornographer. In describing the ways in which our culture demonstrates its contempt for women, in using the language that expresses contempt, she penetrates to the heart of it. She reveals obscenity even as she describes it.

Carter then constructs a metalanguage out of the shorthand of literary history itself, out of "the master's tools," as it were. Barthes offers the image of fissuring, of contesting the symbolic, which in turn becomes an effective model for investigating Carter's persistent use of mythological or canonical narratives.[3] Inside her deployment of mythological narratives, Carter contests their symbolic value. In showing that historical narrative itself is fictive at the same time that history is material, she exposes myth as doubly abstracted from the conditions of history.

In addition, Carter's allusive language acknowledges that the condition of patriarchy is *a priori*. To invert it simply serves to reinscribe its power. Wyatt writes, "Critics have objected that Carter's early novels (*The Magic Toyshop*, 1967, *Heroes and Villains*, 1969, and *The Passion of New Eve*, 1977) critique patriarchy without offering any positive alternatives" (565). But Carter's critique entails a positive assertion: in profaning those high-cultural or ideological tools with which the house of literature has been constructed, Carter accounts for them, takes pleasure in them, and begins to penetrate into the culture of contempt that they have helped create. In this way, Carter's narratives of obscene or perverse sexuality become queer, as they begin to depict "a world of absolute sexual license for all the genders" (*SW* 20).

There is more to Carter's allusive pillaging of the Western canon than the epigrammatic shorthand that literary language offers. She also reveals the limitations of such language itself. Gamble discusses Carter's "Camp" esthetic:

an eccentric and eclectic assemblage of literary forms in which the likes of Shakespeare and Keats are placed on an equal level with references to Hammer Horror, folk-tale and the Marquis de Sade. In this way, the method by which mainstream culture allocates categories of value, taste, and morality is systematically dismantled [41].

We see here a calculated strategy by which Carter takes apart the regime that "high culture" represents. In Sage's reading of *The Magic Toyshop*, she quotes a conversation with Carter: "The house stands for 'the culture I was born to' (*not* the nature) and for that whole sense of the past as a storeroom of properties and costumes to try on — including, more narrowly, literature's past, the house of fiction's heritage" (*Flesh* 6). Philip, then, is the ruler of that house. He makes Melanie into Leda: virgin and victim, mother of disaster. Throughout the novel, Melanie is incapable of articulating agency, of constructing some autonomous self, while she lives in that house. Instead, Carter dresses her in the costumes and props of the literary tradition, letting them reveal their own inadequacy, their own failure, their own lack.

> So I feel free to loot and rummage in an official past, specifically a literary past, but I like painting and sculptures and the movies and folklore and heresies, too. This past, for me has important decorative, ornamental functions; further, it is a vast repository of outmoded lies, where you can check out what lies used to be à la mode and find the old lies on which new lies have been based ["Notes" 41].

Carter gives us two narratives of eroticism in the novel: the incest narrative, and the 'erotic violence' narrative of Leda and the Swan. The former frames the latter in the novel. How does the incest narrative affect the novel's depiction of the eroto-political violence of patriarchy? The novel closes with Uncle Philip's discovery of Francie and Margaret together. He becomes enraged and burns the house, hoping to kill all those inside. Finn and Melanie escape, but the fate of the rest of the family remains uncertain. Incest has, in effect, destroyed the house of patriarchy. It has torn the master's house down. In *The Magic Toyshop*, the apocalyptic conflagration of the Flower house *is* the explosion of the old bottle. For Carter, demythologizing begins by tying myths back into history, by revealing the circumstances out of which they were born. It continues in the systematic profanation of mythical and canonical narratives, by the introduction of such contaminating elements as incest. Carter proves that myths, ideological or etiological, although they claim to be both sacred and eternal, are ultimately neither, and that perversion and profanation — the breaking of taboos — offers a means of representing relationships that subverts the operations of naturalizing patriarchal order. She represents a heterosexuality that is queer, and because it is queer, it also has the potential to be liberatory. Incest, therefore, Carter's version of queer heterosexuality, works in the service of women.

# Notes

1. Sarah Gamble writes: "One of the most controversial areas of her work as far as feminists are concerned is [...] her graphic depictions of violence against women in her writing, which [has] led some critics to conclude that, in spite of the feminist opinions she began expressing from the late 1960s onwards, she actually only furthers reactionary portrayals of women as objects of male desire" (*Angela Carter: Writing from the Front Line* 4).
2. In this case, I am working with an idea of sexual *practice*, or sexual *behavior*. My definition is based on readings of sexual activity, as opposed to sexual identity.
3. "mythologies are succeeded by a more formal, and thereby, I believe, more penetrating idiolectology, whose operative concepts are no longer sign, signifier, signified, and connotation, but citation, reference, stereotype" (Barthes 1989, 68).

# Works Cited

Barthes, Roland. *Mythologies*. New York: Hill and Wang, 1985.
\_\_\_\_\_. "Myth Today." In *The Rustle of Language*. Berkeley: University of California Press, 1989.
Butler, Judith. *Gender Trouble*. New York: Routledge, 1999.
Carter, Angela. *The Magic Toyshop*, 1967. New York: Penguin, 1996.
\_\_\_\_\_. "Notes from the Front Line." In *Shaking a Leg: Collected Writings*. New York: Penguin, 1998.
\_\_\_\_\_. *The Sadeian Woman*. New York: Penguin, 2001.
Gamble, Sarah. *Angela Carter: Writing From the Front Line*. Edinburgh: Edinburgh University Press, 1997.
Jouve, Nicole Ward. "Mother is a Figure of Speech." In *Flesh and the Mirror: Essays on the Art of Angela Carter*. Ed. Lorna Sage. London: Virago, 1994: 136–170.
Lorde, Audre. "The Master's Tools Will Never Dismantle the Master's House." In *Sister Outsider*. Freedom, CA: Crossing Press, 1984.
Sage, Lorna. *Angela Carter*. Plymouth, UK: Northcote House, 1994.
\_\_\_\_\_. Introduction to *Flesh and the Mirror: Essays on the Art of Angela Carter*, ed. Lorna Sage. London: Virago, 1994.
Wyatt, Jean. "The Violence of Gendering: Castration Images in Angela Carter's *The Magic Toyshop, The Passion of New Eve*, and 'Peter and the Wolf.'" *Women's Studies* 25 (1996): 549–570.

# 17 "If thou art God, avenge thyself!"
## Sade and Swinburne as Christian Atheists
### Carol Poster

There is a strong historical association between queerness and damnation. Both are marked behaviors, violating the norms of their respective (sexual and religious) categories, and either passively silenced or actively transgressive. Just as in nineteenth-century Britain sodomy was the "love that dared not speak its name," so the term damnation is etymologically related to the "damnatio memoria," statutory erasure of a person's posterity. The relationship between sodomy and damnation was not, however, merely one of analogy. In both eighteenth-century France and nineteenth-century Britain, sodomy and blasphemy were both illegal, their illegality deriving from an ideological conflation of civic and religious behavioral codes in which morality was internalized via its religious articulation and externalized as civil penal enactments of Levitical and Mosaic Law.

This essay will examine, from a theological perspective, how two men, the French aristocratic libertine Donatien Alphonse François, Marquis de Sade, and the upper class English poet Algernon Charles Swinburne (who was strongly influenced by Sade), combined sexually and religiously transgressive elements in their writings and personal lives. Both Sade and Swinburne were baptized Christians and members of the aristocracy (Swinburne was the grandson of George, 3rd Earl of Ashburnham, while the Sade family was old Provençal nobility), who were self-proclaimed republicans and atheists. They both frequented flagellation brothels and wrote extensively about sado-masochistic sexuality.[1]

Perhaps it might be possible to describe both Sade and Swinburne, albeit anachronistically, as queer heterosexuals.

If, as Jonathan Dollimore writes, "[p]erversion was (and remains) a concept bound up with insurrection" (104), we can see Sade and Swinburne's writings as self-consious acts of defiance and transgression. One could, within a framework of contemporary gender theory, examine Sade's sodomy (literary and biographical) and blasphemy as parallel acts of "queer heterosexuality," deliberately transgressive acts of libertinage by a baptized Christian who was married and had numerous female mistresses. Swinburne's replications of Sadean positions could be similarly theorized. As understood by contemporary gender theory, both the personal habits and literary productions of Sade and Swinburne, and the positions from which it is possible to observe them raise complex questions of gender identity and identity politics, concerning the relationship between straight and queer, hegemonic and transgressive, and oppressor and oppressed. It is less common, but equally fruitful, however, to see these oppositions from a theological perspective, a perspective perhaps closer to the ideological situation in which they were originally enacted.[2]

Starting points for thinking about "queer heterosexuality" within a Christian context are the notions of salvation and damnation and their relationship to grace and sin. The range of positions concerning these phenomena in different Christian faith traditions is very broad. There is an extreme Calvinist position, in which all people are considered predestined either "elect" (saved) or "reprobate" (damned) before the beginning of the world, a position which might correspond to the notion of "queer" and "straight" as unalterably biologically determined. At the opposite extreme is the concept of salvation by works, most clearly articulated in the Roman Catholic Church (of which Sade was a member), in which one has no fixed identity as saved or damned but every minute has the choice of performing good or bad actions, a position analogous to one in which gender is considered an ongoing performance rather than an essential characteristic. The Church of England, of which Swinburne was a member, takes an intermediate position,[3] not technically claiming that salvation is possible through works alone, but insisting that good works are, in some fashion, necessary. In both communions, baptism, which indissolubly "grafts men into the church,"[4] is a first stage in progress towards salvation. Like the choice of same sex or other "unnatural" acts, which defy the traditional forms of gender identity, a deliberate choice of damnation, which works against the promise of baptism, is a radical challenge to Christian beliefs and hierarchies, especially when it appears not essential (predestined by God or genetics) but intentional. Sade, especially, explicitly claims that his preference for sodomy and his transgression of religious norms were both willed rather than instinctive. In Swinburne's case, both sexually and theologically, what is being willed is an imaginative return (poetically and sexually) to paganism. In both cases a baptized Christian attempting to assume the position of a pagan, like the heterosexual assuming the subject position of the queer, appears paradoxical and quixotic. Even the ritual of excommunication (to which, in fact, neither Sade nor Swinburne was subjected) does not undo baptism for no human action (even the most extreme of Sade's imagined transgressions) can, at least according to Christian belief, undo the special relationship of the baptized to God, nor even guarantee damnation. Thus, it is possible to locate the attempts of Sade and Swinburne to stand outside their baptismal relationship with God, by means of libertinism and blasphemy, as structurally similar to that of heterosexuals assuming queer identities, a similarity amplified by the particular nature of the sexual acts about which both men wrote (and, to a lesser degree, performed) which violated the religious/civil laws of their periods.

## *Sade and Swinburne as Transgressive Christian Atheists*

To read the sexuality of de Sade and Swinburne through the lens of Christian theology might seem unpromising at best and eccentric at worst. Both men were self-proclaimed "atheists," whose works explicitly condemned all versions and manifestations of Christianity. Despite the superficially paradoxical nature of the enterprise, there are, in fact, reasons why such an approach is productive. The first, most obvious, and strongest reason is historical, namely that their sexuality and its literary expressions existed within a Christian context. Even if Foucault is correct in arguing that homosexuality did not exist as a conceptual category of personhood, "sodomy," "fornication," "adultery," and "bestiality," *inter alia*, existed as clearly defined theological categories of "sins of the flesh," and the associated literary endeavors of both men fit equally well under the category of "blasphemy." Sade's sodomites (M. Rodin, e.g.) appear to define their sexual interests not so much by the gender of their sexual partners but by the orifices being used. Similarly, British flagellation literature displays more variation in gender than activity (Gibson, 1978). These "sins of the flesh" which both men perform in their anti-Christian and anti-salvific literary and sexual productions, are theologically significant in having a special relationship to original sin, as is emphasized in the Book of Common Prayer, a central theological as well as liturgical standard for the Church of England:

> Original sin standeth not in the following of Adam ... but it is the fault and corruption of the nature of every man that naturally is engendered of the offspring of Adam, whereby man ... is of his own nature inclined to evil, so that the flesh lusteth always contrary to the spirit; ... And this infection of nature doth remain, yea, in them that are regenerated, whereby the lust of the flesh, called in Greek *phronema sarkos* (which some do expound the wisdom, some sensuality, some the affection, some the desire of the flesh), is not subject to the law of God.... [T]he Apostle doth confess that concupiscence and lust hath itself the nature of sin... [Article IX].

Since the regeneration of baptism refers primarily to its relationship to original, rather than actual, sin, if a baptized Christian wishes to reject the promise of baptism, and assume the subject position of the unbaptized, either imaginatively or actually, the sins of the flesh, because of their connection to original sin, take on a particular significance.

The second reason why Swinburne and Sade should be considered theologically is that the works of both men frequently and overtly engage theological issues. The Marquis de Sade's *Justine,* for example, does not differ greatly in plot structure or in details other than narrative viewpoint, from martyrologies (e.g. Foxe's *Book of Martyrs*). Moreover, Sade's narrators are almost obsessively theological, in the sense of explicitly discussing religious issues. Similarly, religious issues recur with surprising frequency in Swinburne, both in his openly published works and in his privately printed burlesques, parodies, and pornography. Pierre Klossowski points out that Sade's struggles against God are not evidence of dispassionate disbelief, but of active engagement (1966, 65 sq.), something that applies equally to Swinburne.

## Atheism in Context

One problem for understanding pre–twentieth-century "atheism" is that the term has undergone a significant shift in meaning. The term "atheos" is Greek, meaning "without god(s)" and is linked to a related Greek term, "pistis," usually translated as "faith" or "belief." As James Kinneavy (1987) points out, the twentieth-century Christian notion of faith collapses two conceptually distinct attitudes towards deities, namely belief in their existence as a matter of empirical fact, and belief in them as a matter of trusting, following, or worshipping. In Graeco-Roman polytheism, these two aspects of the relationship to divinities were not generally conflated. The overwhelming majority of people acknowledged that innumerable divine and quasi-divine beings existed, but belief in the existence of a given deity did not necessarily entail worship or admiration of it.[5] Moreover, a deity's existence was no guarantor of its goodness. A cultured Athenian might react to one of the more flamboyant imported eastern cults, not by disbelieving the existence of its titular deity, but by considering the deity one not worthy of worship by a cultivated Greek. Ancient atheism was generally not existential — there were very few in antiquity that doubted the existence of divine beings — but rather had to do with performance, or, more precisely, non-performance of religious rituals. The actual crime of "asebeia" (impiety), for which Socrates, Protagoras, and other ancient "atheists" were tried, was not one having to do with abstract belief, but with refusal to participate in the required rituals of state religion. In fact, the best known "atheists" in antiquity were the Christians. They were considered "atheists" because they refused to participate in the worship of pagan deities (in particular the imperial cults), not because they did not believe in the existence of pagan gods. In fact, Christian (and Jewish) monotheism consisted not in refusal to acknowledge the existence of various divine beings other than their god (the pagan gods and spirits, the "daimones" which became "demons," were certainly believed to exist by Christians), but rather in the restriction of cult participation to that of a single god.

There are two ways in which this historical context provides a basis for re-interpreting the self-proclaimed atheism of Sade, Swinburne, and other writers (such as Shelley) of their period, one having to do with their relationship to the institutional structures of Christianity and the other having to do with their beliefs. In terms of belief, this historical analysis suggests that claims to "atheism" do not necessarily reflect disbelief in the *existence* of the Christian God; but instead a refusal to *worship* the Christian God, for moral, philosophical, or personal reasons. As Swinburne phrases it in "Hymn to Proserpine," a dramatic monologue written in the voice of a pagan reflecting on Christianity becoming the official religion of the Roman empire: "Though all men abase them before you [the Christian God and saints] in spirit, and all knees bend,/ I kneel not neither adore you, but standing look to the end..." (45–46).

On an institutional level, both eighteenth-century France and nineteenth-century Britain were analogous to Graeco-Roman antiquity in having state religions which required of all citizens performance of ritual acts, especially participation in Easter communion. The Marquis de Sade's legal difficulties, in fact, were in part due to violations of state laws pertaining to religion. One of the more dramatic scandals of Sade's early career concerned an affair with the prostitute Jeanne Testard. After asking her about religion and discovering that she believed in "God, Jesus, and the Virgin Mary":

> Suddenly the marquis burst out in a stream of dreadful insult and blasphemy ... He then masturbated into a chalice, profaned the names of Jesus Christ and the Virgin Mary ... and told a story about having gone to Communion with a women with whom he had slept: he took two hosts, placed them in the woman's vagina, and entered her, shouting, "If thou art God, avenge thyself!" ... At [one] point he took down two ivory Christs and trampled on one while he masturbated with the other, after which he ordered her to do the same [Lever 1993, 119].

When Jeanne complained to the police about mistreatment, it was not Sade's sexual activities which resulted in prosecution (none actually occurred, except his own autoerotic acts and, possibly, a modest amount of flagellation), but the far more serious charges of "blasphemy, disrespect toward the crucifix, and incitement to sacrilege" which "by light of the criminal code of the times, were far more serious" (Lever 1993, 121). Sade's abduction and flagellation of Rose Keller on Easter Sunday, similarly, combined relatively minor sexual misconduct (for a French aristocrat of the period) with rather more serious sacrilege (Gray 1999, 95 sq.). At Oxford, Swinburne would have been required to subscribe to the Thirty-Nine Articles of the Church of England and attend chapel regularly; his being sent down from Oxford reflected an increasing irregularity in his attendance at chapel as well as classes, although the precise reasons are not known. In both nations, nonconformity to state religion would be "atheism" in the ancient sense, an unwillingness to *worship* a god according to the state-mandated rituals. The association of sexual, religious, class, and political rebellion was strong for both men. Swinburne and Sade were both vehement republicans and libertarians. Swinburne was a supporter of Mazzini whose Italian Republicanism, due to the position of the Pope as absolute secular ruler of much of Italy, was strongly anti-clerical. In *Philosophy in the Boudoir*, Sade, whose libertarianism stood in a complex relationship to the French Revolution, argued:

Europe awaits her deliverance from *sceptre* and *censer* alike. Know well that you cannot liberate her from her royal tyranny without at the same time breaking her fetters of religious superstition; the shackles of one are too intimately linked with the other [1965, 299].

In *The Sadeian Woman,* Angela Carter suggests that Sade's work suggests the possibility for a "moral pornographer," one whose work would advocate "the acceptance of a world of absolute sexual license for all the genders" (19), and who would act as "a terrorist of the imagination, a sexual guerilla whose purpose is to overturn our most basic notions" of relations between the sexes (21). But, as he was bound by the premises of his own Christian heritage, Carter ultimately finds that "Sade is still in complicity with the authority he hates" (136).

Since Sade and Swinburne were both members of the upper aristocracy assuming the political position of republicans while retaining many of their aristocratic attitudes and manners, just as they were Christian atheists and sexually ambiguous sodomites, it is possible to trace a consistent thread of oxymoronic subject positions in their sexual, religious, and social relations.

## *Rituals of Damnation*

Two separate notions of "works" inhere in the phrase "salvation (or damnation) by works," one being good (or evil) moral acts and the other being sacramental, or ritual, acts. Sade, in particular, attempts to combine verbal blasphemy, moral, and ritual transgression simultaneously. Blasphemy, whether verbal or ritual, only has meaning in religious context: defecating or ejaculating on a consecrated host would have no more resonance than using an unconsecrated piece of bread for the same purpose for someone without a strong emotional relationship to Christianity. Both in Sade and Swinburne, there are numerous simultaneous and conscious transgressions of Christian moral, sexual, and ritual rules.

At his chateau, La Coste, and in *120 Days,* Sade created libertine communities which resembled inverted churches. Where Christian congregations praised God and consumed his flesh and blood (under the form of bread and wine), in the Sadean community, libertines consumed the excrement, ejaculate, and flesh of each other and their victims and blasphemed God. Christians confessed sins and performed penances in order to be forgiven. Sadean libertines also confessed and performed penances (forms of flagellation indistinguishable from those practiced in the Roman

Catholic religious orders) in order to seal their damnation. The communal nature of the Sadean debauch not only mirrors the community of the church into which he was baptized and the religious orders to which many members of his family belonged, but guarantees its efficacy:

> Almighty God, who hast given us grace at this time to make common supplications unto thee; and dost promise that when two or three are gathered together in thy Name thou wilt grant their requests [Prayer of St. Chrysostom, *BCP*].

Just as the prayers of "two or three" are more effective than solitary prayer in the Christian Church, so the gathered blasphemies of the Sadean libertines are more efficacious than solitary acts of libertinage. Similarly, as in the Christian communities of France and England, blasphemy was regarded as a particularly heinous crime, so in the Sadean community, the Duc de Blangis tells the young victims, "You have seen with what stringency you are forbidden anything resembling any act of religion whatsoever. I warn you: very few crimes will be more severely punished than this one" (*120 Days*, 251).

A particularly significant inversion of Christian sacramentalism is defiling a consecrated host (as Sade was well-aware in his affair with Jeanne Testard and is described in greater detail in *Juliette*). Such desecration is an important step towards damnation, as can be seen in the phrasing of the "Invitation to Communion":

> So is the danger great, if we receive the same unworthily; for then we become guilty of the Body and Blood of Christ our Saviour; we eat and drink our own damnation [Order for Communion, *BCP*].

Swinburne also sees the Eucharist as central to both Christianity[6] and rejection thereof, most obviously in his "The Cannibal Catechism:"

> Preserve us from our enemies,
> Thou who art Lord of suns and skies,
> Whose meat and drink is flesh in pies,
> And blood in bowls!
> Of Thy sweet mercy, damn their eyes,
> And damn their souls.
>
> The cannibal of just behaviour
> Acknowledges the Lord his saviour,
> With gifts of whose especial favour
> He hath been crammed,
> To whom an offering of sweet savour
> Are all the damned.

To one raised in the Anglican liturgical tradition, this immediately brings to mind the Prayer of Humble Access,

> ... Grant us therefore, gracious Lord, so to eat the Flesh of thy dear Son Jesus Christ, and to drink his Blood, in these holy Mysteries, that we may continually dwell in him, and he in us, that our sinful bodies may be made clean by his Body, and our souls washed through his most precious Blood.

For Swinburne, seeing the Eucharist as a literal form of cannibalism is also assuming the subject position of the ancient pagans who accused Christians of cannibalism,[7] an imaginative act for one baptized and raised as a Christian not dissimilar from his sexually ambiguous male appropriation of lesbian voice (discussed in Prins 1999).

Swinburne's inversions of Christian ritual and worship emphasize the fallenness of modern Christians from an Edenic pagan state in which sensuality was not deformed by religious repression, the human spirit not trammelled by oppressive government, and art not constrained by the perverse judgements of prudery.[8] Especially in the early decades of his long literary career, Swinburne appropriated the Graeco-Roman pagan voice as a subject position from which he could critique the degeneracy of Victorian society, a degeneracy having its source, for Swinburne as for Matthew Arnold, in a morbid self-consciousness (the "dialogue of the mind with itself") and the repression of Hellenism by Hebraism. In "Hymn to Proserpine" (especially 20–30), love is characterized as the pagan Eros displaced by the "pale Galilean" under whom "love hath an end" (1–35). What Christianity offers in place of love is "...leavings of racks and rods ... ghastly glories of saints, dead limbs of gibbeted gods!" (43–44). Venus and sensual love are replaced in the Christian dispensation with the Virgin Mary, whose cult demands of women not "life and love" but virginity and martyrdom:

> The life and the love thou despisest,
> These hurt us indeed, and in vain,
> O wise among women, and wisest,
> Our Lady of Pain ["Dolores," 37–40].

The Virgin Mary, and female Christians, have thus a double role, being both martyred and commanding martyrdom, as victims and dominatrices. It is in that latter role of dominatrix that Swinburne portrays the Virgin Mary, a mortal intercessor with an immortal God, being approached by a worshipper, in his "Dolores (Notre Dames des Sept Douleurs)":

> I have passed from the outermost portal
> To the shrine where a sin is a prayer;
> What care though the service be mortal?
> O our Lady of Torture, what care?
> All thine the last wine that I pour is,
> The last in the chalice we drain,
> O fierce and luxurious Dolores,
> Our Lady of Pain ["Dolores," 129–136].

## *Sex and God*

God, for both Sade and Swinburne, exists at the absolute limits of power, capable of greater control and greater scope for inflicting pain than any human sadist, and simultaneously at the limits of possible suffering and renunciation of power, in the sacrifice of Jesus Christ on the Cross, "who made there, by his one oblation of himself once offered, a full, perfect, and sufficient sacrifice, oblation, and satisfaction for the sins of the whole world" (Order for Communion, *BCP*). By acting as sadist and masochist, the libertine simultaneously imitates God as both powerful and suffering, while resisting God's dictates. But the human libertine can never accomplish enough to equal God, no matter how much various acts are multiplied.[9] Just as Luther realized that no matter how many good works he performed, being imperfect, he could never earn salvation, so Sade, especially, is perpetually frustrated because, by quantity or quality of evil acts, he can never earn damnation, nor even a response from the God he abuses and challenges with every transgression. Sade's rage at God in part follows from God perpetually frustrating both the desire for freedom and for control. God's existence implies no human is perfectly free to determine the consequences of his actions. On the other hand, God, never intervened, no matter how directly challenged, to limit Sade's freedom of action. Salvation and damnation can be predestined; grace can be irresistible. Religion also becomes a site of resistance to Sade's sexuality; Jeanne Testard, a whore and a peasant, defied the aristocrat Sade on the basis of her religious beliefs and had him imprisoned for his violations of laws against blasphemy. Justine's faith gives impetus to internal resistance to the various debaucheries inflicted on her; when, at the end of the novel, she is subject to the temptations of luxury, God strikes her by lightning, so that she might die in a state of grace, following martyrdom,[10] rather than being placed so that she might yield to temptation. Sade's rebellion against God can only take the form of an increasingly desperate heaping up of sins of the flesh, which still are never sufficiently evil to exceed infinite goodness. As Swinburne points out, in the discipline of libertinage Sade becomes "a Christian ascetic bent on earning the salvation of the soul through mortification of the flesh.... If ... [Sade's] energies turned back into the old channel they ran in some centuries since, [he] would revert to the chain and the top of a pillar and ascetic worship ... a very serious Simon Stylites — in an inverted posture" (Lang 1959, 57).[11] Swinburne saw himself, by contrast, as trying, through sensuality, to reconstruct a pagan subject position within "this ghastly thin-faced time of ours" ("Faustine"). Both efforts, however, are equally quixotic, in that they presume the possibility of placing themselves completely outside their own historically and socially constructed identity position.

## *Conclusion*

The phenomenon of passing, that of the subaltern striving to imitate, join, or speak within a dominant paradigm has been far more common and well-theorized than its inverse, blackface or queer heterosexuality, just as Christian theology and practical religion typically concern themselves with the problem of humans, who are by nature corrupt, striving towards salvation, or heathens and apostates converting to Christianity, rather than those deliberately seeking damnation. Just as both Sade and Swinburne present us with cases of willed transgressive sexuality (Sade's libertinage; Swinburne's evocation of lesbianism, homoeroticism, and masochism), which can be understood within a social-sexual paradigm of queer heterosexuality, so they also present to us paradigms of a cognate transgressive religiosity, partially sexual in its mode of transgression, the case of those who are trying to escape the Christian and salvific orientation of their childhoods and cultures, but within an environment in which it is almost impossible to do so. The libertinage of Sade, which is that of a baptized Christian actively seeking damnation, and the "paganism" of Swinburne, that of an Anglo-Catholic rebelling against "the supreme evil, God" ("Atalanta in Calydon") exemplify the merging of queer heterosexual with Christian atheist and aristocratic republican as oxymoronic subject positions.

## Acknowledgment

Research for this essay was supported by funding from York University. I owe thanks the British Library, Robarts Library of University of Toronto, and Scott Library of York University.

## Notes

1. Much of Swinburne's flagellation poetry remains unpublished or only available in very limited private editions. The most readily accessible of his flagellation poems appear in *The Whippingham Papers, New Writings by Swinburne* (1964), and an appendix to Gibson (1978). Several flagellation scenes occur in his novel *Lesbia Brandon*; and are discussed by Vincent (1997). A relatively recent biography by Rikky Rooksby (1997) is less reticent about Swinburne's sexual proclivities than earlier accounts.

2. See Maynard (1993) for extended discussion of Victorian sexuality and religion.

3. The Church of England is traditionally described as "Popish in her liturgy, Calvinist in her theology, and Arminian in her clergy." In practice, within a common liturgical tradition, the actual beliefs of Anglicans vary tremendously. Reardon (1995) provides an overview of nineteenth century British theology. This essay emphasizes the Anglo-Catholic (the party in the Church of England which originated in the Oxford Movement) tradition in which Swinburne was raised (discussed in Louis 1990) as the most pertinent branch of Anglicanism. For Roman Catholicism between the Council of Trent and Vatican I see Heyer (1969). For Sade, Gallicanism, the dominant strand of French Catholicism in his period, which emphasized a close relationship between crown and altar, is theologically central.

4. "Baptism is not only a sign of profession and mark of difference whereby Christian men are discerned from other that be not christened, but is also a sign of regeneration or new birth...." (Article XXVII) All references to the Thirty-Nine Articles, creeds, and Anglican liturgy are from the 1662 revision of the *Book of Common Prayer* (hereafter *BCP*), in use in the nineteenth century. Biblical references are to the Authorized Version.

5. For the nature of Greek religion as consisting of ritual observance rather than "faith" in the modern sense, see Burkert (1985). It should be noted that just as it was not necessary in antiquity to worship all the gods one believed to exist, it was also not necessary to believe in a particular god (or the stories about the god in any specific detail) in order to worship it, as discussed in Veyne (1988).

6. For Swinburne's childhood piety, see Lang 1959, 1-4; Louis 1990; Rooksby 1997, 25-27.

7. McGowan (1994) summarizes the evidence for Christians having been accused of cannibalism, primarily found in Tertullian and other second century authors. It is also worth noting that Swinburne's epiphanies during encounters with the sea function as a form of (pagan) baptism.

8. Swinburne articulates these positions quite strongly in his *Notes on Poems and Ballads*, a response to the critics of his volume of poems, *Poems and Ballads*. For examples of the outraged responses of Victorian critics to Swinburne, see Hyder 1970.

9. The literary styles of both authors depend heavily on amplification and repetition. In "Dolores", Swinburne states: "Seven sorrows the priests give their Virgin;/ But thy sins, which are seventy times seven,/ Seven ages would fail thee to purge in...," in many ways suggesting the same amplification as Sade enumerates in *120 Days of Sodom*.

10. French sermons of this period often portrayed infant mortality as a blessing; the sooner one died after baptism, the shorter the time one would be subject to the torments of purgatory for post-baptismal sin.

11. For Swinburne's reactions to Sade, see Mitchell (1965).

## Works Cited

Burkert, Walter. *Greek Religion*. Trans. John Raffan. Cambridge, MA: Harvard University Press, 1985.

Carter, Angela. *The Sadeian Woman: An Exercise in Cultural History*. London: Virago, 1979.

Dollimore, Jonathan. *Sexual Dissidence: Augustine to Wilde, Freud to Foucault*. Oxford: Oxford University Press, 1991.

Gibson, Ian. *The English Vice: Beating, Sex and Shame in Victorian England and After*. London: Duckworth, 1978.

Gray, Francine du Plessix. *At Home with the Marquis de Sade*. London: Chatto & Windus, 1999.

Heyer, Friedrich. *The Catholic Church from 1648 to 1870*. Trans. D. W. D. Shaw. London: Black, 1969.

Hyder, Clyde K., ed. *Swinburne: The Critical Heritage*. London: Routledge and Kegan Paul, 1970.

Kinneavy, James L. *Greek Rhetorical Origins of Christian Faith*. Oxford: Oxford University Press, 1987.

Klossowski, Pierre. "Nature as a Destructive Principle." In *The 120 days of Sodom and Other Writings*. Ed. Austryn Wainhouse and Richard Seaver. New York: Grove Press, 1966.

Lang, Cecil Y. ed. *The Swinburne Letters. Vol.1: 1854–1869*. New Haven: Yale University Press, 1959.

Lever, Maurice. *Marquis de Sade: a Biography*. Trans. Arthur Goldhammer. London: HarperCollins, 1993.

Louis, Margot Kathleen. *Swinburne and His Gods: The Roots and Growth of an Agnostic Poetry*. Montreal: McGill-Queen's University Press, 1990.

Maynard, John. *Victorian Discourses on Sexuality and Religion*. Cambridge: Cambridge University Press, 1993.

McGowan, Andrew. "Eating People: Accusations of Cannibalism Against Christians in the Second Century." *Journal of Early Christian Studies* 2 (1994): 413–442.

Mitchell, Jeremy. "Swinburne: The Disappointed Protagonist." *Yale French Studies* 35 (1965): 81–88.

Prins, Yopie. *Victorian Sappho*. Princeton: Princeton University Press, 1999.

Reardon, Bernard M. G. *Religious Thought in the Victorian Age*. 2nd ed. London: Longman, 1995.

Rooksby, Rikky. *A.C. Swinburne: A Poet's Life*. Aldershot: Scolar Press, 1997.

Sade, Donatien Alphonse François de, Marquis. *The 120 Days of Sodom and Other Writings*. Compiled and translated by Austryn Wainhouse and Richard Seaver. With introductions by Simone de Beauvoir and Pierre Klossowski. New York: Grove Press, 1966.
\_\_\_\_\_. *The Complete Justine, Philosophy in the Bedroom, and Other Writings*. Compiled and translated by Richard Seaver and Austryn Wainhouse. With introductions by Jean Paulhan and Maurice Blanchot. New York: Grove Press, 1965.
Swinburne, Algernon Charles. *Notes on Poems and Reviews*. London: John Camden Hotten, 1866.
\_\_\_\_\_. *The Cannibal Catechism*. Ed. Thomas J. Wise. London: Printed for Private Circulation Only, 1913.
\_\_\_\_\_. *The Complete Works of Algernon Charles Swinburne*. Ed. Sir Edmund Gosse et al. London: W. Heinemann ltd, 1925–27.
\_\_\_\_\_. *New Writings by Swinburne or Miscellanea Nova et Curiosa. Being a Medley of Poems, Critical Essays, Hoaxes and Burlesques*. Ed. Cecil Y. Lang. Syracuse, N.Y.: Syracuse University Press, 1964.
\_\_\_\_\_. *The Whippingham Papers*. Ware: Wordsworth Classics, 1995.
Veyne, Paul. *Did the Greeks Believe in Their Myths?* Trans. Paula Wissing. Chicago: University of Chicago Press, 1988.
Vincent, John. "Flogging is Fundamental: Applications of Birch in Swinburne's *Lesbia Brandon*". In *Novel Gazing: Queer Readings in Fiction*. Ed. Eve Kosofsky Sedgwick. Durham, NC: Duke University Press, 1997: 269–295.

# About the Contributors

**Celia R. Daileader** is an associate professor of English at Florida State University. She is the author of *Racism, Misogyny, and the Othello Myth: Interracial Couples from Shakespeare to Spike Lee* (Cambridge University Press, 2005) and *Eroticism on the Renaissance Stage: Transcendence, Desire, and the Limits of the Visible* (Cambridge, 1998).

**Susannah Mary Chewning** is a medievalist teaching at Union County College. She is editor of *Intersections of Sexuality and the Divine in Medieval Culture: The Word Made Flesh* (Ashgate Publishers, 2005).

**Richard Fantina** teaches English at the University of Miami. He is the author of *Ernest Hemingway, Machismo and Masochism* (Palgrave Macmillan, 2005) and co-editor of *Victorian Sensations* (Ohio State, 2006).

**Denise Hunter Gravatt** teaches and studies at Florida Atlantic University. She specializes in Victorian literature and has presented papers at numerous academic conferences. Her current project is an extended study of Braddon's novels.

**Deborah Kaplan** has a master's degree from the Center for the Study of Children's Literature at Simmons College and a master's in library and information science. She writes about children's literature and fan culture, both of which she thinks are touched by queer heterosexuality.

**Madeleine Monson-Rosen** is a Ph.D. candidate at the University of Illinois at Chicago. Her interests include literary postmodernism and classics.

**Richard Nemesvari** is professor of English at St. Francis Xavier University. His edition of Hardy's *The Trumpet-Major* was published by Oxford University Press. His edition of *Jane Eyre* and co-edited version of *Aurora Floyd* (with Lisa Surridge) were both published by Broadview

Press. His most recent article, "Romancing the Text: Genre, Indeterminacy, and Televising *Tess of the d'Urbervilles*," appears in the Cambridge University Press collection *Thomas Hardy on Screen*. He has also published on Joseph Conrad, Mary Elizabeth Braddon, and Emily Brontë.

**Kate Faber Oestreich** is a Ph.D. candidate in English, studying nineteenth-century British literature at The Ohio State University. She is currently working on her dissertation, "Fashioning Sexuality: British Marriage Plots and the Tailoring of Desire, 1790–1930."

**Carol Poster** is an associate professor of English at York University. She has published many essays in periodicals and essay collections on the history of rhetoric, the rhetoric of religion, and Victorian literature.

**Rebecca Rabinowitz** has a master's degree from the Center for the Study of Children's Literature at Simmons College, where she was a Virginia Haviland Scholar. She reviews for *Kirkus Reviews* and writes children's literature criticism. She lives in Cambridge, Massachusetts.

**Lorena Russell** is an assistant professor at the University of North Carolina at Asheville, where she teaches in the Department of Literature and Language. Her research interests include queer theory, postcolonial studies and film studies.

**Ashley T. Shelden** is a Ph.D. candidate at Tufts University. Her interests include twentieth century British literature, psychoanalysis, and queer theory.

**Melissa Shields Jenkins** is completing her Ph.D. in English literature at Harvard University. Her dissertation focuses on the work of George Meredith, George Eliot, William Makepeace Thackeray and Elizabeth Gaskell. She has also presented and published papers on African American and multi-ethnic American literature.

**Zachary Sifuentes**'s work in gender and sexuality has included the "imminently queer" context of early modern anatomical images, gendered rhymes in English prosody, literary responses to rape and sexual assault, and the idea of sacrifice in contemporary gay men's poetry. He teaches at the University of Miami.

**Grace Sikorski** has taught courses in American literature, comparative literature, technical writing, business writing, and rhetoric and composition at Penn State, Juniata College, University of Maryland University College, and Strayer University. She is currently an assistant professor of English at Anne Arundel Community College in Arnold, Maryland.

**Anne Stiles** is a 2006–2007 Visiting Scholar at the American Academy of Arts and Sciences in Cambridge, Massachusetts. She recently completed her Ph.D. in English at the University of California, Los Angeles, where she wrote a dissertation entitled "Neurological Fictions: Brain Science and Literary History, 1865–1905" under the direction of Professor Joseph Bristow. In fall 2007, she becomes assistant professor of English at Washington State University in Pullman, Washington.

**Calvin Thomas** is an associate professor of English at Georgia State University in Atlanta. He is the author of *Male Matters: Masculinity, Anxiety, and the Male Body on the Line* (1996) and the editor of *Straight with a Twist: Queer Theory and the Subject of Heterosexuality* (2000). His next book will be called *Adventures in Abjection*.

**Shelton Waldrep** is an associate professor of English at the University of Southern Maine. He is the author of *The Aesthetics of Self-Invention: Oscar Wilde to David Bowie* (Minnesota), editor of *The Seventies: The Age of Glitter in Popular Culture* (Routledge), and co-author of *Inside the Mouse: Work and Play at Disney World* (Duke).

**Shannon Young** teaches writing-intensive literature courses at Pace University in Manhattan. She focuses on literature that promotes peace and intercultural understanding and exposes the repercussions of oppressive structures. She has published in Victorian and postcolonial studies, as well as writing pedagogy.

# Index

Acker, Kathy 15
Altman, Dennis 12
anchoress 18, 68–79
Andalzúa, Gloria 13
Anders, D.H. 131
Archer, Bert 13, 15, 21
Archer, William 221, 224, 225, 226
Aretino, Pietro 18, 25–43
Auerbach, Nina 84

Bach, Sebastian 10
Bakhtin, Mikhail 31
Baldwin, James 183
Barreca, Regina 137
Barthes, Roland 234, 238, 243n3
Beerbohm, Max 225
Bennett, Judith 180n13
Berlant, Lauren 2, 6n3, 16, 112, 140–41
Bernard of Clairvaux 71
Bernau, Anke 77n3
Bersani, Leo 2, 3, 51, 54, 58–60, 79n16, 168n5
Blackmore, Josiah 78n4
Block, Francesca Lia 21, 196, 204–207
Bloom, Harold 4
Bloomsbury Group 215
Boehrer, Bruce Thomas 42n26
Boose, Lynda 41n7
Bornstein, Kate 15
Bowers, Frederick 42n15
Boykin, Keith 183–84
Braddon, Mary Elizabeth 19, 109–23, 227
Bray, Alan 35, 41n2
Brenner, Gerry 47, 50
Bristow, Joseph 11, 222–23
Brooke, Rupert 21, 210
Brooks, Peter 176–77, 180n11
Brown University Department of Molecular and Cell Biology and Biochemistry 151
Brydon, Diana 213, 217n1
Buckley, J.F. 55

Buñuel, Luis 153
Burger, Glenn 69, 78n4
Burkert, Walter 255n5
Butler, Judith 2, 5, 11, 12, 17, 83, 131, 137–38, 146–47, 149, 152, 153, 190, 193, 202, 236
Butler, Octavia 22

Califia, Pat 61–62
Campbell, Mrs. Patrick 220
Carlson, Cindy L. 78n3
Carroll, Lewis 217n3
Carroll, Traci 186–187
Carter, Angela 22, 178, 179n1, 181n14, 232–43, 250
Castle, Terry 180n3
celibacy 18, 82–93
chastity 18, 70–79
Chesnutt, Charles 186
Chewning, Susannah 18–19, 77n2
children's literature 21, 196–97
Cixous, Hélène 71
Cleto, Fabio 180n2
Cohen, Cathy J. 180n2
Cohen, Ed 69–70, 77, 79n14
Cohen, Jeffrey J. 78n4
Collins, Wilkie 19, 95–108
Craft, Christopher 16
Currah, Paisley 68

Daileader, Celia R. 18, 41n1
Davidson, Guy 217n4
Davis, Lloyd 83
Dekker, Thomas 31–32, 36
de Lauretis, Teresa 2, 6n1, 162–63, 168n1, 178–79
Deleuze, Gilles 47, 49, 51, 61, 63, 111, 112, 122n5
Derrida, Jacques 3–6, 6n5
Dinshaw, Carolyn 69–72, 76, 77n1, 78n4
Dollimore, Jonathan 16, 112, 245

263

Dolty, Alexander 2
Donne, John 238
Doors 25, 37
Doty, Alexander 196, 208
Douglas, Lord Alfred 209–10
Douglas, Mary 83
Dowling, Linda 100
Dreger, Alice Domurat 146, 149, 151, 154
DuBois, W.E.B. 186
Duncker, Patricia 181n14
Dworkin, Angela 181n14

Eby, Carl P. 47, 53, 61, 64–65
Edelman, Lee 1, 3, 4, 5, 36–38
Egerton, George 224
Eliot, George 9, 19, 82–93, 112
Elliott, Ira 56
Eltis, Sos 230n3
Eugenides, Jeffrey 20, 145–57
Evans, Ruth 77n3

Fabian Society 220, 223
Faderman, Lillian 12, 13–14, 180n6
Fantina, Richard 6, 18
Farwell, Marilyn 179–80
Faulkner, William 186
Fausto-Sterling, Anne 152
Feinberg, Leslie 15
Fiedler, Leslie 54
Findley, Timothy 21, 209–18
Ford, John 36
Forter, Greg 48
Foucault, Michel 2, 12, 17–18, 41n2, 69, 95, 147, 156, 246
Freeman, Elizabeth 16
Freud, Sigmund 20, 36–37, 86, 111, 112, 158–69
Friedkin, William 217n4
Fuss, Diana 135, 141, 159, 168n6
Fussell, Paul 210

Gagnon, John H. 159
Gamble, Sarah 241, 243n1
Gamman, Lorraine 91
Garber, Linda 13–14
Garber, Marjorie 126, 131
Gaskell, Elizabeth 227
Genet, Jean 59
Gibson, Ian 246, 255n1
Gilbert, Sandra 137
Gilman, Charlotte Perkins 224
Gissing, George 22
GLQ 2
Goldberg, Jonathan 16, 17, 33, 40, 41n2, 42n27, 43n27, 43n28, 59–60
Grand, Sarah 21–22, 223–24
Granville Barker, Harley 22, 219–31

Gravatt, Denise 10, 19
Graves, Robert 210
Griffney, Noreen 7n7
Gross, Larry 180n6
Grosz, Elizabeth 184–85, 189
Gubar, Susan 137
Guen, Leah 42n12
gynosodomy 25–43

Haggard, Rider 20, 134–44
Halberstam, Judith 16, 126, 128, 147, 180n4
Hall, Donald E. 3
Hall, Stuart 4
Halperin, David 2, 3, 14, 134, 148
Hamilton, Lisa 223
Hannen, Nicholas 219, 229
Hardy, Thomas 22, 227
Harper, Frances Ellen Watkins 186
Harris, E. Lynn 21, 183–95
Hemingway, Ernest 9, 18, 46–47, 183, 191
hermaphroditism 20, 145–57
Heyder, Clyde K 255n8
Heyer, Friedrich 255n3
Heywood, Thomas 26
Higgins, D.S. 135, 143n1
Hocquenghem, Guy 42n22
Hollywood, Amy 78n8
Hopkins, Pauline E. 186
Horne, Lewis 126
Howlin' Wolf 25
Hoy, Cyrus 42n17
Hughes, Winifred 122n4
Hutcheson, Gregory S. 78n4
Hyder, Clyde K. 255n8

Ibsen, Henrik 21, 220, 227
incest 22, 232–43
Irigaray, Luce 78n8, 79n13

Jackson, MacDonald P. 42n16
Jacobus, Mary 168n4
Jagose, Annamarie 1, 3, 4, 13, 197
James, Henry 2, 212, 215
Jankowski, Theodora 69, 78n3, 85
Jenkins, Melissa Shields 19–20
Johnson, James Weldon 186
Johnson, Samuel 130
Joyce, James 59, 132
Julian of Norwich 70–71, 73

Kaplan, Deborah 21
Katherine Group 75–76
Katz, Jonathan Ned 12
Keller, Rose 249
Kelly, Kathleen Coyne 78n3
Kennedy, Dennis 228, 230n2
Kessler, Suzanne L. 146, 148

*Index* 265

Kingsley, Charles 84
Kinneavy, James 247–48
Kinsey, Alfred 12–13
Kipling, Rudyard 142
Klein, Fritz 184
Klossowski, Pierre 247
Krafft-Ebing, Richard von 111
Kristeva, Julia 4–5
Kruger, Steven 69, 78n4
Kushnier, Jennifer 122n4

Lacan, Jacques 7n5, 161, 162, 236
LaGrace, Del 16
Lake, David J. 42n16
Lang, Cecil 255n6
Larsen, Nella 183
Lathan, Aaron 47
Lawner, Lynne 37–39, 41n4
Lawrence, D.H. 16, 58–59
LeGuin, Ursula 22
Leslia, Marina 78n3
Lever, Maurice 249
Levi-Strauss, Claude 236
Livingston, Ira 180n10
Lochrie, Karma 69, 76–77, 78n4
Lorde, Audre 13, 238
Louis, Margot Kathleen 255n6
Lukes, H.N. 168n4

Madonna 15
Makinen, Merja 91
Mansfield, Nick 62–63
Marck, Nancy Anne 89
Marcus, Steven 17, 122n7
Marks, Elaine 128
Marx, Karl 5, 6n4, 239
masochism 46–47, 109–23, 167
Masten, Jeffrey 33–34, 42n22
Matta, Christina 151
Matus, Jill L. 84
Maynard, John 255n2
McCarthy, Lillah 220
McCullers, Carson 183, 191
McGowan, Andrew 255n7
McInerney, Maud Burnett 77n3
McKenzie, Sister M.L. 213
Merck, Mandy 159, 168n3
Meredith, George 9, 19–20, 124–33
Meyers, Jeffrey 64
Middleton, Thomas 18, 26–43
Miller, D.A. 98
Miller, Henry 135
Miller, Jacques-Alain 20, 167–68
Millett, Kate 185
Mitchell, Jeremy 256n11
Moddelmog, Debra A. 23, 47, 54, 60–61, 64

Monson-Rosen, Madeleine 22
Montenegro, Giovanna 10
Moraga, Cherrie 197
Morgan, Margery 223
Morrison, Jim 25–26

Nemesvari, Richard 19, 114–15, 121, 122n1, 122n2
NEMLA (Northeast Modern Language Association) 10
New Woman 21–22, 220–30

Oestreich, Kate Faber 18–19
Oliphant, Margaret 122n3
O'Rourke, Michael 7n7, 78n4
Owen, Wilfred 21, 210

Paglia, Camille 115
Palmer, Paulina 178
Parker, Andrew 2
Paster, Gail Kern 39
Phillips, Anita 58
Pinero, Arthur Wing 220, 222, 227
Poster, Carol 22
Powers, Ann 7n6, 15
Presley, Elvis 26
Prins, Yopie 252
Protagoras 248
Puff, Helmut 41n3
Pugh, Tison 69, 78n4
Pykett, Lyn 122n4

Qulilligan, Maureen 157n1

R. A. 27
Rabinowitz, Rachel 21
Rae, William Fraser 121
Reardon, Bernard M.G. 255n3
Renevey, Denis 78n10
Reynolds, Michael 50
Rich, Adrienne 12
Rimbaud, Arthur 7n5
Roberts, Neil 126
Robertson, Pamela 179n2
Robins, Elizabeth 220, 228
Robinson, Sally 180n11
Roof, Judith 159, 168n3
Rooksby, Rikky 255n1, 255n6
Ross, Robbie 209
Rousseau, Jean-Jacques 3
Rudat, Wolfgang E.H. 55
Ruggerio, Guido 41n9
Russell, Lorena 20
Russo, John Paul 50

Sacher-Masoch, Leopold von 19, 46, 51–52, 59, 61, 111, 121

Sade, Donatien Alphonse François de, Marquis 22, 244–57
Sage, Lorna 239, 242
Said, Edward 64
St. Alphonsus Ligouri 17
Sala, George Augustus 122n10
Salih, Sarah 77n3
Sarduy, Severo 131
Sassoon, Siegfried 21, 210
Sauer, Michelle M. 78n4, 79n12
Savage, Anne 78n7
Sawday, Jonathan 42n18
Schiavi, Michael 10
Schlichter, Annette 7n7, 5, 12, 15, 16, 116, 110, 148
Schlovsky, Victor 4
Schreiner, Olive 21–22, 112, 223
Schroeder, Natalie 115
Scott, Jay 211
Sedgwick, Eve Kofosky 2, 3, 5, 12, 98, 100, 137, 142, 153, 180n4, 203, 206, 212, 215–16
Shaffer, Peter 217n2
Shakespeare, William 16, 27, 39–40, 51, 121, 129, 132
Shaw, George Bernard 21, 220–21, 222, 227
Shelden, Ashley 20
Shelly, Percy 248
Sheppard, Matthew 148
Showalter, Elaine 122n4, 221, 229
Siegel, Carol 47, 61, 63, 112–13
Sifuentes, Zachary 10, 20
Sikorski Grace 21
Silverman, Kaja 48–49, 55, 57, 61, 63
Sinfield, Alan 16, 130
Smith, Bruce R. 41n2
Smith, Clyde 15
Smith, Patricia Juliana 173–74, 180n6
Snead, W.T. 122n8
Socrates 248
sodomy 17, 25–43, 54–65, 244
Solomon, Alicia 68
Spilka, Mark 47, 52, 55
Spivak, Gayatri 11
Starks, Lisa 51, 115
Steibel, Lindy 134, 143n1, 143n2, 143n4
Stevens, Wallace 5, 6n4
Stevenson, Richard 126
Stewart, Suzanne R. 62–63
Stiles, Anne 22
Stonewall 13, 217n4
Stott, Rebecca 134
Studlar, Gaylyn 51
Sullivan, Nikki 6n1

Summers, Claude J. 16–17
Surridge, Lisa 114–15, 121, 122n1, 122n2
Swinburne, Algernon Charles 22, 244–57

Taormino, Tristan 15–16, 60, 61
Taylor, Gary 42n22
Testard, Jeanne 249
Thackeray, William Makepeace 130
Thomas, Calvin 6n2, 10, 11, 15, 16, 122n4, 180n2
Thomburg, Mary K. Patterson 213
Titian 51
Tourneur, Cyril 27, 41n10
Traub, Valerie 14
Trice, Elliott 42n20
Tromp, Marlene 122n4
Tynan, Kenneth 41n5

Vesalius 34
Veyne, Paul 255n5
Vicinus, Martha 126, 128
Vincent, John 255n1
Voigt, Cynthia 21, 196–204, 206–207

Waldrep, Shelton 21
Walker, Alice 21, 183–95
Walkowitz, Rebecca 221
Warner, Michael 2, 4, 6n3, 14, 16, 110, 112, 140–41
Watson, Nicholas 78n7
Weeks, Jeffrey 11, 95
Weisl, Angela Jane 78n3
Weldon, Fay 20, 170–82
Wheeler, Bonnie 78n4
Whigham, Frank 27
Wiggins, Martin 42n13
Wilde, Oscar 19, 21, 135, 209–10, 215–16, 220, 222–23, 227
Wilke, Sabine 62
Wilkes, Wetenhall 85, 88
Wineapple, Brenda 160
Winstead, Karen A. 78n3
Winterson, Jeanette 179n1
Wittig, Monique 22, 70, 75, 79n15
Wooing Group 71–72, n78
Woolf, Robert 122n9
Wyatt, Jean 236–37, 241–42

Yeats, William Butler 239–40
Young, Shannon 20

Žižek, Slavoj 160, 162
Zorach, Rebecca E. 41n8

www.ingramcontent.com/pod-product-compliance
Lightning Source LLC
Chambersburg PA
CBHW051213300426
44116CB00006B/558